R. A. Leeson

Travelling Brothers

The six centuries' road from craft
fellowship to trade unionism

D1407831

A PALADIN BOOK

GRANADA
London Toronto Sydney New York

Published by Granada Publishing Limited
in 1980

ISBN 0 586 08302 2

First published in Great Britain by
George Allen & Unwin Ltd 1979
Copyright © RA Leeson 1979

Granada Publishing Limited
Frogmore, St Albans, Herts AL2 2NF
and
3 Upper James Street, London W1R 4BP
866 United Nations Plaza, New York, NY 10017, USA
117 York Street, Sydney, NSW 2000, Australia
100 Skyway Avenue, Rexdale, Ontario, M9W 3A6, Canada
PO Box 84165, Greenside, 2034 Johannesburg, South Africa
61 Beech Road, Auckland, New Zealand

Made and printed in Great Britain by
Richard Clay (The Chaucer Press) Ltd
Bungay, Suffolk
Set in Monotype Ehrhardt

Granada ®
Granada Publishing ®

RA Leeson was born in 1928 and started his career in journalism as a local newspaper reporter at the age of sixteen. For over twenty years he has been a reporter, Parliamentary Correspondent, feature writer and Literary Editor on the *Morning Star* as well as a contributor to trade union journals.

He has written *United We Stand: An Illustrated History of Trade Union Emblems* and *Strike: A Live History*, 1887–1971. He is also a successful writer of novels and non-fiction for children, and his books have been translated into German and Hungarian.

He is married, his wife is a teacher and they have a son and a daughter. They live in Hertfordshire.

Also by RA Leeson

United We Stand
Strike: A Live History 1887–1971

For Gunvor

Contents

List of Illustrations

PLATES

DRAWINGS IN TEXT

Acknowledgements

Acknowledgements and thanks are due to the following:

For permission to reproduce extracts from texts, or illustrations:
Mrs Beryl Aspinall (*The Early English Trade Unions*), The Amalgamated Society of Boilermakers, Shipwrights, Blacksmiths and Structural Workers (*A History of the Boilermakers' Society*), the British Library of Political and Economic Science (The Webb Collection), The National Union of Brushmakers (*The Old Trade Unions*), Jonathan Cape, Ltd (*Rolling Stonemason*), Cassell and Co. (*The London Compositors*), Professor W. H. Challoner (*The Reminiscences of Thomas Dunning*), The Union of Construction, Allied Trades and Technicians (*Our Society* and *Foes to Tyranny*), J. Fyrth and The Amalgamated Union of Engineering Workers (Foundry Section) (*The Foundry Workers*), the Felt Hatters' and Trimmers' Union of Great Britain (*The Hatters*), Professor E. J. Hobsbawm (*The Tramping Artisan*), the Iron and Steel Trades Confederation (*Men of Steel*), James Klugmann (The Klugmann Collection), Lawrence and Wishart (*The Story of the Engineers*), the London School of Economics and Political Science ('The Webbs' *History of Trade Unionism*), the University of London (W. McLaine's unpublished thesis on 'The Engineers' Union'), The Mansell Collection (hatters' emblem), The Merlin Press (*The Unknown Mayhew*), A. E. Musson (*The Typographical Society*), A. Plummer (*The Weavers' Company*), the Quattuor Coronati Lodge (*The Medieval Mason*), the National Union of Sheetmetal Workers, Coppersmiths and Heating and Domestic Engineers (*History of the Tinplate Workers*), the Transport and General Workers' Union (Vehicle Building and Automotive Section) (coachmakers' emblem), Truman Taverns, Ltd. (The White Hart, Witham).

For Providing Facilities for research and access to documents:
Librarians and staff of the British Library, the Guildhall Library, the Marx Memorial Library, the Library of the Grand Lodge of Freemasons, the Modern Records Centre, University of Warwick, who kindly assisted with hospitality and other matters, the Nuffield Library, Oxford, the University of London Library and in particular the Goldsmiths' Library, the Research Department of the Amalgamated Union of Engineering Workers, Librarians of the City of Westminster, Stockport, Denton and the Curator of Stockport Museum, the Working-Class Movement Library, Manchester.

For the Loan of precious books, copying of documents, guidance on sources:
Ted Brake, Gary Brain, George Barnsby, Sid Brown, Dr J. G. Dony, John Foster, Eddie and Ruth Frow, Jim Fyrth, Ron and Anita Gray, Phil Leeson, Pat Mantle, Ken Sprague, G. E. Tapp, Angela Tuckett, Ray Watkinson, Mrs D. Wilson.

For editorial advice and encouragement:
John Bright-Holmes, Peter Sommer, Victor Thorpe

Author's Preface

The idea of writing this book came nearly ten years ago while I was looking at the origins of nineteenth-century trade union emblems with their inset gild coats of arms. The emblems clearly arose from the needs of the travelling or 'tramping' system of the early trade societies, about which I then wanted to know a good deal more.

Research, in the intervals of earning a living, has taken its time. This is fascinating but rather obscure territory, with, so far, only one scholarly general explorer, Professor E. J. Hobsbawm, whose article 'The Tramping Artisan', written nearly thirty years ago, is the starting-point for any student (though union historians have paid some attention to the system in relation to the trades they were studying). The sources are widespread and far from exhausted by my searching – I have been obliged to concentrate my attention chiefly though not exclusively on the craft companies of London and the trade unions of England.

I have taken up the question that most attracted me, and which Professor Hobsbawm left open in his study: what were the origins of 'tramping' or 'travelling'? These origins, as I understand them, said something about the origins of the early trade societies and the unions which followed them.

So finally the book has attempted to describe some six centuries of craft organisation in one form or another with the figure of the travelling brother to link them together.

The book is fully annotated but, to avoid cluttering up the text, reference marks are not given. Instead, the notes are given in page order and each is introduced by a key word or phrase from the text.

To all good Yeomen of the Gentle Craft

Travellers by sea and land
Each country's ways to understand,
Wrong they wrought not any man,
With reason all things did they scan.
Good houses kept they ever more,
Relieving both the sick and poor,
In law no money would they spend,
Their quarrels friendly would they end,
And never yet did any know
A shoemaker a begging go.
Kind they are one to another,
Using each stranger as his brother.

Cordwainers' Company, traditional

Our only load as we trod the road
Was a pipe and an OSM book *
We had little to eat and drink and think,
Of what we had got to cook.
If we wrought for the 'Bleeder' on Rylands job,†
Or a country mansion or church,
We would never let a 'roader' down,
If fate found him in the lurch.

'Rolling Stonemason', by Fred Bower (1936)

* Operative Society of Masons
† The Manchester Central Library

12

Introduction

On 28 May 1812 the journeymen hatters of Manchester wrote a letter to their craft brothers in Glasgow, and marked it 'with speed'. The letter travelled speedily enough, for the mail coach service had steadily improved since the 1780s, and it was delivered by the end of the month. But before it reached the Glasgow hatters there was a slight bureaucratic delay.

The postmaster, noting the address, opened the letter, read it carefully, and then sent a 'confidential copy' to London for the eyes of the Home Secretary. He was obeying orders: to open the mail of certain persons and look for evidence or subversion or insurrection. He saw there was nothing insurrectionary about it, but he was well informed enough to know that the hatters were doing something illegal – if not under the Combination Acts of 1799–1800 then under the Correspondence Societies Act of 1797 or the 1799 Act for the Suppression of Seditious and Treasonable Practices, both aimed at organisations with this kind of inter-city contact.

This is what the Manchester hatters had written:

Gentlemen – from daily experience of the various impositions practised upon the trade by means of so many blanks and turnhouses being kept in country places about this town, where there are such quantities of foul men, who in slack time obtain blanks and travel the country, to the great injury of the trade, we have determined as far as lays in our power to put a stop to them and compel the men to join the turnbooks of either this town, Rochdale or Stockport, and by that means prevent these frauds. Therefore we request you not to treat any blanks from the undermentioned places dated after the 1st of June, 1812, they being under 12 miles from Manchester, nor clear any man who shall come from any of the places mentioned until you have first wrote to one of the three places above mentioned, inquiring whether they have served their time and treated to any of the three books. [A list of thirteen Lancashire and Cheshire towns follows.]

In doing your utmost endeavours to detect these imposters you will much oblige yours . . .

The journeymen hatters of Manchester.

The Manchester hatters were ensuring that the benefits of their organisation were shared only by properly paid-up members, men who had served a proper apprenticeship, worked in workshops where trade rules were observed, and belonged to those hatters' societies which had agreed to act together by 'correspondence'.

This indeed was why they were spied on. The government whose authority over certain parts of the country, notably the new 'manufacturing' areas, could not be guaranteed without the moving to and fro of regular troops or local militiamen, found it intolerable that journeymen hatters, framework knitters, shoemakers, weavers, moulders, coachmakers and other trades should, by means of letters dispatched from the upstairs rooms of back-street public houses, give instructions which were heeded in scores of towns in England, Scotland or Ireland.

Not only letters passed to and fro, but a constant stream of men arrived at these same public houses, emissaries, missionaries, agitators, wanted men of all kinds, to be entertained and lodged, and to depart as mysteriously as they had come. A force was at work in the land, beyond the knowledge and comprehension of those in power. If this force were directed towards the overthrow of that power, how might it be met and dealt with?

Yet of all those letters seized and opened, leaflets collected, posters copied from walls, rule books impounded by officious JPs and sent in haste to London, only a fraction could by any stretch of the imagination be seen as moves to overthrow government. Imagination there was in plenty, of course, among the magistrates and the informers they employed. The Glasgow postmaster was one of the well-informed exceptions.

For the most part those papers seized from the early trade societies and stored by the Home Office (for which we may be grateful today, if the Glasgow hatters in 1812 were not) dealt with humdrum everyday trade affairs, as did the hatters' post, though the suspicions of conspiracy might have been sharpened by the jargon in which the letters were written.

Just what were the hatters so concerned about? They were tightening up on their 'tramping' system, an activity already more than a century old in their trade, and in 1812, almost at its height, with another century's declining life to come. The hatters' rules, like those of other early nineteenth-century trade societies, whether in old trades like shoemaker or tailor or new ones like boilermaker or steam engine maker, were basically concerned with four matters: control of entry to their craft and its organisation (the two things being the same in their eyes) by apprenticeship, and a strict ratio of employment of 'boys' to men; the administration of friendly benefits for sickness, old age and death; the regulation of behaviour in workshop or clubhouse; and the tramping or travelling system.

And of these four, the most remarkable and in some ways the most important was 'tramping'. Almost every trade of the day 'tramped'. Brushmakers did, so did bricklayers, boilermakers, bookbinders, calico printers, curriers, cordwainers, coachmakers, carpenters, compositors, coopers, cabinet makers, founders, framework knitters, hatters, joiners, leatherdressers, lithographers, mechanics, masons, machine workers, millers, millwrights, plasterers, plumbers, sawyers, steam engine makers, smiths, tailors, tanners, tinplate workers, woolcombers, weavers, etc.

It would be simpler to say who did not. The cotton spinners, the potters and the miners (except those in Northumberland) did not. But almost every other trade did. It was almost universal among the skilled workers and their organisations, though the potters alleged incorrectly that tramping only took place among the trades of lesser skill.

Universal as the system was, it remains an obscure and little studied corner of trade union history. Small wonder, for it is a strange business to the modern mind, and even active unionists today might have difficulty in understanding what the Manchester hatters were urging their Scots brethren to do.

At the head of their letter is a strange design. A traveller with stick and bundle bends over a table, where a craftsman in apron is registering his arrival in a book. Beside them stands a woman holding a tray with two foaming 'pots' (quarts) of beer. Strangest of all, two rabbits play around their feet. If we could see more minutely into this preserved moment in time from the early 1800s, we would find that the traveller has with him a card which bears the same design. It is the trade sign of the hatters, incorporating a potted history of the craft, its gild and later union organisation. (See Plate 2.)

He is the 'tramp', the card he carries is his 'blank' and the place where they have met is the 'turnhouse' or inn where the local hatters' society has its headquarters. His blank, properly filled in and signed in his home town, is the guarantee that he is a 'fair' and not a 'foul' man, that he will not work under the agreed rate for the job, or enter any workshop which employs too many 'boys' in place of grown men. A 'turn' is a complete circuit of all the society 'houses' or inns in the country, and if the tramp is a fair man he may take one complete turn every six months. In each town he is greeted by the local secretary, offered his pot of beer, given supper, perhaps attends a meeting of the local club, if it is their 'night', where he may speak, provided all others have said their piece, but not vote. Having exchanged news of the state of trade along the road, had another pot, perhaps told a story or sung a song or two, he is taken to

15

sleep in a bed which the local club have inspected to be sure the sheets are clean.

In the morning after breakfast he is given an asking ticket and a society man who has time off for the task (known confusingly as the 'short turn') takes him round the local workshop or shops. If there is work available he will be taken on, whether the local master likes the look of him or not, though such objections are rare. A man thus 'shopped' dips in his pocket if he has money, a lad is sent back to the club house for a jug of ale. His health, the master's health, the society's health, everyone's health is drunk, and a new 'shopmate' has been installed.

But if there is no work, then the club secretary gives the traveller money, a penny or a halfpenny per mile over the distance to the next society town, and then, stick and bundle on his shoulder, he sets off.

Anyone who looks at the membership emblems or certificates of the early trade unions – hatters, cordwainers, boilermakers, coachmakers, ironmoulders (see Endpapers) – will find the figure of the traveller, slogging along the road, being 'signed in' by the secretary, or shaking hands with the foreman of the local shop or yard. In the early ironmoulder's emblem we see the tramp address the foreman:

'Brother craft, can you give me a job?'

And the foreman answers:

'If we cannot, we will relieve you.'

This message, also stamped around the pot from which the traveller drank his customary quart, is what the whole business was about. The tramping system was the trade societies' answer to unemployment. If a man was out of work, he must not hang about, tempted to get a job in a lower paid 'unfair' house. He took to the road and his craft brothers welcomed him, found him work, or helped him on his way.

While the system flourished, and its life was long, it attempted to share available work and aimed to keep up the 'legal' rate and maintain the 'fair' house or shop. In disputes it lent power to the local club, spiriting away the labour force from under the offending employer's nose to disperse it throughout the country, to return only when he was ready to come to terms. A master employing too many 'boys' might find them gone overnight, on the road north or south or bound across the Irish Sea for Dublin, and out of his reach. And when the law tried to take hold of trade club leaders, the system made possible their escape. To serve a warrant needs a body and many a magistrate was frustrated by the disappearance of accused or key witness. Even men who had agreed to be informers vanished from the scene in this way.

Such was the system at its height – a nationwide employment exchange, a mobile strike force, an underground railway.

Yet, within a few decades, this universal system had fallen from favour among many of the unions of skilled workers, collapsing under the strain of repeated economic crises and the mass unemployment they brought with the culmination of the Industrial Revolution. By the mid-nineteenth century, many were turning away from the system they had practised and admired and were seeking other ways of dealing with the workless –

Shop-mate greets tramps in more austere style, post 1850, from a letterhead of the journeymen hatter's union.

emigration, co-operative production, and, above all, unemployment benefit paid *at home*, first by the union only, later by the state.

In 1850 the hatters had a new emblem. A shirt-sleeved worker greets two tramps, top hats on heads, bundles on shoulder. They stand on the bare planks of a workshop floor: no buxom maid, no foaming tankard, no frisky rabbits. In the contrast between the earlier and later emblems, forty years apart, is an aspect of that colossal social, economic and psychological change which rolled through the working population of this country between the 1780s and the 1850s. In the words of G. D. H. Cole, the eighteenth-century artisan who had been 'very much a peasant at heart' had become a worker. His place was in the sprawling industrial towns – goodbye to tankards, goodbye to rabbits, farewell to the jovial tramp.

During that crucial period, skilled workers developed their organisation and slowly, painfully, abandoned their efforts to hold on to craft rights and privileges inherited from ancient days, turning from fading past to pressing future, finding new ways of defending their interests in the new world of the factory system with its large numbers of non-apprenticed 'hands', – men, women, even children – for whom the machine had levelled many former distinctions between skilled and unskilled.

With this change the tramping system had served its purpose and had begun to disappear. Its critics often proclaimed it dying or dead long before it finally lay down and formal burial took place during the 1914–18 war, when the great modern amalgamated unions counted their members not by the hundred but the hundred thousand.

It was, as said, a strange business, and anyone looking at the growth of the trade union movement from the vantage point of the twentieth century is bound to ask 'Why?' Why did the trade unions, born of the Industrial Revolution, choose as one of their most basic methods of organisation a system which could not meet the enormous challenge of headlong industrial development?

The answer is that they did not choose it. It was bequeathed to them by an earlier age. In one sense the unions did not make the system, it made them, the unions, and shaped them in their earliest years.

Some historians have compared the tramping system with the German *wanderjahre* in which the apprentice, after three or four years, was sent out to travel round the country to complete his training by 'wandering'; and with the similar though less widespread *tour de France* of the French *compagnons*. But, having made the comparison, one looks in vain for traces of such customs in the history of the English crafts.

Yet the same processes are at work, under different names and in different forms. The English system was not invented in the nineteenth century, or even in the eighteenth. It grew from some three or four centuries before, and provides a link, now clear and now obscure, now definite and now tenuous, between the ancient craft organisation and the modern trade union.

Between the former with its local loyalties between masters and journeymen of the same trade, its suspicions and sometimes hostility towards outsiders, and the latter with its all-embracing unity between workers of the same trade in every town, confronting every employer, there seems a great gulf fixed. Or if not a gulf, then a no-man's land dark with the smoke and upheaval of the Industrial Revolution. But perhaps neither gulf nor no-man's-land will do to describe the process of continuous change whose cumulative effect made up that which we call a revolution.

The process by which hand work gave way to the machine, master and journeyman to employer and worker, local sectional loyalty to class loyalty, and old craft gild and company to trade club and union, is one which has its continuities as well as its breaks and departures.

The tramping system is one of those continuities, linking the old with the new, acting indeed as a catalyst of change, and being discarded when the change was completed because it could not change itself.

Its origins, where they can be traced in the pre-capitalist past, seem to be connected with the old ways in which the local town crafts dealt with the outsider. The travelling craftsman, welcomed, tolerated, or turned away, became a vital part of craft history and development, just as did the artisan who held on to his place at home and aspired to become a master with his own workshop. A change of fortune and the man who stayed at home might find himself on the road. The 'brother' might become a 'stranger' in his turn.

And so, in time, when change became general for the town craft worker, the 'stranger' in his turn became a 'brother'. And that is what this book is about.

Part I:
The 'Tramp' Arrives   1300–1850

1 If a stranger comes . . .
1300–1450

If a stranger to the city comes in, he may upon giving a penny to the wax work among the bretheren and sisteren and his name shall be written on their roll.

Fullers of Lincoln, 1337

A penny was the price of a ticket to work among the Lincoln fullers in the 1330s and a century and a half later, among the shoemakers of Norwich, the 'stranger' was still charged a penny. It was as if a hundred and fifty years in the making of England, change and upheaval, foreign and civil war, punctuated by popular revolt, had passed over the craftsmen of the walled cities. And in a sense this was true – the needful continuity of work in fulling mill or shoemakers' workshop, the self-perpetuating team of master, journeyman and apprentice, was a stable element in the violent decades as the old feudal world fell apart. In another sense, it was a wish, an illusion of stability, a holding on to tradition in the face of change, change which came all the same, sometimes despite the resistance, sometimes with greater force because of it. That, it seems, was the story of the crafts in medieval England, and within that story the stranger at the gate of the town played a crucial part.

A 'stranger' was someone not born within the town or village; he might also be called a 'forren' from the medieval Latin *forinseci* – those 'from outside', or even, in the jargon of London, an 'uplander'. Anyone from 'beyond sea' was an 'alien', and as we shall see, by the logic of work organisation, an alien was a stranger writ large.

Rules for the 'entertainment' of the stranger varied according to trade, place and circumstances. Tilers who came to Lincoln were told simply: 'Join the gild or leave the city'; hatters who came into London were quizzed to make sure they had not left their last master owing money. London coppersmiths, so it was alleged, forced strangers to 'take an oath to conceal their misdeeds'. Denying this slander, the coppersmiths said that strangers were examined and admitted to the trade after promising to abide by the rules, which included paying into the common fund to care for the 'poor' or unemployed of the craft.

Ideally, none were allowed to start work without a test of skill. Let the stranger be 'known and tried' said the pewterers. Let him be 'tried and proved' said the founders. Let us, said the carpenters, 'see what he can doe'. There was a trial period, 'a week upon his well working' at York Minster, two weeks among the London blacksmiths, or, more rarely, the month allowed by the Exeter cordwainers (shoemakers). Their brothers of Norwich charged the stranger a penny 'even if he only work one week'.

If the stranger were found competent, this might lead to a 'covenant' of twelve months, a guarantee of work for the 'covenant hynd', a guarantee of a year's work at a fixed rate to the master, for covenant men were paid 'as good cheap by the year as they may be hired', which in the baking trade often meant half the local wage. Or the trial period might be a gesture of hospitality, up to a month while waiting for a ship among some Bristol crafts, a fortnight to 'pass and repass' the area of the Beverley Minstrels, or simply a period of work before moving on among the masons and stonecutters. The quarrymen of Portland, who preserved the skeleton of their ancient craft organisation well into the nineteenth century, allowed strangers a week's work after which they were expected to quit the island by the normal route or by way of a plank 'projecting over a cliff'. This apart, the Portland quarrymen treated strangers with 'great kindness'.

But if there were no work, or the trade were in dispute, the stranger might be utterly barred. Early in the fourteenth century, the London weavers refused to admit strangers during a running battle they had with the 'burrellers' or merchants. They used other weapons familiar today, restricting the hours and even the seasons of working and laying down precisely how much time might be taken to weave a piece of cloth. Protective measures of this sort were already well established. Wyclif, the Lollard and church reformer, anticipated the work ethic of the Puritans two centuries and more ahead, when he attacked 'men of sutel craft' such as masons who observed demarcation between hewers and layers and controlled the pace of work, 'when they might profit their master twenty pounds a day by legging on a wall'.

Masons and carpenters who came into London on royal contracts in 1306 and 1339 were met by pickets who instructed them to work at the London rate and no less. The carpenters, who specified sixpence a day and an after-dinner drink, were accused of beating the upland men to enforce the minimum. The masons' leader Jean de Offington was jailed. He crossed the path of Walter de Hereford, master mason to the King, and perhaps his action was one of those which inspired a Royal Proclamation in 1306 against 'congregations and chapters' of craftsmen, perhaps the first state move of its kind in the field of labour relations.

To safeguard their livelihood the crafts relied first of all on solidarity between all those in the trade, master or man. In the 1330s the London carpenter agreed to 'work his brother before any other'. This solidarity depended upon the discipline of craft organisation.

As the Middle Ages saw it, society was in three mutually respecting and dependent parts or 'estates', knighthood, church and the working rest, the third estate, embracing all from peasant and craftsman to merchant. The gild in all its shapes and forms in village or town was the chief form of organisation among the third estate, though it did not include the majority working on the land.

Gilds arose – in ways which are still obscure because most left no documents behind before the fourteenth century – out of the earlier village organisation of pre-Conquest days. Lack of documentation has occasionally caused historians to smile at the claims of the masons to owe their original charter to Athelstan in the ninth century and, indeed, few fraternities made such precise claims. Sincerely they claimed to have existed 'time out of mind' or to date from an age 'whereunto the memory of man reacheth not'.

Modern authority recognises a period of existence for the gilds, varying in length and definition from one West European country to another, before central and municipal government began to fix them firmly in the document record. While 'first dates' are impossible to pin down, 'systematic' involvement of gilds in town government is seen in the thirteenth century and they multiply in the fourteenth and fifteenth centuries.

When, in 1388, the Crown obliged all gilds to set down their rules and other information, it emerged that the network of organisation among the third estate was widespread. Norfolk alone listed some 160 gilds and there must have been thousands throughout the populous south-east of England. The most numerous were those once termed 'social', but now perhaps more accurately 'parish' gilds, groups of people of the 'poorer or middling sort'. (No mayors or bailiffs admitted, said one.)

They banded together for mutual security against poverty and misfortune or better to meet demands made on them by the local overlord of manor or monastery. Gilds provided as well as they could for the poor, the sick and the aged. Should members die away from home, if it were this side of the seventh milestone, stewards would be sent to see them decently buried. Even in the 1840s the Hull masons had a plot of land in a local cemetery so they could see travelling brothers 'decently interred'. Indeed 'cradle to grave' seems a poor description of gild services; they provided payments for apprenticeship, dowries for members' daughters, and in Stamford, 'beyond the reach of memory' the gild bought the beast for the annual bull-running. Carefully worked out rules provided for decent behaviour, above all at annual gatherings, the procession to church and the tavern feast. The rules began with praise of the virtues of society and co-operation, which are echoed down the years by the preamble and rules to many an eighteenth- and nineteenth-century friendly or trade society.

The gilds, counting their members in handfuls or hundreds, are a source of democracy of a deeper and more popular kind than that represented more formally by Magna Charta and de Montfort's Parliament. At a time when the chivalry of Western Europe studied how to cut the next nobleman's throat, ravish his wife and seize their castle in accordance with the highest knightly conventions, gild members were fined for missing meetings, refusing to serve as officers, for being foul-mouthed, for dozing off during the annual dinner, 'keeping the ale cup standing', slandering a brother or sister, or even, among the bell-ringers, 'taking another's rope out of his hand'. Violence was not absent from their way of life, but they made a study to avoid it. In the words of a modern gild historian 'all overt aggression whether by word or deed was ruthlessly penalised'. Help was given in misfortune but not if brought on by the member's 'own folly'.

Each gild was associated with a church whose name it bore. Inside the church burned the 'wax' or 'light' paid for by the members, insuring the next life as they sought to provide for this one. The Church gave spiritual aid, medical care and certainly help in writing and drafting documents. London blacksmiths still sought 'councel' from 'fathers' even in the wake of the Reformation

How much of the charity ascribed to the Church in this period was in fact organised by the gilds is a matter for thought. Some historians have suggested that the great religious houses, famed for hospitality, were more burdened with rich guests than poor.

Where there were enough local people of a certain occupation or trade, in medium- and large-sized towns, they would form their own gild, though artisans rarely used this term, preferring 'craft', 'fraternity', 'mistery', 'brotherhood', or occasionally 'company'. Fraternity members saw no contradiction in ensuring the well-being of members at work or away from it, any more than did the later trade or friendly societies.

26

Men and women were together in the parish gilds, and, to judge from the ordinances of the Lincoln fullers, the early craft fraternities had both 'bretheren and sisteren'. That men and women worked together at the fulling can be seen by a later rule of the Lincoln gild that a man might not work at the trough with a woman who was not his wife or daughter. Restrictions on women in the crafts tended to increase as the fourteenth-century labour shortage gave way to periodic employment in the fifteenth and sixteenth centuries (see Chapter 2).

Fourteenth-century masons were urged to be together as 'systeren and bretheren'; the London carpenters had 'brothers and sisters'; men and women paid 'quarterage' to the blacksmiths; and the coopers' rules included 'sisters' until the sixteenth century. Women were found in a number of trades from brewer to leadbeater. They staged whole scenes in the pageants which marked the annual gild celebrations. Women were more often mistresses, taking over the workshop from their husbands; they were more rarely apprentices, though there was no widespread direct bar to their admission to the trades until the sixteenth century. The Lincoln fullers' rules, though, suggest that the travelling stranger was likely to be a man. Only rarely in the exclusive town crafts does one come across the travelling journeywoman. That is not to say she did not take the road, but she has left a much fainter trace.

Like the parish gilds the craft fraternities grew in the shelter of the Church. Many town craftsmen were Church employees, the richer monasteries employing craftsmen as did the secular barons. And monasteries had their lay brothers. Terms like 'brother', 'sister', 'order' and 'chapter' were borrowed from the Church by the crafts.

Early craft fraternities appear under the name of their patron saint, the tailors under John the Baptist, whose 'decollation' they celebrated each year, the blacksmiths under St Eloi or St Loi. Less officially, the shoemakers celebrated St Crispin and the masons the Four Crowned Martyrs, who like St Crispin and his brother were legendary Christians of old Rome. French and German masons working on the churches and Flemish weavers and shoemakers taking refuge in England probably helped transmit the myths as part of the general traditions of Western Christendom shared by craftsmen of England and her neighbours. Gild organisation in Italy has traditions reaching back to the Roman Empire and influences which radiated through Western Europe.

There were more than spiritual or even charitable benefits to be got from the Church. The London blacksmiths meeting secretly in 1300 to put a farthing each in a 'casket' for the poor were accused of swearing an oath to 'work for no one but themselves'. They were also accused of infringing the liberties of the city by prosecuting people for trade infringements in the Church courts. The Chesterfield blacksmiths went further, threatening 'excommunication without cavil or appeal' for anyone failing to pay craft dues. The Coventry craftmasters, tightly organised in the Corpus Christi Gild, also took offenders to the Church courts.

The London blacksmiths eventually thought better and made their peace with the city. The crafts had other sanctions against rule breakers which needed the backing of secular law. A stranger might come into the city and work if his labour was needed. But on no account would he be allowed to set up shop himself, or to make goods and sell them. On many a day during the fourteenth century, the air over Cheapside in the City of London was black with smoke from piles of blankets, hats, gloves, caps and shoes seized by gild beadles or sheriffs and burned as being 'false, deceitful and a scandal to the trade as well as to the harm of the people'. The seized goods failed to conform to the elaborate rules governing material and manufacture laid down by the crafts.

'No man of the said trade shall garnish . . . tissue of silk or wool or of thread or leather that is in breadth of sixth size, fifth, third or double size, unless it have a double point in the buckle and in the tongue; as also, the bars with a double point down to the rowel below,' said the girdlers in 1327.

The condemnation and destruction of substandard goods by the fraternity was an effective sanction against outsiders. Much of the protesting done at this time by the London trades against 'night work' was probably due less to a concern about the health of those working than to the knowledge that men forbidden to manufacture during the day might well do so when dusk hid them from the 'searchers' of the trade. The blacksmiths, girdlers, weavers and spurriers all took action against night work and the spurriers became eloquent about those who 'compass how to practice deception in their work', and who 'wandering about all day, without working at all at their trade . . . then when they have become drunk and frantic, they take to their work, to the annoyance of the sick and of all their neighbours . . .'.

The master spurriers were protecting themselves against insiders as well as outsiders, against servants who, not allowed to set up in business on their own, were working on the side. Whether the term 'foreigner' used in factories today to denote a job done behind the boss's back has its origins in the evasion of craft monopoly by outsiders is a thought. But competition there was from inside and outside. The master cutlers claimed that while they were in church on Sunday their servants were making and selling goods for their own profit, without doubt 'false, deceitful and a scandal to the trade'.

That these restrictions helped to keep up the standard of manufacture can be believed and in later centuries, long after the craft gilds and the companies which succeeded them relinquished control over the trade at large, the 'strictest' shops were the most skilled, the best organised and the best paid. But the masters probably benefited more from the restrictions than the consumer did.

From the craft master's point of view, control of his livelihood and the quality of work was also assured by apprenticeship. It was to his apprentice, his chosen pupil, usually his son and much more rarely his daughter, that he taught the trade secrets, lack of which knowledge would consign the product to the bonfire on Cheapside. This was the 'mastery' or 'misterie', the 'craft', all words with double meaning, used interchangeably with 'fraternity' to mean both the skill and the body of artisans who used it.

By the 1340s seven years 'servitude' was the London rule, spreading through England until it was general by the end of the fifteenth century and the law of the land by mid-sixteenth century. It was the means by which skills were preserved and transmitted. It was also the means of craft monopoly, of hereditary control and of reducing competition. When one remembers the relatively short life of people in the Middle Ages, then the rate at which new masters came into the business would thus but gradually overtake what we call 'natural wastage'.

The stranger who came to the city or town in this period might be offered the chance of becoming an apprentice. This meant, though, exchanging one year's employment at a fixed wage for seven years' at next to no wage boarded in his master's house. The stranger who came might indeed be an apprentice who had not finished his term, running away from another town. The control of master over boy, including the the right to beat, though not 'unreasonably' for the gild saw to that, often drove the apprentice to wander. But no craft master was supposed to accept any one in his workshop without a clear explanation of why he left his last employ. Until the 1850s, masons' lodges continued to pursue and send back runaway apprentices to their masters or 'disconsolate parents'.

As said, seven years was a large slice from a life that might last only four times as long. Many apprentices in the Middle Ages did not live out their

29

'time'. Even in the seventeenth century, most boys apprenticed to the weaving trade had already lost their fathers by the time they were 14. But 'servitude' was the main channel towards the position of master and with it the freedom to produce goods and sell them within the city or provide other services.

The master was 'employed' as much as was his apprentice or servant, receiving perhaps a fifth more pay than those who worked under his direction. A royal master mason like Walter de Hereford who was paid six times as much as his fellows was an exception. The distinction between 'master' and 'employer' was thus clear and continued to be so understood even in the eighteenth and nineteenth centuries when workshop production was being superseded by the factory. Surveying the decline in 'mastership' in those running the trade, a brushmaker trade unionist who began work in the 1870s remarked contemptuously, 'call them no more masters, call them employers'.

When the apprentice served his time, he was in theory ready to set up shop, but in practice he worked a term as 'journeyman', a worker paid by the day or *journée*. Clothworkers who worked 'by journeys' got a 'groat a day'. The word 'journey', which afterwards came to mean the distance that can be walked in a day, is sometimes taken to mean that a 'journeyman' was a travelling craftsman. In origin this was not so, though in time journeymen did walk for their work. They were certainly more free to come and go than the 'covenant hynd' and freer to vary their wage, though a journeyman would not, any more than a covenant servant, be accepted unless he satisfied his new master he had good reason to leave his old one.

Generally the journeyman was the apprentice out of his time, but not invariably so. In the early fifteenth century some masters were advised not to teach their journeymen secrets as 'they might do their apprentice'. There were clearly some day wage men who had learned their trade in another town, or even picked it up, and the master would not risk their setting up as competitor, perhaps making and selling goods while he was in church like a good burgher.

As towns and cities grew, the hierarchy within the craft fraternity – master, journeyman, apprentice, covenant man or servant – became more complex and the attempts to regulate it by custom and rule more detailed. For other strata were being added.

During the foreign wars the production of saddles grew and became more specialised, involving joiners who made the framework, coppersmiths or lorimers who did the riveting, painters who decorated and saddlers who upholstered, finished and eventually sold the finished article to knight or squire. The saddlers, an arrogant lot by all accounts, tried to subordinate the other trades, accusing the joiners of making saddles on the side in the woods outside the city. It was they who accused the coppersmiths of forcing strangers to swear to 'conceal their misdeeds'.

The other trades countercharged that the saddlers were doing secret deals with the knights' valets, to buy back used saddles, refurbish them and sell second-hand, thus undermining the market for new goods with what must have been the first trade-in business in the city. On Ascension Day 1327, perhaps on the principle of the better the day the better the deed, the parties came to blows. Called to a meeting by the Mayor they made such a commotion that a committee of all trades was appointed as a kind of conciliation panel and the issue was resolved with the temporary defeat of the saddlers.

The saddlers were not the only group trying to insinuate themselves between the crafts and their customers. The burrellers or cloth merchants had already by 1300 interposed themselves between weavers and public. They thus took one step towards being the permanent employers of all in the trade, both master and man. The haberdashers' company, merchants who handled the sale of hats, successfully absorbed the hatters' gild during the fifteenth century. In 1511 only legal action stopped them from flooding the market with cheap imported headgear and thus ruining their junior partners the craft workers. It is interesting that the weavers who fought the burrellers between 1290 and 1320 by closed shop, short-time working and even 'close seasons' were taken to the courts in London and lost the case. To add insult to injury they were lectured about the wickedness of interfering in free trade in a prosecution speech which would have warmed the heart of any nineteenth-century political economist.

The burrellers were bound to win that round, for as merchants they were at the top of the many layers of urban life. The crafts sought to control the making and selling of goods in the town.

The 'gilds merchant' organised in some 160 English towns by the fourteenth century sought to control the trade in and out of the city and the country. While controlling foreign traders in favour of 'denizens', each gild merchant sought bilateral agreements with other towns to secure a privileged position. Thus we have the familiar process of the Middle Ages, the drive to extend influence and control which undermines itself, the impulse towards consolidation and stability which brings change in its wake. The merchants with their ever-expanding trade network and ceaseless activity, turning goods into money into goods, land into money into land, reached upwards and downwards through the social layers, disturbing all. They tempted knights into trade, stimulated barons into more oppressive demands on their tenants, and serfs to raise the purchase price for imported luxuries, and dickered with feudal lord and king for 'freedoms' which would give them monopoly control of a town or a trade.

Henry III thought the merchant barons of London 'clowns, rich to loathing', but neither he, nor even less his successors, the three Edwards, could do without them. Merchants raised the money for foreign wars, sometimes with bland hypocrisy, hastening to meet Edward III's demand for £20,000 for the French wars 'for fear of the indignation of our Lord', and then telling him he could only have £5,000. They chose the right side unerringly in any conflict between town and feudal overlord and they punished men like Waldischeff who in 1322 told Londoners not to subscribe to the Scottish wars – not a pacifist, perhaps, but a hard head who six years after defeat at Bannockburn did not want to throw good money after bad. They earned the king's gratitude for putting down city revolts in his absence and, in the struggles by which town charters were won, the merchants in their gilds acted as co-ordinators and go-betweens rather than outright combatants. But when the citizens won their town freedoms it was the gilds merchant who were the top layer and the town government. In some cities they tried rigidly to exclude the crafts. In Norwich they chose those master craftsmen they thought fit to share the local government.

In Beverley, Chesterfield, Leicester and other cities, craftsmen took part in town government by being members of the merchant gild. In Coventry, the gild merchant tried for a long time to prevent any independent craft organisation from forming.

So the crafts had to deal with the merchants in two guises, as buyers and suppliers of raw material and as local governors and regulators of trade. At first the crafts kept independence and internal solidarity, being accused, as blacksmiths and bakers were, of going outside the city walls to evade the law. Later the craft masters looked to that law to uphold their own position. As they saw it, they had no choice but to strengthen their hold on the craft to protect their livelihood from outside pressures, from interlopers, strangers, 'forrens' and aliens. So they accepted city rule though it meant the rule of the merchant elite.

Thus in this period baron, bishop and burgher all tried to enlarge their own area of freedom of action while seeking to restrict that of others. Each action contradicted the next even when both were taken by the same group. A society which studied stability and 'degree' to the point of obsession set going convection currents which could not be stilled.

The Church was the great symbol of order and degree and through its monasterial estates was active in squeezing feudal dues from its tenants. The lords spiritual were often harsher than the lords temporal and in the Great Revolt of 1381 the rebel axe fell first on Bishop Sudbury's neck, while in Norwich it was the Bishop who led the counter-attack on the upstart rebels and craftsmen. But while the Church preached stability it encouraged mobility – through pilgrimages, drawing the eyes, feet and purses of the free part of the population south-east to Canterbury, which at the peak of the Thomas à Becket cult was said to be attracting 200,000 pilgrims a year (from a population of about three million). Beyond Canterbury across the sea lay the shrines of Compostella, Rome and Jerusalem. The political effect of the pilgrimages was great and the Church knew it. Pilgrimages were a focus of opposition to the Crown from the time of Edward II to that of Edward VI.

The Church encouraged pilgrimages by hospitality in the guest houses at the monastery gates, houses which were often leased out to a lay licensee and formed links in the chain of inns along the pilgrim ways, some of which survive today. The pilgrim routes, draining down through the land and out across the sea to the centre of the Western Christian Church, made easier the draining of wealth out of the English pocket into that of Rome. This in its turn excited opposition and stimulated the demand for secular control of public offices held by the Church. When during the Hundred Years War the French cannily set up their own pope in Avignon, the pressure for secularisation took on the colour of national as well as economic interest. At this point Wyclif began his pamphleteering career with a defence of secularisation and church reform, starting a movement which was to have remarkable effects on the craft organisations during the Reformation nearly two centuries later.

The pilgrimages were religious and political. They were a broad, almost migratory movement and joined in with the flow of commerce down to the richer south-east and out to Europe and the Mediterranean trade routes, reopened after the collapse of crusading banditry. When Walsingham, Winchester and other places encouraged their own pilgrimages one senses rival economic interests at work. And when one reads of thirty English pilgrim ships in Corunna harbour, like package jets on the runway at Palma, coupled with the publicity and fakery of the rival mechanised images, fake Virgin's milk and tons of timber shavings from the Holy Rood, the parallel with today's tourist industry is tempting.

The pilgrimages were a holiday. Chaucer's gildsmen brought their cook with them; others brought pipers and sang 'wanton songs', so the

Lollards complained. Such was the competition that the Minstrels' gild sought royal help to keep out 'artificers and husbandmen of various crafts' who intruded on the craft. Chaucer lets us know how little inquisitive the pilgrims were, provided their companions could tell a good story, and among the crowds trudged others, husbandmen and craftsmen 'going afar under colour of going on pilgrimage' so Parliament complained in 1388.

There were servants cutting loose from lord or master to change their job or their way of life entirely or to plot even greater changes. When captives were interrogated after the 1381 revolt, it came out that they had made contact with fellow rebels in other parts of England by means of the pilgrimages.

The pious, the adventurous, the affluent, the poor, the seeker after experience and pleasure, the discontented and the desperate moved up and down the land and even in and out of the country under the umbrella of the Church. Most returned home, displaying relics as souvenirs widening the horizons of those who had stayed behind. But some did not come home, and those charged with keeping manorial records had to write down 'Ils ne poont estre trouvez' (not to be found).

Merchant, trading and craft or artisan gilds, lovers of stability and control, contributed to the movement. Parish gilds swelled the flow to the cities by sending up their young boys to be apprenticed to masters in the town. Young men 'not cunning' in the art of carpentry came into York or London to learn. The regular flow of untaught youths and trained craftsmen in and out of London continued in this trade up to the sixteenth and seventeenth centuries, during which time only perhaps one in five of boys who served their time in London remained there to work. London was still a finishing school for carpenters in the 1840s, Henry Mayhew reports.

Gilds, parish and craft, including the Lincoln fullers, released members from dues payment if they went on pilgrimage and sometimes clubbed together to help with the expenses ($\frac{1}{2}$d each for Rome, a penny for Jerusalem), walking in a body to the city gate to see the pilgrim away. For sixty years at least the Corpus Christi Gild in Coventry kept a room with beds for poor travellers, a secular version of the monks' guest house, and paid an old woman to wash the travellers' feet.

Merchant and craft gilds in various towns were clearly in touch with one another. There were reciprocity agreements with hundreds of towns. The similarity of rules among the weavers of London, Oxford, Marlborough and Beverley suggest contact.

So perhaps does the coincidence of journeymen's movements within the crafts of different towns, among the Bristol and London cordwainers in late fourteenth and the Coventry and London tailors in early fifteenth century. And there is some suggestion that townsmen combining to throw off feudal control were in contact during the years before the 1381 revolt. The legend of the 'great company' said to have organised the revolt is based on slender evidence, but if such a 'company' (an alternative name for gild or fraternity) did exist then its skeleton would more likely exist among the town crafts than the peasantry. At more or less the same time the gilds of the German cities were linking themselves together as a countervailing force to the anarchy and depradations of 'amateur and professional' baronial plunderers. If a 'great company' did exist, it might have been a shadowy English equivalent.

No less than gild and church, Crown and barons disturbed and set people in motion even as they took steps to fix them in their places. The wars of conquest, Ireland, Wales, Scotland, France, to say nothing of civil wars and private baronial quarrels, drew men from village and town. If they survived, they roamed France and Italy as mercenaries or wandered home again. Warring kings turned to the town gilds as recruiting officers as well as paymasters, encouraging them to create those urban militias which in future times were to be now ally and now enemy of the Crown. Discharged soldiers joined the wanderers of the roads, bringing an element of organisation and boldness which created both the reality and the larger legend of the 'regiment of rogues' beloved of sensation-hungry readers in Tudor times. Any town craftsman who volunteered or was pressed into service took his chance on whether and when he came home. Not until the seventeenth century was there any concerted attempt to provide work for the ex-serviceman.

Edward III's cunning policy of conducting war on the cheap by inciting the subjects of the French rulers to rebel had a far-reaching effect on the English crafts. When the craftsmen of Flanders, highly organised in the processing of raw wool from England, were defeated in their fight for independence, many took refuge in the kingdom of their patron, moving into English towns and upsetting the local trade balance. In the long term their skill helped the development of English export trade from raw to finished wool, part of the transition of England from underdeveloped to developing nation. But in the short term the presence of the 'Flemynges' disturbed the city gilds' degree of control of trade not least because of tax exemptions and other privileges from the King. If one is to judge from the complaints, rumours and actual troubles reported in 1326,

1371 and 1380, these arose more from alien presence as masters and merchants than as journeymen weavers. In 1380 they agreed under pressure to pay contributions in line with their English counterparts. But the move came too late. A year later, when Wat Tyler and his insurgent Kentish men marched through London gates thrown open by contenders for power among the city merchants, some of the London crafts stained the occasion with the blood of Flemish weavers. Yet only a decade later, a chronic dispute between the English cordwainers (shoemakers) and the cobblers (old shoe furbishers and menders) from 'beyond sea' was resolved by a committee elected from both sides.

Another craft group set in motion by the Crown was the building trades, masons and carpenters, recruited in large numbers by monarchs from Edward I to Henry VIII. The Crown's right to conscript builders was still in existence in Restoration times, but in the 1660s, faced with the devastation of the Great Fire of London, King Charles II chose instead the more fashionable solution of the free labour market, to the chagrin of every building craft in the city (see Chapter 3).

In the Middle Ages some 1,500 castles were built, a colossal labour matched by the raising of an even greater number of churches, some of which kept masons employed for decades. In the prime of his reign Edward III kept hundreds of artificers on his permanent staff, with whom he had negotiated agreements about holy-day pay and other conditions. In 1359 he had some 1,600 masons gathered from thirty-odd countries to build Windsor Castle.

The masons, moving about the countryside, organised themselves in flexible lodges before they set up permanent town gilds. Only in 1356 were the London masons persuaded by the Mayor to set up a gild 'as other trades do'. Outside the towns the masons had their lodges, a word derived from 'loggia', the monkish name for the shelter erected by church or castle wall during construction. Then as in the twentieth century, provision of the site hut was the subject for regulation and dispute between mason and church or secular employer. The rules or 'charges' which governed behaviour in 'logge or chambere and such places as masons beth' seem to have been similar throughout the land. It is supposed they were worked out, confirmed and developed at intermittent national 'semblés' or assemblies. The so-called Regius and Cooke manuscripts (1390–1430) describe these rules in verse and prose and suggest that 'felaus' or fellows were under obligation to attend the assembly. Later versions of the 'Old Charges', dated between the early sixteenth and the early eighteenth centuries, suggest that all those working within fifty miles of the assembly point had to attend. There is only third-hand evidence that a masons' assembly, 'national chapter' or 'congregation' did take place. But it is worth a guess that when the masons gathered in 1360 to work on Windsor Castle they improved the occasion by holding a national meeting to swear in new masters and perhaps make rules. At all events Parliament announced the banning of all 'alliances and covens of masons and carpaneters, congregations and chapters, ordinances and oaths', a ban which was repeated sixty-five years later by Henry VI, or rather by his ministers since the lad was only four years old at the time. It was alleged that wage regulations were set at nought by the 'yearly congregations and confederacies made by the masons in their great chapitres assembled'.

Each castle and church was built by the amazing 'misterie' of the largely unlettered master masons. Some historians are amused by the masons' claims to date their organisation back to Euclid's time, but the remaining monuments to their calculations make the fantasy highly appropriate and honourable.

Each mason 'hewer' worked on a bench or 'bank' and on each stone block he put his 'banker mark' so that the overseer might know who made it. Banker marks carved into churches mark the progress of masons (and there are carpenters' marks too) from job to job and an interesting map in Coulton's *Art and the Reformation* charts them round the villages of Norfolk. The masons, too, carved their marks into the wood panels of the trade inns where they took their ease along the roads.

The Crown deplored and banned the masons' craft organisation. But its actions impelled and assisted them to organise. The Minstrels' Gild on the other hand was encouraged by the Crown to take nationwide 'powers of search' to counteract the tendency in those times for interlopers to invade the trade, including perhaps those unofficial 'devisors of tales' who devised them to the discredit of the King and his ministers.

The Minstrels seem to have organised on an area or regional basis, with fines for strangers who lingered in the territory as well as for a member who was guilty of 'stealing another's castle from him'.

Apart from the girdlers (on paper) and an attempt by the pewterers, there was only one effective nationwide monopoly by a craft, that of the printers, granted by Edward IV to the Stationers' Company. Backed by Crown and Church, the rigid control over printing presses – no more than twenty were permitted officially even in the seventeenth century – had explosive social and political consequences as well as causing acute economic tension within the craft.

Gilds, Church, Crown, then, all stimulated population movement, not least that of the craft worker. And one might partly blame the Crown, as war-maker, for the arrival in England in 1349 of that most potent of disturbers of stability, the bubonic plague or Black Death.

In the words of Holinshed's Chronicle, 'the people died wonderfully' and those who did not die and were minded to leave towns and villages where they were underpaid or ill-used were that much freer to do so. The Black Death hastened the trend of falling population and agricultural production as well as rising wages and prices which had already set in by the 1300s. Trades like masons and carpenters, with their mobility and organisation, benefited more than most. But all trades (including the humble land labourer) demanded more, 'immeasurably more' protested London's mayor in 1350, than they had done 'ante Pestem'. The Lord Mayor issued a list of maximum wages which, on paper at least, deprived the masons and carpenters of the after-dinner drink they had defended so vigorously in 1339 and 1306.

On the heels of the Black Death came the Statute of Labourers (1351) which laid down in detail maximum wages in every trade with a much less rigid restraint on prices (a phenomenon familiar to students of twentieth-century legislation). The Statute (25 Ed III c2), which lasted until replaced by a similar law in 1549, was intended to make labour in town or countryside stand still and take the pay offered. Authority was given to employers, if they could, to detain any one who was 'masterless' and refused an offer of pay, and make them work at the rate laid down. It was forbidden to give money to rovers, 'sub colore pietatis vel elemoisine', under colour of piety or charity, a provision which seems in part aimed at craftsmen on the move seeking alms from church or gild. The White Friars and the Black were closely associated with the rank and file of the cordwainers' and curriers' trades in London, York and Canterbury and with the 'inferior' crafts in Coventry, just as the merchant gilds and superior crafts were catered for by the wealthier religious houses. John Ball, the hedge priest and inspirer of the 1381 revolt, had his lesser known counterparts.

Langland, poet-critic of clerical corruption much as he sympathised with the poor, particularly on the land, could understand no more than Wyclif the craftsman who preferred to move on rather than accept the pay offered, 'And can some manere craft an he wolde hit use' (And has a trade if he would use it).

The Statute of Labourers appointed several hundred Enforcers including many priests (clearly no John Balls) to tour the country and punish labourers refusing the statutory wage. They heard cases involving tens of thousands of people and their passage through the land was marked by discontent and rioting. Significantly both in 1364 and 1373 it was laid down in court that the Statute applied to the artificers of the crafts as well as land labourers. Town craftsmen were better able to circumvent or defy such a wage freeze, but the workers on the land were not helpless and were egged on by landowners who were ready to pay a penny a day more even when they had voted in Parliament to make it illegal. The labourer could and did 'suddenly depart into another country' (county) despite the Parliament plea in 1376 that runaways should go to their 'pays propre' and there 'abide'. Some serfs, it was noted, ran away to the towns and became artificers. Perhaps some came back along the pilgrim route with a friendly craftsman, say a Lincoln fuller, and passed through the city gates, paid a penny, and began a new life. Where cities were building up their population to challenge the manpower assembled by the feudal overlord, runaway serfs from elsewhere might be welcome, though craft regulations often laid down that no serfs could be admitted. There was more than one motive for this. The Masons' charges of the fourteenth and fifteenth centuries said that new entrants to the trade must be free men. A curious and interesting reason is given. It might happen that if a serf became a mason then his former 'lorde to whom he is bonde' might come into the lodge with his men. The one-time serf's brother masons might 'debate for him' and 'peradventure manslaughter might thereoff arise'. What is surely known is that the attempt by a knight to drag back a former servant from Gravesend where he had been accepted as a freeman led to a mass protest, one of the initial tremors in the 1381 earthquake.

Though 1381 is known as the Peasants' Revolt, town and village craftsmen were largely involved as well and craftsmen on the move played a part in the revolt's preparation. Masons, tailors, dyers and 'tilers' or 'teghlers' were seized and interrogated after the defeat. It is from the evidence of a renegade mason that we know that pilgrimages were a means of contact between rebels. After the trials and executions were over, near Buntingford in Hertfordshire a tailor led a small outlaw band for several months, no doubt adding a page to the Robin Hood legend. A recent Marxist history of the revolt has described it as a 'broadly based uprising of the Third Estate'.

After it was crushed, and the rebels slaughtered until the king realised that 'too many of his liege subjects would be undone', he told the survivors, 'serfs you were and serfs you are'. But seven years later Parliament was calling for sterner measures to control the movement to and fro of the 'poor'. They must remain where they were born, or return to their birthplace, the first of many similar directives which over the next five hundred years, under the peculiar heading of 'Settlement' law, were to harry the poor without alleviating their poverty.

Craftsmen and other 'servants' might 'freely depart' provided they knew their next employer and carried with them a certificate or 'passport' signed by a 'prodhomme' or someone of repute in village or town. How far this was enforced would be difficult to say, but it must have reinforced the custom in the crafts to examine the credentials of the stranger.

In the same year, 1388, the gilds were ordered to deliver up to local sheriffs details of all 'brotherhoods' their 'origins, governance, oaths, meetings, liberties, ordinances, usages and any charters or letters patent as well as how much money they had'.

How far the Crown suspected the gilds were involved in any rebellions, one cannot say. But with the order, the chapter of independence of the town craftsmen from local and national law was clearly at an end. For some among the crafts the step was welcome and right; for others not so.

2 The serving men called yo'men
1450–1550

From henceforth when any stranger cometh to London to have a service, any of the servants . . . [who] knoweth that he will have a service shall bring him to a master to serve and to warn the warden that is their governor that he may be at the covenant making.

Agreement between Masters and Yeomen of the Blacksmiths' Company, 1434.

Two years after the Great Revolt, the Mayor of London, 'on behalf of the king', proclaimed that 'no person should make congregations, alliances or covins of the people, privily or openly; and that those belonging to the trades more than other men, should not, without leave of the mayor, make congregations, conventicles nor assemblies, alliances, confederacies or conspiracies, or obligations to bind men together'.

The London proclamation of 1383, like the Royal decrees of 1306 and 1360, like the Statute of Labourers of 1349–51, seemed designed to control the crafts on behalf of the customer or employer. On the face of it, the actions of the local or national authorities were directed towards the crafts as a whole, to make the mason or carpenter serve the king more willingly, or the weavers weave more cheaply for the burrellers, the blacksmith obey the city ordinances more exactly, or to resolve disputes between the saddlers, lorimers and joiners. No obvious distinction was made between master and man and disputes were solved by meeting or committee. The numbers involved, after all, were not large. The crafts formed but a small part of the population. Though the move to the city continued against the national trend of falling population, yet by mid-fourteenth century the seven premier cities of England made up only 3 per cent of the total population, with London having the lion's share. Today a comparable figure for the seven largest cities would be 25 per cent of the population.

But at this time we are talking of a London population of 30,000–40,000, York 11,000, Bristol 10,000, with Manchester and Birmingham smaller. In booming Colchester, with between three and four thousand inhabitants, some trades might count their numbers by the half dozen and in Norwich, even by the 1450s, regulations provided for the election of officers by craft gilds of seven and more members.

At such a stage in the growth of the crafts, the key figure was the master craftsman and in all but the biggest trades the number of masters might equal or exceed that of the journeymen and servants. At such craft meetings there was little to complicate craft democracy. Only in the larger crafts did distinctions creep in and it was necessary to lay down, as the bowyers did in 1370, that the fraternity's officers shall be elected 'as well by serving men as masters'. Disputes between masters and serving men could be regulated individually. These disputes could be violent on occasion but when in 1358 the master and journeymen weavers of Chester came to blows the pole-axe wielding masters were in sufficient numbers to win the day.

But the steps taken by the craft masters to conserve their position, as town and trade population grew, slowly but surely shifted the balance. Measures like the seven-year apprenticeship, the need to purchase the 'freedom' of the city before setting up a workshop, or taking apprentices, held down the number of masters while the journeymen and covenant men increased around them. Financially this suited the masters who grew richer and more secure by being able to hold down the rate at which their pupils might rise to compete with them.

But such an imbalance had an inevitable result. In two disputes involving the shearmen (who cropped the woven wool level) in 1350 and the alien master weavers and their servants in 1362, it was observed that the servants instead of settling the dispute man to man would go around among themselves and agree that none of them would work until the said master and man 'had come to agreement'. In such a situation, a meeting of the trade, where serving men had the majority, would have meant the defeat of the masters. But they had a card to play. Their ace was municipal and state regulation.

This they used increasingly in arguments over wages or, rather, how to divide the price asked of the customer. Price lists were the subject of disputes in city companies until the nineteenth century. The master shearmen and the alien weaving masters went to the mayor for help. The master cobblers of Bristol in the 1360s cited the Statute of Labourers as proof that their servants' demands were unreasonable. By the 1380s, and in particular in London where the process of differentiation among craft members was urged on by population increase and concentration of wealth, disputes of an open kind between masters and men were more common. During the reign of Edward III (1327–77) craft ordinances began to lay down that the servant who 'behaves ill' should be dealt with by the mayor.

Four years after the proclamation of 1383, the mayor imprisoned three men, spokesmen for the cordwainers' serving men. In defiance of the proclamation they had held a 'great congregation of men like unto themselves' in the church of the Blackfriars. They were clearly discussing a wage demand 'to the damage of the commonalty and the prejudice of the trade'. Brother John Bartone, one of the friars, had promised he would take their case if need be to the 'Court of Rome' and they had collected money for that purpose. The mayor grew indignant over this deed 'which notoriously redounds to the weakening of the liberties of the said city'. So the three men went to jail.

The case was brought by the 'overseers' of the trade, the leading masters. Over a period of some thirty years, all trades in the city, willingly or unwillingly, had seen their regulations publicly set down and vetted by the Mayor and Council, in effect by the trading elite. Most crafts did it willingly for in return the city government's power now backed that of the gild in enforcing control of the trade. The bonfires of false and deceitful goods on Cheapside were official. In exchange, 'overseers' were chosen on terms approved by the city council.

The masons chose 'twelve of the most skilful', the helmet makers 'their best workmen', the hatters 'the most lawful and best befitting', the tailors the 'most honest and sufficient'. The range was wide, but the trend was towards choosing the more substantial masters. A minority of the fraternity's members – even a minority of the masters – was placed in a position of authority and backed by the city traders among whose ranks the richer craft masters found their place. Even if chosen by the whole craft, their authority no longer depended on solidarity alone, by the recognition of all who worked in it. A division had appeared that was to widen decade by decade and which in the late fourteenth century appeared to reach a complete break.

Nine years after the jailing of the cordwainers' servants the master saddlers complained that the 'serving men called yomen' were holding meetings outside the city, causing 'inconveniences' to the trade. More than holding meetings, they had been wearing a 'like suit' or livery and they had appointed a 'bedel' who would suddenly summon them to 'vigils' for dead brothers when they ought to have been working. The saddlers' servants replied they had done this 'time out of mind'. The masters retorted that they had only done it for thirteen years. If the masters told the truth, then the saddlers organisation dated from 1383 and, like that of the cordwainers, was in open defiance of the proclamation.

Worse still, 'under false colour of sanctity', alleged the masters, the journeymen had caused the wage to rise from five to twelve marks a year. The Mayor cannily told both sides to get together in committee and later ordered that the journeymen must 'come under the governance and rule of the masters' but they on their side must treat their servants better.

Some twenty years later in 1415 an even wider dispute arose between the 'yomen taillours' and their masters. If the account is accurate, the serving tailors had their own fraternity, rules and church services, and lived apart from their masters in 'houses of ill-repute' near St James's Church in Garlickhythe.

They lived like fighting cocks, beating any unfortunate master who dared reprove them, assaulting Sheriffs' men who arrested them, and rescuing prisoners. The tailors told the Mayor they simply wished to continue the customs of their fraternity and the Mayor after lecturing them on being 'youthful and unstable' told them to be under the 'governance and rule' of the masters.

At roughly the same time, the serving tailors of Coventry fought a running battle with the ruling 'Corpus Christi' gild. Their fraternity, forbidden under one saint's name, was resurrected under another. Similar but less acrimonious disputes involved the Bristol cordwainers, the Northampton weavers, the Norwich and Oxford shoemakers and the London bakers, who kept their own 'livery and revelling hall'. Revelling was as much a part of fraternity activity as rule making and one writer put down the urge of the servants to organise to their envy of the high time their masters had in their 'observances'.

But there were serious common factors in these incidents. They show that the masters, or the 'overseers' among them were no longer able to govern the craft without the aid of an outside authority and that the distance between master and man was such that wage and other questions were being dealt with by collective action and sometimes with violence. Unlike the master weavers of Chester, the craft masters of the other towns no longer felt able to match blow for blow. Among the London cordwainers, journeymen sometimes outnumbered masters eight to one.

But a more ominous sign from the overseers' point of view was that among the saddlers 'the serving men had influenced the journeymen among them'. The cordwainers' journeymen were alleged to be acting 'with their accomplices' and the serving tailors included both journeymen and serving men. The day wage and covenant men, some of whom came

44

from outside the city, were making common cause. The old craft loyalty was giving birth to a new kind – loyalty of man against master.

Thus the 'yomen' or 'young men' fraternities suddenly appearing in the feudal era were once seen romantically as early 'trade unions'.

This in turn led other writers to point out that the fundamental conditions for a class division between capital and labour were not in sight at the time. Indeed the ties and loyalties between master and man in a multitude of small workshops were to last another four centuries and more. But, if not embryo trade unions, what were the 'yomen taillours', weavers, cordwainers, saddlers and bakers in London and other cities? The opposing theory is that they were 'ephemeral' combinations of wage earners later crushed out of existence by authority. Just what was happening in the crafts at this time is worth discussing (see Chapter 16). But the 'yomen gilds' were not early trade unions, nor did they disappear.

At least as they 'disappear' something else appears. During the fifteenth century in most crafts where there were a sizeable number at work, a 'yomandry' or 'yeomanry' was formed. This is the rule among curriers, cutlers, cordwainers, brewers, blacksmiths, carpenters, leathersellers, drapers, iron-mongers and tailors in London, while variations of the same appear, sometimes fleetingly, in the craft histories of Bristol, Coventry, York, Exeter, Northampton, Hull, Oxford and other cities. Scarcely a company in London was without its yeomanry says one authority; yeomanry organisation was universal, is another verdict. The yeomanry was not separate but an integral yet self-contained subordinate section of the craft company. The subordination is sometimes not so obvious and the masters and journeymen appear as equal partners, sometimes with the mayor as arbitrator, in disputes over payment for altar lights, prices and other 'necessary and good matters', or more often arguments over the poor fund which was kept in a 'great chest lokkid with three lokkes' (a custom in craft organisation which was to last into the nineteenth century).

The yeomanry, in fact, was a compromise, giving the masters control over the men and the men a form of organisation which they could and did use on occasion, access to funds to relieve poverty, and the backing of the company to preserve their livelihood.

What sort of compromise it was depended on the strengths of the two parties. The tailors' and blacksmiths' yeomanry retained a good deal of their identity, including membership of the fraternities of St John and St Loi. Among the matters agreed in both trades, by the blacksmiths in 1434 and the tailors in 1458 was that the yeomanry would be responsible for the 'search for forrens'. It would be their job to check that no stranger

45

was employed in any workshop without leave of the craft. The black-smiths' journeymen were to appoint a brother who was to take any new arrival to a master who had vacancies. In smaller cities like York, Hull and Exeter, the responsibility for reception of the stranger and approving or vetoing his employment was shared. The 'brother' assigned to the task might be master or man. The chief interest in seeing the control was exercised would be the journeymen's. The way of the blacksmiths and tailors was the pattern of the future, the yeomanry watching entry to the trade and dispensing charity to the 'poor', the unemployed and aged. These internal changes occupied the crafts through a long period of social disruption – the end of the costly and disastrous French Wars, the Jack Cade Revolt and the Wars of the Roses.

During a lull in civil strife, Edward IV, keen to raise money, not only taxed and borrowed from the merchants but joined their ventures. He busily granted charters of incorporation to trading and craft bodies, thus urging forward their already well-advanced transformation into 'livery companies'. Earlier, in 1411, to reduce baronial power, Henry IV had banned retainers from wearing uniform or 'livery'. But the crafts were allowed to keep their 'cloathing' and it is evident that the yeomanry of saddlers, tailors, bakers and other crafts had their livery. When they were brought firmly 'under the governance' livery became more and more the privilege of the masters. Worn at the prestigious annual feasts, Lord Mayor's Days and processions to honour reigning monarchs, livery grew more expensive – 'white garments brawderid with conysaunces of every craft'.

From the 1450s it is evident that not every master has livery and there is talk of brothers 'in' and 'out of the cloathing', or, among the Exeter tailors, 'yowte brodere' or 'out brothers', paying less to the fraternity than those of the livery.

The social stability that came with peace, rising trade and the growing wealth of the craft masters, impelled these changes. By 1500 most of the new companies were divided into livery and yeomanry sections, with the new charters conferring 'perpetual succession' of the craft leadership not on the masters as a body but on the richer section of them. The livery companies once incorporated could own land and property, not only the 'livery halls' which now began to rise but elsewhere as well. Income from this property made the livery more independent of dues paid by the rest of the gild, the 'commonalty'. With the backing of the new charters the liverymen claimed for themselves the right to elect the chief Master of the Company and his Wardens or Assistants who personified the authority of the company. 'They among themselves and none other' had the vote, as the clothworkers' livery put it. The London masons' company charter (1481) is described by the craft historian as 'oligarchical', while in 1487 the carpenters had gone from election by 'common consent' to 'such as "the livery" think convenient'. By degrees the carpenters' company records ceased to refer to the 'brotherhood' but simply to 'this house'. The Hull weavers in 1490 specifically barred the journeymen from the election for Company Master.

From these distinctions flowed others. The London carpenters at the annual feast provided napkins for the livery. Their Coventry brothers ordered 'marmalet and cakes' for themselves, 'bread and ale' for the other ranks.

The changes were prolonged and uneven, varying with the size of craft and town. In 1483 the London mercers had decided that it was 'tedious and grievous' to call so many 'congregations' even of the masters. But in 1477 the Bury linen and woollen weavers – masters, journeymen and apprentices – all assembled to elect the company leadership, as did the Beverley weavers.

The mercers were the richest of the London companies, most powerful of the top layer of merchants and trading masters. City growth and trade specialisation had seen the old 'gild merchant' split into its constituent mercers, drapers, grocers, etc. Just how far these 'merchant' companies were above the smaller crafts in wealth and power can be seen by the Royal Loan raised in London in 1488 when the mercers put up £740, the grocers £455, the carpenters £8 and the masons £4.

The gild pageants of the fifteenth century, a colourful part of the nation's cultural history, take on a new light – and the growing cost and magnificence of the tableaux a new meaning – when seen as part of the competition for economic leadership and public importance. Not for nothing did the mercers of Norwich undertake the staging of the 'Creation', while smaller crafts were obliged to amalgamate to meet pageant expenses. Strangers were obliged to contribute to the cost of the pageant if they wanted to stay in the city. The race was never equal but the competition for 'precedence' down to the last position in the procession was fierce. In England, long after the pageants lost their importance, the fight for 'precedence' continued, involving the crafts in London in dispute right into the sixteenth century. Even in the eighteenth century an argument over which craft forged the needle which sewed the fig leaf for Adam and Eve could enliven a pot of ale in a house of call. But at earlier times the struggle was grimmer and in London it was finally resolved only by a compromise agreement which fixed 'The Order of Precedence' for good.

By this agreement, reached between 1514 and 1516, the twelve major companies, known as 'The Great Twelve', formed themselves into what has been described as a 'self-constituted oligarchy'. The Great Twelve were mainly trading companies and at the head of course were the mercers, not the oldest company, but definitely the richest. Goldsmiths, skinners, merchant tailors and clothworkers were included in the Great Twelve by virtue of their power as financiers and traders rather than their eminence as craftsmen. In his *Utopia* (1516) Sir Thomas More bracketed goldsmiths disparagingly with usurers as unproductive. The tailors were so far involved in trading that in 1502 they had royal permission to name themselves Merchant Taylors and to alter their charter so that men who never learnt to sew in their lives might be admitted to the company. This began a trend in other companies. To the traditional methods of entry by 'servitude' (apprenticeship and journeyman time) or 'patrimony' (inheritance) was added the new one of 'redemption' – a peculiar perversion of the language, meaning 'buying in'. The master who turned into a trader, the trader who 'redeemed' himself into a craft company by his wealth (on which wealth the buying and renewing of charters depended) – these men came through control of the market to dominate the company. The separation of the trader and the manual worker and the domination of the second by the first has been seen as the fundamental difference between the old fraternity and the new livery company.

The process was external as well as internal. The Tudor period saw wealthier companies absorbing or taking over smaller crafts and subordinating them to the status of employees – the leathersellers taking over the glovers, the blacksmiths absorbing the spurriers, the haberdashers the hatters; the clothworkers combining the older shearmen's and fullers' gilds. Thus within one company a merchant elite bore down on an entire working craft, both master and man.

And within the companies the stratification went one stage further. By mid-sixteenth-century, within the livery appeared an inner clique, the Court of Assistants. The Merchant Taylors prescribed penalties for any liveryman who joined in illicit meetings of the craft. The status of the richer, trading master was enhanced as he became interchangeable with the merchant. The status of the poorer master was reduced.

In theory a craftsman who served seven years and then paid the 'upstart' or 'upset' fee could take on an apprentice or employ a journeyman and thus advance himself. But unless he could gain a place in the livery he was limited by craft rule to one apprentice. A liveryman was entitled to two or three according to trade and the chief master of the company to three or four. Thus the hierarchy and balance of the trade were apparently preserved. But it was an unstable balance.

For the liverymen racked up the 'upset' fees to hold back journeymen from becoming masters. They held down the numbers allowed in the livery to prevent the smaller masters from expanding. There were complaints of 'cunning devices' to stop journeymen competing with the masters. Some towns, like Oxford, stepped in to limit fees to twenty shillings. When first the ministers of Henry VII and then Henry VIII intervened to try to peg the entry fees, the average sum was already two or three times as large. Officially the fee to become an apprentice was half a crown. In London it was ten or fifteen times that amount.

Another 'device' was to extract a promise (sometimes under company rule) that the journeyman would not set up for three years after his 'servitude' had ended. So general was this rule by the 1530s that it was automatically applied to pauper apprentices, who, it was laid down, should remain journeymen until the age of 24. In 1556 this age limit became the law of London and in 1563 the Statute of Artificers declared that 24 was the age at which a young man was ready for responsibility.

Three years' delay was not the limit (in Scotland five years was often prescribed) and in London the printers' journeymen protested that eight years apprenticeship followed by five years as a journeyman was a 'lifetime of servitude'. With the life expectation of Tudor times this was small exaggeration.

Thus the yeomanry became the place not only for journeymen but small masters waiting for promotion to the livery. By 1571 the carpenters' company was made up of 40 liverymen and some 300 yeomen, journeymen and small masters. The company historian says the distinction between livery and yeomanry was that between the 'relatively' and the 'less prosperous carpenter'. In the Bakers' Company yeomanry 'servants' were in the majority but the masters, 'mainly single-oven men', took the lead. The tailors' yeomanry became the 'working or labouring part' of the company. As the cutlers' company historian remarks, since the livery was fixed, the yeomanry began to fill up with masters either waiting for a vacancy or having abandoned any attempt at rising.

Some clothworkers' masters were so poor that they paid their fees by instalments of one shilling a month. Such a division in the crafts between livery and yeomanry was above all a matter of economics and was bound to harden. Relations were bound to worsen.

Social divisions within the crafts were widened during the period of the Reformation, as the drive to secularise public life and drive corruption out of the Church reached its climax under the Tudors. This dovetailed with the drive for self-enrichment among the new men who rose with the dynasty. Crown ministers and their associates plundered the wealth of the monasteries and the secularisation process radically affected the companies. By an Act of 1547 companies were told by the King's Commissioners to hand over and then buy back any religious charitable foundations connected with them. At the same time they had to reveal any 'peculiar brotherhoods' existing within the companies under the 'pretended colour of piety or charity'. In this way the old fraternities of pre-company days, in a number of cases coexisting with the yeomanry, vanished from independent life. Their charitable function was to be absorbed by the companies and at the same time a number of the yeomanries were 'remodelled' with a further reduction in their independent rights.

In many trades, notably in building, the opportunity was taken in the name of secular reform to abolish a number of saints' days, which in the past had been holidays and for which even Edward III had to pay his masons and carpenters. With the old holidays gone, the custom grew in certain trades of taking 'Saint Monday' – not working on the day following a holy day.

As Firke the journeyman declares in Dekker's *Shoemaker's Holiday*, 'Say what they like, Monday's our holiday.' 'They' in historical terms were a strange alliance of rich masters and Puritan reformers who from the days of Wyclif and Langland had agitated both against clerical corruption and craft custom.

At the same time (1547 in the case of the clothworkers) restrictions were placed on the employment of 'any mayd or womankind'.

The Bakers' Company would allow no 'mayde servant' to do work which might 'supply the service of any man servants'. The place held by women workers in the crafts, sometimes as unskilled labour, more rarely through apprenticeship, was thus increasingly restricted. But the right of widows to take over their husband's business remained, vested as it was in property right.

The whole process of reform and discipline through the late medieval craft structure is sometimes seen as the 'suppression' of the craft gilds, accompanying the suppression of the monasteries. The old fraternities did indeed disappear. But skilled work cannot be done without organisation; nor can skilled workers live without it. The 'handytrade' found their place within the reformed yeomanry, and in the bigger, better organised trades like those of weavers, tailors and clothworkers, the rank and file resisted the livery's attempt to have complete control, contesting above all the use of charitable funds and the powers of 'search'.

The livery's powers within the company were backed by municipal and state law, and that of 1548-9 (ED VI 2-3 c xv) prohibited craft 'confederacies' with sworn oaths which tried to lay down the price for work and the rate at which it was done. A first offence under this law brought a £10 fine (six months' wages) and twenty days' jail on bread and water; a second offence, £40 and the loss of the accused's ears. These laws replaced the old Statute of Labourers and the law of 1549 was itself to be renewed until repealed together with the Combination Acts in 1826. One historian has spoken pointedly of a centuries-long conspiracy against working people.

Against this background the yeomanry of companies like the founders, tailors, curriers, bakers and clothworkers fought running battles with the livery over elections, control of funds for the poor and the use of the right of search. These disputes might be resolved or rendered less sharp by arbitration and compromise, as was the 'variance and discord' among the founders over their poor box in 1508. Or rupture might be postponed. In 1538 the Bakers' livery warned the yeomanry to 'keep the King's Peas' on pain of utter expulsion from the Company Hall.

Thanks to a well kept company minute book, the threat was carried out – 150 years later.

Beneath the organisational squabbles was the basic economic divergence: for some few the opportunity as liveryman to become richer, for others, to remain a poor master limited for life to one apprentice, or to work as a journeyman in the employ of a liveryman of the same company. This stretched the meaning of brotherhood beyond the bounds of the old loyalties.

It was stretched to breaking-point when the yeomanry discovered they were competing with cheap labour employed by the wealthier masters, some of whom were dodging the company controls and taking on more apprentices than they were entitled to. Complaints of 'disregard' were heard from Norwich to London. The bakers' yeomanry 'brought in' the names of offending masters; clothworkers and cutlers' yeomanry added their complaints. In the 1550s, seventeen craft companies seeking a way out of internal dispute asked the Common Council to fix by law the number of apprentices each master might take. But this did not put an end to the problem. For the richer masters had developed a double standard. They enforced regulations which held back the journeymen and small masters from competing while ignoring the restrictions on themselves. As a modern authority on the gilds has pointed out the richer members respected the rules of the crafts if business was steady or expanding slowly. But in times of rapid expansion they impatiently broke through any restraining rules.

The merchant masters of the expanding wool trade had the arrogance of confidence. Rejecting the demand of their journeymen for guaranteed employment, the clothworkers' liverymen said: Let journeymen and servants take what work they were offered. If not they ran the risk of being 'beat at a cart's arse' and banished from the city. They agreed, however, with the rank and file of the craft that company members should have priority over 'forrens'.

Not only 'forrens' were seen as a threat to employment; a renewed influx of 'aliens' also excited hostility. In 1514 a petition went to Parliament, backed by 'various trades' from the haughty mercers to the humble joiners, complaining of the 'grete multitude pepyll, estrangers of dyvers nacions, Frenshemen, Galymen, Pycards, Flemynges, Keteryckis, Spuryars, Scottis, Lumbardis and dyvers hother nacions'. By this influx, it was alleged, 'the King's naturall subjects would be utterleye decayed'.

Three years later, on Evil May Day, 1517, came riots and violence against the 'aliens' with punitive executions to follow. May Day had always been a time for grievances to come to the fore. As early as 1356 the Shrewsbury journeymen's May Day Festival was suppressed, and the association of blacksmiths and other crafts with disruptive celebration of 'Robert Hude' and 'The Lord of Misrule and the Abbot of Unreason' on May Day is on record. In the Elizabethan pamphlet, 'The Commonweal', the Merchant is heard to complain of the bad influence of both May Day and pilgrimages. On London's 'Evil' May Day, after which twelve apprentices were hanged, the scapegoat for trades discontent was the 'arrogance of the Genoways' (Genoese) merchants, just as privileges for 'Flemynges' excited hostility in the 1380s. But, as at the earlier time, a wider discontent lay at the root of the chauvinistic outbreak. After 1517 it is noted that the trades masters 'went in fear'. The rank and file of the crafts now numbering thousands in and around London made up a formidable body. Thanks to the organisation of the journeymen by 'quarters' of the city, protest crowds were swiftly assembled. The organised crafts were in a minority in city populations, but as an 'artisan elite' had great influence. London's situation applied to other ancient cities and later James I sourly noted that if anyone displeased the

Edinburgh crafts they would take to the streets and 'up goeth the blue blanket' (the blue banner of the amalgamated companies). City masters had good cause to look warily at their 'brothers'. And outside the cities were even more potent forces of discontent.

Along the country roads trudged the vagrants in hungry and desperate bands that grew in number as the ending of the French wars, the thirty years of civil war that followed and the disbandments that accompanied the Reformation added to the flood of discharged retainers and other 'masterless men' who continued their marauding under their own 'captains'.

The decline and suppression of the monasteries with their network of charity-hospitality, limited as it was, put more beggars on the roads and by Henry VIII's reign one estimate put their number at 72,000.

The new men in power felt no obligation to the poor, 'impotent' or 'sturdy'. A popular poem of the time spoke of 'putting away cloisterers' and getting 'extortioners' in their place.

For two centuries the law had demanded that the poor stay where they were born and take service with those who offered work. Even charitable Sir Thomas More would have no casual wanderers in his Utopia. Travellers without passports were sent home 'disgraced'. But, as More knew, there was a new breed of landlord, eager for the profits of the expanding corn and wool trade, eager for land even more than labour. Unlike their forerunners, they no longer pursued labourers to force them back to the land but urged them on to the roads. 'By force or fraud ... away they go, poor silly folk,' said Sir Thomas. The notion that there were people who were idle and rootless not out of will but out of circumstance, because the livelihood had been taken from them, had taken shape. But the law (1496 and 1527) doggedly demanded that the poor go back to the place where they were born or had lived three years and (1530) told the 'sturdy' beggar to submit to a whipping till the blood ran and then to 'put himself to labour'. In 1547, if the sturdy beggar refused, then he should be branded 'S' for slave and if he falsely claimed to belong to a certain town he could be branded 'V' for vagrant. The children of the 'idle' were to be taken from them and 'apprenticed' by the parish, thus setting in train a 300-year saga of cheap labour employed at the expense of the organised craftsman.

No one, on pain of heavy fine, should offer meat and drink to the vagrant. But if a 'valiant' beggar submitted to a whipping and had a testimonial to prove it, he might go every ten miles to a constable and get food and lodging (1535) – a grotesque parody of the relief system beginning to develop among the crafts.

Faced with such charity it was small wonder that the poor – man, woman, child – sometimes turned to the security of the roving bands under their leaders the 'upright men', with their crude organisation and hierarchy.

Fanciful writers of later Tudor times excited their fearful, prurient readers with tales of a 'regiment of rogues' under a range of captains from Jack Straw in the 1380s to Jack Cade in the 1450s, with internal rules and strange sexual customs and a headquarters at Devil's Arse-a-Peak (Castleton) in Derbyshire. (Strangely, in the early 1960s there were rumours of a secret 'hippy headquarters' in this location, which demonstrates the persistence of prejudice and legend.) What is interesting, though, is that the Elizabethan 'low life' writers show the rogues' regiment as having rules couched in the terms of a trade fraternity with meetings, points of order, petitions and fines for unacceptable conduct, the fines to be drunk by the whole company. This reported influence of craft custom and rules on the roving population shows itself again in Victorian times (see Chapter 13).

There is little doubt that among the rovers were craftsmen on the move who had no prospect of work. In an authentic-sounding poem written in 1536, when legislation against vagrants reached a height of ferocity with whipping, branding, gristle-cutting, mutilation and hanging, the writer asks the porter of the 'hospice' who comes for relief. He answers with a list of the unfortunate and irresponsible and includes:

'Craftsmen who work both day and night
'Their labour great and their gains light.'

Thus the trades added their quota to the unemployed as economic change beyond their control put traditional ways and forms to great strain. 'Our dyers go vagrant for lack of work,' said the Bristol dyers in 1408. But they were the victims not of 'bad trade' but of free trade. The wholesale cloth merchants, whom we see already in the fourteenth century trying to force down the prices of the operative weavers in London, had by the fifteenth century begun to outflank the closed shop of the town crafts. Taking their raw material to the countryside they found new weavers in the villages less able to impose conditions on price and production time. The burreller was transformed into the clothier and while the weaving trade went down in the old walled towns it rose in the smaller places of the West Country and East Anglia.

By Henry VIII's reign there were clothiers who employed hundreds of weavers and spinners, not under one roof like the legendary Jack of

Newbury but in their own cottages, with a little land, perhaps some livestock, but partly, at least, dependent upon the wealthy man who sent them wool and took away their cloth. By Tudor times the clothier was a power in the land with influence over the livelihood of thousands. The authorities, Crown and Star Chamber, were increasingly aware of the danger of crowds of 'idle' weavers with clear-cut social grievances, aggravated by the new barons of the wool trade whose greed and arrogance like that of the big landowners and the richest city merchants could disturb the social calm the rulers sought.

Something of the class hatred is echoed in the writing of the time. Thomas More, noting how the rise in the price of wool ruins the poor weavers, attacks the 'insatiable cormorants' and contrasts them with the labourer and craftsman without whose work 'no Commonwealth can continue' yet who are left in poverty. Crowley speaks of 'cormorants, greedy gulls' whose 'idle bellies devour all that we shall get by our sore labour'. Both echo the sermon of John Ball in the 1380s: '. . . by that which cometh of our labour they keep and maintain their estate.'

In the *Commonweal*, published in 1549, a knight speaks of 'lack of occupation' and says: 'When our clothiers lack vent a multitude of idle stir the poor commons to commotion.' Thomas Cromwell, Chief Minister to Henry VIII, tried to force the clothiers to keep the weavers at work, for any 'murmur or sedition' for lack of work would be 'laid to their charge'. Cromwell, son and son-in-law of shearmen, was shrewdly aware of the state of the wool industry.

The journeymen of the crafts reacted defensively to the threat to their livelihood represented by the great moving stream of unemployed on the road outside the town gates. The prospect of a lifetime's work for someone else was not made easier by the more imminent prospect of being cast off in favour of a stranger or alien working for lower pay. Already among the London and Norwich masons there were regulations to ensure 'foreyns' did not compete with local journeymen. Masters were instructed that the stranger must be employed only as an 'allow' or hired man.

Some Hull crafts would not employ a journeyman at all from outside the city if he had wife and children and might settle them there to perhaps become a charge on the poor box at some later date. The demand for job protection by the local journeymen, coupled with the skill difference between the locally trained craftsman and the newly arrived foreigner, helped along the development of a grading among the labour force which matched in its way the hierarchy among the masters. The 'free sewers' of the Exeter tailors' company paid a larger quarterage than the outsider, although the new arrival could establish himself as a free sewer by paying a lump sum.

Among the strangers coming into the towns were more and more artisans who had served their time as well as wanderers who had picked up the trade and had to be 'tried and proved'. The London founders at this time kept a separate list of 'journeymen strangers' who were 'free of the company' but probably did not have the freedom of the city and thus were barred from setting up. Freemen, said the London carpenters, must have work priority over those coming in from outside. This rule was general. Among bakers, masons and brushmakers alike, freemen journeymen had priority over others well into the nineteenth century. The London tailors distinguished in their quarterage payments between 'men free of this mistery and free of the city' and those who were not, while in Exeter, the bakers required a special fee to be paid by masters taking on non-apprenticed labour.

Thus the growth of a skilled labour force, some of whom were freemen, full company members, and others not, went on steadily through the sixteenth century. However, the number of surplus though fully apprenticed men forced to take the road clearly grew. So the custom of quizzing, registering and entertaining the stranger became more regularised. The bakers in every town began to demand that travelling journeymen or servants should have a certificate from their last master to show their trade standing. Bury weavers demanded that strangers explain why they left their last employ. They were then given a certificate and allowed to start work. Bristol and York tailors asked strangers to show their indentures to prove they had served their time. In this way craft organisation with its reputation for restrictiveness in fact enhanced the mobility of labour.

Reduced prospects of mastership and periodic unemployment added to the craftsmen's restlessness.

The state of trade in the clothing trades varied with the season in any case, and there was still great variation from one city to another, with great sprawling London trebling in size during the sixteenth century to dwarf all others. When trade was bad the journeyman could hang around the company hall, or more likely the inn or 'house of call' patronised by the trade, and wait until a master sent for him, meanwhile living on the 'box' or on his shopmates' goodwill. Or he could take the road.

If that was his choice he could set off, tools on his back, apprentice lines or certificate of good standing in his pocket. That paper would protect him from the attentions of constable or beadle who had power to demand from any wayfarer a paper signed by someone of good standing ('prudhomme'). The pass system which dated from the fourteenth century worked erratically. Elizabethan lawmakers complained that vagrants would rather pay a shilling for a 'jarkman' to forge a paper than twopence to come by one honestly. Not all trades were formal in their demands for credentials. The cordwainers or shoemakers were prepared to welcome as brothers the man who came bearing 'St Hugh's bones' or the tools of the trade. The legend of St Crispin the martyr whose bones after death were transformed into tools for shoemakers was still performed as a play by the Cordwainers' Company on 25 October in Elizabeth's day. But in shoemakers' lore the legend was changed into the 'Ballad of Sir Hugh' who was not only a Christian martyr but a 'prince and lover' who tramped with the shoemakers and they:

> brought him relief
> when trouble and grief,
> in travel had him dismayed.

They stood by him when he was imprisoned as indeed any fraternity were in rule bound to stand by a member who had not 'wantonly' brought on his own misfortune. St Hugh's bones marked the shoemaker.

In Dekker's *Shoemaker's Holiday*, Lacey the hero enters the master shoemaker's shop disguised as a Flemish shoemaker. Firke the journeyman says:

'Master, for my life, yonder's a brother of the gentle craft ... if he bear not Saint Hugh's bones ...'.

The master is reluctant to employ the alleged traveller but when Firke and his fellow craftsmen threaten to 'goe play' or take a 'Saint Monday' off, the master is quickly persuaded by his wife to think again. The supposed Fleming having duly paid his drink money is admitted to the shop.

The masons, wanderers above all, maintained their lodge organisation by church or castle and in town during the Middle Ages and it seems that the travelling 'felaus' made themselves known on arrival by passwords, signs and handshakes (the mason's grip). As the castle trade declined, the country house trade rose and so the network of organisation stabilised closer to town and village.

The original documents in verse and prose which laid down the masons' rules in the fourteenth and fifteenth centuries were amended and updated (perhaps in the annual 'semble' or 'chapitre', though there is no absolute proof of this). These rules have been preserved in some seventy or eighty separate documents known collectively as 'The Old Charges'. They date from the sixteenth to the eighteenth century and embody rules made earlier. They have been found in most parts of the country.

Most of these 'Old Charges' specifically name the travelling mason or 'strange felau'. The earliest document dates from Elizabeth's reign, from five years before the Armada in fact, and is full of the spirit of craft solidarity which the masons working in small groups of masters and journeymen together were able to preserve: 'That every mason receive and cherish strange felaus when they come over the countries (counties) and set them awork, as the manner is, that is to say if they have mould stones in his place, or else, he shall refresh him with money unto the next logging.'

Out in the countryside, away from their homes the master masons in their lodges could not board strangers in their own homes. The traveller was found bed and board in a local inn associated with the trade. To this day there is hardly a town of any size which does not have its Masons', Carpenters' or Bricklayers' Arms. To maintain the goodwill of the inn-keeper, travellers were instructed to 'do no villainy where you go to boorde, whereby the craft may be slandered'.

And they were to 'pay truly' for their meat. Villainy evidently included departing without paying the bill. Three centuries later under more or less the same basic system of work or hospitality and assistance, the travelling mason was still on the road, and regrettably now and then did 'villainies' which slandered the craft.

It seems likely that the masons were the first to apply system and rule to the custom of travelling among the trades. Only in the seventeenth and eighteenth centuries do we find so organised a system in other trades, first among the weavers and combers of the wool trade, who may have copied it from the ubiquitous builders.

When other rules and by-laws laid down by the crafts began to break down under the stress of economic and social change, the rules and customs dealing with the stranger or traveller tended to multiply and become more definite. For they coped with mobility rather than attempting to deny it, and in the coming age, as old relationships were disrupted and old restrictions broke down, change and mobility were the order of the day.

3 Queen Betty's Law
1550–1700

From those who would our rights invade
Or Break the Law Queen Betty made,
Domina Nos Libere
Weavers' song, seventeenth century

In the fifth year of Queen Elizabeth's reign, Parliament passed 'An Act touching Divers Orders for Artificers, Labourers, Servants of Husbandry and Apprentices' – 5 Eliz. I c 4 (1563), the Statute of Apprentices, or, as it later became known among the crafts, 'Queen Betty's Law'.

It was impressive in scope, aiming to regulate the economic life of an entire section of society. Like the Poor Law which followed at the end of her reign, it summed up and drew together more than two centuries of custom and legislation, and like the Poor Law it lasted more than two centuries, into the period of the Industrial Revolution. But unlike the Poor Law, which survived because whatever its inefficiencies its basic purpose suited the ruling class, the Statute of Apprentices became a part of the long struggle between craftsmen and their employers. Unlike the Poor Law it was not in the end reformed and embodied in new legislation, but destroyed piece by piece by the employers who saw it as a hindrance to industrial development. In this destruction they had the active backing of Parliament and the whole-hearted opposition of journeymen and small master craftsmen. Once a symbol of stability, Queen Betty's Law became a battle cry in the class struggle.

A law to control the activities of the 'handicrafts' and the traders who more and more dominated them seemed a practical proposition in 1563. This part of society, after all, included perhaps 5 per cent of the population. Even a century and more later, when Charles II was on the throne, craftsmen, merchants and their families still made up no more than 10 per cent of the people, 80 per cent of whom were still living and working on the land. But in the sixteenth and seventeenth centuries the nation's rulers saw this section of society, numerically small as it was, as a source of turbulence and anarchy. When 'our clothiers lack vent' weavers joined with husbandmen against enclosing landlords in local uprisings even in the 1650s.

Craftsmen and merchants might be few in number but they were concentrated in certain areas – the eastern counties, the cities, and above all London. The capital continued to grow, tripling in size again during the seventeenth century, from just over 3 per cent of the total of the population to nearly 12 per cent (almost its present proportion). The traders and craftsmen with their ancient and tried organisation were formidable in the Stuart period when they were the nucleus of opposition to the Crown. This was the biggest single factor, a combination of wealth and quickly mobilised manpower, in the overthrow of the Crown and its allies during the Civil Wars of 1642–51.

At the centre of the disruption of the age was the rapidly accumulating wealth of the merchants, which the Crown encouraged while seeking to regulate its effects. There was wealth from the trade plunder voyages to the West and East Indies, wealth from the great export of cloth which the Crown channelled through London to the distress of other cities, wealth which flowed into larger-scale farming and larger-scale manufacture, with London's clothing trade employing thousands (even the glovers numbered 400 shop-holders and 3,000 workpeople). This wealth the Crown sought to tap by tax, excise, and charter fee, or by joining in the business ventures which seemed to make money out of nothing. If there was advantage (the seventeenth century name for profit) in trading in spices, cloth or the lives of Black Africans, there was even more in trading in money. Worthy Puritan merchants were ready to make 50 per cent on loans to brothers of the faith colonising the bleak New England shore, though the Bible said usury was a sin and even Parliament said 8 per cent was enough. Those who had money hastened to invest or 'venture' it, trusting to make more without raising a finger. ' 'Tis a vain thing to say money begets not money,' wrote John Selden, 'for that no doubt it does.' Selden voiced the conviction which gripped the new class with a deeper fervour even than their religion.

That money begets money was the grand illusion of the next four centuries, but as Spanish silver earned by trade – or plundered from the plunderers – poured into London it seemed like a revelation. To the merchants who made the fortunes and dominated the trading life of the nation, it must have seemed an outrage that their doings should in any way be governed by meetings of craftsmen and small shop-holders because they were all nominally members of the same company, and that men whom they could buy and sell ten times over should lay down how many men should be employed, how many boys apprenticed and thus how the market should be divided. This fundamental dispute over the nature of democracy within the trades swelled through the Stuart decades to break out on a large scale during the excitement of the Civil War and the Commonwealth that followed. In 1647 the radical trooper Ed Sexby confronted the parliamentary generals in the Army Council during the debate over the franchise for the new House of Commons. When told that the vote would be based on property rights, he declared with biting irony: 'We *ventured* our lives,' and added, 'I wonder we were so much deceived.'

That these economic contradictions would lead to a social rift was anticipated by the Elizabethan lawmakers. The Statute of Apprentices declared that a controlled entry into trade through seven years' servitude was needed lest the crafts should 'eat out and consume each other', a sentiment reiterated in Shakespeare's plays, most pointedly in *Sir Thomas More* ('men like ravenous fishes would feed on one another'). Each main part of the Statute sought to balance the interests of one group against another, sometimes seeking to embody two interests within the same clause. The ban on the children of poor husbandmen entering the trades (unless their parents' income was over twenty shillings a year, which excluded a large part of the rural population), a ban which was first laid down in 1406, was justified in two ways. On the one hand it was argued that the gentry and yeoman farmers could not otherwise get labour 'without unreasonable wages'. On the other hand, a commentator added ten years after the passing of the Statute, artificers would 'go vagabond' if husbandmen's children were apprenticed.

Seven years' apprenticeship – not in every trade as is sometimes said, but in the sixty-one trades 'above remembered' – would restrain mutually destructive competition, it was thought.

It would protect the journeyman from an untrained, cheaper rival, the master from too great a rush of apprentices eager to replace him, and the trade and public from the effects of 'evil and unskilful workmen'.

For the masters there was added protection, for the Statute confirmed the rule in many crafts that a journeyman must serve until the age of 24, by which time he would have learned to 'govern himself' before becoming master.

The Statute also confirmed in certain trades – textile, clothing, shoe and hat making – the rule existing in many crafts that there should be work for three journeymen before any extra apprentice was taken on 'work for three felaus' in the masons' charges. The custom in many trades of one apprentice for a master, two for a liveryman and three for the company Master probably amounted to just this in effect. But in the large-scale textile and clothing trades the added force of law was given. But it was precisely in these trades that the labour force grew fastest, and in the country areas outside the main area of gild regulation. So, from this time on until the nineteenth century, textile and clothing workshops and, by customary extension, other trades which employed the correct proportion of journeymen to apprentices were known as 'legal' shops or 'fair' shops.

Thus the control was placed just where it chafed the bigger master most and where it was most likely to be disregarded. It was a hostage to the future.

Justices of the Peace were given the power to regulate wages if need be. It was no new power. It had existed from the time of the Black Death, but changed circumstances brought a change in emphasis. In the fourteenth century wage regulation was attempted against a background of labour shortage. In the sixteenth, seventeenth and eighteenth centuries, the population was rising steadily and in the end rapidly and the labour supply, not least in the less organised country areas, turned in the employers' favour. Now the workpeople looked to the Justices and it was the masters and employers who began to kick against wage assessment. In the organised trades of the towns wage fixing largely remained a matter for collective bargaining.

To complete the system of external control and internal discipline which already existed in the craft companies, the Statute laid down (as the law had done several times since 1349) that 'servants', including artificers, who changed their work must have a certificate from the previous master.

More important still, it embodied the main terms of the 1549 Act against 'confederacies and conspiracies' of working people to decide rates of pay or how much work should be done in a given time. These two clauses gave unalloyed satisfaction to the masters, or rather to the richer masters who set the tone in the crafts. Until 1726 at least, the livery of the Bakers' Company had the 'certificate' clause of 5 Eliz. I c 4 reprinted as a leaflet underlining the fact that a travelling craftsman without a certificate was legally liable for a whipping.

The anti-'combination' clause was noted complacently as a 'sufficient guard' by the London Common Council at the end of the seventeenth century and when, in the early nineteenth century, the employers' lobby in the House of Commons were busy dismembering 5 Eliz. I c 4 they did so secure in the knowledge that the Combination Acts of 1799-1800, latest of forty such laws on the statute books, protected their interests while they busily undermined those of their employees.

The Statute of Apprentices was carefully worked out and comprehensive, designed to make the handicrafts serve the larger feudal interest and to be at peace within themselves. But relations among the crafts were destined to be the major social battleground of the future and the two groups whose mutual welfare was supposed to be assured by the Statute were destined to be the main antagonists. Almost every point of the Statute was to become an area of conflict and the main principles were the first to be disregarded.

The apprenticeship rules were supposed to protect both master and man. In practice they were needed chiefly by the men, or rather the journeymen and small masters. For the richer masters, economic developments were their best defence. The price of an 'upset' or fee to become master rose steadily. The year's income required for promotion to the livery rose tenfold during the seventeenth century.

The fee among the London clothworkers was equal to two years' wages for a journeyman. If he could raise the fee, then he might wait years before being admitted to the livery. Among the clothworkers, and in other companies, the yeomanry ranks during the pre-Civil War years were crowded with embittered small masters. Their grievances, like those of the journeymen yeomen, were aggravated by the behaviour of the larger masters, who enforced or disregarded company rule and the law as it suited them.

In the 1590s came complaints that the clothworkers' apprentice rules were being disregarded. Similar complaints had come from the journeymen printers. Their situation was even more difficult. The printing monopoly held by the Stationers' Company was reinforced by censorship exercised by Church authorities and backed by the weight of the Star Chamber. This kept the number of master printers down to twenty. Thus the journeymen, though 'freemen' of the company, might remain wage earners for life. If the masters were to take on more boys, then their situation would become intolerable. They demanded and got a rule that no new apprentice would be taken on while a journeyman lacked work.

But the printers' trade was booming, fed by the religious and secular pamphlet war of the time in which the opposition elements, loosely termed 'Puritan', contested Church–Crown control of thought and conscience. When the printers renewed their rules in 1635, the five most important, included on the insistence of the journeymen, re-stated apprentice control and the prior right of 'freemen' to employment. The employers, it was said, used 'tricks' to introduce an 'irregular body' of apprentices and it was clear that a number of journeymen had lost patience with company control. The appearance in these days of pirate printers, working secretly 'in corners', some ready to risk jail and mutilation to print illegal pamphlets, testifies to the impulse of free trade, entangled with that of free speech.

In other trades, like those of the founders and carpenters, new rules enforcing the customary apprentice proportions enabled the trouble to be postponed. The Hull bricklayers proclaimed at the head of their rules that 'all men are equal, made by one Maker of the like mire, the meanest beggar as the greatest prince'. But the rules equally laid down the number of boys each degree of membership might take on and train.

In the country weaving areas, not only did the bigger masters ignore the apprentice clauses of the Statute, but, following the 1620 slump in the wool trade, weavers in the eastern counties complained that their wages had been 'abated' savagely, with apparently no help forthcoming from the Justices. The Wiltshire weavers called on the JPs to regulate their wages in face of imposed cuts, and Gloucestershire weavers, less fortunate still, were thrown out of work and, it was reported, 'do wander' the roads.

Such wandering had little point for the whole trade was in the same plight, hit by a slump induced by the failure of the Cockaygne Project, a plan to bring woollen exports under the control of a handful of royal nominees and channel a good deal of the profits into the royal purse. Many weavers emigrated to the new settlements in North America, Stuart economic policies acting along with Stuart religious policies to shift some 60,000 people from old England to New England, Virginia and other colonies during the 1620s and 1630s.

Those who wandered were liable to be driven back home, for the 1600 Poor Law reaffirmed that each parish must see to its own poor. Whipping took the place of mutilation as deterrent and some villages, often reluctantly, provided their poor with certificates promising that they would not be allowed to become a charge on another parish. If the poor stayed at home they might in some places be set to spin or weave municipal flax, wool or hemp in newly founded 'workhouses' – the ultimate indignity since the state of the trade rendered the labour often useless.

The country poor, however, took the road to the cities and above all to London which by late sixteenth century had already some third of the country's 'badged beggars' though only one thirtieth of its population. There some joined the ranks of the 'forren' weavers and tailors, working in garrets in dark 'alleys and back stayers', hoping to escape the company searchers.

Power of search granted by company charter was the crafts' chief power to protect members' livelihoods. It might also be used by one craft to keep another out of its territory, or by yet others to dominate related crafts. In some smaller cities one craft would take the lead in an amalgamation of various trades, perhaps to meet the expenses of buying a charter. The joiners, who often acted as contractors on big building jobs, tried to make other building crafts submit to their 'search'. The blacksmiths took a leading role in metal amalgamations, both in England and Scotland – the 'hammermen's gilds' or companies.

In London during the Commonwealth period, fourteen small crafts asked for 'right of search', compelling all traders in their business to join their company. This was a blow at the merchant trader who had money to invest in other people's work. Thanks to the opposition of the 'Great Twelve' companies, the smaller crafts lost the day.

But the 'search' was most important to the yeomanry, particularly in the big London trades – clothworkers, tailors, weavers. The weavers' company organisation, as the wool men left the city, was taken over by silk weavers, many of them Huguenot refugees from Catholic France, who began to arrive in London in the 1570s. By the 1630s they had spread to other cities, Canterbury, Reading, Coventry – where they were admitted to the Woollen Weavers' Company – and even as far as Manchester. Under the leadership of their 'sixteen young men' the rank and file of the London weavers divided the city into quarters and by 1594 had signed an 'Indenture of Tolerance' for the 'discovery and reform of abuses'. This was a common definition of yeomanry functions; the cutlers' yeomanry, for example, were responsible for 'the righting of wrongs and abuses'.

At this time the tailors' yeomanry or 'bachelor company' revived their ancient custom of search. Journeymen and masters of the two companies must have been in contact for later in the seventeenth century a special parlour evidently for the weavers' 'young men' was erected on land leased from the Merchant Tailors Company, perhaps in imitation of the meeting place used by the tailors' yeomanry.

Such contact between organisations mobilising thousands of craftsmen (in one search the tailors dealt with one thousand 'foreigners') must have made them a formidable force. Indeed, the pikemen drawn from these London companies proved the rock on which King Charles' cavalry broke more than once during the Civil War. The tailors searched their territory with great ceremony, summoning 'strangers' to account for themselves at ceremonial dinners held in various City inns. When the Merchant Tailors complained of 'needless meetings' at company expense the yeomanry defended themselves so well that the liverymen reduced their strictures to a plea that they 'should hold as few dinners as conveniently'. The 'bachelors' were not lightly to be put down: they claimed rights of election 'on the eve of the Decollation of St John the Baptist' going back two centuries and paraded on Lord Mayor's Day, the leading master bachelors in suits trimmed with 'foynes' or marten skin and the lesser in 'budge' or sheepskin.

When they searched for the foreigners, they demanded first to see their indentures. If they had none they might be expelled from the trade. But the tailors were neither merciless nor foolish and had no intention of creating an uncontrolled pool of labour to undermine pay and conditions. 'Ancient dwellers' who had children born in the city were allowed to stay. By such admissions the ranks of the company swelled until it was estimated that during the seventeenth century more or less all working tailors were members. In Bristol travelling tailors were admitted on showing their indentures and paying a fee. In Hull stranger tailors were admitted up to a certain limit and in no case were they allowed to work for a tailor who was not a 'brother'.

The London weavers, led by their 'young men', were equally judicious. Weavers from other cities were generally admitted as 'foreign brothers' on production of a certificate showing previous service and if 'honestly departed from his country and of good name and a sufficient workman'. If the stranger had no documents he was allowed a month's work to 'get his bearings' before moving on.

Ann White, of Manchester, the only travelling 'sister' I have met with in company histories, was given one month's grace on arrival in London, to get her certificate 'out of ye country'. Ann, apprenticed by her father, was one of the girls whom the company historian estimates made up one per cent of those serving their time. Widows of deceased weavers could keep their husbands' place in the trade, and in the early eighteenth century they made up 3 per cent of the London company members.

There was evidently a good deal of movement of journeymen weavers between the main silk-weaving centres, and in the days before the Civil War Charles I, on the look out for more revenue, offered the London Weavers' Company a national 'right of search' over other cities on payment of a tax based on the amount of silk handled. It was, however, seen to benefit only those who could afford to pay it and it encouraged certain masters to break the apprentice rules to earn more money for that purpose and so was rapidly abandoned.

The rank and file weavers were well organised and determined not to let the richer masters entirely evade the rules. They claimed right of search persistently, appealing to the Mayor when the liverymen removed it, or rather the livery majority for a minority sided with the yeomanry. In the 1630s, the sixteen young men had become a 'thorn in the flesh' of the company leadership and were allowed to make use of the journeymen's quarterage payments specifically to finance the searches, as had been agreed in the 1590s.

At several points from 1616 to 1675 the weavers used their right of search to do something of historic significance – to block the introduction of the engine loom with its multiple shuttles. This was in the interests of master and journeyman alike for the engine loom was being used by total outsiders.

Embodied in the 'right of search' was the power to 'break and deface' (blacksmiths' charter), 'cut in pieces' or 'seize' (framework knitters), and 'seize, carry away and dispose of' (tinplate workers) goods that were considered to be 'deceitful'. This right to confiscate or destroy, applied to goods made by outsiders from the fourteenth century on, was automatically transferred to the 'engine loom'.

The new loom was indeed judged by the Government in 1637 to be 'deceitful'. When the 1637 legal ruling proved ineffective the force of the strong right arm was applied. The weavers seized illegal engine looms and burned them in the streets in 1675. The framework knitters, using similar powers, extended them to knitting frames worked by illegal apprentices. The offending masters, driven from the city, fled to Holland or to the Midland counties of England and set themselves up in Leicester, Nottingham and Derby. Here they were to be pursued by 'deputies' of the framework knitters' company. With the full backing of law, custom and tradition, the era of machine breaking had begun.

The framework knitters sought to back their action by appealing to Queen Betty's Law, but were told that since their trade had appeared only after the Statute was passed they were not covered. Undeterred they held to their charter and enforced it by their combined numbers against 'interlopers' and later against backsliders among their own company members.

The problem was the same for clothworkers, tailors, weavers and other companies. The powers of the company charter were used by the rank and file, small masters and journeymen together, not only to keep out intruders but to compel all masters within the company to respect the rules. To disputes over the right of search were then added rows over the use of funds. The clothworkers' yeomanry accused the livery of making away with the profits of land which should have been used to finance the relief of the poor. The merchant tailors accused the 'bachelors' of 'promiscuous' handing out of charity and after some argument it was agreed to limit payments to 300 'poor' annually. It seems likely that the tailors' yeomanry were using the charity payments, which came out of 'quarterage', donations and bequests from richer members, to ensure the loyalty of unemployed members.

Two factors aggravated these disputes. The livery of more than one company had lost all connection with the 'handytrade'. By 1623 the 'tailoring element' in the livery of the Merchant Tailors Company had all but vanished. By the 1650s the weavers complained that their leaders had filled the livery with 'unskilful members' and by this time 'no manual clothworkers' were to be found in that company's livery. Admissions by patrimony or inheritance and redemption or cash payment and admissions of 'love brothers', another euphemism for the nominal membership of businessmen who had not served their time at the trade, far exceeded those of time-served members. In the case of the masons, 'accepted' or 'speculative' masons, professional men and scholars attracted by masonic craft mystery and ritual, became more numerous as the seventeenth century drew to a close. In 1677 the 'operative' masons in London used the last of the money from the 'acception lodge' to buy themselves a banner, before the 'speculatives' broke away to form their own lodge, the forerunner of freemasonry in the sense now understood.

A legal ruling in 1614 that seven years' apprenticeship in one craft gave the right to trade in another enabled a master to intrude into the business while not having to observe the rules of the company. Masters who had turned merchant but wanted to keep capital in the manufacturing processes were not slow to adopt this device. It was against this intrusion that fourteen London crafts appealed in vain in 1653. Such was the extent of the occupation of livery places by trading members that by the mid-seventeenth century the yeomanry of the carpenters had begun to 'accept their lot as wage earners'. The division of the companies into trading and handicraft layers – the 'vital difference' between livery and yeomanry at this stage, in the view of one historian – might arrive by default. But more often it was achieved only after a sharp struggle in which the 'handytrade' confronted the 'non-manual' element. In some cases, especially where a complete craft had been forced into subordination by a merchant company, the manufacturing element broke free. The glovers escaped the clutches of the leathersellers, the feltmakers (hatters) threw off the dominance of the haberdashers and both gained separate charters by the joint efforts of masters and journeymen. The feltmakers fought above all for a limit on apprentices, for by now workshops of twenty and thirty craftsmen were becoming common in London.

The glovers stated their case for independence in a way which is significant. The rich shopkeepers among the glovers, they said, treated them like underlings, but 'yet suffer them to become like themselves'. The leathersellers, however, would not allow them to trade at all and they were in danger of being converted, master and journeyman alike, into a uniform wage-earning labour force employed by the dominant merchants.

King James I, who viewed merchants and crafts alike with cynical detachment based on his experience of company struggles in Edinburgh, was prepared to help groups like the glovers and feltmakers with new – and expensive – incorporation charters. His favoured would-be monopolists sought to gain control of a trade by enticing the craft element of a company away from its merchant masters. Those who succumbed to the temptation like the playing card makers and beavermakers found that under their new patrons they were more rigidly controlled and subordinated than ever – out of the frying pan into the fire. In preparation for the 1620 Alderman Cockaygne project to monopolise wool export the master and journeymen clothworkers were offered help in forming a separate company free of their merchants. The invitation was not accepted, and one reason was prophetic: the small masters who had come during the latter part of the sixteenth century to lead the yeomanry had no wish to find themselves at the mercy of the journeymen who would outnumber them in any separate incorporation. The situation was to come home with force to the master feltmakers at the end of the seventeenth century.

Like the clothworkers, the yeomanry of most other companies preferred to stay in and fight for their right to have a voice in company affairs. The merchant tailors at first avoided the issue by promoting the leading members of the 'bachelor' company to the livery, as did the cutlers. The joiners utterly denied the yeomanry any share in the government of the company and at a later date the bakers' livery even took away from the yeomanry the right of free election to their own organisation. Among the tailors, pewterers, clothworkers, weavers, founders, saddlers, clockmakers, cutlers, carpenters and other companies, the dispute spread.

A vital part of the swelling social discontent and opposition to arbitrary Crown–Church rule in the 1630s and 1640s was this inner struggle of the crafts, reflecting as it did powerful economic undercurrents.

The liverymen under attack had recourse to the law. The company rules declared that the officers should be chosen by the 'commonalty'. The question was, what did 'commonalty' mean? To the journeymen and small masters it meant clearly enough the freemen. The weavers' livery countered with a ruling from none other than the redoubtable lawyer Coke, in his *Case of Corporations*, which they claimed meant elections should be by a 'certain select number of rank and degree', to avoid 'popular disorder'. The clothworkers' company went one better with a ruling that the Master and Wardens 'be likewise the Commonalty'. The founders' yeomanry, accusing the liverymen of 'reading the charter at their pleasure', refused to pay quarterage in protest.

This dispute over democratic forms, inspired by the growing antagonism over apprentice and other regulations between the richer and poorer members of the crafts, had tended to be submerged during the years immediately before the Civil War when, in face of economic and fiscal incompetence and arbitrary rule by Charles I and his ministers, craftsmen, shopkeepers and merchants made common cause. They marched together in the trained bands and later in the ranks of the Parliamentary armies. At least the journeymen and master craftsmen and junior merchants marched and fought against the Royal armies, while the bigger merchants subscribed to war loans, and contributed to Parliamentary funds by purchase of impounded Royal and Cavalier estates, jewels and plate. The combination of craftsmen and small farmers as pikemen and troopers, the enormous concentrated wealth and technical expertise of London and other cities, and the overriding conviction of justice in the cause brought victory to the Parliamentary side, though not without sacrifice. Some had grown richer, some poorer, some had lost everything. 'We ventured our lives,' cried Trooper Sexby to Cromwell in 1647. In 1648 the London weavers issued a manifesto which underlined the point. It declared that many of them had marched to battle, fought and died. Those who returned found that their places had been taken by 'intruders' and, what was more, 'these governors' (the company livery) 'gain by intruders'. They might well have added, with Sexby, 'I wonder we were so much deceived.'

In a number of companies, notably that of the weavers, the Commonwealth saw a brief extension of democracy. The weavers elected 'deputies', including 140 from the militant suburb of Southwark alone. The movement among the crafts gave powerful support and inspiration to the Leveller wing of the City's population. John Lilburne the Leveller tribune and Gerard Winstanley, leader of the Diggers, were both from the rank and file of London trading companies.

The democratic principles of the Levellers, as well as the shifts and contradictions within them, can be better understood if one looks at the crafts and the battle for company control between the richer trading masters on the one hand and the smaller working masters and journeymen on the other. This rank-and-file alliance was bound to be unstable as long as any of the masters retained an ambition to grow greater, or any of the journeymen retained an ambition to 'set up' on their own account.

The confusion and disruption of the Civil War flooded the roads again with wanderers. In 1646 as the King's troops were surrendering to victorious Fairfax and Cromwell's men, it was reckoned there were 80,000 vagrants abroad. Even forty years later, the number was estimated at 30,000. Most of the vagrants were discharged soldiers and freed prisoners, those lucky enough not to have been 'barbadozzed' or sent to forced labour in the plantations of Barbados colony. But neither Cromwell's Protectorate nor Charles II's Restoration government 'suffered them to wander' to the extent that soldiers of previous wars had done. In 1654, Cromwell issued an order that discharged soldiers were to be free to follow any trade 'without let or molestation'. When General Monck took over after the Protector's death he repeated the order and once back on the throne Charles II endorsed it, but added the proviso that ex-soldiers must take the oath of allegiance.

Thus began the tradition of the 'King's Freemen' which lasted for two centuries until the craft companies had utterly ceased their attempt to regulate entry into their trades. 'King's Freemen', claiming the right as former servicemen to set up in any trade (and the forces, particularly the navy, must have given many a country boy an opportunity to acquire trade skills, even of a rough kind), were a disruptive factor, particularly in Scotland where the attempt to maintain craft control lasted longer than in England.

It is not easy to say exactly what was the effect of the various orders. The London weavers protested that they had been driven to work as labourers and porters by intruders taken on by the richer masters while they were away at the war. In Wiltshire the older weavers complained that they had been 'set beside their work' by young men who 'ought to have been their servants' but who had set up with a loom without training on return from the war. Towns like Rye took corporate action to keep disbanded soldiers out of their crafts. In 1663 Pepys gives a complacent picture of a booming economy with returned soldiers busy at their work: '. . . this captain a butcher, this lieutenant a cobbler . . . every man in his apron and frock etc., as if they had never done anything else.'

But a popular song of the time tells another story of the disbanded man:

> In Red-coat rags I wander up and down
> Since Fate and foes conspired thus to array me
> Or betray me to the hard censure of the Town.
> My buffe doth make my boots, my velvet coat and scarlet,
> Which us'd to make me credit with many a Sodom harlot,
> Hath bid me all adieu, most despicable varlet,
> Alas, poor soldier, whither wilt thou march?

To the 'censure of the town' was added the authority of the 1662 Act of Settlement. This could dislodge a newly arrived wanderer if the town or parish officers decided he might become a 'charge' on the poor rate. Unless he owned 'estate' worth £10 a year within the parish, the wanderer could be told to clear out within forty days and go back to his native parish.

Men and women who travelled about to work in the harvest were required to have a certificate from their local vicar or a leading citizen, a guarantee that they would not linger after the corn was in. In certain other cases men and women were allowed to stay if their own parish gave them a paper saying it would support them if they became unemployed and 'chargeable', something not many parishes were willing to do. The Act of Settlement, like the Elizabethan Poor Law which it carried a stage further, kept the whip as deterrent for vagrants without papers, as the bakers' liverymen reminded their journeymen when they set off to work elsewhere. In such circumstances it became more important than ever for the travelling craftsman to carry with him a certificate of his former service. It has been shown that the craftsman on the road was rarely disturbed by the Act of Settlement, but that does not mean that organised craftsmen were in no way affected. Craft companies in certain towns were reluctant to take in married journeymen from other cities. The Hull tailors would admit a married journeyman only on payment of £5, a pretty impossible proposition. It was no doubt calculated among the masters, who were also the ratepayers, that a married stranger would mean extra mouths to feed. One of the Rye burghers objections to ex-servicemen's entering their town trades was that they might become a charge. In later years only a very few trade societies made provision for the married traveller who left family at home, and fewer still for the traveller who brought his wife along. It is difficult to say how much this was the result of the Act of Settlement and how much it arose from the tradition of the journeyman staying single until he could set up, and later for the single young man to be first to be discharged if trade was slack. But if anything the Act of Settlement would have reinforced all these traditions.

There is some argument about the effects of the Act. Liberal historians criticise it for denying poor folk the right to seek work freely but recent opinion has reacted against this view. Others say that the fact of thousands on the roads show that the Act was effective. But the point perhaps lies between these two views.

Most poor people have always sought work even when they would have been well off idle. In 1698 the parish dole was reckoned well above the land labourer's earnings. Yet thousands did trudge away seeking work. What the Act of Settlement did, and its full effect became apparent during the mass migrations of the Industrial Revolution, was to reduce the migrants' security in the place where they might find work. It achieved not an imprisoned workforce but a rootless one, at the mercy of the new employer (see Chapter 5). The Act of Settlement might well have been called the Act of Disturbance in fact.

With thousands of discharged soldiers on the roads after the Civil War, men nominally free to take work at any trade, the richer masters could take advantage of the swollen labour force, hence the complaints in London of 'many intruders'. The printers declared that they were 'very much in excess' of those needed. The feltmakers and tailors entered into a long period of internal dispute of growing bitterness over the influx of labour from outside. For the weavers, too, a time of turmoil was beginning. The 1670s brought a fresh wave of French immigrants. But the company organisation stood the stress; the 'aliens' proved to be willing and active members, easily mobilised through their churches which reinforced their solidarity. Before 1700, though, the whole trade was disturbed by the import of Indian 'callimancoes' cheaper than the home produced silks, very profitable to the powerful East India Company, ruinous to the rank and file weavers. They then had the alternative of staying on 'the box' or taking the road in the hope that Canterbury, Coventry, Reading or Manchester might have work. Already in the Commonwealth period there are signs that wool and silk weavers, in Coventry for example, made payments to unemployed brothers on the tramp. The payments were small enough, sixpence or a shilling, but they confirmed the custom that a brother from another town who could not get work was entitled to help.

The masons' system of employment or hospitality and payment to help the travelling 'fellow' on his way is on record from the 1580s. It continued through the seventeenth century, as the amended versions of the 'Old Charges' show.

A Staffordshire observer noted the custom by which the roving mason would identify himself to local lodge members by a secret sign as potent as any document. The traveller's signal would bring a fellow mason down even from the top of a steeple.

In London, where masons were governed by a more formal company structure, it was laid down that journeymen 'alien or English' must show a paper from their former master and contribute threepence to the box for the relief of the poor. But the masons like other London building trades suffered in this period a blow from which their organisation never fully recovered. After the Great Fire in 1666, King Charles II who had powers of conscription over the builder chose instead to stimulate the reconstruction of the City by letting loose the forces of free trade, setting aside company controls and allowing 'forrens' in from outside, both as master and journeyman. The London building crafts united in a petition against loss of their rights, but were ignored. They continued their 'searches', the carpenters inspecting the indentures of men working on the rebuilding and masons trying to levy contributions. But the degree of success was smaller as time went on. The searchers were met with evasions, with promises to pay which were then broken, and sometimes with blank refusal, though it seems from the masons' records that the bigger sites, churches for example, responded better to company control than others. Here the more skilled men, keener on craft control, would be more ready to keep out intruders who had not served their time in the regular way. In smaller cities craft organisation was more stable. In Worcester new arrivals among the carpenters had to register and either show proof they had served seven years or work as 'a servant'.

Seven years' apprenticeship, the law of the land, was in most crafts written into the charters of incorporation granted by Charles II to London companies, including the new skills of coachmaker and tinplate worker. Restrictions on the sons of 'husbandmen', it seems, did not prevent many of them becoming apprentice weavers and carpenters, though whether this came about because the law was ignored or because the families were able to meet the financial demands of the law is hard to say.

74

In one respect the Statute of Apprentices was occasionally strengthened. A special Act passed in 1662 limited the number of apprentices taken into the Norwich worsted trade to one per journeyman. This move was specifically designed to protect those who could not set up as masters in the trade, that growing body of time-served men who had to face a lifetime of employment by, as the printers journeymen put it, 'a very small number' of rich masters.

This 'small number' was not interested in limits on apprentice numbers. Their wealth, the high cost of 'upset', protected them from competition from below. They were interested in taking on more boys, who after an initial period of training could contribute more to the profits of the business than a time-served journeyman demanding the full rate. In their new charter, the feltmakers (1667) set the limit at two apprentices per master. But within two years masters and journeymen were at loggerheads over the number of 'sindging boys' employed. Ten years later the London masons' charter stood by the old 1:2:3 ratio of apprentices for each grade of master. But, with builders moving into the City from outside, the building contractors could ignore rules made by the separate crafts. The journeymen and small masters among the framework knitters faced with the threat of unlimited apprentices appealed to the protection of Queen Betty's Law, but in vain.

From the country areas, too, came complaints to Parliament that wealthy clothiers, whose trade was specifically covered by the law on this question, were flouting it. Wealthy masters in the cities whose trades were not so covered were equally arrogant, the bakers' liverymen declaring that despite company custom they would take as many apprentices as they saw fit.

For the non-manufacturing merchants and bigger craft masters who now controlled the top layer of city company organisation, the usefulness of controls on the trade (with the exception of course of the rules banning 'confederacies' of workmen) was at an end. Free trade, which later Parliaments were to equate with individual freedom, became their slogan and free trade meant as large and as cheap a workforce as possible. Pamphlet writers attacked 'the strange stubbornness and idleness of our poor'.

English cloth was dear because English artisans were too highly paid, a cry familiar to twentieth-century newspaper readers. The principles of the Statute of Apprentices were attacked as 'common errors'. The lines of future class conflict began to take shape, with the satirical song 'The Clothier's Delight' echoing the most ancient hostility to the rich, but foreshadowing what was to come. The clothier remarks that his trade is secure while the comber, the weaver, the tucker and spinner work for him:

> We will make them to earn their wages full dear
> And this is the way for to fill up our purse
> Although we do get it with many a curse
> We heap up riches and treasure great store
> Which we get by griping and grinding the poor.

The larger and more profitable the trade, the bigger the workforce, the more open and violent the breach. In the Merchant Tailors' Company the livery, now entirely traders, were more and more reluctant to sanction the search. The bachelors' company offered to pay for the search themselves provided the company gave its legal backing and the livery reluctantly agreed. But in 1691 they roundly refused to swear in the wardens of the bachelors. They obtained a convenient legal judgment that 'of late' the search 'hath bin altogether useless'. From then on bachelors' company and livery parted company, with a final dispute over funds which the bachelors claimed were theirs. In 1696, when the bachelors vanish from the company records, they were appealing to the King's Court for return of the money they claimed. The rump of the company membership, the livery, then turned, as the records show, to more congenial matters, the feasting and very occasional dispensing of charity. It ceased to have or to seek any control over the trade with which it had been associated for nearly four centuries.

During the Restoration period the painters' livery 'suppressed' the yeomanry for demanding a greater control over the search, and in 1684 the bakers' livery carried out the 130-year-old threat to expel the yeomanry from the company hall. They took the matter to court, with less success than the working tailors.

The bakers' yeomanry leader was dismissed as a 'prating coxcomb' by a judge who sided entirely with the liverymen. His name was Jeffreys and the following year he passed into history for his judgment on the poor rebels of the Battle of Sedgemoor. The bakers' yeomanry had been withholding their quarterage payments perhaps in protest at the way the company was run. But the bigger masters retaliated by deducting the payments from wages. The masons' yeomanry were also voting with their feet, for the first page of the company records after the new incorporation of 1677 shows nearly 200 names under the heading 'yeomandry arrears'. The Master and Wardens of the company decided to cut their losses and to try and collect a smaller sum each quarter for the box, though it does not seem that a lot was raised in this way. The new companies – tinplate workers, wheelwrights, coachmakers – took no chances and laid down in their charters that both masters and journeymen would pay quarterage, the wheelwrights specifying that no man would be employed unless he were a member.

The journeymen feltmakers withheld their quarterage payments, it seems, to raise money for local action in their dispute with the masters over 'boys'. There were legal actions in plenty before the end of the century, when the master feltmakers tried to bring in journeymen from the country districts to undermine the wage rates of the well organised London men.

Over the questions of apprentices and strangers, the labour supply in fact, the old company structures were strained often to breaking-point. Where the company merchant elite was wholly separated in interest from the rest of the company, the manufacturing side split off, formally in the case of the feltmakers who set up a new company structure. In the case of the tailors, the split was as clear but no formal incorporation followed. But the split between merchant and manufacturer was the prelude to further divisions as one craft after another found. Among the bakers and feltmakers, and later the curriers, wheelwrights, coachmakers and others, the richer masters tried to use the apprentice intake to discipline the journeymen, though, as the bakers' company found, they had to think again to avoid ruining the small master as well.

While new organisational forms appeared amid the old city company structure, among the country wool trades which had never had the same traditional craft controls a militant spirit showed itself. Where the law was unable or unwilling to protect their earnings from the attacks of the clothiers, the wool workers took to the streets. In Colchester and Trowbridge they marched to the sound of horn and fiddle and in Colchester the militia were called out. But in seeking independence from the clothiers, the woolcombers of a number of centres sought formal incorporation of the traditional kind. The Devon combers found Royal Charter too costly for them. In Coggeshall, the combers withdrew from the clothiers' company and formed a 'Woolcombers' Purse'. A friendly or benefit club in form, it sought to apply the old restrictions on 'intruders'.

Friendly societies began to appear in various centres. Sometimes as in the case of the Newcastle keelmen or the Bo'ness seamen they were an offshoot of older craft organisation when journeymen and masters parted company. The journeymen aided by a minority of masters maintained the organisation with its mixed trade and benefit rules while the rest of the masters went their own way. Splits were not inevitable, and in the British Library there are rules of a friendly society set up by master and journeymen coachmakers in the 1690s, when both were members of the same company, a society which lasted into the nineteenth century, while the official craft body was rent by industrial dispute. 'Box' clubs among different groups of workers are a regular feature from now on, looking after the 'poor' since the richer masters were increasingly unwilling to do so.

The Coggeshall Woolcombers 'Purse' was, as said, no simple insurance society, but neither was it an incorporated company. It was something which was to become familiar in the wool textile trade in the eighteenth century, a 'corporation without a charter'.

For, on the eve of the eighteenth century, new incorporations even when they could be paid for were not so easily had. The London sawyers trying to escape the domination of the joiners' and carpenters' companies sought their own charter but were rebuffed. They were told it would be an 'evill example' if employees had a separate organisation.

But such separate or 'separating' organisations were a fact of life and the Woolcombers' Purse was a sign of the future. As well as looking to their members' social welfare they raised money to take intruders to court – 'from such as would our rights invade, or would intrude into our trade, or break the law Queen Betty made', as the popular rhyme put it.

Masons, carpenters, tailors, weavers, shoemakers, woolcombers – all had customary contact, through members travelling in search of work, with craft groups in a similar position in other parts of the country. The old craft organisations and loyalties were disintegrating. But as they did, new ones were in the making.

4 'The Liberties of the Subject'
1700–1800

Our combers have for a number of years past erected themselves into a sort of Corporation (tho' without a charter) . . . when they become a little formidable, they give laws to their Masters, as also to themselves . . . And that they may keep up their price . . . if any of their club is out of work, they give him a ticket and money to seek work in the next town . . . by which means he can travel the Kingdom round, be carressed at each club, and spend not one farthing, nor strike one stroke of work. . . .

A short essay upon trade in general (London, 1741)

History does not tell what answer the woolcombers had to their appeal to the Lord to deliver them from those who broke Queen Betty's Law and invaded their rights. But it does tell what answer they got when they appealed to the lawmakers. Turning down their petition in 1702, the House of Commons declared: 'Trade ought to be free and not restrained.' By 1753 the framework knitters, too, had learned that their attempts to control entry into the trade were 'injurious and vexatious' and 'contrary to the liberty of the subject'. The freedom of the master to run his business was taken as the model for the rights of the citizen. The House of Commons pronouncement was almost word for word that of the master clothiers when they declared the principle of Queen Betty's Law to be 'repugnant to the liberties of a free people'.

Asked for his judgement on whether 5 Eliz. I c 4 applied to the new cotton industry, as the smallware and check weavers were anxious that it should, Lord Mansfield ruled that it was out of date, belonging to 'the infancy of our trade' which had now attained 'perfection'. Such parliamentary votes, legal rulings and public statements of wealthier masters were to multiply through the eighteenth century.

These voices grew in enthusiasm as the fever for trade, manufacture and the profits they brought seized those who were able to have first helping from them. John Selden had written a century before that it was no use saying money did not beget money. By the 1700s there were fewer prepared to deny this law of financial genetics, whether they had the wherewithal to experiment or not. The capacity to make money by trade abroad, reinforced by force of arms if need be (for even a natural law should not be left to act unaided), was demonstrated time and again. With the Dutch defeated at sea, London established itself as the financial centre of the world, taking the lead in the East Indies. The weakening Spanish Empire in 1702 surrendered to the British the right to trade in black human beings shipped to the West Indies, thus ending a 150-year resistance and giving over the Caribbean to a British dominance which the navy held against repeated challenges by France. By the 1750s the French rival had also been displaced in India and Canada and by the early 1800s the flag had led British trade dominance into the Mediterranean and Middle East. The world paid its tribute and free trade overrode opposition abroad as at home. By its very nature it increased the total wealth of the nation and the inequality of its division.

Tobias Smollett observed 'the general tide of luxury which hath overspread the nation and swept away all even the very dregs of the people. Every upstart of fortune harnessed in the trappings of the mode, clerks and factors of the East Indies loaded with the spoil of plundered provinces, planters, negro drivers and hucksters from our American plantations enriched they know not how, agents, commissaries and contractors who have fattened in two successive wars on the blood of the nation, usurious brokers and jobbers of every kind.'

Smollett noted too that the new rich, like the old, who were not averse to becoming richer, employed a growing army of servants, lads and girls from the villages. Often enough when fashion or fortune changed they were thrown on to the streets of London and other cities to join the rootless and unskilled, future recruits for industry's expansion.

Fortunes did change rapidly in speculations like the South Sea Bubble. Many, believing too readily in the natural operation of Selden's law, lost all or much of what they had, or rather had the chagrin of seeing it turn up again in other people's pockets. The mania affected all sorts of people. The London master curriers fined their journeymen for taking part in an illegal 'combination' and put the proceeds into the South Sea Company. The new wealth did not stand still but went into other ventures, more solid but no less exciting. Already by the first decades of the eighteenth century the blacksmiths' company sought to amend their regulations to bring in the foreigners who were moving into the London suburbs. They said they needed the expanded workforce for 'engine work on new inventions'. With new manufacturing techniques in view the smiths had already taken a lead in the hammermen amalgamated companies of the smaller town. They had swallowed up the spurriers' company, allied themselves in wartime with the gunsmiths and tried without success to absorb the clockmakers, whose skill, along with that of the smiths, millwrights and turners, was later to be drawn together in making machinery for the textile industry. The turners already had a variety of lathes for the shaping of wood, and many parts of the new machines were made of timber.

So the skills were gradually switched from wood to metal as the mills of the countryside switched their function from the grinding of corn and logwood to the power manufacture of silk, wool and then cotton. By mid-century, engineers, who made pumps to raise water in mine shafts, had appeared among the London trades, and fire-engine makers engaged in furious competition over new inventions while new horse-powered mills to grind and mix colours threw London painters out of work by the 1740s.

New inventions upset old skills and the author of the *London Tradesman* (1741) waxed sarcastic at seven years' apprenticeship in trades he said could be learnt in as many months or even hours. He warned indeed that in many trades apprentices were 'mere slaves'. As the engine loom with its multiple shuttles had invaded the silk weavers' craft, so the Dutch loom invaded the new cotton trades, throwing established hand weavers out of work and increasing the fortunes of the larger masters. By the 1760s the new men in manufacture, part entrepreneur, part technologist, were making more far-reaching transformations. Wedgwood with his new mass production methods brought in 'fresh hands' from the villages, Watt developed the steam engine and the Kays and Cartwright pioneered technical change in textiles. Expanding manufacture, and enclosing landlords who destroyed farm cottages to stop labourers having a 'settlement', thus subsisting on the poor rates, added to the crowds of the restless and the rootless on the roads. The poor were shuttled to and fro by the forces of free trade so bewilderingly that they had little time to reflect on its benefit. While London's population doubled again during the century, Lancashire's trebled. People moved by tens of thousands through the land on roads and canals improved and dug at the behest of the entrepreneurs. It was the beginning of a nightmare period for many of the poor, worse perhaps than that of the early sixteenth century. They were denied work in the villages and towns of their birth, but when they moved into new 'manufacturing' areas they were not guaranteed the right to stay there should their new employers find that in the fluctuation of trade they had no further use for their labour. Successive wars, as Smollett observed, enriched some. But others they drew from the country to return discharged to beg or starve or, if they were lucky, to compete as 'King's Freemen' with the organised city craftsmen. It was a century of dislocation and insecurity for many.

The organised craftsmen were to be increasingly hard pressed to keep themselves above the tide level. Workforces among the larger crafts had swollen. In the 1720s, the London silk weavers had a membership of 6,000 under a livery of 200, the organised tailors, reckoned at 7,000, were said to be 'as numerous as locusts and as poor as rats'. In the weaving towns and villages alarmed master clothiers spoke of many thousand woollen workers on the march. Each trade fluctuation with its pump-like action drew and pushed ever greater numbers in and out of work.

The East India Company brought wealth to its 'nabobs'. To the silk weavers of London and the smallware and check weavers of Lancashire it brought the competition of cheap imported 'callimancoes', swiftly becoming fashionable even when they might be torn from the back of the wearer in London streets by enraged weavers. For thirty years from 1690 until 1720, when the import of cheap Indian cloth was banned, the whole weaving trade was in an uproar and workless craftsmen left London to tramp the country roads. With them trudged 'great numbers of experienced tailors', forced out, said the journeymen, by the richer masters bringing in raw labour from the countryside and later by many framework knitters. Journeymen of every trade, having served their time in 'legal' fashion, were 'suffered to wander', as the cordwainers put it in the 1790s. And it was not always from the simple lack of work for the whole labour force, as the journeymen tailors pointed out bitterly, but the demands for cheap work from the larger masters who 'had their country houses, their chariots and saddle horses'. The smaller masters turned garret 'captains' or foremen looked after the bigger employers' workshops.

The new rich were ostentatiously greedy. They were also brutal. To the distress of his manager, one of the owners of the Newland Iron Co. at Furness ordered that 'every useless widow and family' be evicted, adding: 'I cannot see any reason why we should maintain the widow of every deceased workman.' As families were evicted, the houses should be pulled down. This, with other measures of 'reform' might 'learn' the men 'industry, attentiveness and gratitude'.

The new rich were also, like the Wedgwoods who prided themselves on their paternal care for their employees, liberal, intellectual, enlightened and coolly calculating. As he drove down the wages of his potters by more than a third, Wedgwood remarked: 'The infallible consequence of lowering the price of workmanship will be a proportional increase of quantity got up ... the vast consequence in most manufacture of making the greatest quantity possible in a given time.' The logic of it all was a thing of beauty to a man like Wedgwood.

Wedgwood would stump the country making speeches against slavery in the West Indies but would tolerate no opposition from his workpeople to his plans to make 'such machines as cannot err' of his green village hands at Etruria. He needed skilled men too, but could not abide the independence their organisation and training gave them. He gave his reasons frankly: 'It is very probably a settled plan that this man, this best hand, shall make the first onset upon his new masters; if he succeeds the rest, both those we have at present and shall engage afterwards are sure to follow the example and there is no knowing where it will end.'

At his Birmingham works, James Watt would not tolerate, and neither should his partners, even meetings of the journeymen millwrights they employed. The millwrights were the travelling kings of the new age, in whose shoulder bags rattled the tools of all trades in wood or in metal, as skilled men as could be found anywhere, as knowledgeable and often more so than the men who employed them, given to fighting in pubs over the principles of engineering and just as pugnacious with anyone who dared tamper with their rights.

There is hardly a great name of the Industrial Revolution – Wedgwood, Watt, Boulton, Fairbairn, Naesmith – who did not clash with the skilled workers, the millwrights at their head. Their powers of organisation, their cunning way with cherished trade secrets and above all their determination to control entry to the trade through apprenticeship and through a fixed ratio of journeymen to apprentices made them formidable. The millwrights, many of whom had served their time in older trades, carpentry or clockmaking, carried forward the old rules and customs into the new age, the demand for their skills boosting their negotiating power. The repeated cry of the bigger employers that the old craft rules denied them labour for their work must, however, be taken with a large reservation. Labour they could have had, if they had employed the journeyman and paid the skilled rate. But it was not just labour they wanted, and in this the greatest innovator of the Black Country was at one with the most notorious sweater of the London garrets – it was cheap labour, as cheap as they could get it.

The seven year apprenticeship and the limit on apprentice numbers through the ratio of boys to men stood in their way. So they waged a prolonged battle to break the 'legal' or customary 'fair' limits, thrusting them to one side in workshop or factory if they could and imploring the government to wipe it from the statute book if they were thwarted. They evaded the limits even when to do so meant breaking the rules of their own craft company, laid down 'time out of mind'. Some masters – the hosiery and printing trades were notorious – took in large numbers of children, often orphans, from the workhouses, taking a premium from the parish funds. The overseers were glad to see the back of their charges. Having done this, masters demanded that their journeymen train the new labour. Finally, when the apprentice was trained, they would have pupil replace teacher at the loom or bench. This process was still able to provoke the skilled worker to fury in the 1890s. Often, though, when the children had grown they were turned adrift to wander to the next town where they would join the reserve army of 'foreign' labour threatening the journeymen's livelihood. The calico printers quoted examples of fifty-five apprentices employed alongside two journeymen in one shop. Worse was to come with technical change. With the arrival in 1785 of the cylinder printing process, the calico printers found themselves outnumbered and then supplanted. They severely controlled the introduction of the new processes for twenty years at least, to their employers' fury, but by the 1820s they, like their brother compositors, as well as shearmen, wool-combers and other proud hand-trades, were unemployed in large numbers. Cartwright's claim that his new machine would enable the wool manufacturer to discharge all his combers and employ children at a fraction of the cost was exaggerated. Another half-century was to pass before the prophecy was fulfilled, but it was the beginning of the end for these independent men.

Whether the threat to livelihood from cheap labour came with the added backing of new technology or not, the resistance particularly among the traditional town trades was tough and prolonged. The battle over the employment of 'boys' and 'forrens' between the bigger masters and the journeymen with their allies the smaller masters widened the split in craft organisation. The division which appeared in the seventeenth century with the separation of 'handytrade' from merchant members developed into a much more significant class breach between manufacturing capitalist masters and the general body of craftsmen in the trade. These were no longer seen as craft brothers but as a labour force which properly handled and 'free' could create great wealth. The bigger masters calculated that apprentice regulations would be the journeymen's Achilles' heel. In 1718, when the journeymen coachmakers of London demanded more pay, the City aldermen advised the company's court of assistants to counter by changing the by-laws to allow more apprentices.

Two years later the master curriers decided that each liveryman should take an extra apprentice for the same purpose.

In the earlier part of the century though, once the dispute was over, the *status quo* was restored and the apprentice regulations observed once more. In 1753 the coachmakers' court agreed that the restoration was to the benefit of all, fearing that in outright confrontation with the journeymen who now outnumbered the livery by ten to one, they would be the losers. Many of the skilled men were ready to set up in opposition to their employers and some demanded to have work by the 'piece' rather than daily wages, which the masters thought an 'intolerable insufferable usurpation'. In 1717 the clothworkers' livery was advised by an investigating committee to leave well alone and not provoke the company rank and file by tampering with the regulations. In 1731 the Court of Aldermen was similarly reluctant to disturb the *status quo* at the request of the masters. But the situation could not remain unchanged when trade rules were under attack from all quarters and the richer masters saw advantage in abandoning them. In a further dispute in 1760 the master curriers decided on a 'desperate step' – to take on as many apprentices as they saw fit – and in the 1780s the Tinplate Workers' Company not only took on extra apprentices but broke off wage negotiations with the journeymen. Twenty years later they sold copies of the 'price' book to raise money to prosecute them instead.

The rank and file of the companies fought back by industrial action. It was a time-honoured custom, said the journeymen cordwainers, that if any shop employed more than its quota of apprentices the men should all leave without more ado. In enforcing company regulations they might have the backing not only of the small masters but of some larger employers who favoured industrial peace. In 1782 the 'Father' of the wheelwrights' company was censured for supporting journeymen's demands.

The journeymen fought back by using the law. A shop with too many apprentices was an 'illegal' shop in some trades, under 5 Eliz. I c 4. Trades like hosiery and cotton sought its shelter to protect jobs and prevent wage cuts, but the Manchester check weavers were told by a friendly magistrate that the Statute did not cover them, and further that it laid down maximum, not minimum pay. Though other JPs interpreted the law otherwise on other occasions.

The employers, whether new men in iron foundry and engine workshop, country clothiers or rich new craft masters in their London suburban villas, fought the battle under the flag of free trade, with the eager help of Parliament. The tide of government opinion turned by mid-century decisively against the old sixteenth- and seventeenth-century regulations. State intervention from now on was on the side of the masters, with few exceptions. The direction of state policy allegedly was towards industrial freedom, the term *laissez faire* being most commonly used to cover the period. But it is misleading. Government was as active as ever in industrial regulation. Its effort, however, was thrown in one direction.

Even legislation in other fields reinforced this change. The 1723 Workhouses Act, which led to workhouse masters providing the poor and above all the young poor as cheap labour for industry on an increasing scale, undermined the bargaining power of the journeymen. Those 'private contracts honourably made' which the clothiers told Parliament in 1756 should be the rule for industry rather than state regulation, were in fact not made on an equal basis. By the early 1800s the Nottingham workhouse supervisors openly protested at the role they had been obliged to play in undermining the framework knitters' wage rates.

Parliament intervened directly, too, and almost always on the side of the employers. It removed the protection of the seven year apprenticeship from the West Riding broadcloth weavers, ten years after an Act of 1724 had apparently reaffirmed it. The employers' lobby had been at work. It took from the woollen cloth weavers generally the protection of legal wage assessment in 1756. In the 1770s, the hatters were deprived of any assistance they might expect from the law on apprenticeship, while the cotton workers who sought legal protection had been told their trade was too new for the advantages of Queen Betty's Law. Not too new for its disadvantages however. In 1779, that part of the Acts of 1549 and 1563 aimed at stopping workers from combining to improve pay and conditions was embodied in an Act covering cotton workers.

In the field of labour discipline, of course, there was no lack of state intervention: in 1718 a Royal Proclamation against journeymen's clubs, in 1719 an Act to punish frame breaking in the hosiery industry, in 1721 an Act at the request of the master tailors of London to discipline their journeymen, in 1720 an Act to make combinations generally illegal among the London crafts, in 1726 an Act against 'unlawful clubs and societies' in the woollen trades. Of such intervention there was no lack and by the end of the century the Combination Acts of 1799–1800 made a grand total of some forty laws specifically aimed at controlling employees. If this were a period of 'leaving alone' in industry then some were surely left alone more than others.

In their pursuit of greater production and profit, the employers undermined the inner, mutual discipline of company rule and custom. Assembling larger and larger workforces, they suddenly found themselves at the mercy of men over whom they had no control – if trade were truly free. They appealed to Parliament and not in vain. It was discovered that the law of free trade was not so natural that man could not improve on it. The eighteenth century was in fact a century of active industrial legislation, but of a distinct class character.

However, if the picture of *laissez faire* is not a true one, neither is that of a helpless, desperate, destructive class of working people. They appealed to the law, in elaborately respectful petitions, but their stance was anything but humble. The weavers in silk and cotton fought a thirty-year campaign culminating in massive street demonstrations in London when their demands for control over cheap 'callimancoe' imports were ignored and evaded. The weavers' movement, led by the company yeomanry with its rank and file organised in the quarters or divisions of the City and its suburbs, must have been a powerful stimulus for the 'combinations' in other trades which the master tailors declared an 'evil example' in 1720.

London framework knitters, finding the non-manual majority of their company court unable to prevent intruders filling sweat shops with illegal frames worked by apprentices, poured from their house of call in Old Street Square in 1710 to cast the frames into the street. Ten years later West Country woolcombers ransacked merchants' houses for cheap imported wool which threw them out of work. Gloucestershire weavers, enraged when the clothiers cut their wages in defiance of the law, seized the employers by force and dragged them back to the negotiating table. Time and again, from Banbury to Glasgow, the weavers petitioned for legal rights, won their point, saw the clothiers evade the traditional law, appealed to the State, were rejected, and then, not in desperation but rather in exasperation, marched, broke the looms in 'illegal', 'unfair' or 'foul' shops, or cut the web from the loom and paraded it on an ass's back to the sound of trumpet, drum and fiddle through the town.

The 'cutters' in the silk trade of the 1760s, finding their own company unwilling or powerless to help them, undertook to enforce their ancient laws. They called the masters to pay contributions at the Dolphin Inn in Cock Lane, off Spitalfields, while men with cutlasses held the door. Surprised by police and guardsmen, they fired and fled, but later saw five of their leaders go to the gallows. The outrage of these men, who in the words of the *London Tradesman* 'make but poor bread', is the undercurrent below the London street battles of the era. The 'mob' which appears so spontaneously in the history books is more often than not led by craftsmen who were seeing the law and custom that sustained their trade for centuries giving way to cut-throat competition. The Spitalfields Acts of 1773, an attempt to stabilise wage rates in the trade, was a rare example of the law intervening on the side of the rank and file of a trade. It was intended, according to Henry Fielding's magistrate brother, John, to divert the weavers from the House of Commons to the courts.

Yet force in defence of old rights and laws was a last resort. The drive to break them down and open the breach between master and man came from the other side, the bigger employers, who were assisted in the name of 'freedom' by a House of Commons whose electoral base in most parts of the country was as narrow as that of the masters and wardens in the companies. At every stage and in every way, the journeymen of the crafts, the time-served men, nucleus of the growing body of lifelong wage earners, sought to uphold and continue the form of industrial organisation which held master and men together and preserved traditions of skill and sentiments of fraternity. 'This beautiful branch,' said the Lancashire check weavers. Their object, said the London cordwainers, was to 'provide proper and legal journeymen for the master' and anyone who stole his master's goods should be deemed a vagabond. Our rules, said the Belfast cabinet makers, are 'for the good of the trade'. 'None but good workmen need apply,' said the Birmingham tailors. 'None but honest men' receive our benefits, said the woolcombers. 'None but those who left their last master fairly,' said the compositors. And the silk weavers summed up the outlook in a poem at the end of a negotiated wage list:

> 'Let masters still increase their treasure
> And journeymen pursue their work with pleasure'

These considerations were reflected in nineteenth-century union rules; not only the old hand trades but the new trades, the boilermakers and engineers, demanded that new members be skilled and moral too. The same spirit flowed from the ancient to the modern trades, flowed indeed uphill against the gradient of change.

As the small workshop production team, which was the typical until well into the nineteenth century, held small master and man together, so these sentiments were shared whether by cotton and wool weavers, compositors or tinplate workers.

In what must be the first definition of a 'scab' in industrial history, the cordwainers in 1792 declared:

What is a scab? He is to his trade what a traitor is to his country; though both may be useful to one party in troublesome times when peace returns they are detested alike by all. . . . He first sells the journeymen and is himself afterwards sold in his turn by the master, till at last he is despised by both and deserted by all. He is an enemy to himself, to the present age and to posterity.

This 'definition' was so popular that it turns up again in the records of the tinplateworkers' union (1820). The wording is the same, but 'scab' has been altered to 'rat'.

The ancient 'chapel' organisation of the print shop dating from the fifteenth and sixteenth centuries, with affinities in mock religious ritual to the French journeymen's gilds, was designed for the 'well-ordering' of the work, its rules endorsed by master and man alike. Among the bookbinders family relationships could be shattered by trade disputes. In one harrowing case a striker, imprisoned at the demand of the masters, led by his uncle, died of jail fever. His coffin carried (deliberately?) past the uncle's house caused his aunt to fall down in a faint.

Before the avenues to setting up were completely closed, masons, moulders and hatters often became employers in a small way. 'Many of you,' the journeymen hatters were to tell the masters in the early 1800s, 'have risen from our ranks.' 'There is no one of sufficient weight' to have authority in Sheffield, reported an army officer in the 1790s. The cutlers' company was the only thing like a 'resident jurisdiction'. In the older craft companies of the smaller trades, the yeomanry organisation renewed itself well into the eighteenth century, and among founders and blacksmiths it went on disputing the rights of election to company leadership.

Where journeymen and small masters through craft company franchise had the local vote, the limited electoral roll made them formidable in Sheffield, Leicester, Nottingham and Bristol. The crafts could influence who went to Parliament and formed the backbone of 'constitutional' societies.

As the government sided more openly with the wealthier manufacturers, so the politics of small masters and journeymen became more radical – fertile soil for revolutionary ideas from France or America. The collapse of the great Principle of Subordination which Defoe lamented, 'that subordination which ought to exist' as the master shoemakers said, was no chance or spontaneous happening. It was the other side of the deliberate destruction of the old working unity of the trades by the men who controlled them. 'Subordination' depended on respect for hallowed rules. Once this shell was broken then subordination rushed out and dispersed. 'The other side of the picture of the Bakers' control over their workmen is their recognition of the men's right to employment,' writes the company historian.

The democratic aspect of craft tradition gained radical impulse from economic discontent. Its new organisational form, growing in an age of international upheaval, was a force to be feared by government and, in the era of the Napoleonic Wars, to be repressed. How far this new class in the making became consciously seized by revolutionary ideas in the terms of the time may well be discussed. But the primary impulse of the main body of craft workers was not to change but rather to conserve, to hold on to something slipping from their grasp. Those who did look to the future in a visionary way looked with a view tinged by ideals of fellowship and a way of life being relentlessly undermined.

Under the same pressures, small masters and journeymen stood together. Even an organisation described as a journeymen's club could contain small masters. The wheelwrights' company decided none from the journeymen's club should be elected to the Court of Assistants – an unnecessary distinction if only journeymen were in question. The rank and file used company law as long as they could and where no formal structure existed with legal sanction they made it to their own satisfaction, 'illegally presuming to use a common seal', as the woolcombers were said to do. In smaller companies the 'right of search' lasted until the 1830s. In other companies the search and the collection of quarterage from master and man were abandoned together.

The one could not be maintained without the other. This was recognised by the coachmakers' court in the 1750s, while the blacksmiths dropped the search and the attempt to compel quarterage payment in the 1780s. The disbandment of the clothworkers' yeomanry in the 1750s and the abandoning of the search followed rapidly one on the other.

In each trade, from the feltmakers in 1708 to the curriers in 1796, a distinctive body, mainly journeymen, parted from the big master-dominated companies. The economic dissension reflected itself meanwhile in the social life of the crafts. In 1716 the master masons decided that the 'whifflers' or stewards at the Lord Mayor's procession should not dine with them but have three shillings and sixpence to eat elsewhere. In 1724 a surgeon was called to attend to a master coachmaker following a 'riot' at the annual celebration and several journeymen were prosecuted. In 1771 the annual dinner was abandoned as the 'proper members' could not dine in 'decency'. In 1781, founders' journeymen were barred from the annual dinner because of their 'behaviour'.

As the old forum for debate, the old mechanism for resolving disputes broke up, so in one company after another – feltmakers, masons, bakers, curriers, coachmakers, wheelwrights – the leading masters turned to the

Mayor and the courts for help. 'By admitting an unlimited number of apprentices,' says the curriers' historian, the masters 'had undermined their hold over their workmen and the two parties were in active conflict.'

The master wheelwrights, with the aid of peace officers, in 1782 seized the subscription book of the journeymen's club (perhaps from the public house where they met) and used it to pick out the names of seven men who were, incredibly, indicted for 'petty larceny' for 'trying to extract large sums of money' from their masters. With such actions, the breach was more or less complete.

Equally dramatic was the 1752 meeting in a Nottingham inn called to seek parliamentary backing for a new framework knitters' company charter. The larger master hosiers stormed out and the journeymen with the small masters set up a new organisation which tried unavailingly for the next sixty years to have Parliament regulate their trade.

The old alliance within the craft and within the town walls had been reshaped time and again over four centuries – gild, mistery, fraternity, livery company, craft corporation. But the confrontation within the body over wages, apprentice rules and ratios, and payment for the unemployed had become irreconcilable. The richer masters, speculating on unlimited profits to come from unlimited markets (the world was England's oyster), provided the labour force was also unlimited, found the old craft structure a hindrance and the craft philosophy an embarrassment and, in the light of the new economic wisdom, quite irrational.

What had once been peace interspersed with internal battles became an armed truce with the threat of unbroken war ahead. The battlefronts were shaped more and more on modern class lines; masters with the capital to employ larger numbers of men faced those selling their labour. At first both sides fought under the old articles of war. In the long dispute between the master and journeymen feltmakers, which spanned the seventeenth and eighteenth centuries, both sides interpreted the company by-laws as seemed right to them. In later decades rules were broken and patched up again. Until the 1760s master coachmakers were convinced that abandoning controlled entry to the trade might lead to a free-for-all which would push up wages. At the end of the century, the master curriers, who had thrown off all restrictions to try and defeat their journeymen, then appealed to the men for help when outside entrepreneurs invaded the trade. The most hallowed of craft rules could not stand the strain for ever.

Where the employers had the whip hand, as with the clothiers, they would talk of 'private contracts honourably made'. But when on occasion the boot was on the other foot, as with the woolcombers, tightly organised in small mobile work gangs roving the country like masons, then it was said 'they give laws to their master as to themselves'.

Both sides turned to the law, at first with mixed results and later almost invariably to the advantage of the employers, save where the outrage was so great that legal regulation (as in Spitalfields) was the price of social peace.

The skilled workers, much as they appealed to the law, believed that their chief strength lay in controlled entry to the trade, regulated by workshop custom and practice. Traditionally the weak spot, in a locally based workshop manufacture, had been the stranger, the 'foreigner' who when trade was bad in his own town moved on to the next or settled in the sprawling suburbs of the capital outside the company frontiers and beyond the reaches of the yeomanry searchers. When the blacksmiths found their trade expanding in 1700, with metal replacing wood in various branches, they took the bold step of 'admitting foreign brothers', just as the silk weavers, when the 'engine loom' could no longer be stopped, admitted the 'engine' men to their company. The feltmakers' or hatters' journeymen finally broke from their masters in 1708 and made common cause with the stranger journeymen.

Such a process could not stop short at the suburbs, for the whole country lay beyond and each year brought more strangers along the road, toolbag on back, indentures in pocket, by tradition and custom as much entitled to work if such there was as the man of the town. At this stage, the old custom and rules for reception of the travelling craftsmen, evolved over three centuries, took on a new significance. As laid down by the masons in the sixteenth century, they embodied work, hospitality and help on the way, provided the traveller observed the rules, behaved decently at the house of call and paid his bills when leaving. The traveller announced himself by sign, password, handshake, certificate or apprentice lines. A 'brother' would take him to a master who needed a 'hand' – the rule among nineteenth-century blacksmiths as among those of the fifteenth century.

By the eighteenth century a network of contact existed between the main towns. Since during the livery company period reception had been the function of the yeomanry organisation, so in the larger cities it was continued by the journeymen's club. Where fewer men were involved, the job was done by the masons' lodge, the printers' chapel, the hatters' or cabinet makers' workshop. Thomas Gent who earned his 'freedom' in the Stationers' Company in 1717 speaks of 'the fraternity' relieving

'On Tramp' after a Bewick print, a fair idea of one of the hazards of tramping in the late eighteenth century.

printers moving across the country or coming from Ireland or Scotland. Relief was often informal and among tailors and calico printers it was given voluntarily at the workshop door. Yet other trades had begun to set down rules concerning the traveller. In the 1750s the Salford smiths decided that a traveller did not need to pay for his drink, and during the Napoleonic war a brother balloted for military service was 'deemed a traveller'.

Craft workers became more mobile in the second half of the century as roads improved and the number of turnpike Acts sanctioning new roads increased four-fold. These were dirt roads; durable tarmac surfaces came only in the nineteenth century. In summer the traveller walked in a dust cloud. In winter he trudged in mud. If he could afford it he rode on the outside of a coach and sometimes with a friendly coach driver he had a ride on the steps in as much discomfort as the later American hobo trade unionist 'rode the rods' on the railway. More often, though, the traveller would be seen by stage coach passengers trudging along, pack on back. There were dogs to be fended off outside farmhouses, as celebrated by Thomas Bewick in his print *On Tramp* (*previous page*). In the 1780s villagers chased and hooted at a foreman tailor known to Francis Place, the radical reformer. But, if the obstacles could be endured and overcome, when the traveller who reached a town where his trade had a 'house of call' there would be in the tailors' words 'good encouragement'. Though if there were a dispute in the trade the traveller who tried to get work might find there would be 'no entertainment' in the words of the Liverpool tinplateworkers in 1756.

Travelling conditions for the poor – fording a river to evade a tollgate after a Bewick print.

Reception varied from town to town and organisation to organisation but the rule was to welcome a bona fide brother even if only to wave him on. 'Receive and cherish' was the rule of the masons in 1726 as it had been when the Tudors were on the throne. Members of the wool-combers' clubs which show themselves in East Anglia and the West Country from 1700 onwards would be 'caressed' at each club on showing their ticket, but only if they proved themselves honest, the House of Commons was assured in the 1790s. A Royal Proclamation of 1718 shows 'lawless clubs' of weavers in touch with one another and the hatters began a similar town-to-town correspondence and contact when they broke with the feltmakers' company in 1708. The curriers had a 'tramp-ing' link-up by mid-century while the London journeymen, at least, were still members of the ancient company though at odds with their masters. The brushmakers' clubs of the main cities made permanent contact with one another from the 1770s and the woolstaplers likewise from 1785. The 'blanks' which the brushmakers carried, stamped with the town coat of arms and the Russian boar, 'authentic sign of the trade', became their passport on their journeys to seek work, just as the 'emblematic engraving' of the West of England shearmen was later copied and recognised by their fellows in the Yorkshire textile areas.

Thus the rank and file of the town crafts developed their links with artisans elsewhere, independent of the bigger masters and eventually in opposition to them. The sudden outburst of activity by tailors' journeymen in London, Sheffield, Newcastle, Dublin, Cambridge and Aberdeen in the 1720s suggests some contact and Francis Galton, the tailor-historian, thinks the links were made by out-of-work men from London.

'I am a rambling woolcomber, regardless of your pity,' says one broadsheet version of the old song, and without doubt the growing links with journeymen in other towns, equally determined to maintain trade rights, increased the independence of the men. In the 1770s the hatters' journeymen, deprived of the legal protection of Queen Betty's Law, called a congress which laid down rules valid for the whole country. Twenty years later a fully fledged travelling system was in force, with 'blanks' and certificates for the journey and a nationwide network of 'turn houses' as the hatters' inns were called, a 'turn' being a complete tour of all the club towns in the country. During this period, too, the brushmakers began to elaborate their travelling network into a national organisation and the curriers, faced with the alliance of their masters with masters outside the company, worked to transform their travelling federation into a society.

The example was infectious and in the 1790s the London cordwainers took the first recorded step to transform custom into more formal organisation. The curriers, the hatters and the cabinet makers, they said, 'do not suffer their members to wander like vagrants'. Organisation was the only way to deal with the 'scab' who undermined journeyman bargaining power. Funds were essential, they added, for 'a lasting union among journeymen of any trade ... benefits more lasting and advantageous than any supper'. The trade and friendly societies of the time were still attached to the centuries-old custom of the annual feast, which in some friendly clubs was both the occasion and sometimes the means of sharing out all the money put in. Nearly a century later, the chairman of a patternmakers' club prevented his members from sharing out the funds and rushing down into the pub bar to spend them by putting his back against the clubroom door and keeping the meeting in session by force.

The crucial word in the cordwainers' statement, made in 1796, is 'union'. This may not be the first use of the word by wage earners, but as far as I know it is the first time it is used in the meaning of the future – the 'trade union'.

Journeymen's clubs with contacts through the land by means of their travelling brothers had more than a new organisational form. They had a new weapon in trade disputes. We cannot be positive that the disputes in the tailoring trade of the 1720s were linked by travelling journeymen, but in 1794 when Francis Place, the radical reformer, was a working tailor it was 'well known' that striking tailors were sent on the road, depriving the masters of potential 'scabs' or strike breakers and easing the burden on friendly society funds. In 1764, 6,000 striking London tailors 'dispersed' into the country. The tinplate workers in the 1750s already knew the value of keeping travelling journeymen on the move during a dispute with a local employer and the woolcombers were ready to 'break the combing pots', and 'abandon their work'.

But the most significant case of the use of the town-to-town link came from the millwrights, best paid and most independent of all the tradesmen, meeting in their club house on Friday nights to inspect strangers' indentures.

Fairbairn, the pioneering engineer, told how the millwrights working on London Bridge refused him a ticket to work, a woeful tale which has often been repeated. In fact he was shown the door because they discovered his indentures were faked. The millwrights were as independent as the woolcombers. But they had the future on their side as well as the past. Like calico printers, shearmen, handloom weavers and framework knitters, the woolcombers were destined to be humbled by the new machines. But the millwrights, like their brother mechanics, smiths, steam enginemakers and boilermakers, grew by what the woolcombers sickened from. The new capitalist inventors of factory, mill and potbank needed their skilled labour, and, unlike the labour of the new production hands, theirs could not so easily be cheapened. The master millwrights fought a running battle through the 1790s with their journeymen in London, with the aid and comfort of *The Times* which was then involved in a similar running battle with the compositors, who were trying to stop the owner using cheap boy labour. *The Times* announced (16 July 1795) that the master millwrights were determined to 'put a spoke in their wheel'. The masters had decided, as James Watt advised his partner ten years before, to find a good lawyer.

The advice was acted on, but unfortunately for the masters, who proceeded under common law, when the warrants came to be served the journeymen had all 'run away into the country'. For by now there were clubs of millwrights and allied tradesmen in many of the main towns, not least in the increasingly industrialised north. By 1799 these infuriating habits of the journeymen had become so much a pattern of the trade that the masters were at a loss. They decided to appeal to Parliament for an Act to control the journeymen, such as the master tailors, for example, had secured earlier in the century.

The appeal met with a response which must have amazed the master millwrights, a response which was to be a landmark in the history of organised labour – an act to ban combinations not among the millwrights alone, but in every trade.

The 1790s saw England at war with France. By 1797 Napoleon's armies had disposed of all other opponents and England was confronted with a trade boycott, the menace of the seizure of her rich West Indies colonies and the threat of invasion. At home there were bad harvests, rampant inflation, disputes in almost every trade from tailoring in Edinburgh, through weaving in Halifax, to baking in London. The calico printers, woolcombers, shearmen and handloom weavers had engaged in a prolonged stand against disruptive technological change and journeymen's societies had begun to develop national networks of contact, correspondence and organisation in some seventeen trades. The famous corresponding societies, where journeyman and master tradesman debated the notions of liberty, equality and fraternity, owed a good deal both in their 'divisional' organisation and their inter-city contact to the existing craft network. The Spitalfields silk weavers, not least, must have brought to the formation of the London Corresponding Society their organisational traditions.

To this ferment was added mutiny in the navy and rebellion in Scotland and Ireland. The sense of crisis among the ruling class can be appreciated, stimulated as it was by ignorance and the direst suspicions about the motives and intentions behind the new force in the land. 'The spirit of insubordination increases with the increase of manufacture,' said one report from a government officer in Scotland. In Sheffield where there were no persons of 'sufficient weight' the mechanics in their organisation included the 'lowest' admitted on payment of sixpence. The local magistrate had conveniently left the county. The 1797 naval mutinies at

Spithead and the Nore followed a succession of highly organised and successful strikes in the great merchant fleets of the northern ports in which masters and men stood together against the shipowners. Surely only profound ignorance of the ways of the new class could have led the authorities to conscript striking tailors into the armed forces as they did in Scotland during the year of the mutinies.

Just as baffling and suspicious were the friendly societies which since the 1690s had multiplied to some 7,000 in number, many based on craft organisations but containing altogether perhaps ten times as many people as were organised in the crafts. Those advising the government, even the liberal-minded Sir Frederick Eden, felt that many of the friendly societies, with their passwords, loyalty oaths, and their drinking habits, were breeding grounds for rebellion, offering, in the words of the Board of Agriculture in 1793, 'commodious opportunities to foment sedition'.

The authorities guessed friendly society funds were being used to support unlawful activities like strikes. Suspicions were mutual. In 1793 an Act was passed to encourage friendly societies, which, intelligent observers recognised, took an enormous burden of care for the sick and unemployed from the shoulders of the ratepayer. But the Act had an unexpected result. Nearly a quarter of the societies refused to register for they feared it would mean scrutiny and perhaps seizure of funds by the magistrates. The Act, though, had an advantageous feature. It specifically protected members of friendly societies from being removed under the Act of Settlement and forced to go back to their home town. This perhaps more than other factors must have impelled the journeymen's societies to regularise their travelling, for the man on the move whose club membership also entitled him to friendly benefits would find his blank or certificate ample protection against interference from parish authorities.

It was a confused and contradictory time. The economic drive was towards loosening all ties that bound workers to one place in order to make them mobile for the sake of the rapidly expanding manufacturing industries. The political drive was towards clamping down on the freedom of action of the same workers. The contradictions between the two make no sense if free trade and *laissez faire* are taken to mean simply what they say. But, in terms of class warfare and the demands of manufacturing capitalists claiming more and more backing from the country's aristocratic rulers, the contradictions are both clear and logical.

In 1794 the government suspended Habeas Corpus, making easier imprisonment without trial, restricted the freedom to hold meetings and arrested leaders of the London Corresponding Society. Acts 'utterly suppressing' the Scots and Irish nationalists, the Corresponding Societies and, by extension, any society composed of branches in contact with one another followed shortly, making the activities of the developing trade societies more risky. The letters sent by trade clubs to one another, however innocuous, now came under close scrutiny from government agents who opened the post and reported what they read to the Home Secretary.

And in 1799, under increasing pressure of discontent at home, and the threat of Napoleon abroad, the government took more far-reaching moves. The appeal of the master millwrights, fruitlessly chasing their strike-and-run journeymen, came in the spring of that year. In June the masters were persuaded to withdraw their Bill.

In its place went a more general Bill, roughly based on one intended to curb the papermakers' organisation, swiftly put together, and rushed through both Houses of Parliament in the space of six weeks. It went through at such a pace that only a few organised workers were aware of what was happening, let alone able to react. But there were protests inside and outside the House of Commons which brought limited amendments. By the summer of 1800 the second version of the Bill was on the statute book. What one historian called 'an odious piece of class legislation', the fortieth Act of its kind and the logical end of a century's development, was now the law of the land.

5 'Association . . . the malady of our times' – the Combination Acts and after 1800–1850

The first Combination Act, tightening up on all loose ends in existing legislation, was a renewed invitation to all employers to rule their employees by force of law. Any workers in any trade, who called or attended a meeting, or spoke to one another to put in an application for wages advance or to oppose a cut in wages, to seek to alter hours, let alone call a strike, persuade or oblige others to join it or not to break it, could be rushed to a magistrate. On another's accusation or their own admission, they could be jailed for three months, sent to hard labour for two months or fined £20 (three months' skilled wages). Even giving or asking for money for their own funds or those of other workers could bring a £10 fine, half to go to the informer.

There were protests from trade organisations in London and Lancashire and some MPs found certain things about the Act hard to stomach even when they accepted it in principle. It was too much, they said, that masters could combine but workers not, that workshop- or factory-owning JPs could try offenders from their own industry, that one magistrate should be enough to convict. The government responded with an amending Act in 1800, increasing the number of magistrates needed to two, excluding JPs from trying cases involving their own industry and introducing a £20 fine, but not jail, for masters who combined. No masters were ever tried or convicted. Throughout the twenty-five years of the Acts, masters met in public to decide their action and make their demands on the government with impunity. The Nottingham Mayor demanded that publicans should be forced to disclose details of journeymen's meetings, while the master hosiers of the same town met quite freely in the Police Office Tavern.

Together with the Corresponding Societies Act and the Treasonable and Seditious Practices Act of 1799, which made contact between branches of the same body illegal, the Combinations Acts of 1799–1800 were designed to prevent or make hazardous organisation among those who, during this period, came to be known as 'the working classes'.

'Combination', philanthropist Wilberforce told the House of Commons, is a 'general disease'; and even Sir Frederick Eden, who welcomed friendly societies as a form of self-help for the poor, said that 'association is the malady of the times!' and warned of the 'contagions of assembly'.

The government perhaps feared that the contagion of assembly might spread from the old craft-organised towns to the newer areas where manufacture was on the increase and a labour force was gathering which was an unknown quantity, a 'fresh race of beings', in the words of one Lancashire magistrate. Among the Scots weavers insubordination was seen as arising from a potent blend of whisky, Calvinism, constipation and the spread of manufacture. Fears that subordination would vanish were sharpened by the belief that trade societies had learnt the technique of linking together from the radical Corresponding Societies. From them Jacobin ideas of revolution would flow like an electric charge into a human mass already restless from the pressure of war-famine prices and savage wage cuts. The government had things the wrong way round of course, for the Corresponding Societies probably learnt the techniques of contact from the trade clubs. Indeed there is no reason to suppose that the many craft organisations which had 'For King and Country' clauses in their rules were being hypocritical or indulging in deceit for the sake of security. The skilled workers were often people of very conventional politics, while being highly militant on trade matters. The appeal of Lancashire weavers in 1799 with its side kick at 'wild democratical fury' is not untypical. But to a remote aristocratic government industrial militancy was as subversive as any avowed revolutionary activity. At all events, the Combination Acts achieved what they were meant to prevent: they drove together radical and conservative artisans in mutual defence. From Lancashire with the passing of the Acts came the report, 'The Radicals are drinking Pitt's health.'

The period of the Combination Acts saw the seeds of independent working-class politics sown. Some of the inspiration came from across the Channel, some from across the Atlantic, with English-born Thomas Paine the epitome of all three sources of radical notions. Paine, like many a lesser known spokesman for the journeyman politicians, drew his inpiration from the mainstream of English popular tradition. When Cobbett said, 'Without the journeyman and the labourer, this country would be a wilderness not worth the trouble of an invader,' he was paraphrasing Sir Thomas More's notion of the value of labour, without which 'no Commonwealth were able to continue and endure one year'. The radical workers wore the green ribbon, memento of the Agitators of Cromwell's army and the rebels of Sedgemoor, and critics of the rich were known as

'Levellers' in the newspaper language of the early 1800s. To sharpen and refresh memories of old struggles there was the mixture of upper-class hatred, fear and guilt which saw the freedom of trade organisation as a 'worse than universal suffrage . . . a mob oligarchy', in the words of one government spokesman. Thus the inevitable result of the 'gagging' Acts of the 1790s was that a growing number of workers, most of whom suffered from the law without being able to influence it, would increasingly demand the right to vote in order to change it.

But, though the powers of observation of the government were limited and their understanding of the journeyman's mind was small, their class instincts were unerring. Beneath all the wild talk of Jacobins and 'mobs' there was a real battle in progress, greater in scope than the Napoleonic wars. 'The industrial revolution,' said Engels, looking back from the vantage point of 1844, 'is of the same importance for England as the political revolution for France.'

He summed up the transformation which took place in past decades:

Sixty, eighty years ago, England was a country like every other, with small towns, few and simple industries and a thin but proportionately large agricultural population. Today it is a country like no other, with a capital of $2\frac{1}{2}$ million inhabitants, with vast manufacturing cities [Lancashire's population had increased ten times in the period.] with an industry that supplies the world and produces everything by means of the most complex machinery.

In 1799–1800 the revolution which had been gathering momentum for several decades was about to go into top gear. It is an interesting point that one of the early mass-production techniques, for block making, was introduced into British naval shipyards by the Brunels, refugees from revolutionary France. The skills employed in forging cannon for Trafalgar were interchangeable with those used to make boilers for the new power-operated mills of the cotton industry. There was indeed a kind of revolution, an industrial civil war in progress. And it was to be fought out over the next half-century through the introduction of machinery and mass techniques, the reducing of the old hand skills, the lowering of wages (Wedgwood's equation of wages and production was well learnt) and the creation of a labour force of millions intended to serve the needs of the machines and their owners. The crux of the struggle was the breaking of the power of the old style craftsmen, master and journeymen alike. At all points during the next fifty years – the builders' head-on struggle with the contractors in 1833–4, the engineering lockout of 1851 – the employers saw the issue as one of control. 'Dominance' was a word they used freely.

It was the age-old question: Who shall decide the running of production, the 'handytrade' or those who own the means? In its early nineteenth-century form, that question was revolutionary. In one sense – the technological – the issue was decided; the coming of the machines and the concentration of capital made the dominance of the minority of contractors, mill and factory owners inevitable. The machines and the factory structure they demanded came to dominate over small workshop and hand production; the number of workers in 'manufacture' overtook those in agriculture (by the 1830s); and the skilled workers, the 'aristocracy of labour' as they came to be known by the 1840s, were slowly but surely surrounded by a multitude of unskilled and semi-skilled workers enabled by mechanisation to compete more and more with them.

But the issue was not decided in a day. The Industrial Revolution had contradictory though temporary effects, which seemed to strengthen the resistance. By 1817 industry was processing six times more wool than in the 1730s, and in the 1830s about twelve times as much. Raw cotton imports multiplied a hundredfold in seventy years. But this great leap in production was still largely the work of the handloom weavers. In the 1810s there were just 2,000 power looms and a quarter of a million handloom weavers. In 1834, there were 110,000 power looms yet the number of handloom weavers was barely reduced. Of the $1\frac{1}{2}$ million at work in cotton, only 20 per cent were in the new mills. But the change had been accomplished and by the 1840s the number of hand loom weavers was to melt away to a few tens of thousands. For the first thirty years of the century though, with their traditional craft organisation, the weavers were still a power in the land, even though machine-induced unemployment was affecting them from 1810 onwards. Only with the 1840s and 1850s was the battle seen to be won and the handloom weavers, like the woolcombers, shearers, framework knitters, the organisational kings of the past, were in decline.

Yet as they went down before the machine, the men of the metal trades, blacksmiths, boilermakers, steam engine makers and millwrights rose up, bringing the old style craft organisation to bear on trades that needed their skills. The new employers, unlike the old masters brought up to the trade, had capital not skill and found the combination of craft cunning and organisation highly frustrating.

Cashing in on these frustrations in 1839, Andrew Ure published his 1,200-page *Dictionary of Arts, Manufactures and Mines* 'to instruct the manufacturer, metallurgist and tradesmen in the principle of their respective processes so as to render them in reality the masters of their business and to emancipate them from a state of bondage to operatives too commonly the slaves of blind prejudice and vicious routine'.

The craftsmen's strength was real, though their opponents exaggerated it. With their time-honoured exclusive approach to work and skills, they were often opposing not only the employers but their potential allies among the less skilled. Yet the organisations they built in the decades of turmoil enabled them to survive, to fight again and eventually to find those allies.

What is remarkable in their story is that crucial changes and advances in their organisations were made during the first quarter of the century, precisely during the period of the Combination Acts when every power – industrial and legal – was ranged against them. During this apparently 'underground' period they not only preserved their fighting capacity but extended it. The Combination Acts were a dark period for the skilled worker, they were not a blank period. It might indeed be called a 'chrysalis' period for in that twenty-five years the embryonic 'union' movement of the 1790s was transformed. The upsurge of trade union activity which followed the repeal of the Combination Acts in the late 1820s was the logical outcome not of the repeal itself but of everything that had gone before. The weapon of the Combination Acts was quite largely blunted by resistance before it was discarded.

By 1814, Maudslay and Donkin, powerful leaders of the master engineers, declared at an openly held meeting in the Museum Tavern, London, that the Acts had been 'evaded and defeated'. By 1818 the Home Secretary himself declared them 'almost a dead letter'. By 1822, Hume, the Radical MP, profiting from an evident desire on the part of the government to be rid of the embarrassment the Acts represented, put forward his proposals for repeal. These were followed in 1823 by a repeal Bill sponsored by Gravener Henson, the framework knitters' leader. Eventually in 1824–6, prompted by Francis Place, the radical master tailor and skilled lobby man, and his journalist ally McCullough, Hume produced the strange flesh-fish-fowl notion of doing away, in the name of free trade, with restrictions on the export of machinery, the emigration of artisans and, almost as an afterthought, the restrictions on artisans' trade organisation.

During the hearings in 1824–5 of the Parliamentary Committee on Artisans and Machinery and the Select Committee on the Combination Acts, 1825, employers from Donkin the engineer ('it helped in no degree') to a prominent Ayrshire mine owner ('it never weighed with the miners') emphasised that the Acts had not succeeded.

It is true that witnesses to the inquiry were prompted by Place, who had convinced himself and others that 'combinations' largely existed because of their illegality, to stress the ineffectiveness of the Acts. But Donkin was merely saying what he had said ten years earlier and what the Home Secretary had concluded six years before.

The Combination Acts, and other laws that sent union members to jail for two years or transported them for seven, did give employers immense power. The workers were convinced, whatever the political economists (including Place) told them about population, supply and demand etc., that the Acts had held down wages. They declared them to be 'savage and injust' and said that in 1818 there were 'an immense number' in jail. Yet in their main purpose the Acts were seen by their supporters to have been 'evaded and defeated'.

Both Tory and Whig cabinets were ready to crush what they saw as insubordination by jail, transportation, execution if need be, and were ready to occupy working-class areas with troops for years as though they were foreign territory, as in effect they were in government eyes. But, having provided the laws, the government expected the manufacturers to do their share of the dirty work, so that they might preserve some appearance of standing above the struggle. By 1804, the Home Secretary was told by legal advisers that the nationwide organisation of shoemakers was illegal, and there was 'no difficulty' as far as the law was concerned. But if the State prosecuted, then the masters would expect the same service next time. Suppose, then, that the journeymen asked the government to prosecute the masters? Better leave the actual prosecution to the employers, with the government footing the bill (students of history may recall similar arguments during the period of the Industrial Relations Act, 1972–4).

In 1816, while the government often used informers against trade and radical clubs, it was reluctant to agree formally to bend the rules of evidence still further to make conviction easier, as some masters demanded. At least it was unwilling to be seen to make a policy of bending the rules. The government was ready to use repressive measures but kept a certain reserve in face of the enthusiasms of its underlings.

One vicar-magistrate vainly asked permission to close public houses at 6 p.m. to stop meetings. For Lord Sidmouth the Home Secretary had already shrewdly noted that he would rather have the workers gathering where his men could watch them. Many magistrates, vicars among them, were eager prosecutors and gatherers of intelligence, though not always as skilled as they were willing. But not every public authority would follow the most vindictive of the masters in a vendetta against their workers. In Nottingham there were no prosecutions under the Act until 1814, and then, since it was the first time, it was not thought 'politic' to impose more than one month's hard labour. When the seamen struck at Shields in 1816, the local magistrate only ordered the arrest of the strike leaders under pressure, being convinced that the masters were in the wrong. At Merthyr Tydfil, in 1818, a local JP said roundly that violence had been avoided thanks to the restraint of the soldiers who had moved in, not thanks to the masters. In 1817 the poor overseers around Nottingham were so shocked at the masters' insatiable desire for cheap labour that they refused to allow any more paupers to go to the hosiery factories. During weavers' strikes in Scotland local landowners gave the strikers work on the land and in many towns shopkeepers and others gave to strike funds, though this was illegal. The rising industrial bourgeoisie was not a pretty sight and did not always find favour in the eyes of the onlooker, middle- or upper-class.

There were other problems of 'proving the necessary facts' in the face of craft solidarity. The Law Officers (1816) might encourage informers to 'infuse a great degree of jealousy and distrust' among trade club members, but informers were often as ignorant as the men who paid them and as ready to commit perjury (one declared that the meetings of London trades' delegates were connected with the plot to kill the Prince Regent – a statement made on the prompting of his eager paymasters). But even the minimal proof needed to convict could often not be obtained.

The pattern of prosecution varied widely. In 1819, strike leaders in Lancashire were fined. In the same year, the 'Robin Redbreasts' (Bow Street Runners) stormed the inn where Wolverhampton tinplate workers were meeting. After a pitched battle and the destruction of club records, the leaders were arrested, tried and transported for seven years. Master boot- and shoemakers in London, seeking to intimidate the men, had handbills printed warning of penalties, not under the Combination Acts which many employers regarded as derisory, but under the Treason and Sedition Act, 1799, which was probably used against the Wolverhampton tinplate men. The journeymen, too, sometimes thought Combination Acts sentences derisory. 'They laughed at one month,' complained an Abergavenny JP. They would send convicted men to the jail 'in a chaise and four, and the same back again', came a report from Sheffield.

Many masters were unwilling to prosecute. Reports speak of 'great indisposition' and 'a want of spirit'. When Yorkshire clothiers wanted action against the woollen workers they asked if it could be done without anyone knowing they were responsible. In Lancashire, where the industrial struggle was fierce, there were signs that during the last six years of the Acts there was a 'reluctance' to prosecute, a 'want of courage' among the masters. Why 'reluctance'? One reason may be sought in the state of affairs which prevailed in manufacturing until the 1840s, the predominance of small production based on hand work, already mentioned, and thus the greater intimacy of master and man. In Oldham in the 1820s 50 per cent of the workforce were handloom weavers and only 7 per cent were in factories. In the same town by the 1840s 60 per cent were in factories. Two of three firms employed 80 per cent of the engineering workers while the small workshops were reduced to subcontracting. In the 1850s, engineering masters ranged from those employing two men to those employing 1200, but the latter sort came to dominate. In the building trade, the contractor rose to dominate the old master–man set up with a new breed of employer like the 'tyrant' of Accrington who in the 1830s dismissed all the journeymen masons and all but three of the masters who sided with them, cut off supplies of stone from the quarries, and dismissed the masons' children from the factories he owned. But this development was only getting under way during the period of the Combination Acts.

Thus, such statements as 'controlling powers over their masters', 'the fiats of our workmen', 'in the hands of our united rulers' and fearing to 'incur their displeasure', may be exaggerations but not untruths. Explaining the reluctance of the master shoemakers to prosecute, a memorandum to the Home Secretary in 1804 says that 'any individual' doing so 'would probably be deserted by his men'. In that year a single master shoemaker took out 107 warrants, and then, to the chagrin of his fellow employers, refused to serve them. Government agents found it remarkable, though amusing, that framework knitters should summon master stockingers to a public house meeting to discuss terms 'with as much consequence as if they had been the Prince Regent'. The Manchester hatters asked the masters to 'kindly come forward' to a meeting or have their names given 'to the public'. Defaulting master blacksmiths were warned that if they did not comply with regulations 'all the police in the barracks will not save you'. The journeymen and many of the masters too did not see why the trade should not govern the trade. This was still true even in later decades when master masons came to the lodge house to accept terms after a strike. 'If I may be trusted with 50 masons', said one, who only wanted to 'die decent' after defeat in a dispute. Let the masters 'meet us in open lodge,' said the masons' corresponding secretary on another occasion. This cooperative-coercive relationship where it existed during the period of the Combination Acts helps explain their limitations. The real crux of the struggle lay not so much in the law but in matters the masters and men were trying to control.

Most drastic in its impact was technological change. The battle which had begun many years before among the London trades, the fight back of shearmen, croppers, framework knitters, woolcombers, calico printers, and handloom weavers, has been lumped together under the general heading of 'machine breaking' or 'Luddism', a synonym for mindless opposition to 'progress', or as desperate illegality in a harsh situation. But neither view gets to the heart of the matter – why skilled, intelligent, well organised workers should go in for machine breaking. Gravener Henson, leader of the framework knitters, lucid, passionate historian of his own trade, believer in the perfection of 'thirty generations' of gild-style craft control, was not 'King Ludd' himself as later Victorian writers suggested. Sam Slater, the frame smith, as the historian, Felkin, suggested, seems nearer the mark. The smith, marching hammer in hand, primeval figure of vengeance at the head of a torch-bearing crowd, moves among the machine breakers of other trades carrying 'Great Enoch', the hammer which smashed the shearing frames in Yorkshire.

> Great Enoch now shall lead the van,
> Stop him who dares, stop him who can
> Oh the cropper lads for me
> The cropper lads for me
> Who with lusty stroke
> The shear frame broke . . .

Machine breakers of any trades, like the weavers, were driven by 'distresses . . . beyond all description', as Lord Sidmouth was told in 1819. In 1814 in Nottingham, centre of the hosiery industry, half the population were on the poor rate.

But one and all in every trade were driven by the conviction that the machines which enabled skilled men to be replaced by children were 'illegal' or, as the London weavers said of the engine looms they broke in the seventeenth century, 'deceitful'. In the seventeenth century the law backed the weavers for a time. In the nineteenth century it had turned against weaver, cropper, comber and framework knitter. Or, as they saw it, the law had turned against itself. Up to this point the crafts-men tried persistently to use the law as they understood it. Gravener Henson sought to the last to use the powers of the Framework Knitters' Company Charter. To break the 'illegal' machines was both an extension of that attitude and a departure from patience with it. Gravener Henson and men like him were King Ludd in spirit though not in body. Behind the violence of Luddism was a moral force based on generations of old law and custom.

Machine breaking was only a part of the struggle over the labour supply and entry to the trades. Can anyone imagine that, had the employers guaranteed to the journeymen that their livelihood would be secure, the machines would have been opposed? It was the machine as destroyer of their livelihood they opposed, and the machine as the means of cheapening labour which the employers were bringing in.

Cheap labour was the crux of the struggle over apprenticeship regulations. A journeyman speaking to the Artisans and Machinery Committee in 1824 put his finger on the essential point: 'The men are more naturally in the power of the master if entry is not limited.' But five or seven years' apprenticeship was simply a barrier to the bigger masters, whose capital represented their power. On the other hand, the journeyman–apprentice ratio, which irritated the masters even more (more than two apprentices per man denotes 'a foul shop', said the hatters), was no absolute barrier to the employer who wanted a larger labour force. He could, after all, take on more men, and boys. But it was a barrier to a larger, cheaper workforce. As the calico printers said, offending employers took on more apprentices while journeymen looked in vain for work. We want more apprentices, a master printer told the Select Committee on Combinations in 1838, 'to increase the quantity of work done and to get it done at the cheapest rate.' It was the compositors' opposition to his wholesale employment of cheap labour that led the owner of *The Times* to have their leaders jailed with the aid of the judge, Sir John Sylvester (known as 'Bloody Black Jack').

Printing masters, though not unique in their greed for child labour, went to great lengths to get it. A Dublin employer proudly told MPs how during a strike he worked his presses with children, taught by apprentices. The children were locked up in the print shop day and night and taken out to the countryside by cart at the weekends for exercise. His 'novel scheme' was sabotaged when the journeymen spirited away his apprentices.

In some industries, 'apprentice' was a euphemism for slave labour. The children of the poor, including parish orphans, were taken by cart and barge load to the manufacturing areas, the high point of this 'migration' coming in the middle of the Combination Acts period. Such were the conditions of their transportation that London parents and others protested and in 1816 the removal of children over a distance of 40 miles was made illegal. Arthur Redford, who tells the harrowing story of this traffic in unskilled labour in his *Labour Migration in England*, says that parish apprenticeship which began as an extension of the normal trade training 'degenerated into a form of disposing of unwanted children'. The poor, recruited under appalling conditions, with the help of workhouse supervisors, were in some cases sent back home to their native parishes as soon as unemployment made them a 'burden' on the rates of the town where their employer was a ratepayer. Redford speaks of the 'parasitic action of the manufacturer in using up labour quickly and then rejecting it (through the poor removal system) in favour of a fresh supply of human material'. This was indeed the worst aspect of the use of the so-called Act of Settlement, or as one recent study has said 'abuse' of the Act, though the distinction between use and abuse seems a narrow one, and of course non-existent to the victim.

Even where apprenticeship was normally carried out, the apprentice might be turned adrift when trade was bad. By mid-century workhouse wards abounded in such half-trained 'craftsmen' youngsters with nothing to thank respectable society for, as Henry Mayhew discovered.

But the process by which apprentice regulation and custom were undermined was still too slow for the bigger employers. They demanded and got from Parliament the abolition of a series of ancient laws that stood in their way. First went the laws barring machinery, then those regulating wages in various trades, and finally, in 1814, the House of Commons, in the teeth of mass opposition, threw out the final legal bulwark, the apprentice clause of 5 Eliz. I c 4. Tens of thousands of journeymen and masters signed petitions against the repeal; only a handful of signatures supported it. But Parliament ignored all protests and nine years later threw out the Smithfields Acts protecting silkweavers' wages and conditions. This was done at the request of a minority of employers, though 11,000 signatures to preserve the Act were collected in a few days by the journeymen.

The vote of the House of Commons in 1814 shocked the journeymen much more than the passing of the Combination Acts. As they saw the matter, it struck them more directly and weakened their powers. But the journeymen refused to accept the legal verdict. Only in 1852 did the engineers cut from their rules the clause on apprentice–journeymen ratios. Though by 1849 the masons recognised that the seven-year apprenticeship was dead, they still negotiated local agreements for five years' apprenticeships and recognised ratios, and until the 1870s observed the understanding that runaway apprentices should return to their masters.

London compositors re-established apprentice regulations in 1848 and the boilermakers maintained them through the century, while in the 1850s the iron founders managed to hold the proportion of boys in the foundries to one in thirteen of those employed. Only in 1857 did the coachmakers moderate their entry terms to admit those who had 'worked at the trade' for five years before the age of 40. As with the fight over machinery, it was a long, rearguard action to maintain rules which had had the force of law for centuries. It was no traditionalist sentiment, but practical economics. 'Such trades as are strict' on these points 'are most powerful and best remunerated', said the masons in 1836.

The 1814 vote following on the Combination Acts added to the workers' conviction that they were on their own resources. In 1818 the *Gorgon* newspapers echoed the sentiments of Fielding's Jonathan Wilde in saying that Whigs and Tories disagreed only as thieves falling out over division of the spoils. Expecting no good from the legislature, they strengthened craft organisation. 'The sun of your independence is setting,' John Gast, the shipwright and leader of the London trades, warned his fellows. The new employers thought the old master–man relationship a 'grovelling state of affairs'.

Strengthening of the organisation came about in two ways: one more naturally and swiftly, the union of workers within each trade; the other more slowly and with difficulty, union among the trades.

Information is not complete, nor will it ever be, though one must be grateful to the bureaucrats of the Home Office and even to the spies they employed for having seized so many letters, pamphlets and rule books. It is ironic that the government during those decades when it tried to suppress the nascent trade union movement did something which that movement was incapable of – it preserved much of its documentation. These documents make Aspinall's *The Early Trade Unions* the most valuable of all source books in this area of history.

Using these sources, those of Parliamentary Committees, and such early trade society and union independent sources as are to be found, I estimate that whereas when the Combination Acts were passed there was some kind of inter-town contact in seventeen trades, by the mid-1820s, when the Acts were repealed, such a contact existed in twenty-eight trades at least. What is more, these 'federal' networks (37 branches among the steam engine makers, 20 among the mechanics, 29 among the foundry workers or moulders, 70 or 80 among the boot and shoe workers) were often well developed: six divisions of branches among the brush-makers in 1823, several 'divisions' among the papermakers in the 1820s, a congress and rule book among the woolcombers in 1812, a central 'government' and rules among the framework knitters in 1813, a general secretary among the coachmakers in 1819 and a union of 'confidential representatives' among the tinplate workers in 1821.

Between 1820 and 1826, steam engine makers, mechanics, smiths, papermakers, shipwrights, pottery workers and others were making contacts to sort out their accounts between societies, and the system of the 'acting branch', by which one society took charge of headquarters work, had been established. The move to unity varied from trade to trade. In 1803 the Home Office spies learnt that delegates from various towns had been summoned by cotton printers to discuss wage rates. The various friendly society 'orders' began to 'affiliate', the Oddfellows leading the way in 1810, their main object being to ensure that members moving from one town to another might retain benefits paid for at home.

'Equalisation' carried out loyally and efficiently between societies in the millwrights and other metal trades enabled the experience of long-standing members of one society to be carried to the next. With the travelling member went the rule book and the verbal laws and customs which existed side by side with it, thus hastening the process of unity and uniformity.

The almost universal reason for contact was the system of relief accommodation and employment of the traveller, or, as he came to be 'commonly called' by the carpenters around 1800, the 'tramp'. By 1800, woolcombers, hatters, curriers, papermakers, cordwainers, calico-printers and others had begun their tramping contacts with 'tickets' or 'blanks' and 'houses of call' where hospitality and news of work were to be found. By 1802 the government had news that the shearmen had similar nation-wide connections, as did workers in hemp and flax manufacture in 1804. In that year it was reported: '. . . it is too notorious that similar combinations exist in almost every trade.' In the early 1800s, there are signs that joiners, cabinet makers, brushmakers and printers had provision for hospitality, the cabinet makers making it clear there were no jobs for strangers while disputes were on. In 1819, the coachmakers' general secretary was warning branches to halt tramping temporarily and save money for a strike. In 1818 the ironmoulders had a 'plate' or engraving from which 'blanks' were printed with the union emblem, and in 1822, during an extended strike, the tinplate workers were urged to 'support the tramp'. From this time on the activity becomes general with hardly a major trade uninvolved. And all these developments were watched by the government. All of them, as the Glasgow postmaster observed when he opened the letter from the Manchester hatters to their Glasgow brethren (see introduction), were on the face of it illegal. Yet so widespread were the networks, involving altogether many hundreds of clubs, that action against all was impossible.

George White, secretary to the Committee on Artisans and Machinery, asserted that the Combination Acts had been 'in general a dead letter upon those artisans upon whom it was intended to have effect. . . '.

They had their 'travelling societies' and 'houses of call, as though no such act was in existence'. This point was confirmed by a master hatter who told White's Committee: 'The law cannot take hold of these men for they leave gradually, man by man and get employment at other places; thus the Combination Laws are by that means completely avoided.' In short the whole exercise, designed to remedy the trouble the master millwrights complained of in 1799, seemed to have failed.

To complicate matters, many trade societies were also friendly societies, registered or unregistered. The authorities were convinced that many friendly societies were 'frequently made the cloak' for other activities, offering 'commodious opportunities to foment sedition and form illegal combinations'. On the other hand there were many friendly societies with trade rules which had once been registered by magistrates and now could not automatically be deregistered. By 1803, three-quarters of a million people, or 10 per cent of the adult population, were members, perhaps ten for each active trade unionist, an immense reserve of moral and financial support in all kinds of misfortune. Earl Fitzwilliam, no friend of the organised workers, asked: 'What is the objection to men laying aside money for future need?' And the members of friendly societies saw little difference between acts of God and men in time of need. Master engineers Maudslay and Donkin might grumble that the London journeymen evaded the law 'under the mask of friendly societies' but to the trade society member and his family there was no contradiction.

Solidarity grew with class antagonism and with mutual hostility. The shoemakers of Bath told their London brothers of their 'late contest with our tyrant' and bade other societies make their news 'as public throughout the trade as possible'. Town-to-town contact made financial support during strikes easier, and during the Wolverhampton tinplate strike already mentioned large sums were raised in other towns and the strikers found work elsewhere.

Unity went beyond the bounds of each trade. As the government intervened on the side of the employers, so trade exclusiveness began to melt away. Journeymen in different trades had in any case had friendly personal contact for many years. But what now emerged were new forms of active mutual support, for political action to secure trade rights or freedoms or financial solidarity during strikes.

In 1795 journeymen and masters in ten London trades made a joint protest over government attacks on free speech. In 1800 a joint trades demonstration over rising prices was banned by Royal Proclamation. The passing of the Combination Acts united artisans and labourers in Liverpool, journeymen of London and Westminster and workers of different trades in Manchester, Stockport and Bury. In 1803 the government was told there were plans to 'disseminate the system' of correspondence among various trades and in 1809 comes an intriguing rumour that delegates of different crafts (perhaps around the textile trade) had met in Carlisle to improve communication with one another. The campaign to prevent the repeal of the apprentice laws in 1814 brought together the London journeymen in a joint committee which Maudslay and Donkin claimed could mobilise large numbers in a short space of time. Caldecott, the informer, may well have exaggerated in 1817 when he said that the London tailors with their club network were involved in regular meetings of a Grand Union of all trades, but in November 1818 an editorial in the *Gorgon* newspaper urged all trades to join in one 'band of social fellowship'. The knowledge that simultaneously in Lancashire Doherty and others had set up their 'Philanthropic' union of all trades, including cotton workers, must have sharpened government alarm. It would seem that, while the London joint trades committee was mainly concerned with lobbying on trade rights and to some extent with suffrage, the Lancashire organisation was above all concerned with organising solidarity and co-ordinating strikes.

In the disturbed years that followed the ending of the Napoleonic Wars, the roads were crowded with soldiers and sailors discharged 'before the mills were ready for them', with men and women driven out with the aid of the Settlement Act, by employers who no longer needed them as workers and did not want them as paupers.

In the clothing towns of the North and Midlands the machine breaking and mill burning reached their climax and troops marched in to control what master and magistrate could not. On the roads between towns moved the tramping artisans, as the socialist printer Bray later wrote, together with 'men in need of the goods each could provide but the other could not buy', drinking in the evenings with fellow tradesmen, sharing the same club house and sometimes the same room or bed with men of other crafts. Fellow feeling in misfortune was a powerful bond.

Among the tramps were men with a purpose, letters and rule books in their pockets along with their 'blank' and indentures, on their way to set up new societies in towns where none existed, carrying messages secure from the post office spies. They ran the risk of being searched on the road and they were closely watched. Government agents reported emissaries of the Manchester mechanics collecting money from workers in the potteries in support of their strike. In London the brushmakers entertained three calico-printers from the North and lent them £20 for their funds, some of which could only be paid back eight years later. Along with the organisers and collectors were 'itinerant orators' preaching sedition, it was alleged, despite the 1817 act aginst 'delegates, representatives and missionaries' sent between groups in different areas of the country.

Sometimes the messengers and letters were concerned with momentous matters, but more often with the everyday, and above all with the regulation of tramping. Bring your blank, the Portsmouth shoemakers advised their 'loving shopmaites' in other towns. Entertain only 'fair' men, wrote the Manchester hatters. Sixpence for every tramp who crosses a member 'with a union blank', said the woolcombers, drawing up their elaborate travelling rules in Congress. All houses of call to come under the central government, said the framework knitters at their conference. Let all societies meet to regulate tramping, appealed the mechanics. Later, in 1824, the Committee on Artisans and Machinery listened in wonder to the elaborate explanations of papermakers and printers of their nationwide system of aid and relief for the workless.

Just as incredulous, some forty-three years later, members of the Royal Commission on Trade Unions listened while the boilermakers' leader patiently explained that yes, unemployed men were paid to travel the country (see Chapter 12). Impelled by the facts of economic life, the new 'unions' had no choice but to extend and consolidate their tramping networks and in the interests of good accounting, if nothing more, to introduce some measure of central financial control. The law of free trade dictated it and the laws of Westminster could not hinder it.

By 1824, then, the trade clubs were stronger than in 1800, their links with one another had become more regular and solid and the links between 'unions' of different trades, both local and regional, for political lobbying and trade solidarity, while not permanent, were renewed with increasing frequency. By the time Francis Place and his allies, the Radical MPs, had produced their over-ingenious plan for repealing the Combination Acts, the government was almost openly seeking a way of removing the Acts as more of a liability than an asset, or at the least amending them. The possible repeal of the Acts must have been in the air in the early 1820s for the number of 'union' delegate meetings taking place openly begins to increase. So, with the mid-1820s and the repeal of the Acts, the 'labour question came into public view', as Mr Gladstone quaintly put it in 1892.

The formal repeal of the Combination Acts was followed not only by the appearance of many fully organised trade unions. It was followed by a strike wave in which many workers tried to recover ground lost in previous periods of bad trade. Place seemed to take this as a personal affront and he wrote to some unions urging them to desist. He had after all assured the government that with the repeal combinations would cease to exist. But the unions had urgent business on hand that could not stay for personal appeals.

Employers' organisations now swiftly lobbied a receptive government and in 1826 some of the restrictions on union activity removed in 1825 were restored, particularly on picketing. But the employers' attack was met by a vigorous counter-lobby. With Place as co-ordinator and the London trades delegates bringing up one detachment of workers after another to Westminster, the situation was brought to something of a stalemate.

Some historians have complained of the failure of the unions to respond to appeals for moderation in 1825–6. But if they did not respond it was not out of a failure to appreciate benefits conferred on them. It was rather that the repeal of the Acts had simply, in the words of a hostile observer, Nassau senior, adviser to the Home Office (1830):

confirmed in the minds of the operatives the conviction of the justice of their cause, tardily and reluctantly but at last fully conceded by the legislature. That which was morally right in 1824 must have been, they would reason for 50 years before. They naturally regarded themselves as creditors on their masters or on the State for all they had undergone and if the relation between master and servant was before ameliorated by gratitude attachment or respect, those feelings were totally extinguished.

It has been argued that the unions were in some way abusing a freedom which had been conferred on them (by a legislature for which only some of them had the vote). But this is to see freedom of organisation as an abstraction which must be granted by Parliament in order to exist at all. Freedom to organise as a reality depends upon the real existence of the organisation, without which any debate is academic. The unions not only maintained their organisation during the period of the Combination Acts but in face of every obstacle they developed, extended and transformed it.

This is not the occasion to argue in detail the controversial qualities of Place or what he accomplished in terms of trade union law (for in most historical accounts we have only his word for what went on). His efforts made union organisation easier, but that organisation would have developed with or without the formal repeal of the Combination Acts. The greatest and most difficult part of the fight against them had been carried through before 1825–6. Once the Acts were repealed and the attempt to reinstate them in full warded off, the unions turned with vigour to the task which had occupied them for the past three decades. This was the more efficient organisation, with regular officers, proper accounting systems and uniform rule books, of the 'unions' which were growing out of the tramping networks. In 1826 the brushmakers established their central accounting system, and the mechanics of Lancashire extended their contacts. In 1827 the first national carpenters' organisation known as the 'General Union' was formed. In 1829 the first bricklayers' union appeared, and delegates of a 'grand general union of all the operative spinners in the United Kingdom', under their redoubtable leader John Doherty, met in the Isle of Man, where they celebrated the occasion by carousing 'not to a late, but to an early hour'. In the same year the cotton unions and a number of other trade societies came together in the short-lived National Association for the Protection of Labour.

In 1830, the compositors of some forty towns formed their Northern Union; a year later the plumbers and the Scots masons formed theirs; and then, most famous of all, the Operative Builders' Union appeared. It lasted for three years and brought together the stonemasons, painters, plasterers, plumbers, carpenters, bricklayers and slaters in a single body, said at one point to number 40,000, though this must now be seen as a considerable exaggeration. Just why and how the builders first jointly organised in this manner would be worth a book in itself, though I feel it cannot be unconnected with the amalgamations of the older building craft organisations in many towns outside London which date from the seventeenth and eighteenth centuries, just as the roots for the sudden storming growth of the Operative Masons, the hard core of the OBU, must be searched for in earlier craft forms.

At the height of this drive for union organisation, Robert Owen, 62-year-old Welshman, successful, genuinely benevolent factory owner, inspirer of Co-operative organisation, utopian socialist writer and speaker of tremendous appeal and reputation, came to the 'Builders' Parliament' in Manchester in September 1833. There he successfully appealed to them virtually to take over the building industry by organising a Grand National Gild which would begin to replace the capitalist general contractor with a form of co-operative ownership, starting with a big 'Guildhall' project in Birmingham. Within six months Owen had reached yet higher, joining with leaders of trade societies in launching a Grand National Consolidated Trades Union which would bring together workers, irrespective of trade, into one body. The unions within it were in the middle of a tremendous drive to increase their membership, and the 'Grand National' drew into its net, though briefly, previously unorganised workers from women gardeners to chimney sweeps.

Farm labourers in Tolpuddle, near Dorchester, joined the GNCTU and a local magistrate found them guilty of administering illegal oaths. Not far away in Exeter a much larger crowd of masons had done exactly the same, but they were let off with fines. The Tolpuddle men, however, were sentenced to be transported. Faced with demands from employers for the Combination Acts to be brought in again, the Government seized its opportunity, endorsed the savage sentence on the men of Dorset, swiftly thrust them on a prison ship and had them ready for their voyage to Australia while the movement of protest against this 'legal' outrage was building up.

In the wake of this determined counter-blow, with disagreements over strike and lockout solidarity, which had been its main business, the 'Grand National' fell apart and so did the Operative Builders' Union.

This double failure is sometimes seen as the collapse of trade unions, whose development was only resumed in the 1850s when the engineering workers launched their famous amalgamation.

But since the 'trade unions' had not suddenly developed during the early 1830s, but over the previous forty years, they could not suddenly fall apart. The Operative Builders' Union which lasted three years was above all a fighting alliance or coalition among building workers against the hated 'contracting system' in which one big capitalist employer dealt with the customer and placed all the 'operative' builders in a subordinate position. The small masters hated 'contracting as much as the journeymen did and when in 1833 the OBU launched a 'general attack all along the line upon the new system' the small group of large firms were at first forced into a retreat.

For a moment it seemed that the traditional master–man working relationship, traditionally very strong in the building trades, had been preserved and that the 'operatives' would have the say in how the industry was run. Soon the big employers were to counterattack and the 'operatives' had to make a fighting withdrawal. Robert Owen's Guildhall project for the entire trade to be self-employed came at the triumphant height of the anti-contracting movement.

It should be remembered, too, that it was not uncommon for striking workers to go into production on their own account during disputes, for in those early days strike funds were small and workshop production was on a small scale too. In the 1790s London tailors on strike, Francis Place reports, made breeches and sold them to supplement strike funds. In 1764 Edinburgh masons in dispute offered work direct to the public and in 1816 London carpenters, organised in eight public houses, did the same. Blacksmiths employed out-of-work members on making tools. There was a tradition maintained by the master–man closeness of the small workshop of which later co-operative production schemes among engineers, brushmakers, tinplate workers and others were a part.

Robert Owen's grasping at the future and the builders' grasping at the past met at that point in time – Autumn 1833. To say nothing came of the whole episode would be a mistake. It seems a grand gesture with which to turn from the hope of recreating ancient conditions in the building trade to the hard business of winning better conditions in an industry which was to feed on giant contracts for railway viaducts, new industrial plants and the vast towns that formed around them. Ironically, only six years after the Guildhall episode, the Newcastle lodge of the Operative Society of Masons proposed that the union should undertake public building contracts as the answer to unemployment. The Newcastle brothers were chided for 'visionary schemes' which were 'about a century too soon'.

That the grandiose Guildhall scheme owes a lot to Owen is true, but to allege as one historian does that the builders 'swallowed Owenism whole' is to credit Owen, like Place, with superhuman powers and suggest that the men who formed the unions had no minds of their own.

Had they uncritically supported Owen, they would have joined the 'Grand National', but they did not. Many of them regarded the Operative Builders' Union itself only as an alliance, while others wanted it to be a union in fact with all trade distinctions abandoned.

In short, 1831–4 was a time of tremendous experiment and debate in action, in which none of the participants, neither the most visionary of socialists nor the most pragmatic of non-political 'society' men, had any previous experience on which to base their union of all the trades. The year 1834, far from being a time of defeat and collapse, was an arrival point for the union movement which was in every sense creating something new out of something very old, tried and tested, which the workers involved sensed was no longer enough for the challenge they had to face. Those 'trades' which marched out on 21 April 1834, under their society banners, 30,000 strong, in their top hats and ribbons, their leaders on horseback, to Copenhagen Fields to protest at the deporting of the Tolpuddle Martyrs were performing a historic act. The rules of every single one of those organisations would have barred the men of Dorset, who had served no formal apprenticeship, from joining them. Yet those craft-proud journeymen recognised that brotherhood had a wider meaning than the old exclusive one.

The GNCTU failed in its efforts to help some thousand men, women and children, locked out by their employers in Derby, but the solidarity efforts made by the skilled trades who raised huge sums to help those unskilled factory 'hands' were not unworthy. In these and in many other actions they had begun to give expression to the wider meaning of union. 1834 showed the strengths and weakness of the unions; it showed the limits of their development. But 1834 was not followed by a dead period.

Before the year was out, coachmakers had shaped their tramping federation into a permanent national union. Boilermakers had founded theirs. The boilermakers included in their rules initiation ceremonies, loyalty oaths, passwords and signs. The 1830s and 1840s saw both success and failure in the drive to build the trade unions.

The printworkers, pottery workers, boot and shoe workers, tailors, basketmakers – all made attempts to amalgamate separate national organisations which did not entirely succeed, and stable union organisation was built only slowly. But national union development went on steadily among the carpenters and joiners, masons, plumbers, steam engine makers, blacksmiths, ironmoulders, brushmakers, cabinet makers, shipwrights and many other trades. The complete collapse of organisation in a trade was the exception rather than the rule. But attempts to link unions in different trades took second place to the consolidation within each trade, to the shaping of the new organisational forms, the executive committee taking the place of the 'acting' or 'head' branch, the delegate meeting replacing the traditional method of balloting by letter 'round the societies', the conversion of separate lodges and clubs into 'branches', with uniform subscriptions and benefits throughout the country, and above all, uniformity in the vital matter of 'tramping'.

A first stage had been accomplished. The stranger from the club in another town had become the brother of the nationwide union. And the traveller or tramp had now become a part of the rules of the organisation he had helped bring into being.

6 Bread, Cheese and Beer – How the Tramping System worked

A simple everyday need first brought the separate societies in each trade together, gave them regular cause to correspond between towns, and led them to agree common rules and common benefits – to create a 'union' in fact. This was the 'enabling of the workman to maintain himself while casually out of employment or travelling in search of it'. By 1860, this was declared by outside investigators to be the 'simple and universal function' of trade societies.

It turned out to be a far from simple function. But it was universal. Organised workers in every trade from masons to millers, from basket makers to boilermakers, evolved or copied the system from others. The boilermakers copied their first tramping rules from the blacksmiths, for example. Only certain trades like cotton spinners had no such tramping system. When their union delegates met in the Isle of Man in 1829, the Carlisle delegates proposed a tramping system, but Doherty, the national leader, moved 'previous business' and the discussion was closed. The spinners used one aspect of the system, a 'certain device' by which a member moving from one town to another might be recognised. Nor did the miners, whose organisation was strongly localised like that of the cotton workers, have a tramping system, with the exception of the Northumberland men whose out of work members had to tramp round two or three pits searching for work to qualify for benefit.

Unions in England, Ireland and Scotland often co-operated over tramping as they did over strike solidarity. But 'reciprocity', the key word, was not easy to achieve. In time it led to disagreements among the English, Irish and Scots members of a number of trades. It was a source of 'recrimination' among the printers for decades. Among the workshop trades of Ireland and England tramping was widespread. But in Scotland hatters, tinplate workers, boilermakers, masons, plumbers, tailors and compositors used the system with less enthusiasm and some trades did not use it at all. While the English moulders tramped the Scots moulders took their 'idle aliment' or unemployment benefit at home.

In Wales, where industry was strongly localised and often isolated, in quarry and mine, some trades, like the 'copper ladies' who broke ore in the quarries, were itinerant, but there is little sign of any system of organised relief. When the main industrial development reached Wales in the second half of the century, however, the steelworkers adopted the system and masons and other building workers from England carried it into Wales with the aqueducts and viaducts they built to carry away the coal and water out of the country for English industry. By 1875 the masons' rule book was translated into Welsh.

In England, tramping was almost universal. During the eighteenth century, the word 'traveller' had begun to replace the word 'stranger' in trade society rules, although 'stranger' was occasionally used in rule books until late in the century. The term 'foreigner' for a non-local man was used in workshops even after 1900. But during the nineteenth century the more common usage was 'traveller', 'travelling brethren', 'tramping brother' or 'tramp'. The hatters told the Committee on Artisans and Machinery that the object of their club was merely 'the treating of strangers and paying attention to one another'. In the words of their historian, the moulders 'made no provision for keeping in touch with each other than the travellers'.

It is difficult to say when the travelling journeyman was first called a 'tramp'. Perhaps in the late eighteenth century. The Birmingham carpenters who in 1808 looked for a suitable public house for their club had in mind the needs of those members 'commonly called tramps'. The Leeds mechanics (1824) and the Derby smiths (1822) used the word 'travel' in their rules, the tinplate workers (1822) used the word 'tramp'. The brushmakers in 1829 spoke of having brought their 'tramping system to its present enviable state of perfection'. By the 1830s it was in general use. In 1844 Engels, explaining the practice to readers of the *Condition of the working class*, said simply, '. . . this is tramping and the traveller a tramp.'

There was nothing derogatory in the use of the word. It simply meant that the member in question was 'on tramp' looking for work. Today it was an unknown brother arriving at the club house, tired, dusty, hungry and thirsty. Tomorrow it might be you setting out. In the second half of the nineteenth century, the increasing use of rail travel began to make the term redundant and it was changed back to 'traveller', though the change was more complex than that. (see Chapter 12.)

The principles of the system had been laid down three centuries before by the masons, and it is an interesting speculation whether the little known 'assembly' of masons' lodges to which all fellows within fifty miles of wherever it might be held 'must nede gon' gave rise to the 'moveable' or 'head' lodge or branch which co-ordinated the early 'unions' and 'orders' of trade and friendly societies. The legacy of the masons to the movement is indicated anyway in the wide use of the term 'lodge' and the widespread diffusion of the tramping system.

The essentials were common to each trade: a friendly reception, a night's hospitality, and a job or a hand on the way to the next town. At first the help might be casual. Anyone calling at a mill would be given money, said the papermakers; and the same applied to the tailors or hatters workshop – a coin from the master, a whip round from the men, threepence or sixpence, said the hatters, according to the number of men at work. Unofficial loans among the moulders continued after the union rules forbade them.

If the tramp arrived late and the workshop gates were shut (later critics said some tramps arrived at sundown by design) then the tramp went to the local club house or turn house where the 'trade' did its meeting and drinking. His chances of meeting a brother were good. 'I went into the bar at the White Lion,' said a sawyer, questioned by police in Stalybridge in 1840, 'and the place was full of sawyers.' He might make himself known by an agreed sign, if his toolkit did not make him immediately recognisable (like 'St Hugh's bones' among the shoemakers).

'How would you recognise a fellow boilermaker if you saw such in a bar?' an applicant for union membership was asked. The laid down reply was: 'I would raise my glass and make the boilermaker's sign – thus'.

The masons' sign which could charm a fellow member down from a steeple, was well known and the 1834 scare over oaths, passwords etc., in the wake of the Tolpuddle Martyrs' case, deterred neither them nor the boilermakers. In 1838, though with a special government inquiry into Combinations in the offing, the masons proposed to abandon all 'initiations', oaths and other paraphernalia. They did so officially, but unofficial ceremonies on building scaffolds continued into the twentieth century. Blacksmiths issued passwords to tramps in 1839 and the steam engine makers were reluctant to give up the use of passwords even in the 1840s, while the Oddfellows, most ancient and powerful of the 'affiliated' friendly society orders, went on using passwords on travel, issued by the 'Noble Grand' or chief officer, until much later.

As numbers increased the reception became more formal. Secretaries were paid a small allowance, sometimes in 'liquor' to 'attend' at certain times in the day at the club house. The sums of money for the tramp ceased to be casual and voluntary and for the sake of fairness and efficiency were laid down by rule. Thus the use of 'tickets', 'blanks' and 'clearances', in use already among woolcombers, hatters and others in the eighteenth century, became general. Mechanics issued a 'testimonial', framework knitters a 'diploma' and 'blank', and other trades a 'certificate' – the traditional craft usage from the sixteenth century. The document became quite elaborate in some trades; the brushmakers' was a book of several pages like a passport, which was a record of the tramp's journeys and the amounts received. Stamped with the 'sign of the trade', a copperplate engraving uniform throughout the country, it took on all the aspects of a passport, was specifically seen as such by the hatters, and it reinforces the Webbs' picture of the craft unions as 'a jealously democratic state within a state'.

One of the duties of the acting branch in the early days was to arrange for the making of the emblem plate. One of the problems with the Northern Typographical Union's system in the 1830s and 1840s was that the branches had indulged in elaborate designs for their own cards and thus it was not easy to enforce a uniform design.

In 1838, the ironmoulders commissioned a new engraving because the old plate was worn out after twenty years' service. The engravings were small works of art representing the trade emblem. In an older trade – tailors, masons, compositors – this would be the authentic arms of gild or craft company. In the newer trades, like the boilermakers, steam engine makers or lithographers, it would be an emblem with coat of arms in craft style, the boilermakers borrowing freely from plasterers, blacksmiths and other sources. The brushmakers' emblem contains the arms of six towns, the first societies to join in union. From these tramp certificates developed the later union emblems which decorated front parlours and hung on public-house walls between the gilt mirrors and almanacs, large, poster-sized, highly coloured, designed by amateur artists or commissioned from Royal Academicians.

To the members the emblem was a thing of pride and beauty and one old boilermaker had the union arms engraved on his tombstone, while the masons' lodges were locked for months in aesthetic, professional and theological debate over their emblem's contents before they would allow the RA they had hired to get on with his work. To the outsider the emblem or blank was a mystery and the Home Office papers contain an interrogation of an informer by a curious magistrate as to its purpose, from which he emerged none the wiser for the informer was quite uninformed. When the Committee on Artisans and Machinery interviewed trade society members in 1824, they too were curious about the blanks. When the hatters explained that a worker who robbed his master would get no blank, his questioner asked:

'Could they go without such an institution?'

'No, it is a kind of passport and a certificate of good character.'

The blank was given to 'honourable' members (compositors) or those 'not illegal' (moulders). This valued document and the membership card and rule book and perhaps apprentice indentures were carried carefully on travel. Some trades used a metal box to preserve the documents and the boilermakers' general secretary describes a clearance box as being flat and heavy, weighing five ounces empty.

Thus carried, clean and dry, the tramp book became a record of the tramp's journeys. As the unions developed and more branches opened, these journeys grew likewise. In the 1830s the blacksmiths had a network of 36 towns, the brushmakers 34, growing to 64 in the 1830s, the printers 43 in 1837, the steam engine makers 37 in 1824, the shoemakers around 80 in the same year. Since relief was given only once every six months in each town, the tramp, once started, had in theory to make the complete 'turn' or 'circuit' and 'not pass a lodge where entitled to relief'. A turn might be a thousand miles or more and might involve two crossings of the Irish Sea to call at Dublin, Belfast and other Irish cities where 'reciprocity' was the rule.

In each town the procedure was the same, a procedure laid down in 1434 by the blacksmiths who delegated a yeomanry member to direct the traveller to a place of employment. The smiths' national organisation laid down in 1822 that the tramp should be directed to the shop foreman who would then apply to the master or masters for work. Among the hatters this was the job of the 'short turn' who took the tramp round with his 'asking ticket'. Woe betide the hatter who refused an asking ticket or the job that went with it, unless it happened that the shop was in dispute. Master hatters with no job to offer might in accordance with ancient custom allow a tramp the chance to earn a few shillings or give him some from his own pocket. Mechanics, millwrights and moulders sought to have shop foremen in their ranks to ensure that work would be given to members in strict rotation on the vacant book. Employers saw this as an invasion of their rights. But until they had succeeded in forcing or enticing the foremen out of the societies, a process which took several decades, they did not get complete control over hiring and firing. 'A new ten-arch viaduct is to be built and since the foreman is the former president of our society you may guess what sort of men he will employ,' reported a masons' lodge in December 1834. So recognised was the procedure that the union emblems of moulders and boilermakers show the yard foreman ceremonially greeting the tramp. The moulder tramp is greeted thus:

'Brother craft, can you give me a job?'

'If we cannot, we will relieve you'

The local 'vacant book' (a term already used in the 1830s) hung behind the bar in the club house and no one, Scots plumber or English engineer, had a 'sight of it' until they had produced their certificate with the branch seal. In the vacant book names were entered in strict rotation and if no local man were out of work the tramp got the job. Shipwrights in London laid down by rule that members on 'job work' should only hire members, recalling the carpenters' 1333 ordinance: 'work his brother before any other'.

But if there were no work, then the tramp got his supper and pint (two pints among the Friendly Mechanics of Leeds, two pots among the London hatters, ale and a piece of bread and cheese among their provincial brothers). If it were a club night, the tramp might attend, but not speak unless called to do so. Informally though he would be questioned on the state of trade. On the general state of trade might depend whether a local society could engage on a strike, sending some of their men off on tramp to ease the burden on the funds. As correspondence developed, local societies lodges and branches were required to report whether the 'state of trade' was 'good, dull or bad' to the acting branch, so that this could be included in the fortnightly or monthly returns or reports sent out to all parts of the organisation. Thus the gossip of the tramp gave rise eventually to the union report or journal.

After supper the tramp slept in a bed provided by the publican. The London brushmakers paid their host at the Craven Arms, Drury Lane, £6 a year to provided 'good clean beds' which they inspected every month and a servant whose job it was to see to the needs of the tramp. In 1839 they 'admonished' the landlady who had been letting out tramp beds on the side. But brushmakers also made gifts, a half-crown to the old woman servant 'who had been many years in that service and always attentive to the tramp', which recalls the old woman employed by the Coventry gilds to wash the feet of poor travellers in the fourteenth century.

It was a 'privilege' of masons' lodges to inspect tramp beds regularly to see 'if they were fit for a decent person to sleep in'. The inspection was no formality, and a masons' leader later recalled that 'though my resting places were never luxury hotels', the accomodation 'was much better than might be expected'.

If the tramp arrived on a Saturday he was allowed to travel no further on the Sunday unless by special permission. In the better off societies like those of the mechanics and smiths three meals were provided for the Sunday. And on Monday the tramp would set off again 'refreshed with money', as the masons put it, to the next 'tramp station'.

The amounts given varied. The Manchester printers gave four shillings to a man from one of the 'Old Societies' which like theirs dated from the eighteenth century, and half a crown to a 'minor society' man. The London compositors gave two shillings, the moulders likewise, the tanners 10d, the masons 6d, the cordwainers 4d. But eventually most societies adopted the mileage system, a halfpenny or penny a mile. The brushmakers added a shilling for journeys over 20 miles and 1s 6d for journeys over 60 miles. In the West of England, society towns were few and far between and the member might have to go 80 miles between one club house and the next. Plymouth masons secured an extra payment on top of the sixpence, pointing out that from Plymouth to Bristol was five days' march, while in more populous areas a tramp might reach two stations in a day, getting one shilling and even more in a week, while his brother was slogging away across Devon. Variation in tramping and other benefit payments was the reason for the drive for 'equalisation' which accompanied the move to union in the 1820s and 1830s. In 1826 the brushmakers' 'acting branch' in Witham, asked all branches to send accounts so they might 'regulate them as equally as possible'. Sometimes there were delays when even the auditors had to go on tramp. Sometimes whole branches were on the road and the local landlord had to take on the job of 'relieving officer'.

Equalisation was particularly important for engineers, boilermakers and other unions where the benefit payments for sickness, travel, burial and old age were relatively high. Affiliated friendly societies took early to 'equalisation' for they had been advised that without equalisation they imposed a form of 'settlement' on the members which prevented them from travelling to another town for fear of losing benefits saved up for at home.

Among building workers, each lodge was supposed to support the tramp station until funds ran out and then ask the acting branch for help. It was not an efficient system and often broke down. Blackburn lodge, we read, can offer only a bed for the night. But Armagh is paying one shilling instead of sixpence according to rule. Equalisation – 'Rochdale desires

Oldham, Burnley and Rossendale lodges to settle their tramp accounts' – was still in its primitive form. But eventually it gave way to centralised accounting, though even in 1867 the Royal Commission on Trade Unions was suprised to hear the general secretary of the oldest carpenters' union say that head office never held more than £500 in funds, when other unions were handling tens of thousands of pounds in benefits each year.

Along with a regularised tramping system went different treatment for different grades of member. A newly enrolled member got a bed for the night (plus what he might receive unofficially at the workshop door). A twelve-month or 'free' member got full hospitality and a penny a mile. The boilermakers, in imitation of the blacksmiths, made it a halfpenny for a twelve-month member and a penny for a two-year man. Among the London hatters in 1824 a 'stranger' got five shillings but if he brought 'a blank from another town however' he had a bed for three nights and two pots of beer. The Glasgow compositors made more interesting distinctions. A man leaving the city got a lump sum of 15s (21s if married). A tramp coming in got 7s if a member of a similar society, and 5s if a non-member but 'free from professional opprobrium'.

Difference in status might be indicated by the colour of the card. Among the tinplate workers there was a blue card for a free member and a black card for a non-free member. The masons gave free members a white card, new members a yellow one. Highest status of all, though, in both trades went to the 'green card' man on tramp because he was on strike (see Chapter 8).

Coachmakers were divided into 'citizens, people and subjects'. This means freemen of the old company and thus freemen of the city with the vote, in first place, then members of the society with twelve months' service, and finally new members. The brushmakers also had their 'free-men' who were a source of friction when they refused to take their turn on the road when trade was bad. Under pressure from political candidates employers would seek to keep the freemen in work during election times for the sake of their vote. This relic of the old city company system, known as 'forcing the freeman', was resented among the brushmakers and disappeared when the civic rights of the old companies were abridged in the 1830s.

In the early days tramping was obligatory. If a craftsman lost his job and wanted unemployment pay then he had to walk for it, though among the brushmakers he could draw 'pension' at home after a complete circuit had failed to find work. With the coachmakers this worked in reverse. The unemployed were allowed a period of relief at home after which they had to walk for work. To make sure the walking was done 'fairly' many trades supplied 'route cards' with a list of towns, club houses and sometimes 'fair' shops.

When the union member went on tramp he was generally parting from his family, with only occasional provision for a tramping wife. The cordwainers' and now and then the early tinplate workers' societies provided a bed for the wife. London tanners gave tramping wives a bed but woe betide the man who tramped with a woman he was not married to. One tramping mason caused trouble when he demanded a bed for his wife and daughter, threatening to work in a non-union site if denied. Greater still was the indignation when a mason arrived with another brother's wife, whom he had so ill-used on the road that she had to have medical treatment at the lodge's expense.

Hatters, tanners, Glasgow and Manchester compositors, and brush-makers gave extra payments to tramps leaving families at home. But these were exceptions, and this was to prove a damaging weakness in the tramping system in later years when heavy unemployment put it to severe test. Though tramping meant a sort of widowhood for the wife, the man was obliged to walk. That was the rule for many years. Among the boiler-makers it lasted until the 1870s, although the out-of-work brother was not obliged to march if he was over 50. Tramp or no pay remained the rule among many building workers, tailors, and boot and shoe workers until the twentieth century when the system was at its last gasp.

On the other hand the eager tramp was carefully scrutinised. Give satisfactory reasons for tramping or bear your own expense, said the mechanics' rules in 1824; no payment for the tramp 'causelessly leaving his employment', said the hatters in 1859; no cheque 'if he refuses employment', said the masons in 1849.

Willing or unwilling, thousands of union members took the roads while the system lasted. Just how many, particularly in the early years, is a matter of guesswork, though an attempt is made in Chapter 15 to estimate numbers at different periods, in times of 'good trade' and bad.

The system was paramount in the early years of the nineteenth century and the reason was clear to union members if not to outsiders. As a carpenter told the Select Committee on Combinations of Workmen in 1838, 'If men were not assisted they would eventually have to take work at the lower rate.' Quizzed by the Poor Law Commissioners in 1834 as to why he preferred to take tramp relief rather than work for a pound or thirty shillings a week, a leatherdresser explained that two pounds was the union rate and he did not intend to be 'turned black' for working below it. As a London hatter told Henry Mayhew in 1850, tramping kept men independent.

That independence of the time-served journeyman in the small workshop was prolonged by tramping. Of this many union men were convinced, and they were attached to the system both by conviction and sentiment long after the mass unemployment of the middle of century put intolerable strain on it.

A picture of the tramp on the road in those early days was given during a trial of sawyers' union members at Ashton in 1840. Thompson, a union tramp, had been taken into custody: his mysterious arrivals and departures were enough to make him appear suspicious to authority. The Court heard that:

Thompson . . . had left Hull on December 6 and after working at Goole, Doncaster and Sheffield, he came to Ashton at 8 o'clock on Wednesday. He went to the Stag's Head, saw the relieving steward and many other sawyers and slept at the house that night. The following day he went to get a job at the first yard along the Stalybridge Road, after trying the next yard, he went back to the Stag's Head, had twopennorth of stew and went away to Oldham which he reached about three o'clock and went to the club house . . .

On the following day, Mr Richard, timber merchant at Oldham, saw Thompson in the sawpits of his own yard with the men. On hearing an unusual noise or kind of loud laugh among the men, who were drinking beer which had been sent out for by them, he went to inquire the cause and they said it was an old shop mate of whom they were glad to see from Manchester.

7 The Craftsman's Lighthouse – inns and pubs

Thompson, the tramping sawyer, was welcomed by his shopmates in Oldham, with beer they 'sent out for'. Within walking distance of every workshop would be the public house or inn the trade favoured, the 'society house', 'club house', the 'house of call'. Indeed, while Thompson and his mates were laughing and drinking together under the eye of the timber merchant, their betters may well have been poring over a book published only the year before which purported to explain to them the curious and reprehensible (when comprehensible) customs of the artisan. The skilled workers, wrote John Dunlop, the temperance campaigner, in 1839, 'supported the trade, or it may more properly be said, supported the tramping and drinking system.'

Like most statements from the militant anti-drink lobby it was exaggerated, but it had a core of truth. The early trade societies put the care and control of the tramping member high on their priority list and within the tramping system the public house played a crucial part, as it did in the life of the early unions as a whole. All their activities depended on or were linked with it.

For the tramp the public house was first of all a labour exchange, a 'house of call' where behind the bar he could get a sight of the list of jobs going. 'Vacant books' were kept in public houses right up to the time of the introduction of Labour Exchanges in the early 1900s. It was alleged that keepers of Victorian lodging houses kept a book with names of local people who were an easy touch for passing cadgers, which book would be shown only on payment of a fee. It was not the only example of the way in which the rules of trade societies were parodied by the professional vagabond from the sixteenth century onwards (see Chapter 2).

In the vacant book the name of the out-of-work man went down 'in order of occurrence', as the Cork journeymen put it. When it reached the top he was next to be taken on.

Just when the public house began to be used as a 'house of call' cannot be said for sure, although there is a tradition that the builders of Westminster Abbey during the fourteenth century took their pay from the Cock Inn in Tothill Street nearby. The craft gilds used convenient inns, some of which bear trade names to this day, for annual celebrations and transacting business. We find the carpenters' company at the Dog and Bear, the weavers at the Black Boy in Cornhill. Here in the late sixteenth century rebels against the rule of the richer masters met and demanded reform and one member of the weavers' livery accused his fellows of 'sucking the profit from the company'. The wheelwrights met at the Swan, the blacksmiths had a hostelry in each of the four quarters of the City. The master masons until the early eighteenth century set out each quarter day to beat their bounds, checking on the presence of strangers and the quality of stone used, collecting dues, and tempering August dryness or November chill in the George at Southwark Bridge-foot, or Martin's coffee-house near the Guildhall. Tailors held their quarterly summoning of 'forrens' at public houses in the company's area and when in 1608 the Court of Assistants accused them of holding too many public-house meetings they produced their statistics proving how vital they were to the protection of the trade. Masters and journeymen of the Framework Knitters' Company looked out from their protest meeting in the Cock in Old Street Square in 1710 and saw across the street the shop of an offending master filled with apprentices working illegal frames. Their fury turned to action; they stormed the workshop, threw out the frames and beat the unfortunate operators. Fifty years later the rank-and-file 'Cutters' Club' among the weavers (so-called because they cut the web on illegal looms) met behind closed doors, guarded by men with cutlass and pistol, in the Dolphin in Cock Lane, off Spitalfields. Here they fought the troops and police and escaped across the rooftops, though later five went to the gallows.

The house of call where the journeymen went or where he was summoned had by the eighteenth century become a 'kind of law'. Houses of call, the master tailors told Parliament, 'encourage and abet these journeymen in their unlawful combination'.

Nearly a century later in 1800, the master tailors alleged that a network of some forty public houses was the centre of organisation for some 20,000 journeymen and they demanded action against the houses as a means of 'destroying communication' among the men. In 1818 the network was in existence still, with forty houses, thirty held by the 'Flints', men who would not yield on trade principles, and nine or ten held by the 'Dungs', who had been prepared to compromise with the masters. But the contempt of the one for the other did not stop them uniting against their masters at times. In 1804 the boot and shoe employers, meeting appropriately at the Crown and Anchor in the Strand, agreed to deliver up to the magistrates the list of public houses used by the journeymen so that their meetings might be suppressed.

With society houses dotted around the City and its suburbs, with landlords whose interests made them allies of the men, with the unemployed reporting at set times during the day, it might be possible, as was alleged, that meetings of thousands could be convened in a matter of hours, even during the period of Combination Acts.

At this time, the framework knitters' organisation, which had been obliged during the eighteenth century to shift its centre from London to the Midlands after the richer hosiers had escaped there in search of cheap labour, had its houses of call in a circle of towns for 'more certain employ' of the members. These houses were 'under the control of their central committee'. It will be seen that the word 'control' is no exaggeration where the trade was well organised and the connection was encouraged by ale house keepers and brewers. During an eighteenth-century dispute among the blacksmiths the company livery alleged that the complaints had been 'managed by ale house keepers' who had access to the then mayor, a brewer by trade. In the 1830s, the master bakers, in a 'doleful diatribe', charged their journeymen with organising industrial action against synthetic yeast on the grounds that this would undermine their connections with the brewers.

For the men to have benefit from the house of call, though, strong organisation was needed. Among the less organised trades and particularly in industries which developed with the industrial revolution with a large proportion of new labour, the public house connection was seen as weakening solidarity. The temperance lobby were not alone in objecting to the paying of wages in public houses and the consequent pressure on the workers to spend part of what they earned in the pub, sometimes while waiting for the agent to arrive with the wages money. In such circumstances the masters' connection with the public house would work against the mens' organisation. A famous masons' strike at the House of Commons in 1841 broke out when a notorious foreman, known for his bullying and arrogance as 'The Black Prince', (the tinplate workers called one of their opponents 'King Pippin'), tried to force the workers to buy worktime beer from a designated pub. To enforce the trade connection he locked up the water pump on the building site. The contractors admitted that it was 'by arrangement with the brewers'.

But even at its best the system of the house of call and the vacant book could not always provide work. Then the second function of the pub as provider of supper, beer, evening's company, bed for the night and breakfast before setting out the next day, came to the fore.

'The tramping routes of particular groups of artisans seeking work, can almost be plotted from inn signs bearing the craft name,' it has been pointed out. This is true of the earliest days, though it becomes less true after the 1820s. Old pubs closed down; new landlords changed the names; local societies changed their pubs not once but several times.

Of some 700 pubs in 135 towns in use by societies and unions in the major trades between 1820 and 1860, about 100 actually bore trade names: twenty Masons' Arms, sixteen Bricklayers' Arms, nine Moulders' Arms, right through a list of forty trades to the Papermakers', Mechanics' and Fitters' Arms. In 1849 about a quarter of the masons' lodges listed in the union's returns had their 'tramp station' in building trade pubs; in 1860 only one in fifty. Among the blacksmiths only one in seventy lodges used a Blacksmiths' Arms.

A typical 'trade' pub is Simon The Tanner, in Long Lane, Bermondsey, whose tanning trade Henry Mayhew described graphically in the *Morning Chronicle* of 15 November 1850. Simon the Tanner was the house of call of the trade, the place where the 'Old Union' gave hospitality to travelling members and, of course, the place where tanners did their drinking.

One tanner who had taken the pledge told Mayhew how he would pass the pub and say, 'Simon, you'll get no more tanners out of me.' (Mayhew explained to his respectable middle-class readership that a 'tanner' was also slang for a sixpence.) Unfortunately from Mayhew's point of view, the lure of Simon had been too great and his informant had finally broken the pledge.

Fortunately for those who like their drink today, this is one trade pub which has survived the demolitions of the area and is still to be seen.

The decades of change brought strange results even when pubs continued to be club houses. In 1860 in Greenwich, the ironfounders met in the Woodman, while the boot and shoe men met in the Ironfounders Arms. In Chesterfield, the tailors took over the Moulders' Arms, the moulders retiring to the Old Angel. In Leeds the boot and shoe men used the Masons' Arms and the masons the Spotted Cow. In Burnley the cabinet and coachmakers met at the Masons' Arms, the masons in the Boot Inn. In Cardiff the carpenters and masons swapped pubs and in Swansea the engineers and the skinners took over the Masons' Arms and the masons went to the Recruiting Office! The masons took over the Fleece in Preston while the weavers (perhaps with one eye on the temperance lobby) met 'Next to the Green Dragon'. In York between the 1840s and 1860s the masons had moved from the Blue Bell to the Masons' Arms and back to the Blue Bell again. In Bolton the Hand and Banner, where the ironmoulders first met as guests of fellow member James Isherwood, was still in use as a union pub fifty years later, by the ropemakers, while the moulders had gone to the Fleece.

Names of pubs changed in union records. The Brazen Head became the Brazen George, the Crown and Thistle the Crown and Cushion, the Blue Boar the Blue Pig, and the Red Bull the Red Cow. Whether the changing of the Pondicherry Arms to the Masons' Arms in Denton was a reversion to an older trade name after an outburst of eighteenth- and nineteenth-century imperial pride or whether the masons had simply taken over is difficult to know.

All that can be said with reasonable certainty is that up to the early nineteenth century all trade pubs were probably used by craft organisations, though not all societies always used trade pubs. As the organisations multiplied, there were just not enough of the old houses to go round. There were, of course, cases of great fidelity. The engineers in the 1860s used the Peacock off Westminster Bridge Road, where the London Society of Engine and Machine Smiths met at the close of the eighteenth century. The Paviors' Arms in Westminster was the 'lighthouse' of tramping masons 'whenever they attempted to approach the metropolis' for sixty years until the 1890s. Their banker marks decorated its panelling and its abandonment, when not enough masons lived within three miles to support a lodge, was widely regretted throughout the country and even by continental masons who had enjoyed its hospitality.

The thought of the 'lighthouse' round the bend in the road kept up the tramps' spirits on a slog of twenty or thirty miles. 'Blow your beautiful scenery, I wish to the Lord I could see a public house,' one mate told the engineer Thomas Wright on their travels. Once arrived, Wright said, the tramp was heartily welcome among the society members who gathered there on club night or other nights during the week. Especially so if he brought useful news about towns along the route, or could do a turn 'singing an Irish song with trousers rolled up and the poker as a shillelagh'. Or even more welcome with the host if he could turn his trade skill to mending the beer pumps or do other odd jobs. During the evening, John Dunlop gloomily pointed out, the tramp would part with some of his allowance buying beer over and above his tramp ration. In the club house, he said, the tramp might 'sleep and spend . . . this is an element of great danger'. Upstairs, the bed or beds rented and inspected by the local members awaited the tramp when evening was done. The Gloucester masons insisted that proper respect be paid to the hosts, for it was the lodge's 'study to ensure clean and wholesome beds'.

Ensuring tramps behaved properly towards landlord and landlady, doing 'no villainy' as the sixteenth-century masons' 'charges' put it, became something of a problem for every union when the tramping system was in decline. Nor were the hosts always consistent in providing beds according to rule. The ironmoulders noted that during the 1840s the tramps were being slept three in a bed and four beds to a room, with some beds 'not over clean', though it was recognised it was not easy to ensure cleanliness 'be the people of the place ever so desirous'.

For many branches the need to see to the tramp dictated the choice of club house. The Greenock steam engine makers decided not to move from one pub because of the need to accommodate tramps. The Chorley bricklayers were in trouble because 'the late landlord has left the place and the present landlord will not lay down any more for tramp relief'. When the London brushmakers quarrelled with their landlord he told them bluntly, 'It is left with you to devise other means to pay the men out of employ.'

The club house was not only labour exchange, hotel and 'lighthouse' for the tramp, it was also the meeting place for the local club. One pub often served the needs of several trades. The Stanley Arms in Liverpool was host to cork cutters, engineers, boilermakers, smiths and sailmakers. Here in the club house the local society held club nights and strike meetings, paid out benefit, held debates, and ran savings clubs. The pub was their post office and even in the 1860s only a minority of local union branches gave a private address for their mail. It was also their reading room, with newspapers provided by the club. So congenial a custom was carried across the sea by emigrating members and in 1841 a letter arrives for No. 1 lodge in England from the local masons at the Crown and Anchor, George Street, Sydney.

The pubs provided an upstairs room for the society, usually on the first Monday in the month, when the agenda and drinking were regulated – if not always limited – by rule. But more than ordinary business was transacted. Government agents reported in 1817 a mass meeting of carpenters at the Argyll Arms, Argyll Street, called to discuss electoral reform. The agents must have attended with some discretion not to be discovered, as did the peace officers who listened in on a trades meeting at the White Bear in Hackney in 1802, returning to report that nothing was amiss that was said there, except that the men ought to have been in church at the time.

The White Hart, at Witham in Essex, which still serves the traveller after some five centuries, was for many years in the early nineteenth century host to the local brushmakers and to their national organisation. From the White Hart during the 1820s went out the call for the two brushmakers' national societies to amalgamate, and from the White Hart in 1826 went out the secretary's urgent appeal for all societies to send in their accounts for 'equalisation'.

White Hart, Witham, Essex, a fourteenth-century inn used in the 1820s by the brushmakers, for tramping hospitality, meetings and conferences; still in existence. (Courtesy Truman Taverns)

Some taverns must have been huge places. During the 1841 strike at the House of Commons, 3,500 turned up for a builders' rally at the Crown and Anchor in the Strand (where the master boot and shoemakers had met forty years earlier). The organisers of the 1841 meeting did, however, say that the rooms were 'packed to suffocation'. Some of the larger public houses provided rooms of all sizes and were extremely popular with the trades. The Craven Head in Drury Lane was host to the London brushmakers and their tramps, and provided for meetings and a 'ball' held by the stonemasons, a genial, rowdy amalgamation conference between rival cordwainers societies, and the regular meetings of the tinplate workers co-operative society during the 1840s. The London silk weavers' Mathematical Society, with its 300 volumes and instruments lent out to members (later reported to have been taken over by the Royal Astronomical Society), met in pubs, while at the Swan in the Strand, where the Clockmakers' Court met in the seventeenth century, journeymen millwrights would debate the principles of engineering until late at night, resolving matters disputed with the weight of a fist when argument failed.

Men would call into the club house to read the newspaper and almost any journal might be had there from *The Times* to the *Voice of the People*, which in the 1830s distributed a third of its copies to pub and coffee-house reading rooms. In 1834, as on other occasions when it was spokesman for the anti-union lobby, *The Times* was unwelcome on the pub table. The 'bloody old Times' said the builders, and its editor was described by the tailors as 'the poor mercenary time-serving tool of tyranny and oppression'. Why read it then? demanded the radical Lovett of his contemporaries, noting that newspapers were read in a thousand 'humble' coffee-houses and pubs throughout London. Where trade societies had 'complete control', he said, they should 'banish the Great Unprincipled'. At the request of striking compositors, the London brushmakers did ban another newspaper – the *Sun* – from their own club houses.

Public-house bars and upper rooms saw the many celebrations and occasions that marked the craftsman's life: the making of apprentices, the 'emancipation' of journeymen, 'wetting the baby's head' when a member's wife had a child. They also saw more discreet and even illegal ceremonies.

One can imagine the fascinated horror with which readers of the Manchester *Times* read of the apparatus of initiation removed from local sawyers' club houses during a police raid in 1840 or of the magistrates who heard the confession of innocent women buttonmakers that they had been blindfolded and swore an oath of loyalty to the GNCTU in 1834. When travelling delegates of the builders union reached Exeter that year, they performed the mass initiation of a crowded roomful of masons at the Sun Inn. Little did they know the intrepid police captain was watching through a hole bored in the wall. At a signal the police forced their way in and those who could not escape were arrested – though unlike the poor Wesleyan farm workers of Tolpuddle they escaped with a fine.

Pitched battles around union pubs were not uncommon. In 1819 the Bow Street Runners stormed the Black Horse in the Horse Fair Wolverhampton and striking tinplate workers were sentenced to transportation. In 1835, the Northwich masons drove off an attack on the Queens Head by strike breakers who were chased from the town with 'bloody and broken heads'. But nothing more extraordinary could have happened than the night in the summer of 1839 when masons' officers were held captive upstairs at the Pump Tavern in the Bull Ring while a crowd of Chartists waited outside. They had driven a detachment of policemen before them who then took refuge with the masons. That the masons were unwilling protectors may be judged from the fact that later that year their union recommended the new Chartist newspaper founded at the Bell Inn London as 'deserving our support'.

More peaceful but still exciting was the meeting in 'Mr Forshaw's large room' at Ranhill, where a member of the masons' executive confronted an opposing speaker, a strike breaker, in debate. Declaring that he would rather dine on red herring as a free man than on venison as a slave, the masons' leader looked his opponent 'in the face' and said: 'You're a rare contrivance of your master's will, a mere machine that he may use at will.' (Cheers.)

To the club house came the post, with letters of instruction, money, tool bags forwarded for tramps, and pleas for news of wandering husbands from sick or abandoned wives. During the period of the Combination Acts government agents opened the letters and copied, resealed and sent them on. The employers were not as discreet as the government and in 1817 London master hatters met the postman outside the club house, paid him off and rushed the letters to the magistrates before whom the men were appearing. When the magistrates refused to open the letters, the masters did so and read the contents out in court. What is sauce for the goose ... In the 1780s a journeyman printer picked the pocket of a master while plying him with spirits and stole a letter vital to a prosecution of the men. But in normal times the public house was a secure address and the landlord a trusted agent – though they were known to impound money and goods in payment of debts.

As his house was all things to the society, so was the host. He was vetted by local officers to see if he was 'approved as a proper person and could give security' (Old Mechanics, 1824). Security meant a good deal. The South Shields shipwrights carried an enormous amount of money in their club box, and the landlord of the Sun Inn was asked for and gave security of £1,000 for holding it. The landlord in most cases was the society's banker and often its treasurer. In 1838, the Manchester masons, who were then 'head lodge', 'owed a considerable sum to Mrs Wood'.

When London brushmakers were in trouble over tramp money in 1829, Mr Hawkins their host lent them £100 on the spot. In 1845 the steam engine makers reaffirmed the custom of making the local landlord treasurer, declaring that this was the only way local clubs could borrow money in time of need. They declared that 10 per cent was very reasonable. Six years later for more or less the same reason the new Amalgamated Society of Engineers rejected by 28 votes to 9 a motion that no secretary or treasurer of a local branch should be allowed to keep a public house.

It was a two-way process. Officers of local societies did become landlords. In the seventeenth century the carpenters had a special category of company membership for alehouse keepers. James Isherwood of the Hand and Banner in Bolton was first treasurer of the ironmoulders who met in his pub in 1809 and in the 1830s a boilermaker, Gabriel Leigh, was landlord of the Manchester No. 1 branch's house (and foster parent to the son of John Roach, veteran boilermaker and Chartist – the son being named Feargus O'Connor Roach). Leigh was a humorist and called his pub the March of Intellect, the sign being a man aboard a donkey which he is urging on with stick and carrot. The boilermakers were still at the March of Intellect in the 1860s. In 1856, a member of the Manchester typographers 'intimated' to fellow members that he had taken the Ring O' Bells in Cathedral Yard, where 'every attention will be paid to the comfort and convenience of those who may favour him with a call'.

Landlords were ready to do more than take the money of local societies and lend it back to them. They signed tramp cards and paid mileage allowance, though this sometimes led to lack of strict control. But in 1846, when every moulder left the town of Reading during the depression, the landlord held the fort, his books being found to be impeccable, though at the height of the period of unemployment he paid relief to 1,000 tramps every six months. It was no light service and suggests more than a commercial interest.

Sometimes this service was given at some cost. During the eighteenth and nineteenth centuries, authority was uncertain whether to trust the public. In the 1740s Scots publicans lost their licences for harbouring militant tailors and some twenty years later London's mayor issued a proclamation that 'no publican do presume to harbour or entertain' journeymen's combinations. In the 1790s publicans lost their licences for lending money to the curriers' journeymen. In 1799, the Treasonable and Seditious Practices Act laid down punishment for landlords who allowed illegal societies to meet on their premises. That year a Yorkshire landlord went to jail for three months for this offence.

Not every landlord was loyal to his clients and during the period of the Combination Acts a Manchester publican betrayed members of the spinners' committee to the police. But on the whole, through the main period of illegality and persecution, the inn and alehouse keepers seem to have valued the custom of the trade societies more than the blessings of authority, or else authority was unwilling to put that loyalty to so sharp a test. As Lord Sidmouth remarked in 1814, he did not want 'every source of information dried up'.

During the Chartist period the issue came up again with landlords threatened with loss of licences if they let rooms to Chartists. In 1848, learning that a landlord was proposing to chair a meeting for the local masons' lodge, a policeman was sent round to express the hope that the meeting would 'have nothing of the republican in it'. Nor did it have, though there was much talk of the 'avarice of the capitalists'.

Loyalty apart, it was worth the publican's while to serve the trade. A considerable traffic in beer went on at all hours of the day, being 'brought in in buckets and cans' according to a journeyman who gave evidence to the Committee on Artisans and Machinery in 1824. He added, however, that the quantity was not as much as 'formerly', being now 'only what a man requires for his work'. Beer and ale at whatever time of day were drunk according to ritual of ancient origin. Thomas Dekker in his *Shoemakers' Holiday* has his hero (disguised as a travelling Flemish cordwainer) pay his drink money on being admitted to the workshop. 'Benvenue' or 'ben' money is written into printers' chapel regulations from the sixteenth century onwards.

Rooms hired out by publicans to trade societies were paid for not in cash but on the assumption that members would drink during the evening. This custom of the 'wet rent' began to die out only late in the nineteenth century. Even today, the hire of rooms over pub bars is cheaper than elsewhere on the assumption that the hirers will drink during the evening. 'Wet rent' like 'ben' money was an old custom. Sir Frederick Eden calculated in the late eighteenth century that one third of friendly society rules dealt with social drinking. And to back the rules went one third of friendly society expenditure, he asserted. The breeches benefit club attended by young Francis Place in the 1790s required fourpence a month per member 'for the good of the house'. The fourpence being obligatory, 'those who attended drank for those who did not.' Francis Place liked to exaggerate such customs but what he said was true and in 1788 the Belfast cabinet makers, whose club and workshop rules were very like those of their English brothers, required each member on the first Monday of the month to put $3\frac{1}{2}$d 'in the chest' and 3d down for drink 'attending or not'. The same rule was followed by Newcastle smiths in 1822. These sums were not exceptional, the blacksmiths allowing 3d out of 2s a month for drink, the Manchester compositors 4d out of 1s 6d, and the boiler-makers 3d out of 1s 9d. William Hughes, who drew up the boilermakers' rules, added a warning about the member who was 'a slave of his passions, too fond of the carousals of convivial parties and by such an aberration of the powers of intellect reduced to the direst distress'.

Hughes, a Christian whose motto was 'nothing human is alien to me', was typical of the most intelligent and independent-minded of the skilled workers, whom a later commentator described as 'entomologists, botanists . . . as fond of a glass as the most graceless of their neighbours'. What outside observers saw as undue attention to drinking, society members saw as controlled conviviality. The brushmakers rules called for a 'pot ticket at eight, a pint at ten and no more'. The pot was a quart pot often drunk from a mug decorated with the trade emblem, and in the case of the moulders it celebrated in its design the arrival of the tramp at the local workshop. Around the society table on club night the only people allowed to 'drink out of turn' were officers or men on travel, who were also exempted from paying for their liquor within the prescribed quantity. 'Waiters' and 'beer marshals' were appointed to see all was in order and the masons and other trades appointed an 'outer and inner tyler' or doorkeeper to see proceedings were not interrupted from outside.

It must be said, though, that on certain special occasions the amount drunk, by rule, seems colossal. The Huddersfield engineers on their audit nights in the 1830s and 1840s got through more than five gallons. The compositors' regular meeting drink took one seventh of the annual expenditure and the moulders', one fifteenth.

One problem with the association of regulations with drinking is that one tended to reinforce the other. A certain proportion of the income of every trade society came from fines for infringements of rules in the course of daily life. The blacksmiths (1839) had thirty separate fine-punishments. And a certain proportion of the fines (Dunlop reckoned three-quarters among carpenters) were taken in drink. So the brother who refused to be beer steward paid for his refusal by buying drink for his fellows. Society club or branch rules were not the only ones that might be broken. In every trade there were workshop rules, some very ancient. Printers' chapel rules are best known and most ancient, and they regulated conduct of both master and man, or at least the master would hesitate to go against them. Among the cabinet makers a man with a grievance could by striking a blow on a 'holdfast' in the shop summon all working there to an impromptu court. Among the hatters these courts were called 'dozens' or 'garrets' according to the numbers involved and the level of the offence. A worker could challenge in these courts anyone who aggrieved him, though a drunken man would have his 'insist' disregarded.

It is said that printers' rules were enforced by beatings, with the victim stretched out over the press. But eventually fines replaced thrashings and fines were paid in drink. So were 'footings', 'benvenues' or 'ben money', paid when a man first came to work in a shop. More money was paid when he came out of his time (the coopers paid for three gallons during the eighteenth century) or when his wife had a baby (the printers paid sixpence for a boy, threepence for a girl). As time went on, custom multiplied the fines and payments, garnishes, plank money, fancy gallons, wagers, etc. among the hatters. It was alleged that among the hatters, when the tramp received his beer allowance on arrival, all or most of the shop would retire with him to drink it. It was evidently so among the sawyers.

Inevitably there were objections. The celebrated Benjamin Franklin demurred at a second payment demanded when he transferred from one department of the print shop to another. He appealed to the master who sympathised but did nothing. When he still refused the 'chapel ghost' got to work on him and he was subjected to the many ingenious torments which can be and still are inflicted upon an unpopular worker. In the end he paid up.

A lesser known worker, a shipwright, who declined on temperance grounds to pay footing money, alleged that his shopmates lit a fire and threatened to roast him. When he resisted, they dragged him off to the pub and kept him there for the rest of the evening, determined he should drink. But like an early martyr he used the occasion to mount a barrel and deliver a lecture on temperance.

The temperance movement did have its effect on the 'drinking system' which Dunlop claimed took a 'very large sum' from trade society funds, though he refrained from saying how much for 'he had no means of demonstrating it statistically'. And this pressure, inspired by a middle class increasingly inquisitive about the ways of the workers, mounted from the 1840s onward. But it would be a mistake to imagine that the argument over drink began in this period.

Employers traditionally kept a close eye on the drinking habits of their workers, with what one historian ironically called the 'touching regard of the capitalist for the welfare of his employees'. In 1538 the merchant clothworkers complained of those 'who would rather sit in ale houses and haunt ill company' than work. At the time city regulations could jail an apprentice or journeyman found in an alehouse during working hours. How often these were enforced is a question, for the working day then lasted from dawn to dusk, with disputes in some trades over 'candlelight' even during the nineteenth century. Often enough concern over alehouse gatherings had less to do with drunkenness than the danger to social order. In the 1790s it was alleged that benefit clubs meeting in public houses led to 'idleness, intemperance and sedition'.

There is no need to take at face value the strictures of city masters and merchants renowned for their feastings, or those of a ruling class noted for its intemperance, any more than those of employers meeting in public houses to condemn the conduct of their journeymen. If the skilled workers had submitted readily to the industrial discipline and work rhythm of the age of the factory and machine, one doubts whether so much would have been heard of the evils of 'the drinking system'. James Naesmyth, the master engineer, preferred machines to men because 'they never got drunk, their hands never shook from excess, they were never absent from work'.

Celebration led to taking time off, celebrating 'Saint Monday' in fact (or 'Blue Monday' as the German masters called it) in stubborn continuance of the lost medieval holy days. The determination to resist inimical social change was remarkable and Saint Monday or 'Cobbler's Monday' was celebrated even in the twentieth century. In his memoirs Harry Pollitt recalls how as a boilermaker he joined in the mock ceremony of throwing up a brick outside the workshop gates on the day after a holiday. If the brick stayed in the air they would work. If it came down, they would go home. Nor has this resistance to 'progress' been entirely in vain. After yearly attacks in the press for their 'absenteeism' after Christmas and New Year, the miners have had the satisfaction of seeing the whole nation follow their example, thus creating (or recreating) a holiday of civilised length.

The shrewder observers of the journeymen's way of life never imagined that intemperance alone was at stake. In the 1790s, a government agent writing from Sheffield reported that it was 'pretty generally the practice for them to work for three days in which they earn sufficient to enable them to drink and riot for the rest of the week'. No place, he added, 'is more fit for seditious purposes'.

A picture of a skilled working class of Bacchanalian habits frowned on by Puritan outsiders would, however, be a false one. The most active, organised craftsmen saw no merit in drinking for its own sake but only as an aid to 'conviviality' and good fellowship. It has been argued reasonably that all the regulations governing workshop and club drinking helped control what was then developing into a social disease during the period of disruption that accompanied the Industrial Revolution. Certainly from the eighteenth century onwards organised workers tightened up on regulation at the expense of custom. At various points – 1780, 1787, 1795 – the journeymen coopers forming their independent society within the old company decreased their fines and footings until with the formation of their union in 1821 these were done away with. Following the example of the curriers and hatters, the cordwainers in 1794 were emphatic that one of their objects was to limit the drunkenness traditional in their trade: 'No more sotting and swearing in public houses on Monday like vagabonds as usual.' Society stewards coming to a meeting 'disguised in liquor' were fined half a crown. The early engineers' societies condemned those who came 'disordered in liquor'. The custom of birth ales, said the Newcastle Coachmakers in 1807, is 'extremely oppressive'. It took money away from the family when they most needed it, and was 'contrary to the object of true benevolence'. In 1826 the brushmakers considered the matter but decided to 'leave the rule on footings where it is for the moment'.

But the desire to cut down on the drain on funds was reinforced by the the wish to have businesslike conduct of affairs. The 'success of our cause . . . its solemnity and good conduct', said a leader of the National Union of the Working Classes in 1833, would be enhanced by meeting away from public houses. But unfortunately, he noted, the move caused attendances to drop.

He had at least partly in mind a middle-class 'public opinion' now paying closer and mostly unwelcome attention to the organised workers. In May 1836, the Sheffield filesmiths noted that the local press was 'teeming with daily abuse, holding them up to public scorn as idle insolent drunkards, plotting the ruin of themselves and the trade, meeting in pot houses to concert their schemes'.

They quoted the *Sheffield Globe*: 'Thousands are passing the time in idleness; the streets, the beershops and the Fire King's Palaces swarm with men, determined it seems to ruin themselves, their masters and as far as they can their country.'

Respectable opinion, however, could make little headway while its expression was uniformly negative, even hampering the reform it urged. Recalling the 1840s, an active member of the Oddfellows' Friendly Society spoke of the regrettable hostility of the 'largest dissenting church' on the grounds that their lodges met in public houses. When he tried to obtain land to build a hall for meetings, the landowner blankly refused on the grounds that this would ruin the local publicans.

The main influence in the reform of the drinking system was internal, the drive within the societies for discipline and order. In 1838 the Glasgow spinners were looking for a public hall where the 'idle men' could be entertained away from public houses. The moulders began to cut down on 'liquor allowance' at meetings and the Manchester printers symbolically removed the society's pewter pot from the meeting table. By 1838 the steam engine makers had declared 'footings' to be 'exactions ... injurious to morals ... inconsistent with our character ... as a society'. Four years later they were ready to remove the liquor allowance altogether. The move away from the public house began slowly to gather pace. The moulders' leaders encouraged all branches who wished to hold their meetings 'aloof from the public house' to write in. The Brighton cordwainers claimed that having moved from pub to schoolroom they felt the 'importance of the change'. The Dublin carpenters by 1838 had begun to build a special hall which would accommodate meetings and travelling members.

But it was not easy. In 1843 the Manchester printers voted to do away with the 'wet rent' and pay cash for the hire of the room, and went with £2 to the landlord. 'The landlord, being a publican but not necessarily a sinner, formally received the cash with an appropriately modest protest, being unwilling to accept rent in that form. Finding the deputation inexorable, he of course took the money but declined to pocket any of it and so spent the whole amount in suitable refreshment.'

Some members were just as unwilling to alter old custom. A chairman of a tinplate workers' branch forced through the vote to ban liquor from the club room only by lining up the two parties for and against on either side of the room.

And there were other more real obstacles to change. The London bookbinders quitted their pub in 1840 only to return eight years later. The London compositors, deciding that the atmosphere of the Red Lion in Fleet Street, with the 'jingle of the pots' was 'repugnant', indeed 'positive corporeal punishment', moved to a private address but returned three years later.

The compositors, like the Greenock engineers, needed the pub because of the obligation to the unemployed. The needs of the tramping system indeed kept the drinking system going. And the merits and advantages of the former were as yet too clear to most organised workers for them to depart from it.

8 Travelling Delegates – the Tramps at their best

On St Crispin's Day, 25 October 1833, the shoemakers of Nantwich in Cheshire staged a craft procession in honour of their patron saint. They also celebrated the establishment of the new Cordwainers' Amalgamation, which was in turn part of the new Grand National Consolidated Trades Union.

Recalling the occasion many years afterwards, Thomas Dunning, veteran shoemaker, made a special point of the colourful presence on the parade of a 'shopmate in full tramping order, his pack on his back'.

They honoured the tramp and with good reason. The cordwainers' union had grown over forty years from the first links established between local societies to care for unemployed members. Tramping was their first reason for union and the tramp himself had played an active part in the process. The tramp was a symbol not only for ancient trades but for newer ones who had adopted the old custom. Hatters, coachmakers, moulders, and boilermakers all featured the figure of the travelling craftsman in 'marching order' on the union tickets which men carried in their pockets or the emblems which they began during the 1830s and 1840s to place on the walls of their parlours or in society club rooms. The tramp's figure – his dress and gear changing with the times, knee breeches and stockings giving way to trousers, and side whiskers disappearing – appears on the emblems and reflects the continuity amid change which the old custom represented.

The unions in their formative period were proud of the tramping system. A short story called 'The Difference' published in 1840 expresses this feeling strongly. The narrator watches two blacksmiths on tramp approach an Irish town. One, a union man, says he is sure to find friends there. 'So saying, he drew from his pocket, a small tin box, from which he extracted a paper and opened it. As at this time they were very near to me, I immediately recognised the beautiful arms of our society and immediately knew it to be one of our travelling cards.' The 'difference' is of course between the union member and the non-union man. Leaving his companion to take supper and a night's rest with congenial company while he depends on casual charity, the non-union man reflects that he too will join up as soon as he can.

The tramping system, said the Leeds masons in 1837, is 'our main support'. It is 'our greatest bulwark', declared delegates at a moulders' conference in 1846. When, during a bad period, the brushmakers considered that since tramping had taken the whole income of their union the system should be dropped, the notion was called 'a violent remedy, the amputation of a valuable limb'. When in 1837 the masons debated whether to cut tramping benefit, the Weedon lodge declared its 'contempt and regret' for the proposal, affirming that the tramps were 'the best members we have got'. Men like William Sandy offered living proof of it. A shop steward (the masons already used this term, which is, I think, much older) who was sacked for union activity in 1838, Brother Sandy refused the victimisation pay of eighteen shillings (two-thirds of the full rate) and chose to tramp off and look for work rather than be a burden on the funds.

Such was the credit that the union tramp had built up in the early years that later critics of the system had to phrase their remarks carefully. There are many men 'who have tramped long and hard and have never brought the least disgrace on our society', said the compositors. The tailors declared: 'We must all respect those who rather than idle about go on the tramp.' The brushmakers said that tramping was a 'great preservative against the torpor and supineness produced by the receiving system'.

The view that to remain at home living off the contributions of fellow members was unthinkable was embodied in the rules which in most trades made tramping obligatory, or in the determination of the moulders that members should 'walk fairly', which meant a round trip through some fifty towns with two crossings of the Irish Sea. The president of the Huddersfield Old Mechanics, returning from five weeks on tramp, instructed the secretary to record every sum of money he had received on his march.

This would convince, he thought, any who doubted the value of the system. Each member knows, said the Worcester masons' lodge, that 'he must 'ere long go on the road'. Engineers, said Thomas Wright, were 'wondrous kind' to the tramp. 'They either have or know they may go on tramp.'

The tramp and tramping were a symbol of independence. Later in the century, the tailors' general secretary said that in the old days 'a man was scarcely considered a good tailor until he had done his turn on the road'.

149

'It helps to keep a man more independent,' an old hatter told Henry Mayhew, who was firmly convinced the system was demoralising. Thanks to the system, said Thomas Wright, 'the road is deprived of half its terrors, it relieves all apprehensions of starving'.

Moving from town to town with tool kit on his back the builder tramp learnt his trade on the move. Tailors would stop off at isolated farms and work with sleeve board and iron doing welcome adjustments and repairs for people isolated by the still inadequate transport services. The skilled engineer who could mend a beer pump was welcome in the roadside pub. And, as one observer of the 'trade tramp' in the 1860s noted, he was the means of spreading knowledge of new technical improvements or labour-saving devices. The traveller, said the observer, was more sharp witted and better informed than those who lingered at home, though perhaps more easy morally. Thomas Wright recalled the lessons he learnt as an apprentice from tramping engineers, one of whom thrashed him to teach him the value of his daily bread when he dropped a crust on the workshop floor.

Wright gives a vivid picture of the man on the road, with 'summer the pleasantest season', marching barefoot to save the well greased lace-up boots, stopping to bathe feet in a roadside stream or do 'extempore tailoring' on clothing, walking by night and sleeping by day during the hottest season, slogging along five weeks at a time, sometimes forty miles a day before reaching an inn where fellow members meet. He added, however, that 'waiting about workshop gates takes more out of you than straightforward walking'.

This latter opinion was confirmed by Will Crooks many years later when, as a Labour MP in early twentieth century, he wrote his memoirs. Or as a stonemason author who tramped through England and America put it: 'I understand why tramps take the denial of work so calmly, the movement in the air, takes a lot off the mind.'

Tramping gave the artisan time to think deeply about life and the world. Moritz, the German clergyman who walked through England during the late eighteenth century and was not always well received, speaks with warmth of the travelling craftsmen, remembering particularly a saddler who treated him to lunch at an inn and entertained him with quotations from Homer, Horace and Virgil. Bray, the pioneer Socialist, typical of the many lesser known thinkers who gave shape to working-class ideas, developed his notions of society on tramp in the 1820s and 1830s: 'I was constantly meeting the shoemaker, the tailor out of work, and each one in need of the goods the other could make.'

A fascinating picture of the independent trade tramp is given by Charles Manby Smith, the printer, who recalled that during his apprentice days in the 1820s a man named Martin came to the shop where he was an 'indoor boy'. Martin, who had travelled all over England, had a 'substantial testimonial for successful advocacy of the rights of working men'. He could argue on every topic and on all (with the exception of Christianity) he 'reasoned gently and modestly'. He took neither beer nor spirits and when finally he fell ill and the priest came to the deathbed to offer prayers, Martin dismissed him politely saying he had 'no time for such frivolities'.

The union tramp, Thomas Wright stressed, was no 'ordinary tramp', no ragged garrotter like figure who lurches along making a show of selling but begging. . . . That is not the working man's idea . . . they are pests to society . . . he is simply a working man on the road who has not the means of paying for railway travel.'

The trade tramp could 'easily be distinguished from the vagabond', a workhouse supervisor told Henry Mayhew. Of those admitted to the workhouses the artisan made up no more than one per cent even during mass unemployment. They preferred 'walking through the night'. They would enter the workhouse only in the last resort for 'only one night's shelter'. The travelling craftsman, Mayhew was told, is 'strictly honest', seeking such relief only when he had 'sold shirt and waistcoat and so weakened he could scarcely reach the gate'. The supervisors would allow them 'several days to recruit their strength' before returning to the road.

This then was the early union tramp celebrated in the tradition, lore and document of his organisation, admired for independence, ingenuity and integrity. There was a solid basis for the sentiment. The tramping system had helped make the unions, passively, by the problems it presented such as the need to 'equalise' relief between smaller and larger societies. But in the process of unity, the tramp played an active as well as a passive role. He spread the union. 'If no society existed in the town where the new arrival came, then he who had already experienced the benefits would start one,' says a historian of the early engineering unions. 'The tramps were the first organisers carrying the principles from town to town,' say the moulders' historians. As government agents often noted during the period of the Combination Acts, 'seditious emmissaries' and 'itinerant orators' travelled the country, organising and collecting money. The drive for 'one big union' must have owed much to the tramps of many trades meeting on the road, as Bray said, exchanging views, and sharing supper and often a bed for the night. The *Pioneer* journal describes how in 1834 journeymen bakers from Glasgow arrived in the Midlands, called meetings and recruited members before leaving for Carlisle. Among the masons, the tramps were *the* organisers. During the 1830s we see them at work: tramps from Liverpool opening a lodge at Beaumaris in Wales; tramps seized by the police while conducting initiation rites in an Exeter Inn; Sheffield lodge opening a tramp station 'contiguous to the North Midland Railway'; London reopening the lodge at Hastings; William Oliver, a man punished for having a 'false' tramping card, redeeming his reputation by marching to Goole and setting up a lodge with sixty members.

Over forty years later, the boilermakers of the Wear district saluted their retiring 'delegate' James O'Neill, originally a Birmingham man, with 100 guineas and an address which said: 'You came among us as a stranger.' Most boilermakers' leaders in the nineteenth century, including general secretary Robert Knight, 'visited and worked in various parts'. Henry Broadhurst, later MP and junior minister to Gladstone, spent a good deal of time as a tramping mason and praised the system in his memoirs. So equally did a very different mason, Fred Bower, a rank-and-file militant who was later involved in the campaign to unite building workers in one 'industrial union' in the early twentieth century.

The tramp, it was felt, helped keep up wages and safeguard conditions. The tramp would pass on warnings about employers: 'Do not work for —— a desperate tyrant who has tried to introduce candlelight.' And in many cases he could be relied on not to accept work below the rate, much to the bewilderment of outside observers. In 1815 Francis Place giving evidence to the Parliamentary Committee on Poverty, Mendicity and Crime, tried to explain 'the wisdom of the unemployed in refusing to work under-rate'. All would otherwise be 'reduced to a brute state ... lose independence and self-respect'. Twenty years later a journeyman leather dresser tried to explain to the Poor Law Commissioners why a job at a lower rate was *not* better than no job at all.

A roving compositor, no better than he ought to be, explained the attitude of the tramp to Charles Manby Smith during the 1820s when, on occasions, two-thirds of printers were out of work. He speaks of 'lounging in tap rooms, tramping it to get a job and touch tin, then get on the mop again'. He adds, 'I like a drop of beer myself (here's your health) but I like work too, at the scale figure, and never shirked it yet to go on the swig.'

The anonymous author of an article on 'The Trade Tramp' in the 1860s who felt that the tramp was inclined to the immoral was talking of a different system of morality. To the middle-class observer it seemed immoral that a worker should tramp the roads, living on the charity of his mates, in preference to working at the rate the employer saw fit to offer. To the organised worker this *was* the moral thing to do. To work, however 'honest' the work, under rate was the depth of immorality. There could be no agreement on this moral point in Victoria's time, any more than there had been in Richard II's when Langland criticised the craftsman who 'can some manere craft an he wolde hit use'. As the mason's fortnightly letter recorded, the brothers would 'rather walk about' than take work where the society forbade it. 'The roadsters', wrote Fred Bower the mason, 'were always good union men. They would attend the lodge, tell of outside jobs and if the trade justified it, suggest going in for a rise in wages. If it came to a strike, they would clear out – it gave the home guard a better chance.'

If it came to a strike the strikers could, thanks to the tramping system, leave town and remove themselves from any temptation to accept work. As early as 1741, the striking woolcombers of the West Country left their shops, removing the combing pads so that no one else should be tempted to work, and thanks to their system they could 'hold out several months together'. Francis Place in the 1790s convinced his fellow breeches makers it would be a better use of their limited funds to give each striker a week's pay as a starter and for them to leave town, agreeing not to come back for a month and getting relief from the tailoring shops in other towns. During their great 1812 strike the boot and shoe makers sent many members into the country, giving them no aid unless they left town. Calico printing employers in Lancashire reported at the same time that their workers were being gradually withdrawn from their shops until they were 'entirely deserted'. Even the apprentices were being taken away and 'carried off to Ireland'. Removing apprentices was a necessary tactic if the strike were not to be undermined and in 1792 master woolcombers in Kendal announced in the press that three apprentices had been 'granted tickets' by the union without which they could never have left their employ.

Provided the strike was limited to one town, the tactic of sending off the men a dozen or twenty at a time was highly effective and was used time and again. From Edinburgh it was reported that of 250 masons on strike only 120 were left in the town and the rest were on the road. Dover: 'The turnouts (strikers) have all left.' Drogheda: 'All left except the secretary.' During the 1840s the steam engine makers decided during a strike: 'Eight men to be drawn out each week.'

A system which removed strikers could also remove strike breakers. A Bristol shipowner told the Committee on the Combination Acts in 1825 how he went to the local inn to find men he had hired to break a strike being seen on to the coach again by local carpenters. When he 'remonstrated with the strangers on the impropriety' of their deserting him, the strikers told them 'they should not work in the city' and passed them up spirits to 'drink to the success of the carpenters' union'. A Belfast calico printer who brought over women from Scotland to 'establish our work again' discovered that the strikers had 'been on the look out for them, met them, entertained them a day or two and paid their passage back'.

It did not always work. The same committee was told by a carpenter how the union had spent £80 in treating strike breakers on drinks and beefsteaks and 'everything Dublin could afford'. But still they went in to work. The *Pioneer* newspaper in 1833 printed an item attacking the idea of treating strike breakers. There was, said the writer, 'a sort of rogue' who would take all offered and still work a job which had been struck.

But generally it worked. During a strike at Bristol in 1839, when masons were brought in from Cornwall and from as far away as Scotland, the union enlisted the aid of the Scots masons' society and were able to persuade most to return home, while many of the Cornishmen went 'on the tramp'. During the famous House of Commons beer strike in 1841–2, the strike committee spent nearly £200 each on sending strikers on tramp and 'sending away blacks'.

(Readers may notice that in this book the terms 'black' or 'blackleg' for strike breaker are avoided where possible. Their origin in the early nineteenth century is clearly racial. In the masons' records they are spoken of as 'Africans' and a union pamphlet shows a black figure in 'servile chains', the implication being that the anti-union man is a slave.)

If other members would not 'support the trade, let them support the tramp', wrote the leader of the striking Wolverhampton tinplate workers in 1821, adding that to lessen the burden on strike funds they had 'ordered out' more men on tramp, giving them a special green-coloured card. This practice was widespread and the possession of a 'strike card' would mean a more generous response on the way. A 'backed' card – one with the word 'strike' written across it by the local secretary – together with a lump sum was the rule among the printers, though in some large compositors' societies a 'backed card' meant double relief. Among the masons a strike card meant a shilling a day instead of sixpence, a 'small compensation for the sacrifice', as a later commentator put it. The material value was small, the moral value considerable and rather than break a strike the men would 'walk about'. In 1839 three of the Bristol mason strike breakers who changed their minds were charged by their hirer with breach of contract. On their refusing to work they were sentenced to a month's 'walking' on the treadmill, but said they preferred it to 'working for a deceitful employer'.

No inducement, threat or punishment could turn a good tramp into a strike breaker. And if prison threatened the system could even save him from that. Time and again employers and the State were thwarted by a very effective underground railway. This use of the tramping system indeed helped bring about the Combination Acts. The master millwrights who appealed to Parliament in 1799 for some more speedy means of subduing their journeymen told MPs that when they indicted their employees, before the time of the trial arrived, 'the offenders frequently remove into different parts of the country'.

Since it is 'a long time before they can be brought back to trial', the expenses for the masters were 'heavy when their business is stopped by desertion . . . aware of these difficulties the journeymen carry on their combination with boldness and impunity.'

The Combination Acts, which permitted summary trial and conviction by two magistrates, were intended to remedy this. But, as a master hat manufacturer told the Committee on Artisans and Machinery in 1824, journeymen hatters in dispute would leave the workshops and 'the Combination Laws cannot take hold of them for they leave gradually man by man and get employ at other places so that the Combination Laws are by that means completely avoided'.

In 1838 the Select Committee on Combinations of Workmen noted: 'The Justices can proceed only by summons and if the party summoned does not appear, then by warrant or warrant/complaint. The summons is inoperative if the person is not named.' A boot and shoe worker told the committee of a case where journeymen sued an employer for non-payment of wages. He retaliated by taking out warrants 'for combination' and the men 'were obliged to leave town'.

Nassau Senior, reporting in 1830 on the effects of the repeal of the Combination Acts, was convinced that the system was used to man picket lines 'by the use of persons who though parties to the league are unknown in the Districts in which they are called to Act'. And, as a pamphlet writer in the following year, 1831, claimed, pickets were summoned from a distance because 'a warrant needs a name on it'. In 1840, when the local magistrates tried to pin the death of an Ashton sawyer on his workmates in the local society, a tramping sawyer who arrived in the town was seen as an obvious suspect, arrested and interrogated. The constable reported to the justices that the tramp had told him triumphantly after questioning: 'You see you got nothing from me.' A newspaper correspondent in the town alleged, though without evidence, that when the police pursued their inquiries by raiding sawyers' club houses in sixteen counties, 'emissaries were despatched to destroy papers' in advance of the police.

Not only the accused disappeared. In certain cases vital witnesses vanished. During the 1780s when striking framework knitters were on trial in the Midlands a key witness – suitably named Leavers – was awakened in the dead of the night by the brother of one of the accused, blindfolded, marched across country and hidden in Essex, being well treated until the trial was abandoned for lack of evidence. In 1802, when shearmen were in the thick of their battle against the 'finishing machines', the Yorkshire and West of England men, linked by their ticket with its crossed shears device, had the assistance of a friendly travelling shoemaker to carry confidential messages. During the campaign a man named Beaumont who was to have given evidence against the shearmen suddenly disappeared, although the local magistrate had offered him protection and work in his factory with a 50 per cent wage increase. Knowing of the cross-country contacts, it was suggested that his wife's post be opened and that a watch be set for Beaumont on the road so he might be taken and searched.

The Nantwich shoemakers made good use of their tramping system in 1834 when a local employer, profiting from the Tolpuddle example, took out warrants against them. Some of the leaders, including the 'Tramping President', fled to Manchester. Thomas Dunning, reporting the incident in his memoirs, regarded them as cowards and set about organising the defence of those who had been arrested. William Capper, a young shoemaker who had given names to the authorities, was sorry he had done so. Dunning arranged for him to leave town, taking him first to Manchester where he was lodged with society members and then to Dublin as a safer place. There the witness stayed, supplied with money through the post, and nursed through a dangerous bout of measles. When the trial opened William did not appear, and he returned to Nantwich only when it was too late.

Thus the tramp helped build the union, proved a 'bulwark of strength' in industrial battles, and bore tidings of the trade and notions of a new world round the country. Thanks to the system, the unions were able to grow, defying both the employers and the law. As both a passive and an active factor, 'tramping' brought the nineteenth-century trade unions into being.

9 Duthie's *Wanderjahr* – Tramping on the Continent

One day in the early 1850s, a baker, a goldsmith, a coppersmith, a bookbinder and a woodturner were tramping from Hamburg to Berlin. On the road, they met

> ... a little crowd of men in blouses, little queer caps, knapsacks and ragged beards, all carrying sticks. The were travelling boys, like ourselves, bound from Berlin to Hamburg. 'Halloo' they cried. 'Halloo' we answered, shouting in unison as we approached each other. When we met, a little friendly skirmish with our sticks was the first act of greeting. A storm of questions and replies then followed. We all knew each other in a few minutes: carpenters turners, glovers were there, not a jeweller among them but myself. We parted soon, for time was precious. 'Love to Berlin' cried one of them back to us. 'My compliments to Hamburg' I replied, and then we all struck up an amatory chorus of the 'Fare thee well, love' species that fitted properly with our position.

It was the perfect romantic picture of the *wandergesellen* or travelling journeymen on their *wanderjahre*, their traditional time of tramping round the land, celebrated by many a German writer in poem, novel and comic opera. But the writer, the goldsmith, was no German but an Englishman abroad, and no romantic but a shrewd and often caustic observer of a scene which to him was often baffling and outmoded. William Duthie had come to Hamburg in 1852, joined the town gild, worked for several months to learn the language and then set out on travel. He worked his way through Berlin, Leipzig, Dresden, Prague, Vienna and at last via Strasbourg to Paris, reaching London again four years later, little better off (he kept meticulous account of his income and expenditure) but a good deal better informed.

He wrote of his travels in a series of articles in Charles Dickens's *Household Words* and when the series was made into a book he dedicated it to Dickens. His *Tramp's Wallet* describes in great detail for the English reader a system of trade organisation which had barely altered in five centuries, though, as he wrote, it was entering its final decades.

Duthie had great respect for his work companions, recalling them with affection, not least the master jeweller in one German town who rose at dawn to make him hot coffee and kiss him on both cheeks before he took the road. One does not even begin to think of an English employer doing anything so extravagant.

He compared the trade training given by the gilds to their apprentices with that received by the 'chance-taught' English worker and noted that, despite lower wages, the Berlin artisan with cheaper lodging and food 'is at least in as good a position as his self-vaunted brother of London'. But as a whole he had little respect for their time-encrusted craft system, for the 'feudal usages' of Hamburg and Leipzig, where journeymen still did not marry but lodged in the house of the 'Herr', and the only prospect of mastership for them was a dead man's shoes – if the dead man had no relatives!

Nor was he impressed with the *Wanderjahr* travelling system which set the journeymen of every trade tramping the roads for four or five years after three or four years of apprenticeship. The travelling allowance, the *geschenk* (gift) or *viaticum* as it was called, was a 'mere trifle, sometimes but a few pence and in a large city like Berlin it amounts to but 20 silver groschen, little more than two shillings ... The viaticum is the tramp money that may be claimed from his guild by the travelling workman. Germans, like other people like to take pills gilded and so they cloak the awkward incidence of poverty under a latin name.'

At first, to the bewilderment or irritation of both masters and men, Duthie was inclined to decline the *geschenk*. 'Nonsense,' they told him, 'you pay for it when you are in work and have a right to it when travelling.' But after a week's unemployment in Berlin 'I asserted my claim to the trade geschenk and having fulfilled all the conditions of a tramp unable to find work, received from the Guild twenty silver groschen.'

On his travels he lodged in the trade inn or *herberge* (the English term 'house of call', he said, was 'but an inadequate translation'). But he did this only when he had to, for he had a low opinion of the accommodation offered to the German journeymen (save in Saxony, which had 'the only trade herberges in Germany which are in any way decent'):

The German herberge is the home of the travelling workman. It should be clean and wholesome; there should he be provided together with simple and nutritious food, every necessary information connected with his trade and such aid and reasonable solace as his often wearisome pilgrimage requires. All this is to be rendered at a just and remunerative price and it is usually supposed that the fulfilment of these requisites is guaranteed by the care and surveillance of the police. But this is a fiction.

Our Herberge is in the Schustergasse and a vile, ill-conditioned uncleanly den it is, nor, I am sorry to say are its occupants, in appearance at least, unworthy of their abode. But we must not be uncharitable; it is a hard task this tramping through the length and breadth of the land; and he is a smart fellow who can keep his toilet in anything like decent condition amid the dust, the wind, the pelting rain or the weltering sunshine that beset and envelope him on the implacable high road . . . ragged beards and uncombed locks, soiled blouses and travel worn shoe-leather, horny hands and embrowned visages . . .

We are duly marshalled to bed at eight o'clock with the rest, huddled into our loft where nine beds await some sixteen occupants and having undergone the customary examination as to our freedom from disease and vermin are safely locked in our dormitory to be released only at the good will of the 'Vater' in the morning.

But to Duthie's mind there were worse indignities suffered by the *wandergeselle*, indignities from which his possession of a passport protected him. Travelling with a tinsmith, he arrived at Lubeck.

As we were about to pass in, the sentinel beckoned and pointed us towards a little whitened watchbox at which we stopped to hand our papers through a pigeon hole. In a few minutes the police officer came out, handed to me my passport with great politeness and in a sharp voice bade the tinman follow him.

Such is the difference between a passport and a wander book. I, owner of a passport might go whither I would; tinman carrying a wanderbook, was marched off by the police to his appointed house of call.

But in Altenburg even his passport did not save him from the bureaucrat. There was a scene which recalls vividly the plight of the worker-hero of the German play *Captain from Köpenick*:

One would naturally suppose that a few hours would suffice to pack my little stores and to depart, but there were the guild regulations to fulfil, the railway officials to be waited on and the police to satisfy. The last named gentleman would not consent to vise my passport till I should produce my railway ticket, as a proof of my intention to go; while the railway officials doubted the propriety of issuing a ticket until I had received the authority of the police for my departure. Here was a case of daggers, a dead lock, but the railway was obliged to cede the ground and I departed in peace.

When he set out with his companions on the way to Vienna the bureaucratic farce reached, to Duthie's mind, its climax:

When we had already passed through the most romantic portion of Saxon Switzerland and were slowly descending to the plain we met a poor footsore wanderer with a woe-begone visage who proved to be the dejected object of official vengeance. Four days before he had started from Dresden full of life and hope, but on arriving at the frontier town of Peterswald it was discovered that he had neglected to obtain the signature of one of the numerous gentlemen of whose existence he was scarcely even cognisant and so was driven back to Dresden to seek the required attestation with loss of time, loss of money and almost broken-hearted.

For the English reader, Duthie was confirming an impression already given in a popular work, a translation from the German published some forty years earlier, in which a pastor, P. Moritz, travelling in England, compared the two countries:

It strikes a foreigner as something particular and unusual when on passing through these free English towns he observes none of those circumstances by which the towns in Germany are distinguished from the villages, no walls, no gate, no sentries nor garrisons. No stern examiner comes to search and inspect us or our baggage; no imperious guard here demands a sight of our passports; perfectly free and unmolested we here walk through villages as unconcerned as we should through a house of our own.

(However, Moritz found many people hostile to him on his way and charged the English of being more anti-Semitic than the Germans – a sobering thought for local chauvinists.)

One wonders, though, whether Moritz, or any other German observer, would have gone as far as Duthie in his conclusions:

It must be remembered that the German artisan is ruled in everything by the state . . . he becomes numbered and labelled from the hour of his birth and the gathering items of his existence are duly recorded not in the annals of history but in the registry of the police. Thus he finds that the State in the shape of his Zunft or Guild, is his sick benefit club and his burial society, his travellers fund and his Trade Roll Call; aspires indeed to be everything he ought to desire and certainly succeeds in being a great deal that he does not want.

To drive the point home to the English, Duthie includes a description of the *livret* system among the French workers:

The French workman is taboo until he is registered by the police and can produce his livret. The book costs him twopence halfpenny. Its first entry is a record of the completion of his apprenticeship. Afterwards every fresh engagement must be set down in it. . . . The employer of a workman holds his livret as a pledge. When he receives money in advance the sum is written in his book and it is a debt there chargeable as a deduction of not more than one fifth upon all future employment until it is paid. The workman when travelling must have his livret vised for without that, says the law, 'he is a vagabond, and can be arrested and punished as such'.

Duthie declared:

. . . while the English workmen, by their own collective will, raise up their trade or other societies in whatsoever form or to whatever purpose their intelligence or their caprices may dictate to them, the German on the contrary discovers among his very first perceptions that his position and treatment in the world is already fixed and irrevocable.

And his words were echoed half a century later, by economic historian George Unwin:

At the very moment when the workers of England were laying the foundations of a free organisation, by the establishment of the 'tramping ticket' and the 'house of call' the Governments of France and of Prussia were putting a veto on any such spontaneous popular development by transferring these same institutions into the hands of the police, and utilising them as part of the machinery of a more or less benevolent despotism.

Brentano, the German historian, makes a similar point:

The want of a similar growth of trade societies on the Continent must be accounted for by the military sway prevailing there at the end of the 18th century and the beginning of the 19th century, which suppressed all kinds of meetings and unions and by the absence of a similar disorganisation of trade to that which prevailed at this time in England.

This latter point is made by Unwin as 'the prevalance of the principle of laissez faire'.

Generalisations have their weaknesses and it would be too simple to blame 'military sway' or, on the other hand, see the trade union movement simply as one of the gifts of *laissez faire* capitalism.

These eighteenth- and nineteenth-century developments were the culmination of some four centuries over which the path taken by England had diverged from that of both France and Germany, assisted by the greater external security and internal unity possessed by England since the Middle Ages, greater than that enjoyed by either France or Germany until the nineteenth century. The struggles of the seventeenth and eighteenth centuries which secured English dominance of the world market helped ensure that lead in industrial development which the smaller country held over the two larger ones right into mid-nineteenth century.

Yet, for the fourteenth-century craft organisations of the three countries, conditions were not all that dissimilar. All worked on the general system of a period as apprentice, followed by a term as journeyman, *geselle* or *compagnon* and eventually, after the making of the masterpiece, acceptance as master with the right to do business, train apprentices and employ journeymen. The masterpiece was not as common in England as in Germany (or even in Scotland, where the term 'masterstick' is almost identical with *meisterstücke*), though English hatters, coopers, tinplate workers and others used the custom. But all were organised in fraternities with Church connections which were gradually secularised, changing, as the German historian Schanz says, from the 'rein kirchlichen' to the 'weltlichen'.

But for the journeymen, the *wanderjahre* of Germany and the *tour de France* of the *compagnons* did not exist in England, though as we can see from Duthie's account the English journeymen seem to have been going through the motions of the Continental custom without ever admitting they were doing it – doing informally what the Germans and French were doing formally. The actual similarity is very close, and if we see the French and German customs as being solely part of the traditional training process of the crafts then we shall miss the real reason why the craft workers of the three countries were really engaged in the same activity.

The general rule in England by the fifteenth century was to have seven years' apprenticeship, followed by three more or less obligatory years as a journeyman, thus ensuring that ten years' delay followed before each new apprentice could begin to compete with his master. The German and French masters achieved the same 'balancing' effect by a different means – three–four–five years' apprenticeship followed by up to five years on the road.

Brentano says: 'Some of the Continental Statutes, probably with the object of restricting competition, made it a requisite of mastership that everyone should have worked as a journeyman for a certain number of years.' And: 'As the apprenticeship did not last seven years as in England, but only two to four years, the Craft Guilds in order to diminish competition laid the journeyman under the obligation of travelling sometimes for five years.'

To reinforce the point, Brentano adds that the sons of masters who worked with their fathers were exempt from travelling. But if they worked for someone else they had to travel.

In his book on the *Gesellenverbände* Schanz says that the custom of 'wandering' began among skinners and tailors in the fourteenth century. At this stage the manufacturing towns in the Holy Roman Empire were developing powerfully. Strasbourg with 50,000 inhabitants, Danzig 40,000, Erfurt 32,000, were bigger than any English cities, save London. But their development was separate, and the English cities were all the time being outdistanced and dominated by the faster growing seat of trade and government – London. In the absence of a real central government these German imperial cities sought to impose their influence on the region around and form alliances or 'leagues' with other cities. In such circumstances the journeyman in search of work could not travel casually as he did in England. Schanz says that wandering had become obligatory in the fifteenth century (the *wanderpflicht* or 'travel-duty') and, significantly, 'the need for such an institution arose early when the trade had many hands'. One can see in England also that travelling journeymen (and others of humble status) were supposed to carry certificates with them, and not move without them. But the enforcing of these statutes was never complete, and there were complaints of magistrates not bothering to enforce them. The late and difficult development of national unity in France and Germany, however, must have powerfully stimulated both enforcement and acceptance of regularised movement.

The obligatory travel period no doubt did help the journeyman gain experience. The French compagnons had the saying:

> Quiconque a beaucoup vu
> Peut avoir beaucoup retenu.
> (Those who have seen much, learn much.)

This attitude was not unknown among the English crafts. 'You saw something new every day,' an old hatter told Henry Mayhew in 1849.

But the vital function common to travelling in all three countries was to keep skilled labour on the move in times of slack trade. Its function of reducing the pressure of competition on the masters was in England ensured by the longer apprenticeship.

In Germany, as in England, separate journeymen's organisations appear early in the fifteenth century. But, whereas in England the journeymen became a subordinate part of the craft company 'under the governance' of the masters in the livery, in Germany the *Gesellenverbände* became organisations in their own right. For all that, a similar process was at work; for the German journeymen were expected to meet only in the presence of deputies appointed by the masters. The German and French organisations were responsible for the obligatory and eventually statutory travelling system. But in England, the 'yeomanry' organisation within the gild often assumed responsibility for receiving and dealing with the stranger.

Brentano says that 'the host or herbergsvater was obliged to take in anyone who could furnish proof that he was a journeyman of the particular craft . . . he kept a list of all masters who were in want of journeymen, in order of arrival. Sometimes a special master or journeyman was appointed by the guild to look out for wandering journeymen.' The two latter points could apply also to the unregistered travelling customs of the English trades.

The German masons, like the English, met, master and journeymen together, in an annual 'chapter' to make regulations for the trade, including the reception of strangers identified by the *schenk* or handgrip.

The German mason's greeting, 'I beg thee heartily for God's sake give me employment' / 'With God's help, thou shalt have it', is strangely recalled by the English ironmoulders' 'Brother craft will you give me a job?' / 'If we cannot, we will relieve you'.

As with the English trades, the German mason would get no relief if he left his last master in debt and Duthie points out that the right to a fortnight's work, which was a widespread custom in England, was the law in Germany.

There are other small similarities or parallels – the 'box' with its three keys in which the funds to which masters also contributed were kept; the office-holding senior journeyman, the *Altgeselle* in Germany, *l'ancien* in France, and, among the English tailors' yeomanry 'the ancients'. The French *griffarins* or journeymen printers of Lyons shared with their English counterparts the initiation ceremony in which the father of the chapel poured wine or beer as a libation, a mock religious anthem was sung, and the new entrant was given a 'new alias' (among the English, 'Duke of Pissing Alley', 'Lord High Admiral of all the Bogs in Ireland', etc.). Ellic Howe, the historian of the printing industry, suggests that terms common to the printing industry, including the word 'chapel', came over from France in the early days of print. German and French printers as well as shoemakers and masons did come to England in the fourteenth, fifteenth and sixteenth centuries. The travelling customs of the English crafts may well have been in imitation of their French and German brothers, whose trades were generally more highly developed in medieval times than those in England.

But though similar they are yet different, and the chief difference is that while in England gild control backed by the State began to disintegrate from the sixteenth and seventeenth centuries, in France and Germany the control, modified, was tightened and the regulations multiplied. Over a period of five hundred years through a vast number of edicts the French trade associations 'were encouraged by the Government both as a source of revenue and as a system of police'. The German *wanderjahr* system with its control over movement between cities became linked with imperial police legislation even in the sixteenth century, and in 1731 a Prussian law laid down that every workman should carry an 'information card' and a good conduct certificate, a condition confirmed by a law of 1794. In 1807 it was specified that the *wanderbuch*, while it served as a means of recording the workers' movements for the police, did not act as a passport between the states, as Duthie saw to his disgust.

In 1867, Felkin, the hosiery industry historian, observed that among the German framework knitters the *wanderbuch* is 'now issued from the police office in large towns and by the ordinary authorities in lesser places and every workman must have his pass book ... on reaching another place [he] must present himself to the police authorities and be registered.'

The system of certificates, blanks, etc. among the trades, which in England was confined to the 'state within a state' as the Webbs called the trade societies, was in France and Germany absorbed into that of the State proper.

Noting the 'aristocratic constitution' forced on the German gilds by the masters 'during the latter part of the fifteenth century', a German-based American consul said: 'In many cities the authority of masters over apprentices was absolute and co-equal with that of the state.'

With the French Revolution the old craft organisations were under attack. By a decree of the National Assembly in 1791 the old regulations 'to refuse in concert or not to afford except at a fixed price the benefit of their industry or labour' were declared 'unconstitutional and attacks on the liberty and the declaration of the rights of man'.

Or, at least, the rights of some men. The declaration echoes the claim by the English clothiers earlier in the century that craft regulations offended against the 'liberty of the subject' (see Chapter 4). The 1791 decree was associated with the appearance in French manufacture of a new, larger-scale employer. In the words of a French legal historian, '... the old impoverished master and compagnon found the power of the strike combined with an esprit de corps still very strong afforded them a sanction to the rules nearly as efficient as that of the old laws.'

When Napoleon seized power the anti-worker aspect of the 1791 decree was emphasised by an amendment providing three months' jail for strikers, increased in 1810 to between two and five years for strike leaders. One of the ironies of history, as well as one of the contradictions of bourgeois revolution, is that in the name of the rights of man, France enacted something very like the Combination Acts, which were passed in Britain by a government in fear of the French Revolution and its influence on the English craftsmen and other workers.

Napoleon's invading troops carried the *Code Napoléon* and the 1791 decree into parts of Germany where the old craft organisations were suppressed, or rather, as in France, waited for the storm to blow over. Only with the fuller development in both countries of capitalist industry during the middle and latter parts of the nineteenth century were the old regulations finally done away and the set-up, already familiar in England, of trade union organisation confronting large-scale employers became general. As late as 1885, however, the German General Trade Union urged that: 'The Imperial Government should at last take measures for the preservation and furtherance of the middle trading classes and the trade union considers the only remedy to consist in the limitation of absolute liberty of trade and the introduction of obligatory guilds'.

Throughout these decades, uninterrupted by the shifts and changes of the status of craft organisation, the *wandergesellen* and the *compagnons* kept up their customary round on the roads of Germany and France. In France the *compagnons* combined their *tour* with an ancient religious pilgrimage until the 1830s. To George Sand the *tour de France* was the 'pilgrimage of adventure, the knight errantry of the artisan. Those who own neither home nor inheritance set forth on the roads in search of a homeland, under the care of an adopted family who will not abandon them, neither during life nor after death.'

No such romantic tribute came from any of the English novelists to whom the tramping system was unknown.

In Germany, Goethe, Mahler, Möricke and others paid tribute in words and music to the spirit of the *wandergeselle*, if not to the reality as seen by brother Duthie. Brentano noted: '. . . whilst there exists a rich German literature from the seventeenth century and especially on the position of the workmen in these guilds, nothing on this subject can be found in England.' True enough. Indeed, when one famous German comic opera serenade was translated into English, the *wandergesell* became a 'strolling vagabond', so little was the word understood, though 'vagabondo', a criminal classification, was an insult to a journeyman in France, Germany or England.

But, if no English novelist paid tribute in the manner of George Sand, Bewick the artist celebrated the tramp on his journeys, and trade unionists wrote poems and short stories about him. Tramping featured in a novel, *Harry Welford*, published in instalments in the steel smelters' journal in 1907.

The traditions and legally defined system of the German and French craftsmen had much in common with the *ad hoc* activities of their English brothers. To Duthie, the security offered to the continental journeyman by the age old system was little compensation for the intolerable state interference with the liberties of the artisan. But in contrast, Baernreither, expert observer of the English trade unions and friendly societies, found the English Parliament and government baffled and incompetent when it came to 'the improvement of the condition of the working classes'.

Duthie thought, and probably most English craftsmen would have agreed, that the Germans and French paid too high a price for any benefits derived from their system. Still, the 'freedoms' enjoyed by the English journeyman trade unionist exacted their price, as union members discovered when increasingly through the nineteenth century the full burden of capitalist economic crises fell on their organisations and funds.

Part II:
The 'Traveller' Departs   1850–1914

10 'Grinding the Wind' – the 1840s Depression

Throughout the length and breadth of our native land there has not been a corner or village but what some of our members have perambulated in pursuit of employment; our high roads have resembled that of a mechanical workshop, or a mighty mass of moving human beings; we have various instances where twenty or thirty men in a body of different mechanical trades, wending their way from town to town, asking leave to toil.

The 1846 report of the Journeymen Cabinet Makers' Society tells the story of the testing time through which the early union organisations went during the 1840s when their industries were plunged into two periods of depression following swiftly one on the other. Their effect, on top of the pressures of other industrial change (the industrial steam-engine capacity of British industry doubled during the decade, the number of workers in cotton mills increased by 50 per cent and the railway mileage increased five times between 1840 and 1850) was tremendous and did much to force changes in structure and organisation on the unions.

Unemployment struck at the end of the 1830s and early 1840s, followed by a brief boom period, which then gave way to an even more severe depression. In the print trade the periods of heavy unemployment were 1836–43 and 1846–7. The contemporary records of the ironmoulders speak of their organisation being 'healthful and vigorous until 1837', of the 'horrors of 1840–41', of 1842 being 'dark and gloomy', and of trade being 'generally good in 1846' while in 1847 'commercial stagnation has raged to a considerable extent'.

Since no agency other than the trade societies themselves cared even to number the jobless, it is difficult to say how many of the growing industrial workforce were unemployed. But among the masons the 'unprecedented' number out of work ranged from one sixth to one third; of the moulders, nearly a third, and twenty-six out of their fifty-five branches were in debt; of the cabinet makers in London, one in six.

A meeting of delegates from London trades at the Bell Inn, Old Bailey, in March 1848, spoke of 200,000 'artisans and mechanics' in the capital, of whom one third were employed, one third half-employed and one third entirely out of work. Many of the poorer workers had gone into the workhouse.

Another indication of the crisis level of unemployment is the number of men, women and children classed as 'vagrants'. In the year 1847–8, 1,647,975 are said to have been relieved in workhouses. This figure must contain a large number of repeated reliefs, but if we look at the figures for vagrants relieved during one December night throughout the country's workhouses we see the army of workless growing: 1845–1,791; 1846–2,224; 1847–4,508; 1848–16,026. During 1847–8, some 17,000 passed through the Warrington workhouse, over 12,000 of them Irish, as hunger and need turned great numbers from that country into refugees. In 1842, it is said, the pile of stones worked by Huddersfield paupers reached the incredible total of 150,000 tons.

It is a matter for debate among historians whether the period deserves the name 'Hungry Forties'. But we shall see that for the people who endured it, even the skilled workers with higher pay and savings, it was one of insecurity and misery. The suffering of the voiceless poor can be guessed at by extension of what the better-off craftsmen and their families went through.

A decade of industrial crisis, with many thousands tramping the roads, was the background to the great Chartist agitations when, as one Ashton worker recalled, 'masons, millworkers, colliers, shoemakers were out, little girls marched up and down the street shouting "ten per cent" and "no surrender", the mill masters went about with pistols in their pockets and the soldiers were sent for'. Or, as the Bristol delegate to a moulders' conference in 1848 put it, the past twenty months had seen 'unforeseen and extraordinary events, thrones have crumbled into dust, deadly strife ... commerce and trade now severely injured and that confidence so indispensable to a flourishing and active demand for our labour has been almost totally destroyed'.

The Chartist movement of the 1830s and 1840s reached its first peak in 1842 when the demand for the working-class vote, which had stirred hundreds of thousands, merged briefly into widespread strikes against savage wage reductions particularly in the factory areas of the North and Midlands. These became known as the 'Plug Strikes' because some factories were brought to a standstill as the plugs were drawn from the boilers. The simultaneous declaration by some trade unions in Lancashire that the demands of the 'People's Charter' were 'the only remedy for the present alarming distress' determined the easily convinced ruling class that revolution and not a simple demand for justice was in question. The manufacturing areas were occupied by troops, units being stationed in the potteries for two years, and 1,500 workers were arrested. Some of these belonged to the craft unions, though they had not been directly involved in the main strikes. The engineers collected money for those arrested but when they discovered that their part-time general secretary, Robert Robinson, had been guilty of 'impropriety of conduct during the late excitement', he was censured. To drive the point home the union executive decided that any member out of work because of any 'political or popular movement' would get no out-of-work benefit.

Severe unemployment was not new to the skilled workers. There had been bouts of it after the Napoleonic Wars and in the late 1820s and in the 1830s, but the latest wave was, in the words of the compositors, 'great beyond all former example'. It induced a sense of grim fatalism. We read 'as ten tramp out, ten tramp in', or of members 'tramping for work he knows he will not find'. This was the new element for those skilled workers who had until now relied on the tramping system – the knowledge, made plainer thanks to the newly improved railway and postal services, that there was little chance of work in the next town, or the next.

'Hundreds of men were wandering about the country in search of work and there was little rhyme or reason about the travelling. Men heard rumours of work somewhere else and set off to find it, and at the same time men were travelling in the opposite direction probably passing one another on the road,' says a historian of the early engineering unions. Even if the tramps knew this, and many did, the system demanded that for full benefit they should 'walk fairly through the branches'. While trade was fair or simply 'poor' the unemployed tramp might often be the younger man more recently taken on. But as the workless percentage rose it bit into the hard core of society members, the highly skilled long-serving men, the cadre force of the unions, the men who had set them up in fact. While this is not yet the era of regular union records there are enough figures to give some indication of the number of tramps trudging between the club houses. The Manchester printers saw the tramps treble in number between 1835 and 1841. In 1841, the Reading moulders' branch, with 22 members, relieved 275 tramps. In the winter of 1847–8, when every Reading member was on tramp, the local landlord with union blessing paid out relief to 1,038 tramps. (Tramp figures for this and other periods are discussed more fully in Chapter 15.)

Those lucky enough to have work felt a deep sympathy for those on the roads: 'It is hurtful to see our brothers as they are at present walking the towns and villages seeking employment and without assistance from the funds they have paid to support' (boilermakers).

'Brothers are tramping every day for sixpence ... wet or dry go they must for the want of tin, and have no time to look for a job, too late to see the members, too much fatigued to travel about much which gives the non-society man the chance of dropping into a job while our boys are tramping the road where it is more likely to find a dead donkey than employment' (Exeter masons).

'The humiliation to which these unfortunates who are compelled to take the road are subject calls for the active sympathy of their more fortunate brethren' (typographers).

Such was the impression left by these years that even in the early twentieth century, the Amalgamated Tailors carried this message in the preamble to their rules:

Devoid of humanity must be the man who is not willing to relieve those distresses, by unity to support his fellow men travelling in search of employment ... they wander through the country from city to town, and from town to village, seeking employment, but alas in vain.

Or, as one tramping engineer put it:

> Out in the rain, the pitiless rain
> Suffering from hunger, cold and pain
> The weary tramp pursues his way
> He has travelled many miles today
> And many he must travel yet,
> Though his heart is heavy and garments wet.

Nor was the reception always hospitable when club houses were crowded and landlords not always attentive to the comfort of the tramp. 'Many diseases arise from sleeping in damp beds,' said the Oldham delegate to a moulders' conference in 1848. While in the opinion of the Bradford delegate the dangers were more than those to health:

[Tramping causes] the greatest possible amount of moral degradation. Freed from his home with its thousand little endearments and affection, the silver links are severed and he is destined to wander three months out of six in those districts inhospitable as wandering through a dreary wilderness, under the scorching heat of a vertical sun, or the cold and chilly blasts of winter, without means to evade that punishment which nature inflicts upon such as violate her laws and how frequently is premature death the result. Young men ... the public house becomes his home ... degradation, dissipation and misery ...

Worse, at most club houses, the tramps were 'confined to the tramp room like beasts to their den, by the inhabitants of the town through which they pass they are stigmatised with the utmost ridicule and contempt and designated as vagrants more willing to tramp than work'.

The description may be colourful, but the damage to physical health and well being was real enough. 'Consult your sick lists,' said the Stockport moulders; 'see how much of the sick funds goes on bad feet, swelled legs, surfeits of colds.' Some £300 had been spent in their area on treating travellers taken sick while passing through the town.

Bad as was the plight of the tramp, that of his family was far worse, for they had nothing to live on unless a man could send home part of his tramp benefit. 'After three months wearisome toil he finds his family in worse circumstances than when he commenced.' A man might avoid the workhouse while on tramp and as we have seen most avoided it like the plague, though in 1848 Charles Butley, first president of the Poor Law Board, urged Boards of Guardians to distinguish between those tramps in genuine search of work and those who were 'idle vagrants' and, as Henry Mayhew discovered, most workhouse staff were ready to make this distinction. But on the tramp's return, all benefit money gone, he might find his family already in the workhouse and, in the words of the 1848 London trades delegate conference, be obliged as well 'to accept the hateful badge of poverty'. Or he might find himself, as happened to some moulders, arrested by the parish authorities and destined to the treadmill for 'neglect of family'.

'Treadmill' was a description which by now some were prepared to apply to the tramping system itself. The Stockport moulders eloquently summed up the mounting frustration:

The professed object is to enable us to remove our labour to such place as it may be in demand. Is the system adapted to that end? No. If trade be in a state of universal stagnation and no chance of employment we must still go on the road before we obtain bread. As a labour test it is of the worst description, worse than the stone yard, like when the taskmaster has no work for the 'mill' and the prisoners must go their round even if they only grind the wind. Such is tramping when trade is bad.

The conference at which the Stockport delegate was speaking had been called in all the atmosphere of an emergency. The ironmoulders, with just over 4,000 members, had nearly 1,200 on tramp. Although half of these had exhausted their benefit from the union, tramping and the care of sick tramps had cost over £13,000 in a year. Tramping cost them 6½d per member in 1831 and 2s 8½d in 1837, but by the winter of 1847–8 it was costing some 5s. The word 'bankruptcy' was used by delegates, not in a panic sense, for the moulders were a canny lot, given to deep and shrewd thinking as the conference report shows.

Not only the moulders faced financial crisis. In 1842 the Journeymen Steam Engine Makers (also known as the Old Mechanics), a powerful and well paid body of men, who were to be in 1851 the backbone of the new Amalgamated Society of Engineers, discovered that out of 68 branches, 41 had paid to their unemployed members more than they had taken in subscriptions. It should be remembered that at this stage tramp money was paid from local funds which were 'equalised' once a year by the 'corresponding' secretary. While awaiting this, local lodges and branches borrowed from their landlords. Or, if the strain were too much and local autonomy the rule, the town society went out of existence and the tramp station closed.

In more tightly organised unions there was retrenchment by degrees. In the early 1840s the boilermakers suspended their tramp relief with regret, resuming it in 1845 when trade proved better. The moulders cut their mileage rate from a penny to a halfpenny in 1842 and held it at the lower rate for several years, despite pleas from branches that men were 'holding aloof' from membership because of the reduced benefit. In that year the Liverpool masons proposed that no lodge should give tramp relief without consent of the general body. The loose 'federal' nature of relationship between local and national bodies which the tramping system had helped shape now reacted on it. The strains were mutual.

The Northern Typographical Union, founded in 1830, linked forty societies, mainly in northern England. The tensions between big and small town societies and between the north and London and other areas outside the union grew over the vexed question of 'reciprocity' and its burdens. Manchester spoke of hordes descending on its print shops from outside and the London men claimed that during strikes northern men flooded into the capital and worked there. Relations with Ireland and Scotland were likewise complicated. The Liverpool compositors reckoned they were paying out twice as much as they received and proposed a General Reimbursement Fund. Starting in 1842, this was intended to equalise payments between the disputing areas. It was controversial from the beginning because, as it worked out, London was obliged to pay more. Though the London delegates to the meeting which agreed the Fund loyally accepted this, the London membership later repudiated it. Still the Fund was a step towards more solid national union. Aided by the easier state of trade in the mid-forties, this step took place. In 1844, the National Typographical Association was formed.

The Northern Typographical Union leaders had expressed their dislike of the tramping system in 1843 and earlier, and it was hoped that the new

The tramping hatter signs in. From a pictorial resolution head, 1820.

The emblem of the United Society of Brushmakers, issued in 1840, incorporates the coats of arms of the six towns which make up the original amalgamation.

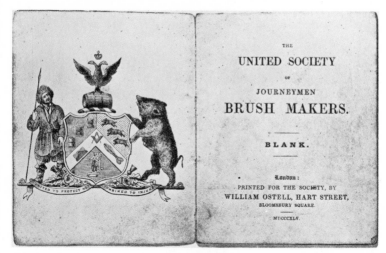

The Brushmakers' 'blank', 1845, an elaborate passport-like document which recorded the journeys of the travelling member.

Tramping shoemaker and his wife – a rare photograph from the late 19th century.

Simon the Tanner, a house of call for the trade and its tramps, known to Henry Mayhew in 1850. It still stands today in Long Lane, Bermondsey.

Close-up of the inn-sign, Simon the Tanner.

Boilermaker's emblem from the late 1830s, showing the tramp being greeted by a yard foreman.

Boilermaker's emblem from the late 1870s when the union official dispensing sick and funeral benefit, took the place of the tramp and the union motto was changed to 'God helps those who help themselves'.

This is to certify that Mr.
is a free Member of this Society
and is entitled to receive the Benefits
Stated in the Schedule

                                    Sec.y

No. Dated this   Day of   18
This Card is renewable in four
Months from the Date hereof

Two centuries of change—the coat of arms of the Worshipful Company of Tin-Plate Workers, alias Wire Workers (1670), is absorbed into local trade society membership cards (Wolverhampton, early 19th century) and finally into the emblem of the General Union of Tin-Plate Workers, formed in Manchester in 1867. The design is modified and expanded, although the motto remains.

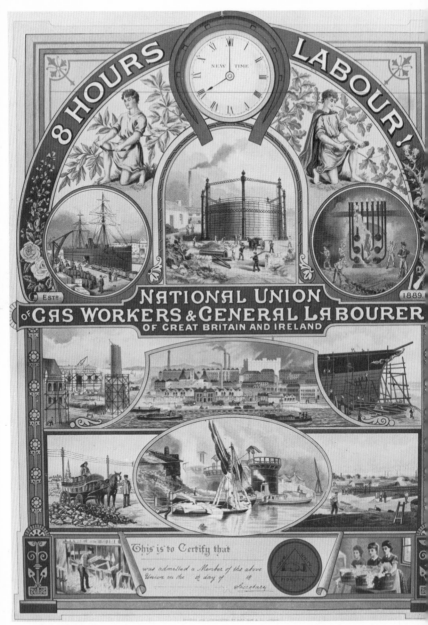

The emblem of the Gas Workers (1889) illustrates the willingness of the 'new' unions to organise workers irrespective of craft and industry.

body, the NTA, would find a solution. For a couple of years after its formation, indeed, tramp numbers dropped, but this was more because of better trade than any organisational improvement. By 1848 tramps were on the roads again in their hundreds and the tension between the north and London became too great. The new body split, the Provincial Typographical Association and the London Union of Compositors remaining separate for many decades to come.

Nor was the printers' amalgamation the only attempt at wider union. During the forties the tailors and cordwainers tried to amalgamate, but the attempts were evidently not successful. In the cordwainers' case certainly, and possibly also in that of the tailors, disagreement over tramping arrangements was the central problem.

The most famous amalgamation was that of the engineering trades in 1851, the latest of three stages of development. In 1822 came the first link-up of local mechanics' and steam engine makers' societies; in 1837 the Old Mechanics or Journeymen Steam Engine Makers was formed, based mainly on Yorkshire.

In 1851 the Old Mechanics and their rule book became the basis for the Amalgamated Society of Engineers. While not quite the 'new model' it has been represented to be, it had two clear advantages over other amalgamations. Mechanisation did not disrupt it as it did the older handcraft unions, since mechanisation was the reason for its existence. And the core of its members were highly skilled, well-paid men who were able to subscribe to benefits which could sustain them through long periods of unemployment.

During the 1830s, the Old Mechanics had added a second string to their benefit bow. They had introduced 'donation', or out-of-work benefit paid at home, of ten shillings a week for full members. In theory this 'static' pay was an alternative to tramping, not a substitute. But it was clear that the union was turning away from the old system. The 1842 delegate conference refused to allow members to draw 'donation' in any branch. 'If such a system were adopted members might place themselves in branches where pleasure was the object rather than a desire to work.' A rule was agreed giving the general secretary the power to 'remove' a member who remained unemployed to where work was available. Along with the security of home 'donation' came the beginnings of a squeeze on the roving member.

When the ASE was formed in 1851, home donation was the rule. Members tramped if they wished or if in certain cases their fellow members felt strongly they should 'move on'. But if there were no work in his own town the member could sit tight and wait for trade to improve.

Despite remarks about the 'supineness' of the receiving system in 1829, by the 1830s the brushmakers had begun to allow home unemployment pay and by 1846 the general secretary claimed: 'Tramping is largely done away with.' By which he meant that the system of 'no walk, no pay' had gone, for voluntary tramping continued among the brushmakers until the end of the century. Those who wished to try their luck in another town could have up to twelve days' 'pension' advanced to them.

Typograpers in large, old-established societies like Manchester paid threepence a week in return for seven shillings a week out-of-work benefit, paid at home in the 1840s, but the attempt to introduce home donation nationally among the printers failed and tramping remained the only system of unemployment relief general throughout the printing industry for another thirty years.

When in 1848 the moulders sat down to thrash out the problem of unemployment, many of their delegates were quite clear that the tramp system was not only hard on the tramp but ineffective too. The cheapness of rail travel 'deprives them of the support which the (union) law allows and thus nullifies the society's objective and also deprives them of the means of getting work on the route they take'. It seems that more and more travellers were heading straight for towns where there might be work instead of meticulously following their route card round the 'circuit'. The great variations in number relieved by different branches at various times seems to confirm this.

But those who 'walk fairly through the branches of the society are frequently exposed to the rigour of inclement weather and bring on themselves colds, etc, which are the foundation of a variety of diseases to which they must inevitably become the victims and these diseases bring them on the sick allowance which augments that item of expenditure.'

The Bury delegate declared: 'As to the travelling system we heartily wish you would do away with it.' And the Oldham delegate thought it 'a great evil to compel a man who is out of work to leave home before he can receive any relief especially in times like the present when there is no prospect of work. It compels him to spend the greatest part on himself and puts it out of his power to share it with his wife and family. .... A great part is spent on beer, beds and riding from place to place.'

Employers, added Oldham, would stand out during disputes 'under the impression that when the men cease to draw their relief they would return to work'.

The Stockport delegate struck the shrewdest blow. The system 'compels us to work again for the money we have wrought for before and obtained after hard toil from our employers and to the sacrifice of many domestic comforts and social pleasures we have paid to our society'.

Not only was the conference unanimous that the system was inade-quate, it was also unanimous in suggesting what delegates saw as the solution – 'a donative system works well with other bodies situated as we are', with 'monthly trade reports to serve as guide to where employment is most abundant'. Home donation would mean the tramp would share his money with his family and not with the publicans and the railway and shipping companies. What is more, several branches had come prepared with elaborate calculations to prove their point.

'We are of the opinion that a man on tramp receives 22 shillings from the funds, a great part of which is spent on beer, beds and riding from place to place. Now the money paid to two men on tramp would keep three better at home at 15s per week or four at 11 shillings or six at 7s 6d' (Oldham).

A traveller calling at every 'box' and getting a penny a mile received £13 19s 11d; 432 travellers would thus receive £5,830; at ½d a mile the traveller received £10 7s or 532 travellers receiving £5,825. (By a rough calculation this makes the moulders' full tramp route around 1,700 miles.)

On the other hand, out-of-work pay at 8 shillings for 13 weeks and 4 shillings for a further 13 weeks would cost £7 16s. The sum of £5,826 then would have provided for 747 unemployed. Donation allowed pay-ment to 315 more men than tramping at 1d a mile and 185 more men than tramping at ½d a mile.

Bristol moulders calculated it a different way. Tramping at 20 miles a day (½d a mile) means 5s a week mileage. Then there was 7s 6d a week supper money, 2s 4d for beds, 2s Sunday money – a total of 16s 10d a week. By the time a tramp journeying round the fifty-two branches – in-cluding 'water stages' London to Hull, Preston to Belfast, Dublin to Liverpool, and Bristol to Cork – had paid all his travelling expenses, he had 9s a week left for shoes, clothes, food and beds between branches more than a day's march apart. Ten shillings a week would be 'infinitely superior' to 16s 10d a week on the tramp. The Newcastle delegate added that the member might 'travel if he thought well', but that the water stages should be done away with except where it was not possible to travel by land.

There seemed indeed no answer to the arguments, that the home donation was more efficient, cheaper, and more healthy physically and morally than tramping benefit. As it turned out in later years, home donation was no cheap solution and more than once the union found itself in a tight corner financially. But the change was made and the old system was relegated to a minor role. Never in all the difficult later periods did the moulders even consider turning back to it.

The delegates having prepared the ground well, the moulders' executive put forward its plan. There was to be home donation of 8s a week for 13 weeks and 4s for a further 13 weeks for members of two years standing, with 6s and 3s for twelve-month members. Those who wished to travel could draw their donation on the road.

Before the end of 1848, the number of moulders listed as on the road had dropped dramatically. The union report judged that members were 'staying at home waiting for donation to come in'. Returns for the second half of that year showed London with 227 on donation and 24 on tramp, and Manchester with 785 on donation and 224 on tramp. By the end of the year the head office recorded an average figure of 90 members on tramp throughout the country. In the early 1850s this dropped to 60.

It is strange that, as far as I am aware, during the whole debate no one referred to the fact that the Scots moulders (who had a separate organisation) had for some time paid 'idle aliment' at home to their members. This they had kept up through the whole depression period. At one time, it is true, it was reduced to as little as 1s 6d a week. The Scots moulders, significantly, had suffered no membership drop comparable with that of the English union, and later depressions, however severe their inroads into the funds, did not shake the English moulders as the 1840s had done. With the introduction of 'home donation', they like men in other skilled trades had begun a policy of cautious consolidation of both membership and funds, under which a more stationary membership was easier to record and keep track of and more susceptible to stronger central control. The turn to home donation was a key part of this change. It made being out of work easier to bear, and it kept the local branch organisation together.

But home donation on its own did nothing to find jobs, nothing to reduce the unemployment which remained a threat to members and organisation. Some union branches and conference delegates called for co-operative production to provide the answer. The newly formed Amalgamated Society of Engineers did, later on, invest funds in union-owned workshops, and the brushmakers set up three bass broom factories, with 'receivers' being given brooms to sell for their own benefit, in lieu of 'pension', when union funds were low. Such projects, though, eventually became themselves a burden on the union funds and the brushmakers found themselves borrowing money from club house landlords to maintain the factories. In 1840 the Newcastle masons' lodge found little sympathy from other brothers for their proposal to undertake work contracts.

The Land Bank with its Chartist Associations attracted some investment from trade unions, but it also attracted scepticism and even hostility. Invited by Hull branch to increase their local subscription in order to take out Land Bank shares, the Leeds brushmakers replied that funds were too low. The Sheffield brushmakers voted 50 to nil against investing in the 'allotments', saying that this would 'do very well for individual speculation but could not answer for a trade society looking for an immediate benefit'.

There was some support among the moulders for the idea of buying 'a few acres of land' to support unemployed members but the steam engine makers were dubious on practical grounds. 'Would they produce as much or anything like the agricultural labourer?' It was asked at the 1842 conference. Some branches, though, must have gone ahead and invested for in 1848, when unemployment was at its height and donation and travel benefit had already been halved as a crisis measure, these branches were told that unless they withdrew money from the Land Bank and used it to aid the unemployed more directly, their travel certificates would not be honoured by other branches of the society.

Trade measures to control work and thus secure employment were part of the craft tradition, and repeated proclamations and laws made worktime regulation illegal, though these did not deter the practice. In 1849, Henry Mayhew, quizzing the London trades, heard about the 'short hours' system, by which available work was shared among members. Linked to this was the more far-seeing campaign to reduce working hours on a permanent basis. At a meeting in the Princes Tavern, Manchester, in November 1833, it was said: 'Eight hours' labour is enough for any human being ... the remainder ... for education, recreation and sleep.' This foreshadowed the slogans of the great campaign of fifty and sixty years later. Though working time in many trades was still twelve hours a day, this was not seen as a propaganda demand. In 1837 the Scots moulders declared that 'eight hours is sufficient for a regular day's work ... and the same to bear in practice as early as possible.' And nine years later, in the midst of the depression of the 1840s, Brother Carter, addressing a mass rally of masons in Liverpool, put the question bluntly.

There were, he said, 8,000 masons in England (he was talking about organised men) of whom 2,000 were 'probably unemployed'. 'If 6,000 gave up one hour', this would put 600 in work again. He had other things in mind and went on to tell the meeting: 'I think I need only ask them the wretchedness they have seen in consequence of the system of tramping, the immorality it has induced and the injury it has done to bodily health.'

One of the issues in the big lock-out of 1852 which nearly crippled the new engineers' amalgamation was the regulation of working hours – the control of overtime. The engineers recognised that unrestrained competition for available work, even in times of good trade, could destroy unity and the ability to maintain decent conditions for all. In times of economic crisis, it could be disastrous. The steam engine makers had previously sponsored inquiries into overtime and invited outside experts to compete for prizes in analysing the problem.

In such ways did the campaign develop which occupied the energies of many trades, from building workers and compositors to cotton operatives in the factories, a campaign first for the ten- and then for the nine-hour day stimulated by the desire to share out work and thus somehow iron out the process of boom and slump which every few years threw more and more workers out of employment.

One possible solution to unemployment found favour for a while at least with almost every union. It was in a way an extension of the tramping system, and in some trades it was seen and treated as such. It was what the carpenters described as the 'natural outlet' for surplus labourers and mechanics – emigration.

'In Every English-speaking Country in the Globe' – Emigration

From the 1840s onwards 'the laws of supply and demand' became a familiar expression in union reports and periodicals. It was not simply a matter of the leaders of the skilled craftsmen being won over to fashionable economic notions – that labour was not the source of all value, but a commodity like any other which should find its correct 'price' on the market according to availability. The mass unemployment of the previous decade had convinced many active union members that there was a 'surplus' of labour not likely to disappear automatically when 'good trade' times came around. This surplus, said the Glasgow ironmoulders in 1851, must be 'grappled with or else it will overpower us'. So lasting did the surplus seem that in 1860 the preamble of the rule book of the new Amalgamated Society of Carpenters and Joiners spoke of 'surplus labourers and mechanics' as though they were a fact of life.

What to do with this 'superabundance of labour', as the *Compositors Chronicle* described it in 1841? Co-operative production schemes seemed to swallow money rather than provide jobs. The shorter working day was a worthwhile object, but had to be fought for against determined opposition from the employers. Even those claiming to be 'well wishers' of the men declared the idea of shorter hours to be 'impractical and of no avail'.

But one solution seemed to swim with rather than against the current both of economic affairs and 'economic' opinion. That was emigration, which by the 1830s was taking workers both skilled and unskilled, though mainly the latter, out of the country in their tens of thousands, in some cases with public assistance. Why should not the unions help unemployed brothers start a new life overseas? The brushmakers had begun in the 1820s to collect money for emigration grants and in the 1830s a levy was imposed.

This was known as 'the emigration shilling'. Branches could nominate members whose names would be forwarded to the 'acting branch' in London. If approved by a general ballot of the membership the nominee would get £15 for his passage. If, having been chosen, he refused to go, he could be fined £2. If he returned within fifteen months, he had to repay his grant at the rate of £1 a month. This scheme was later suspended, though attempts were made to revive it in the 1880s. In the 1830s the Glasgow spinners and Dublin printers also had local emigration schemes. The spinners balloted for their emigrants who had to have two years' membership and no dues arrears. The Dublin printers chosen got £4 if they emigrated to England and £8 if they went to America, and their scheme was still sending some thirty a year overseas in the 1860s, probably some to England where they may have replaced English compositors who in the 1850s began to be assisted abroad by their fellow members.

Such uneasy thoughts occurred to trade union members at the time, as we shall see, but emigration schemes spread among the trades and around the middle of the century carpenters, engineers, flint glass makers, moulders, potters, printers, spinners, steam engine makers and others had adopted them. The potters combined the idea of emigration with that of land grants and lost a good part of their funds in the unsuccessful settlement of Pottersville in Wisconsin, USA in the 1840s. Most schemes, however, were straightforward grants. The London compositors' scheme was more generous and longer-lasting than most, giving £30 to married men and £15 to bachelors; some forty-eight men were sent abroad at a cost of £1,000 during four years in the 1850s. The ironmoulders, after a deal of reluctance, started a scheme in the 1860s with four guineas passage money to the United States via Liverpool. The scheme reached its peak in 1868, when nearly 200 emigrants went mainly to the United States but also to Canada, Australia and Brazil, before the fund ran into debt.

For the London compositors, emigration was the alternative to tramping which they found 'evil and ignominious'. There was little point, they felt, in paying out 'indefinitely, a few shillings', leaving the tramp to choose between pauper relief and starving on the road. Emigration would 'relieve the overcrowded labour market'.

The Liverpool compositors were more cautious and practical. They saw emigration as 'an auxiliary to, not a substitute for the present system of "tramping"', a view endorsed by the leaders of the Provincial Typographical Association. A fund of halfpenny and penny subscriptions should be enough, said Liverpool. They continued:

If a man emigrates it matters very little where he goes for he at once ceases to be that burden on the trade he would otherwise be if he were tramping about the country. If he travels in this country to seek employment he will receive from the various societies in 12 months about £12. For £7 a man can procure a passage hence to New York and have £2 when he lands. ... £12 would send two a week to America at £1 or three in a fortnight to Australia. . . . The recipients would be required to enter into an engagement to pay the money back should they return to the country within a given period, say five years.

By December 1851, an Emigration Society had been set up and in July 1852 the first four emigrants sailed, three for the United States and one for Australia.

The emigration scheme of the journeymen hatters, however, was neither an alternative nor an auxiliary to the tramping system, but a simple extension of it. Members wishing to emigrate to Europe had a 'turn' of £1 which they had to pay back if they returned within six weeks (to guard against a regrettable tendency noted also in other unions for members to take emigration grants rather as a form of holiday subsidy). If hatters travelled outside Europe, they got a 'turn' of £3 3s. The hatters' scheme was still in existence at the end of the century, perhaps because the amounts involved were never larger. The London compositors with their much larger grants ran out of money in the late 1850s and suspended the scheme for fourteen years.

They started again in 1871 with £10 grants and a top limit of £300 a year and in 1890 the grant was increased to £15. Financial strains likewise broke the ironmoulders' or founders' scheme in the 1870s and unlike the London printers' theirs was not revived. The provincial printers' scheme suffered all along from lack of enthusiasm among the branches. Only a handful of emigrants were sent out each year and the funds soon ran out. There were other setbacks when the chosen men began to return home but refused to return the money they had been given, or perhaps were quite unable to do so.

As far as can be seen the numbers emigrating under union schemes cannot have amounted to more than a few thousands altogether – a minute fraction of the total emigration even among skilled workers. The schemes certainly cannot be said to have done much to alleviate unemployment. Perhaps the stringency of the conditions was a deterrent.

The Amalgamated Carpenters were, on the face of it, the most enthusiastic exporters of their own unemployed. The 1860 rule book declared: 'The prolific character of the Anglo-Saxon race rapidly increases the population of these isles. For their surplus labourers and mechanics, emigration is the natural outlet to distant colonies whose inhabitants they are destined to bless.'

The carpenters' emblem included, in a colourful display of its various benefits, a panel on emigration based probably on Ford Madox Brown's painting, *The Last of England*. But, unfortunately or not according to opinion, this was mainly window-dressing. For the carpenters' rules laid down that emigration grants of £6 would be paid when funds had reached £3 per member and when unemployment reached 7½ per cent of the membership. Grants would be given only to five-year members. As the historian of the woodworkers remarked, the combination of 'big cash rate per member and excessive unemployment were not likely to coincide and as a matter of fact no member was able to receive the benefit.'

Stringency of conditions was one limiting factor. Another was a marked lack of enthusiasm among many members for the whole idea of emigration. The executive committee of the Provincial Typographical Association remarked that 'expatriation' is 'still regarded by our profession at least with something like dread'. Assisted emigration, indeed, was regarded with suspicion among the organised workers. It had a bad history and prehistory and was linked with forced emigration or 'transportation' in the minds of many.

This is not altogether surprising for until the seventeenth century such was the only form of emigration. The medieval custom of requiring certain criminals to 'forswear the realm' in some years dispatched about a thousand people abroad and the custom was consolidated into law in 1597 with 39 Eliz. I c 4, an Act for the Punishment of Rogues which provided for transportation. For by then in Virginia the government had a place to which it could send 'rogues' along with the innocent. Many of these settlers in Virginia and the New England colonies further north were poor country folk sent out as 'indentured servants' for seven years and even longer, under conditions close to slavery. There was little to distinguish their situation from the 'rogues' picked up on the roads, or those deemed 'rogues' for the purposes of export. Some 60,000, moved by religion, poverty and the law, emigrated in the early seventeenth century. During the eighteenth century, the choice of colonies growing along with the number of poor, the authorities were able to temper the justice of hanging for petty theft with the mercy of transportation. The framework knitters, though some emigrated to South Africa at the height of their distress in 1817, generally regarded emigration as 'transportation' and so did the Chartists and propagandists like Cobbett and Hunt.

When during the early nineteenth century the authorities began a scheme of 'internal' emigration, dispatching children – including many parish orphans – to the new textile areas, the conditions of their journeying and the way they were used and discarded by their employers caused widespread protest. At one point London parents whose children were bound for the north demanded to have them back for fear they were being transported.

The internal emigration of parish apprentices in the eighteenth and nineteenth centuries was a form of transportation. It was suspected by trade union members as being an attempt to undermine their organisation. Rightly so, for in July 1834 Edmund Ashworth, the sponsor of some of the schemes, thought they would 'have a tendency to equalise wages as well as prevent in some degree some of the turnouts which have of late been so prevalent'.

Active union members were no less suspicious of emigration out of the country. J. F. Bray, the socialist printworker who worked out his theories tramping round England and America, declared that emigration was 'a capitalist remedy' which would 'expatriate the half-famished workman to some foreign clime where his murmurings will be unheard, his threats unfeared and his wants unrelieved by the wretched pittance extended from capital by means of the poor rates'. Bray's charge seems confirmed by the businessman Hurst who at this time was urging his fellow capitalists to make emigration grants which would 'relieve distress' and 'give yourself pleasure', for a 'few hundreds' saving 'thousands from destruction'.

But it is confirmed more precisely by the policies of the Poor Law Commissioners who, in their report five years before Bray wrote those words, went into some detail to show how each town and village could 'get rid of surplus labour'. Benenden in Kent had cut the poor rate by a third in four years. Ewhurst had sent a hundred of its paupers abroad. The Poor Law Commissioners and the local ratepayers were at some variance, though. The national authorities favoured internal emigration because it was cheaper; the local authorities preferred emigration out of the country because the poor were less likely to come back. This could not be guaranteed of course. 'Surplus' paupers did return home with tales of bad treatment and bad food. One unnamed man was alleged to have saved money to return from Montreal because he did not like the beer.

Not all employers were emigration enthusiasts, particularly if the 'hands' going abroad were skilled. Then tales of hardship abroad could be touched up a little and passed around. In his 'Address of the workmen in the pottery on the subject of entering into the service of foreign manufacturers', in 1783, Josiah Wedgwood declared that on the American crossing 'recruits could not be raised from England sufficient to supply the places of the dead men', which proved to be perhaps one of the most ill-founded prophecies in history. Not that the discomforts and dangers of the Atlantic crossing were imaginary. In 1850 Henry Mayhew was told by London shipwrights that an inferior brand of shipbuilding was called 'emigration work' – vessels made to last one voyage and if they survived to be broken up again for the timber.

Wedgwood painted worse horrors of the situation on the Continent, warning artisans who took service with French companies, encouraged by French businessmen and authorities, that they were being hired only to train the locals before being thrown out of work to exist on 'frogs, hedgehogs and the wild herbs of the field'. Certainly some continental employers viewed their English recruits as expendable and one German manufacturer at least could not wait until he had done with the idle drunken English and could whip them home again.

At this stage, in the late eighteenth century, Continental countries had begun to try seriously to catch up with the rapidly growing English industry which was flooding their markets with cheap manufactures. So the discouragement of skilled emigration was backed by a government ban on the export of both artisans and machinery. It was a ban evidently more honoured in the breach than the observance, as MPs on the Committee of Inquiry into Artisans and Machinery in 1824 were told by witnesses. When the ban was lifted in 1825 at least 2,000 skilled English workers were employed by other European firms. So the government came to accept the fact of skilled emigration.

As said, there had never been any reluctance to export the poor. The Parliamentary Committee on the Relief of the Poor said in 1819: 'All obstacles to seeking employment wherever it can be found even out of the realm, should be removed and every facility that is reasonable afforded to those who may wish to resort to our own colonies.'

By this time emigration was going ahead at a tremendous rate. In 1818 the *Gorgon* newspaper wrote of 'swarms' from all parts of London sailing for America at the rate of 200 daily. In 1817, 5,000 had sailed for Canada alone. By the 1830s the yearly figure had passed the 80,000 mark.

But among the organised workers, the suspicions and hostility towards emigration remained. The moulders' emigration scheme was delayed until the 1860s, partly by strong executive opposition. The union leaders warned in May 1848 that for every thousand who left the country 'a thousand fresh hands would immediately rush on to the market to supply their places'. Opinions were divided, though, as the debate among the masons in 1849 shows. In May the Liverpool lodge proposed emigration as an alternative to strikes and a better way of spending union money.

With £4 for passage money and £26 to buy land in America the unemployed members would be well served. Grimsby lodge proposed a compulsory emigration fund and Penzance agreed with Liverpool that a combination of emigration and land purchase would be a good idea, while Bow (London) lodge favoured the land purchase alone.

Nottingham, however, replied that emigration was 'banishment' and some other scheme should be found to employ men on strike. Lichfield declared strikes to be a 'necessary evil' for which emigration was no substitute. Bristol sternly told Liverpool to 'leave the strike laws alone', while Leeds asked pointedly: 'What benefit would it be to the trade if half of our members were to emigrate at the present day, if no protection were offered to those who would be left? In the course of a year or two (for there is no seven year apprenticeship now) we should be as numerous as ever.'

Despite the objections, many lodges proposed that an emigration society should be set up. But the masons, whose funds were already stretched to the utmost maintaining the tramping system, were not ready to put more into emigration.

With or without union backing, however, emigration took workers out of the country in increasing numbers. By the 1880s it had reached flood level with over half a million Britons going to the United States between 1880 and 1882 and tens of thousands to Australia and New Zealand. In one year nearly 6,000 mechanics and nearly 4,000 bricklayers, masons and carpenters emigrated to America, though these figures must be qualified a little by the fact that some masons were given to sailing for America, working the summer, and then returning to Britain. And, to judge from the emigration grant rules of many unions, so were other workers. At any rate, by the 1870s one emigrant reported finding hostels in Canada and the United States filled with footsore compositors, mechanics, shoemakers, coopers and others. They trudged the roads with the native American migrant workers and rode the railroads as earlier tramps in England had ridden the stagecoach steps. Fred Bower, radical stonemason and humorist, relates how he was hurled from a train by an indignant railwayman freemason who was not going to give a free ride to any operative of the breed, particularly not an active union man.

But other unionists who emigrated could count on a better reception. At their 1842 delegate conference the steam engine makers learned that members 'who had been in America ten years had founded a society similar to ours', though the migratory habits of the trade there made organisation difficult. In that year too came news of a Society of Operative

Stone Masons at the Crown and Anchor, George Street, Sydney. By 1853 the new Amalgamated Society of Engineers had a brother society in Sydney and Montreal, while by the 1860s there were branches in France, Constantinople, Bombay, Malta, Buffalo, N.Y., and a decade later ten ASE branches were functioning in the United States.

In 1885 the ASE delegate meeting was told of 'our organisation in every English-speaking country in this globe' and proposals were made for the overseas branches to have their own council within the union. Seven years later these overseas branches numbered eighty-two, with 5,000 members, half of them in Australia and New Zealand. Before the First World War there were twenty-six ASE branches in South Africa alone and nine overseas countries accounted for ten per cent of the union's 170,000 members. Already in Canada, however, engineers were joining native unions and eventually all the overseas branches, which by 1920 numbered 300, were absorbed into their national unions.

The ASCJ had declared in 1860 that emigrating members were destined to 'bless' the inhabitants of distant lands, while declining to assist the blessing with union funds. But clearly many members did emigrate without union help and carried the organisation with them. By 1886 the ASCJ had sixty-seven branches in the USA, Canada, Australia, South Africa and New Zealand.

Emigrants also carried with them the principles and practice of the tramping system. In 1865 the Journeymen Hat Makers had a United States travelling card similar in design to the English version and the Amalgamated Society of Journeymen Felt Hatters had a foreign travelling card. The engineers allowed their travelling system to extend across the world. A Board of Trade Inquiry in the 1890s was intrigued to observe how a member from the Bilbao branch could return to put in his card to the Manchester branch or a Toronto engineer turn up in Luton. It was a very extended system and needed careful control, which must have helped advance centralisation in this increasingly powerful union, by now one of the biggest in the country. The ASE general secretary kept a strict eye open for members who left their jobs to go abroad 'voluntarily'. They were not to have travelling cards. The hatters also kept an eye on tramps overseas and when American unions wrote complaining of English hatters 'working foul' the English union dealt out fines to the offending members.

American unions, too, took up the tramping system. In a leaflet entitled 'Why We Organise', the International Brotherhood of Bookbinders said in 1892:

Any member of the brotherhood leaving the jurisdiction of a local is given a travelling card assuring the holder thereof good fellowship and brotherly assistance from any local in whose jurisdiction he may go. This card is acknowledged to be the greatest asset a travelling member may possess. It is the passport to fraternity, brotherly love and friendship which has aided so much to cement the ties of organisation.

This declaration could have been made a century before by an English trade society.

The spread of union organisation by emigration also increased the caution with which it was regarded. In 1839, J. F. Bray, after his experiences in the United States, had warned: '... there is the same inequality of rights amongst them as amongst us, for they are likewise divided into rich and poor, into capitalists and producers, and the last are there, as they are here, at the mercy of the first.'

If any were inclined to treat Bray's warning as socialist propaganda, confirmation soon came. As soon as they were in touch with the union in the home country, the Sydney masons' lodge sent this warning (March 1842): 'Beware of bounty emigration. It is only a delusion. Employment is scarce, house rents high, provisions dear.' Twelve months later, a letter from Toronto advised masons not to emigrate and in 1861 the Melbourne masons' lodge ironically forwarded to the head lodge a resolution: 'That our society charter a vessel for England to take a few of the unemployed masons out of the country.' A similar warning came two years later from the Buffalo and Boston branches of the ASE about unscrupulous employers who were arranging for people to emigrate to 'keep down the price of labour'. An ASE report in 1873 showed that the situation had become more difficult: 'In consequence of the state of trade in the States and Canada a number of members on donation are returning to this country. The travelling cards issued by our branches there are not registered and we ask for them to be forwarded.'

Three years after this the ironfounders, whose emigration fund was in debt, decided: 'It is unwise and cruel to send out our unemployed members to places where their labour is not wanted.'

Emigration was proving from the organised workers' point of view to have the same weaknesses as the tramping system of which it was to some extent a development. By the 1890s, 'clearances' for hatters travelling in America were suspended because so many were out of work over there.

By the end of the century, indeed, it was already clear that emigration was no more a solution to the problem of unemployment than tramping had been. But emigration did prove to have the same positive features as tramping had had. It spread union organisation around 'the English speaking world', helped no doubt by the action of the authorities in punishing union activists with transportation.

By the early twentieth century powerful union organisation among boilermakers, engineers, building workers and other trades had firmly established itself in every one of the 'dominions' and was already an integral part of the life and history of these nations, although not until the 1920s were the formal links between home and overseas organisations severed.

A year after the outbreak of the First World War, by which time nearly a quarter of the membership of the ASE had enlisted, most of the travelling members who did not intend to settle abroad had returned home. Almost the last 'tramp' to be recorded in the ASE journal was J. Smith, en route from Schenectady USA, to Bolton, Lancashire in the spring of 1815.

12 Respectability and Reorganisation

Do your utmost to consolidate the society and avoid the use of offensive language.
President's appeal to ASE 1852 delegate conference

The slumps of the 1840s signalled the end of the old tramping system as
the universal way of dealing with the unemployed. And they signalled
the end of that stage of union organisation which tramping had helped
bring about – a system in which societies were loosely linked together,
sometimes throughout England, Ireland and Scotland ; cared for each
other's travelling members; and 'equalised' accounts by a cumbersome
process of sending postal packages from club house to club house, with an
'acting branch' to see fair play which changed year by year, so moving
the union headquarters around the country.

The rise and fall of the grand notion of 'one big union' in the 1830s
has overshadowed the completion of this first stage in the development of
the national unions in which the leading part had been played by journeymen of the old hand trades – woolcombers, shearmen, framework knitters,
hatters, tailors, shoemakers, masons, carpenters, blacksmiths and millwrights. By mid-century some of the older hand trades had been pushed
out or absorbed by the machine, national union organisation in wool,
cotton and hosiery establishing itself among the machine operators of the
mills only after some decades. But what the machine took away it also
gave and in the mid-1840s the rising number of engineers passed the
declining number of handloom weavers. The men of metal took the stage
as the old craftsmen left it.

The metal trade unions came to the fore in the second phase of organisation which now got under way. If the hallmark of the first stage had
been expansion and diffusion of the idea of union, that of the second was
consolidation, even if it meant retrenchment. The old sprawling federated
societies gave way to more tightly knit national unions, with local clubs
becoming branches and full-time secretaries with executive councils
replacing 'acting branches'.

Delegate meetings replaced or supplemented the old method of 'voting round' the societies by post. There arrived a new-style, more domineering leader working from an office, even if it was in his own front parlour, a man able to draw up a balance sheet. Men like Shortt, the masons' corresponding secretary who could make a point with a poem in the fortnightly report or thrash a strike breaker who attacked him in a side-street, were on the way out.

The changes were a response to wider changes of which the depressions of the 1840s were a symptom – the growth of industry, the growth of the working class, and the growth of cities it inhabited. Trades from masons to brushmakers allowed their travelling members two, three or more days to 'walk about' seeking work in large towns like London, Sheffield, Manchester, Liverpool and Birmingham. More machines, more power, more workers and bigger workplaces meant the dwindling of a system and way of life based on a chain of small workshops where journeymen and masters shared the same craft traditions, a chain along which the independent artisan might move seeking work or the potential strike breaker might be helped on his way with a square meal, a pint and a slap on the back.

Changes were needed because the opponent in industrial disputes grew stronger. The engineering lock-out in 1852 and the builders' lock-out in 1859 were marked by the tough, aggressive behaviour of the bosses, led by men employing between 1,000 and 2,000 men each. In London a third of the building workers were employed by 10 out of 550 firms. As Thomas Hughes, the author and student of the unions, noted, the 'technical sense' of the terms 'master' and 'journeyman' was 'all but lost'. Such 'masters' could not be beaten by their journeymen packing their toolbags and deserting the shop. The moulders noted the growing readiness of masters to sweat out a dispute, calculating that the men might give in when dispute pay ran out. In that proud and well organised trade it was observed that some tramping members, exhausted after a 1,500-mile trek of the circuit seeing their families go hungry or into the workhouse, could not always resist the temptation to work in a 'struck' shop.

Consolidation, when it went along with 'static' or 'at home' unemployment pay, meant more stable branches, while the old system sometimes put whole branches on the road. It meant steadily growing membership and funds. It meant increasing public recognition, that is to say increasing recognition from a mainly middle-class opinion which had begun to shed the guilty fears of the 1830s (when the engineers were looked on as 'a band of secret desperadoes'). The basis for increased membership was perhaps the industrial prosperity, between bouts of unemployment, of the 1850s and 1860s. But the ability to draw in and hold a larger membership (a two- or threefold increase among moulders, engineers and boilermakers) through times of bad and good trade – when the cost was measured in tens of thousands of pounds – depended upon stronger central organisation. Between 1865 and 1868, when membership of the ASE rose from 28,000 to 33,000, unemployment benefit payments shot up from £14,000 to £68,000 a year.

Those unions which failed to reorganise lost ground or disappeared from view for decades. In almost every case of difficulty or failure, the problem was that of the unemployed, of tramping. In October and November 1844, the Philanthropic Society of Boot and Shoemakers, which had 'jogged along for 50 years' and which we met in Chapter 4, and the Cordwainers' Mutual Assistance Association came face to face in an amalgamation meeting at the Craven Head, Drury Lane, London. There was a good deal of good-humoured banter, and a deal of recrimination about tramps and strike breaking and mutual threats – 'simply this, if you continue to stop our cards, we must stop yours'. But there was more to it than a failure to agree about the mutual recognition of tramping cards.

Clark (Philanthropic): 'I must contend our code of rules is more democratic than yours. Yours is what I call centralised democracy.'

Skelton (Mutual): 'Men go from the Metropolis to other towns and drive men out to become their opponents and this same system is being carried on by all trades for want of an efficient executive.'

The boot and shoe amalgamation was formed and on paper it was a powerful body with the Philanthropic having 3,000 members in London alone. But it was not able to build a stable national organisation. No more was the Tailors' Trade Protection and Mutual Benefit, with '30 or 40 towns now in union with the Metropolis', whose new rule book was published in the spring of 1844. Both boot and shoe and tailoring workers found that the old tramping method of winning a strike was no longer effective when much larger numbers were involved. In 1859, when mechanisation was already seriously weakening their organisation, the boot and shoe men struck. Strike money was shared out among those who tramped out, as was done in the great strike of 1812. But whereas in 1812 some provision was made for families, they were left in 1859 with 'little to subsist on'. In 1812 the result was victory, in 1859 defeat. In 1812 hand work was king, in 1859 boot-closing machinery was already in use in several areas and the manufacturers were able to send away parts to be made up elsewhere.

The tailoring strike in London in 1867 saw 2,000 out of 2,800 strikers leaving town, 200 to emigrate. But in the words of the union history the 'policy of subsidising men to leave London . . . in line with tradition . . . was afterwards seen to have been something of a blunder.' For many of those who set off on tramp got no further than the outer suburbs of the City where they displaced non-union labour and widened the breach between union men and the rest of the workers in the industry.

Still, the newly-formed tailors' 'Amalgamated' of 1867 survived the strike. While the employers were recovering the money they had spent on strike breaking from the profits brought in by the Singer machine, newly imported from the United States, the union built up a membership of between 14,000 and 17,000 during the 1880s. But the boot and shoe union found stable organisation in 1874 only when a group of branches seceded after finding they could not 'amend the laws of the old Cordwainers' Union'. Beginning with just over 4,000, the breakaway kept pace with the old organisation during the 1870s and 1880s but by 1890 was six times as strong.

Both trades, however, retained earlier forms of equalisation and, though reluctantly, the old tramping system, for neither had the funds to introduce static unemployment pay. But the Tailors' 'Amalgamated' insisted on one 'uniform card' issued by the Executive Council.

Another smaller amalgamation, the basket makers', which grew out of a 'federation for trade and tramping purposes' in the 1860s, nearly broke up when one party seceded in protest at an attempt to abolish tramping and bring in home donation.

Much more protracted was the struggle for unity among the printers' societies. The National Typographical Association, joining the northern compositors and those of London, Ireland and Scotland in 1845, aimed at static unemployment pay in order, as the Liverpool delegate charmingly put it at the amalgamation conference, 'to annihilate the Arab-like propensity of those who brought pecuniary embarrassment upon the profession'. The new organisation, the NTA, was to have districts co-ordinated by a corresponding secretary, a centralising move which caused some alarm among the various societies. But not so great an alarm as that pretended to by the editor of *The Times*, who like his predecessor of the 1790–1820 period kept a close, hostile eye on the unions. On 11 November 1845 he declared that the 'little squabbles' of towns or districts were not very important, but 'introduce a foreign power . . . the Great Central Committee, after deliberating in darkness decides in folly.' The compositors defended themselves by explaining that each central decision was the work of '45 practical working men' and went on to lay down the essentials of a new organisation.

Instead of the total confusion of tramp payments, 1s 6d in Brighton, 3s 6d in Manchester, 1s 4d in Leicester – 2s 6d in Birmingham 1s in Aylesbury – there would be a uniform unemployment allowance of six shillings a week: 'Not so great an inducement as to cause idleness'.

By the end of 1846 the new NTA had seventy-four branches; by 1848 it had broken up. The London men and the Scots had withdrawn, the London men in particular being hostile to tramping, or at least to the arrival in their shops of tramps from the country societies. The Irish members remained; indeed money from Dublin helped the organisation stay afloat a while. But by the 1850s the new Provincial Typographical Association, formed from the remains of the 'National', was retrenching and consolidating alone.

At first attempts were made to enforce a uniform tramping card, but 'branches recently have been at some expense in setting up elaborate designs'. But in 1851 a 'register of cards in circulation' was proposed with the Executive alone being allowed to issue cards. It was noted that 'a similar plan is adopted advantageously in other trades'. The 'register' when it finally took effect proved to be the starting-point for the union's journal.

But still further retreat and retrenchment was to come. The Dublin printers pointed out that their society and others 'established for upholding the interests of the trade were under great disadvantage in being necessitated to support members of societies established for the relief of tramps only'. Their protest in December 1850 let loose a flood of demands from other societies trying to uphold trade standards that they were being held back by the 'mere tramp societies'. The sooner a check in the system takes place the better for the profession, declared Shields. In June 1851, the Executive Committee announced the 'temporary dishonouring' of cards issued by societies existing simply for tramping. 'If individual hardship should occur to their own members in consequence they will only have to thank their own supineness and neglect or what is still worse an obstinate refusal to co-operate in a laudable attempt to benefit the profession.'

But the 'mere tramp societies' would not go away, nor would their wandering members stay away from the more organised and industrially militant towns. A solution was found in 1863 when an Association for Relief of Unemployed Travelling Printers was formed with a separate fund. London, Scotland and Dublin kept clear of it.

The Scots decided that the penny-a-mile relief system proposed simply fostered tramping. The Relief Association which took the care of the casual wanderer off the backs of the more active trade unionists had an up and down career, sometimes making a surplus, sometimes draining money from PTA funds. But it led to good in the end for by the late 1870s many of the 'mere tramp societies' had come fully into the PTA and by the time the Relief Association was wound up regular home unemployment relief had been introduced. Even in his declining years the tramp had made a final contribution to the development of trade unionism.

Hatters were among the pioneer tramping unions but in the 1820s their amalgamation split over the question of apprentice regulations. For sixty years the two rival organisations, the 'blue' and the 'white' ticket men, refused to accept each other's 'clearances' and even broke each others strikes until the disputes were resolved in the 1880s.

Rival bricklayers' organisations – one, the more powerful based on Manchester, the other on London constantly invaded each other's territory, and in 1864, after the Manchester men 'under the sanction of their EC had treated our men harshly when they were in search of work', London men from the Leamington lodge had a 'chance of retaliating' by taking over a 'job' in their rivals' base town. This successful tramp raid brought a truce, with each side allowed to attend the other's lodge meetings, though not to speak. The London-based union however continued to advance, its roving organisers penetrating 'Manchester' areas. During the 1869 lock-out these infiltrators worked on jobs where the Manchester men were in dispute. The London leader, Coulson, had gone too far and his own rank and file repudiated him, but the dispute went on and in 1872 Coulson was complaining about 'childish, mischievous and disgraceful conduct' by Manchester. The builders with their long migratory traditions were not able to get away from the tramping system and it proved difficult to avoid such disputes until the much larger scale amalgamations of the twentieth century.

More instructive still is the story of the two carpenters' unions. The oldest, the Friendly Society of Operative Carpenters or the 'General Union', dated from 1827 and during the big anti-contracting struggle of the 1830s was said to have nearly 7,000 members. If correct this is a greater membership than any other single union was ever to have until the 1850s. The General Union maintained an old-style organisation in which local autonomy and the tramp network had precedence over central organisation. Members of the Royal Commission in 1867 were surprised to hear Robert Last, the union secretary, say that his central funds never amounted to more than £500, this at a time when the boilermakers were spending double that amount on their old age pensioners alone.

'Do you mean that you have never more than £500 in hand?' Last was asked.

'Each branch retains its own funds after paying its proportionate share of the expenses of the whole society,' he answered. Local autonomy was complete. Each lodge provided for its own tramps and sent notices to the others ('Rochdale desires Oldham, Burnley and Rossendale' to square their accounts). By the 1860s the General Union was not only down to nearly 2,000 members, but was being challenged by a rival Amalgamated Society of Carpenters and Joiners. The amalgamation was in fact a grouping of London clubs but it had taken a leaf from the book of the formidable ASE, or rather two leaves: the first was out-of-work pay at home and the other, the (for builders) exceptionally high subscription of one shilling a week to pay for it. The masons, for example, stuck at sixpence a week for some time to come.

The ASCJ used its range of benefits to campaign through the country, blatantly poaching the members of the older union. At a rally in Belfast, after leader Robert Applegarth had emphasised the 10s a week out-of-work pay, the chairman, Brother Hunter, then went on to justify the centralised organisation which backed it:

Local societies were certainly a great advance over no society at all and had the means of locomotion remained in the position it was 50 years ago they would be perhaps sufficient to meet the requirements of the present time, but as steam has cast aside the barriers that separated the workmen of different cities and towns and offers them easy facilities for removing their labour from where the market is over-supplied to where it is in demand, draws on the necessity of a society which shall extend the hand of friendship to every worker no matter what locality he hails from.

By the end of the 1860s the new ASCJ had nearly 10,000 members and the leaders of the old 'General Union' responded by taking a leaf out of the book of the Amalgamated. It was not easy, as the union historian reports. 'The change to a more centralised and businesslike [system] ... was not without opposition. Lodges took exception to the replacement of the old tramping system with out of work benefit.' Robert Last, in May 1863, urged lodges not to be 'terrified by phantoms'. The new system would be 'more beneficial, less costly'. So vigorous was the General Union's counter-attack that by the end of the 1860s it had drawn level with its challenger. Although the pace was to prove too hot for the old union, it nevertheless took a fresh lease of life into the early 1900s.

The cabinet makers, who were not over-enthusiastic about the tramping system, concentrated their organisation in 1838, separating the English from the Irish societies. In 1846, the twenty-nine societies in England became branches of the reformed union and the regulations on tramping were tightened up.

In 1840, after some heated arguments over tramp payments in which the Irish were alleged to be twice too generous, the English masons too separated from the Irish. The separations should not be misunderstood, for the Irish masons, like men in other trades, were also on the way to setting up their own organisation. And tramping masons continued to be relieved between the two countries as between England and Scotland, though in the late 1830s the English imposed more stringent conditions on the travelling Scots. This edginess did not, however, prevent English and Scots masons from helping one another generously in other ways.

The English masons had a single organisation from the beginning and thus no amalgamation problems. There was strong tension though between a stubbornly independent rank and file and a centralising leadership, or rather leader, for Richard Harnott, who ruled (and that is no figure of speech) the masons from the late 1840s until his death in the 1870s, dominated the whole of this phase of union organisation. He was often at odds with the lodges and he strove to link them more closely to the executive, to control their spending and their striking, and to streamline the decision-making process among nearly 300 lodges. During the 1859 lock-out in London the men were so incensed by Harnott's attempt to 'settle' the dispute that they kidnapped him and held him under guard in a room at the Sun Inn, Mason Street, Lambeth, a stronghold of the builders' unions and those of other trades.

Nor was Harnott alone in his wish to restrain his members from striking. When the Amalgamated Society of Joiners and Carpenters was formed, one of the rules borrowed from the engineers' book was 'no strike without EC sanction'. *The Times* in its alarm at the decision by the National Typographical Association in 1846 to have sole control over the power to strike, was ignorant of the outlook of the new men. They were concerned to stop rather than to call strikes. 'Would to God', wrote one observer in 1867, 'it were as difficult for an English Ministry to involve the Empire in hostilities as it is generally for a Trade Society to enter upon a strike.'

But facile contrasting of 'militants' and 'moderates' should be avoided. Between, say, Harnott and the masons' rank and file two antagonistic but yet justifiable points of view were clashing. Harnott's is summed up by the building workers' historian as a determination to keep as many men at work as possible and thus build up union funds. His opponents urged militant action in time of good trade to build up the closed shop – 'no non-union member need apply'. This led to a tug of war over the role of the tramp, one side trying to cut expenditure and the other seeing this as a threat to the use of the tramp system to aid industrial militancy. Though Harnott had to caution the more enthusiastic economisers 'to handle this subject in a careful manner' for fear of 'harming honourable members who cannot avoid the use of tramp laws', it is considered that tramping among the masons began to die out during his term of office. And it was during Harnott's time that the masons had a new emblem designed showing, according to the official description, 'Prudence with her bridle . . . restraining profuse and needless expenditure'.

The boilermakers from 1845 on tightened up not only on tramp benefit but on the 'considerable looseness' in the use of lodge funds. Those who, for example, broke into the general fund to buy a banner were told to meet the cost out of their own pockets. In similar tones to those of the Merchant Tailors' Company rebuking its 'bachelors' in 1609 (see Chapter 3) the boilermakers' lodges were warned against spending too much on 'anniversary dinners and excursions'. Boilermakers' organisations outside the main body were accepted into it only on condition they handed over all their funds.

Along with centralised control over spending went increasing discrimination in the treatment of the unemployed. Twenty-year members among the boilermakers could draw their money at home. Others walked for their money getting 1s 6d a day for fourteen weeks. Men with less than twelve months' service ('non-free members') were allowed a bed for the night only when on travel. During the Clyde boilermakers' lockout in 1868, benefit men with less than twenty years were 'ordered out on the road'.

Members of the Royal Commission on Trade Unions in 1867 were baffled by the distinctions between 'too old to work' and 'too old to travel', and the patient explanations of John Allen, the boilermakers' leader, did not seem to make much impression on his audience. They did not understand for example the distinction between 'fares' and travelling'.

John Allen told them that since 1852 his union had a rule: 'If an employer or a foreman has a particular desire for a certain person and that person is out of employment we go to the expense of paying that man's fare or travelling money to send him to that employer.' For fares the union paid £259 in a year.

'But', added Allen, no doubt wiping the smiles of comprehension from his listeners' faces, 'that is different from a man travelling the other way.' 'The other way', the traditional method of tramping, cost the union in the same year £15,698.

'It is a large sum, is it not?' asked the Commissioners. They had good reason to be baffled for, over sixty years of operation, the old bread, cheese and beer system had become very complicated and the rules governing it had multiplied. As tramping became less universal and more 'voluntary' and thus involved a smaller and smaller proportion of union members, a kind of Parkinson's Law developed. The fewer tramps the more rules, until the Amalgamated Tailors, who did all they could to discourage tramping, had as many as twenty-three tramping rules on their books. Given the various grades of membership the complexities which developed were those beloved of lawyers, amateur and professional.

In January 1858, the ASE rule book laid down that non-free members were to get a bed or fourpence for a bed in each town or city, but not more than one bed even 'where there are more branches than one', secretaries disregarding this had to pay out of their own pockets. The next year a branch asked if a non-free member who had lost his job through drunkenness was entitled to a bed while on tramp, adding innocently that 'the rules are silent on this point'. The general secretary, having minutely consulted the rule book, replied with some asperity: 'A free member is not, so quite clearly a non-free member cannot be.'

The new distinction introduced by the boilermakers between selected members dispatched to jobs awaiting them and those paid to travel speculatively caused its own complications. The ironmoulders, or as they now called themselves the ironfounders, adopted the 'fares' system in 1858. And immediately disputes arose. From Southampton to Cambridge 'cannot be a distance of 360 miles', wrote the founders' general secretary, dismissing an over-ambitious branch claim.

The fewer tramps, the more rules; the more rules, the more infringements; the more infringements, the more revisions; and the more revisions, the greater the impulse towards central control. Full-time officials preferred the newer way of revision by delegate conference to the old process of 'balloting' through the branches inherited from the 'federal' days. The struggle between the two forms was protracted in the custom-bound building trades. In 1838 the masons' corresponding secretary demanded of his members: 'Those trades who periodically employ deputies to revise their laws, do they attempt to alter them at any other period?' He asked branches to put forward rules-revision proposals only during the period before delegate meetings. But it was many years before lodges surrendered their ancient right to appeal, through the fortnightly returns, to the verdict of the entire membership. In 1868, during a dispute over whether to cut out the tramps' Sunday allowance (double money), the bricklayers' Executive Committee, finding itself defeated by a branch ballot, had the result reversed by the annual delegate meeting.

As tramp numbers decreased, so concern over the cost increased. Union leaders were preoccupied, if not obsessed, with the funds, and not without reason. In the 1840s they dealt in thousands of pounds. In the 1860s they dealt in tens of thousands. The fluctuations in funds in times of unemployment were sudden and alarming. The moulders/founders saw out-of-work pay leap in one year from £14,000 to £35,000, a 'decrease in funds of £20,000 which calls forth our deepest regret'. 'In two years we have expended for unemployed labour alone (and that not caused by any act of their own but simply through circumstances over which they have no control) the large sum of £66,864 3s 6d.' Average numbers out of work were over 2,000, a fifth of the membership, though on the books, at least, only a hundred or two hundred were on the roads.

The ASE spent £18,000 a year on the jobless during the 1860s when nearly 10 per cent of its 30,000 members were unemployed and around 300 registered as on the road. At this time, too, the general union of carpenters which had now 'fairly established benevolent benefits' spent only £1 on tramps for every £20 spent on unemployed men at home.

Substantial funds meant more than the security of the union in the eyes of the new leaders. They were also a passport to respectability, a signal to public opinion – at least to the opinion of lawgivers and the writers of newspaper editorials – that unions should be recognised. During this period the major unions began to publish not only their yearly accounts, but abstracts not simply for the benefit of their members but to influence public opinion. In 1871, Harnott, the masons' leader, pointed out that in eight years the union had spent as much as in the previous twenty-three. He added that publication of these figures 'defies the anti-unionist to sustain his abhorrence of trade unions as useless and ineffective institutions'. This was precisely the argument of critical pamphlets of the day, which claimed that 'thrift' did more for the working class than any unions.

This was a sore point. As the active trade unionists knew, their organisations and their predecessors had always had friendly benefits as one of their main aims. This had been true in the early years of the century when they had been regarded as 'band of secret desperadoes' and was more true in the mid-century years of consolidation. The working class and skilled workers above all did not need to be taught 'thrift' by their betters. This had long been one of their qualities, as acute observers had been aware since the late eighteenth century. Engels in the 1840s quotes an eminent churchman on the subject: 'The poor give one another more than the rich give the poor.' During the first sixty years of the century the Friendly Society Orders, like the Oddfellows and Foresters had seen their memberships grow to the half-million mark. Such was the thirst for 'self-help' that commercial companies like the Prudential (avoiding insuring people in certain towns and streets where life was considered too fragile) had enrolled a million members. This kind of self-help had its admirers.

Lord Elcho made a speech reported in *The Times* in January 1867 in which he said that the unions 'are the means by their sick fund, their accident fund and their death fund . . . by their funds for supplying men when out of employment, of keeping men off the poor rate'.

Henry Mayhew, writing seventeen years earlier had been a good deal more blunt. With three million members in 33,000 friendly societies paying out £3 million in benefits, a sum greater than the total poor rate, the middle class 'were indebted to the working class'. A writer in the *North British Review* of October 1870 (perhaps Thomas Hughes) took the argument a stage forward, and historically perhaps a stage backwards, when he said: 'The unions perform a work [unemployment pay] which would otherwise be incumbent on employers and towards which in the time of the guilds they contributed.'

Hughes went even further and defended the tramping system in terms of political economy. Thanks to the system, 'freedom of locomotion is a reality'. It assured a 'prompt supply of labour' from places where there was no demand to where it was needed. But he reassured his readers that 'members on tramp are under special control'.

The coin of thrift and benevolence had two sides. What was to the alert middle-class observer a saving on the rates was to the Birmingham masons security against the 'horrid alternative' of the 'Bastille' or workhouse. This was nothing new, for the battle against insecurity and poverty was unending. But what was happening in this period was the recognition by some of the middle class in a spirit, of mingled compassion and self-interest, of this long, silent struggle for survival in decency. Thus a strange dialogue began between the independence and pride of working-class people and the hard-headed social conscience of the well-to-do.

Sometimes it took an uncomfortable turn for the former. The *Typographical Circular* noted in May 1849: 'The trade is partially maintaining a local poor law . . . under which pauper aid is dispersed to its casual poor, the ratepayer being the employed and the guardians thereof the society's officers.'

Indeed, Tid Pratt, who became Registrar General of Friendly Societies, viewed with awe the way this 'poor law' was administered. When he asked friendly society officials if half the basic wage was enough for those out of work they shook their heads and warned against paying more than a third. Some sixty years later, Board of Trade investigators noted shrewdly how 'self-governing associations' were able to help people find work but had a 'financial interest to find solutions and watch that the society is not being defrauded'. Their system compared very favourably as a means of 'checking imposture' with charity organisations and Poor Law grants. Charles Booth noted the 'immense amount of experience accumulated by the unions' in conducting relief, a point duly appreciated in the twentieth century by William Beveridge, as he began to draft his schemes for welfare benefits. The foundations of the Welfare State, with all its blessings and its meanness, were already laid among the working class some two hundred years before. What happened in the mid-nineteenth century was that middle-class opinion awoke to this realisation.

To sustain sick and out-of-work funds, the engineers imposed seventy levies on their members between 1850 and 1890. And the brushmakers noted: 'The men suffer untold levies such as no other organisation dare inflict and none but union men would pay.' That was the crucial difference. The discipline was self imposed – 'discipline actuated by love and sympathy', claimed the hatters. But it was accepted by the members in the expectation that the union would stand by them in work as well as out. Middle-class opinion was not as ready to accept the one as it was the other, that the discipline governing friendly benefits might be applied to 'trade purposes'. Behind the faint smiles of recognition the old hostilities remained and the ironfounders' general secretary said, after the meetings of the Royal Commission on Trade Unions in 1867:

As far as the majority of the Commissioners is concerned they do not seem to be much wiser on trade union matters than when they first began their labours. Their chief aim and object seems to have been to gather together all the bad they possibly could in connection with our associations and forget or overlook anything which would be calculated to put us before the country on anything like a favourable position.

The greater freedom and security of organisation for trade unions which came from the 1871 Trade Union Act following the Royal Commission discussion came as much from union pressure as from the sweetening of 'public' opinion. At the 1867 general election, in which the working men of the towns had the vote for the first time, the carpenters' leaders pointed out:

Several distinguished societies aided by the different trades councils throughout the kingdom . . . most of the candidates of all shades of opinion . . . have been catechised on questions that have a direct bearing on the interests of unionists and upwards of 300 aspirants to seats in the new Parliament have made trade unions the text of their addresses, whilst a great majority have pledged themselves to support any well considered measure for the protection of their funds.

At the height of this agitation, the first meeting of the Trades Union Congress took place in 1868. It was a partial realisation of the attempts at 'general union' but it was primarily directed to seeking public legal recognition of the right to organise. The TUC 'parliamentary committee' was in fact the basis for what later became the 'General Council'.

To the craft union leaders it seemed that public recognition was at last coming to them. To the middle class it seemed that the 'revolutionaries' of yesteryear had become more statesmanlike. But as yet there was still a good distance between respectable opinion and the outlook of the working class generally. Here was still ample scope for the eager reformer, not least in the habits and life style of the rank-and-file trade unionist.

Much of the reforming zeal was directed to urging the workers, and not least the organised ones, not only to thrift, in which they were already well schooled, but also to sobriety, where the schooling was less apparent. A good deal of the money which often goes with moral reform was put into the newspapers and pamphlets of the temperance movement and into some 1,500 coffee-houses designed to win the worker away from the 'beer shop'. As the slogan went:

> A public house without the drink
> Where men may read and smoke and think
> and sober home return. . . .

A great deal of that money was lost on these coffee-houses when workers generally declined to sit around drinking 'sparkling milk' instead of ale. Indeed, the temperance campaign might have had little or no effect on organised workers if there had not already been a hard core of opinion within the union movement linking discipline with sobriety. 'No more sotting and swearing in alehouses on Mondays like vagabonds as usual,' the cordwainers had said in the 1790s. Attempts to limit drinking customs and laws among the unions had been successful on one estimate by 1849. Fines and footings are almost done away with,' claimed Lovett.

Whether one believed, as a Yorkshire union man told J. M. Ludlow, that more regular work meant 'no Saint Mondays or play days' or, with the carpenters' union, that more temperate habits brought better conditions, opinion in favour of drinking control would have developed inside the unions irrespective of outside pressure.

But outside pressure was applied often in a less than winning manner. James Samuelson in his *Trade Unions and Public Houses* (1871) declared that because of meetings in public houses nine-tenths of the 'tyranny and violence of the unions' was 'suffered in silence', because the sober were oppressed by the 'intemperate men' who hatched 'their secret plots over a glass of grog or a pot of beer'. Unions should be encouraged to transfer meetings, as had the Liverpool unions, to an 'Operatives' Hall. They should be compelled to stop receiving union dues in public houses where wives and daughters sent to pay in for the head of the family had to run the gauntlet of the looks and comments of those at the bar.

Internal and external pressure could limit drinking, but it could not so easily stop unions from meeting in public houses. In 1867, the first and only *UK Directory of Trade Societies*, with over 2,000 addresses in some 400 towns, includes only a handful of non-pub addresses and (mainly in Scotland) temperance hotels and coffee-shops. The overwhelming majority of unions still met in public houses. Even in the early 1900s it was reckoned that 70 per cent of trade union organisations met in pubs, despite the efforts of the Trade Union and Labour Officers' Temperance Fellowship (1904), who claimed that because of the custom 'no less than 50,000 men, women and children visited public houses every day'. Arthur Pugh, under whose leadership the steel union branches radically reduced their connection with pubs, indicated one reason why the custom survived. Unions 'had no reason to thank the Temperance Party' which would not let the religious halls it controlled to unions because of a 'prejudice against "agitators"'. As late as 1907 efforts through the press in London to appeal for non-drinking accommodation for unions brought only one reply from a religious organisation.

The unions stuck to public houses. There was the old need for 'conviviality' which in the summer of 1866 took carpenters and bricklayers to the Sun Inn, Maidstone, for a celebration and cricket match. The bricklayers won by four runs. Pub accommodation was friendly and it was cheap. As Samuelson sourly noted, the annual rent was 'trifling'. Few branches had the funds to buy or build their own premises. Nor, one might add, were Samuelson and his allies rushing forward to help.

The pub fulfilled its trade functions, as meeting place, and as labour exchange, with the vacant book still hanging behind the bar. Though, as the London tailors had realised by the 1860s, the house of call without the closed shop worked against the unions, keeping the men 'hanging about' in the bar rooms. Active union bakers out of work resented being greeted by the spongers' cry 'What are you going to stand?'

The most important reason for staying in the public houses remained, however, the needs of the tramping member. For all the introduction of home donation, many union members were still on tramp in the 1870s and 1880s, particularly in slump years. 'Non-free' members, particularly the young, in unions like the engineers and boilermakers, were offered no benefit other than a bed for the night on their travels. Even in 1892 the ASE had to tell its branches to ensure their meeting places, 'where practicable', had sleeping accommodation 'at reasonable cost'. In 1861 the Belfast engineers proudly announced the opening of a new house they had rented with meeting hall and bedrooms for tramps. There is little sign that the example was followed, though. As Liverpool bricklayers found, a move to a preferred public house had to be cancelled because the new host would not accept the tramp. Back they had to go, no doubt in some embarrassment, to the old house.

Some unions gave their non-free members fourpence, leaving them to find their own night's accommodation in a cheap lodging house. In the 1860s the Doncaster branch of the ASE warned tramps to steer clear during race week when the cost of a bed for the night went up to five shillings. But the engineers, who like other unions heard complaints of beds 'not sufficiently good and clean' for members, increased the bed allowance in the 1880s to eightpence, and later to one shilling, though other unions still allowed only sixpence a night in the early 1900s.

The tramp was no longer typical of the union. Where home donation was paid, tramps made up no more than 10 per cent of the unemployed. But he could not be made to disappear, even though in the second half of the nineteenth century much thought and effort was directed to this end.

In this period trade union leaders were beginning to mix with MPs and cabinet ministers. Applegarth of the carpenters was able by personal lobbying of Gladstone in 1865 to obtain permission for union branches to use the Post Office Savings Bank. They were beginning to secure the guarded admiration of some of the intelligentsia. They had become, in the words of the carpenters, 'respectful and respected'.

In this atmosphere, customs and peculiarities like tramping became, if not an embarrassment, then a little difficult to explain, as Allen of the Boilermakers found before the Royal Commission, whose members were puzzled why this worthy body of men should not only pay men to roam the roads, but compel them to do it.

True, only some of the tramps actually tramped. Some were sent direct to new jobs. Even those who moved about the country looking for work made use of cheaper fares to cut across areas where common sense told them there was little point in searching. Thus already in the 1840s the moulders/founders and the coachmakers had already renamed the tramp 'traveller'. The masons made the change in 1861–2 and the compositors a decade later. The masons also amended their records to read not 'on tramp' but 'supposed to be in search of employment', a term with an edge to it. There was indeed, perhaps, another motive for changing the name. 'Tramp', which originally meant someone who walks, had over the years taken on a darker meaning for the respectable. Wright, the roving engineer, protested in 1868 that the word conjured up in the public mind the image of a 'lurching garrotter like figure', when all it meant was a working man travelling on foot to find work. Skilled moulders obliged to go on tramp had been shocked at having to 'mingle with the refuse of society in the tap' and to discover that 'in public estimation' the status of the union tramp was little above that of 'common vagrancy'. Respectable opinion, half-convinced that a man not working is a man who does not want to work, had its prejudices confirmed by finding the man tramping the roads.

'It is vulgarly called tramp benefit,' wrote George Howell, trade union leader and historian. 'To tramp or in politer terms travel the country,' said the writer of a pamphlet about the boot and shoe trade. Slowly then, from the mid-nineteenth century onwards 'tramp' disappears from union official vocabulary to be replaced by 'traveller'.

And slowly his figure, which had adorned the processions and emblems of shoemakers, hatters, moulders, coachmakers and boilermakers, vanished from them. Significantly it began to be replaced by that of the union organiser, Gladstone bag in hand, calling on the grateful sick and bereaved with friendly benefits. The boilermakers, whose first emblem, like that of the moulders, showed the tramp being greeted by the yard foreman above the union motto 'Nothing human is alien to me', redesigned it in the early 1870s. The tramp vanished and the new motto was 'God helps those who help themselves'.

As he vanished in image, he was also expected to become less visible in reality. By the 1850s and 1860s the rules of engineers, masons, moulders and tailors expressly forbade the tramp to call at the workshop, much less shake the foreman by the hand. The foreman in the yard was by now much less likely to be a society man, having perhaps, under pressure from the employer, quit the union to join a separate foreman's organisation.

But the 'don't call' rule had another motive. The arrival of the tramp was 'tending to injure the respectability of the society with the employer', said the founders/moulders.

In being renamed a traveller, the tramp was not rising in the esteem of his fellows, but falling. In the past the roving craftsman as tramp had been seen as something of a hero. Now as traveller he was regarded as something of a villain.

13 Flying Brethren and Common Cadgers – the Tramps at their worst

Slowly transformed from hero to villain, from asset to nuisance, diminishing in numbers and in respect, the tramp did, however, become more and more a preoccupation of the union lawmakers. The masons 'tramp law' had eighteen clauses, the tailors twenty-three clauses and the ironfounders, even in 1917, had fourteen clauses. The tailors, indeed, deliberately multiplied their laws to reduce the number of tramps, until by the 1890s they had banished them from the union records and funds, if not from the roads. The ASE leaders conducted the most persistent campaign against offending tramps between 1899 and 1912, when less than one in a thousand of the union's rapidly growing membership were regularly on the road.

Recurring mass unemployment, more rapid travel, better communication – through the 'state of trade' sections in the union journals not least – had convinced most members it was pointless to set off to the next town in the hope that there was work. On the other hand, the constant growth of industry, heightening each boom as it deepened each slump, convinced them that trade would revive. Meanwhile better sweat out the hard times at home with the family than on the road. This seems to have been true in trades where home donation was the rule and in those where tramping or travelling benefit was the only one paid. The roads, save for times of depression, were left to the voluntary tramp. And as the unions turned from the system, with union officials leading the way in a more stringent interpretation of the rule book, so impatience grew with the minority of members who chose to tramp, the 'roadsters'.

The contrast between the relative comfort with which members might be sent by rail to available jobs and the discomfort and even squalor in which the man 'working the circuit' (what was once a point of honour became a term of discredit) made his way, began to express itself in a distaste for the member who would put up with such conditions. From there it was one step to equating the traveller with the professional tramp, someone the roving craftsmen of the past had viewed with contempt.

Union members as well as their leaders were uncomfortably aware that they had 'professionals' among their own ranks and angrily aware that imposters from outside could exploit the system they had built up to care for their own members. The system was as open to abuse as any system of welfare has always been and the perennial problem of sorting out the guilty while not humiliating and penalising the innocent was more and more a matter of controversy. Those who wanted to discard the system made the distinction between guilty and innocent less frequently. At the same time, deciding who was what became a source of friction between national and local officials, the one upholding the funds and the rules, the other having to deal with the human being, however unpopular, however suspicious. The tramp was going down with the system and his offences multiplied with the rules designed to curb them. Tramps were accused of strike breaking, working foul in shops banned by the union because of bad conditions, of theft, abuse, violence, indecency, fraud and embezzlement of various kinds, but above all with using the system to avoid work rather than find it, with 'chasing the sixpences' or 'working the ticket'.

They had their benefit cut, they were fined, their cards were blocked, they were suspended and eventually 'excluded', which meant that in union shops they would never get a job, as the steel union secretary later pointed out. And as a last resort they were handed over to the law. Thus the system, which in its heyday was a means of guaranteeing employment and safety from prosecution, in its decline turned into the very opposite.

Government officials had been impressed at the severity with which union friendly benefits were administered. But no one from the outside could feel the fury of union members with those they saw as abusing the system they had created, and living as parasites on the money they had subscribed. The violence of language used in union records against defaulting tramps, the scorn and loathing, would give the impression that a horde of scroungers was at work. Yet in the 1890s, when the tailors dealt the death blow to the system by restricting travelling cards to those more than two years in the union, no more than 2 per cent of members were tramping.

A minority of members were still tramping out of choice, and within that minority, to judge from the brief lists of offenders in union reports, an even tinier minority broke the rules and 'brought disgrace' on the organisation. When in 1899 the ASE devoted a section of its journal under the heading 'The lazy and the artful' to the activities of only five men out of a membership of 84,000 one may well suspect the leadership were making a mountain out of a molehill. But the annoyance caused by a few could go a long way.

It would be wrong to suggest that the problem of the bad tramp arose only in the twilight of the system. To travel the roads even as a trade tramp was to live on the wits, and no craftsman could avoid contact with the 'gentlemen' of the roads, avoid influencing or being influenced by them. Just as, in Elizabethan times, vagabonds' organisation was a parody of that of the crafts, so in 1865 the 'Irish cabinet maker' and the 'York spinner' scratched their names on the workhouse walls along with 'Welsh Ned', 'Sailor Jack', 'The Lancashire Crab' and 'The Islington Kid'. A writer in a magazine of the 1860s asserted that common lodging houses had a list of 'charitably disposed persons' in the neighbourhood who might be touched for money – in imitation it seems of the trade tramp's vacant book. Written around 1900, the working-class novel *Harry Welford*, which appeared in instalments in the steel union journal, describes a night's entertainment in a lodging house, a 'tumble down dwelling in an evil smelling lane' where the waiters were known as 'tilers' in imitation of the masons' lodge and there were fines for any tramp who failed to address another as 'brother'.

The ranks of the vagrants were fed by industry's outcasts. In the London workhouses, Mayhew discovered lads recruited as 'apprentices' to almost every trade ending in the workhouse where perhaps some of them had been born. Most, said Mayhew, had developed an 'impatience of steady labour'. Or, one might add, the reward for 'steady labour' being the street, they had learned to live on their wits. As the cynical couplet of later depression years had it:

> He who works and does his best,
> Goes down the road with all the rest.

The professional tramps streamed into the cities during the harsh winters, then made their way out in the springtime, moving north, keeping pace, as one observer noted, 'by the ripening of the grass crop' or, as one old tramp remarked, when he could 'put his foot on two daisies'.

To Mayhew the tramping system was evil in itself. He thought it 'almost a necessity that any such system should be the means of har- bouring and fostering the idle and the vagabond'. The encouragement of tramping eradicated 'former habits of industry' and transformed the worker into the beggar. George Howell shared his view, believing that the tramp system, before the rules were tightened, was 'little better than professional mendicity'. Howell's view echoes that of a writer in the

Pioneer of 1833, who accused some building worker tramps of 'plying the trade of licenced pauper'.

When the depressions of the 1840s threw on to the roads thousands of solid union men accustomed to regular work, many of them had experiences they would thereafter recall with deepest indignation. Tramp life, said the Stockport ironmoulders, was 'disreputable ... without a local habitation and a name ... we are regarded with suspicion and jealousy, the most industrious are classed with the idle. If we dare to have a manly bearing at the house of call we are met with the bitter taunt and sarcasm of the stranger that we would rather tramp than work. In the eye of public estimation we are but as one remove above common vagrancy.'

The workhouse keepers told Mayhew that the travelling tradesman obliged to take refuge with vagrants in the 'spike' was generally 'like a bird out of a cage – he dont know where to turn for a bit'. He might sell the shirt off his back before he entered the workhouse, but there were many intermediate stages of impoverishment he might suffer.

Even if his benefit money did not run out, and that often happened in the worst times, he might be faced with far more than a day's march before he reached the next club house. Then it might be a fourpenny bed in a back street lodging house or, as Harry Welford found, a night's kip in the warmth of the brick kilns, if the police left him to sleep in peace. 'Life on the road knocks men up,' Thomas Wright, the roving engineer, said A speaker at a masons' mass meeting in the 1840s said. 'even young men 'on tramp go off very quickly, diseases of the chest most common.'

Under such conditions, noted the tailors, 'good men are demoralised'. 'If they get a shop,' said the moulders, 'they do not retain it.' Charles Manby Smith was told; '... being so often out of work makes a man apt to get fond of lounging about in tap rooms.' Sleeping sometimes 'three in a bed and perhaps three or four beds in the same room' and the beds not always clean despite union inspection, the man who survived the rigours of this life might well do so only at the cost of learning the survival philosophy of those who made it their living.

In 1862, the Scots printers concluded that 'when a man once acquires the habits of the road, he is compelled through force of circumstances to adopt it as his calling.' The tailors said:

They wander through the country from city to town and from town to village, in search of employment. This continues until (upon the mind of an honest man) the thought rests like an incubus: how shall I relieve myself of this degradation?
Devoid of humanity must be the man who is not willing to relieve those

distresses by uniting to support his fellow men travelling in search of employment and wretched must be the character who voluntarily avails himself of such benevolence as a means of existence in preference to honest and respectable employment.

Union members might get the tramping habit early in life. It might go with the nature of the work. Or it might be traditional. 'At one time a man was scarcely considered a good tailor unless he had done his turn on the road.' This tradition also existed among the engineers. At the 1853 ASE delegate conference those arguing against the application of a 40-year age limit for new members remarked that 'young men anxious to gain experience travelled from place to place for that purpose' while the 'more aged member endeavoured to settle'. Young compositors 'traversed the trade' looking for better pay.

Young men, complained the moulders in 1862, might 'pay ten shillings, draw a blank card . . . travel with it . . . draw out more than they have paid in and care no more about it.' They kept the tramping card and were not punished because 'no one knows anything about them'. Worse might happen, as had been noted earlier in the same trade. Young men, particularly, 'who before they went on the road had been very steady and attentive to work, but when they had been two or three times round become quite altered characters, acquired disorderly habits and when they obtain employment, it generally takes some time before they can settle. In many instances they become habituated to tramping and not very solicitous of obtaining work. If they get a shop, they seldom retain it for any great while.'

Young men who became habitual rovers were a cause for concern while they were young. But if they survived by strong constitution and quick wits to become old tramps, then the concern was liable to give way to something else.

'It was a rule with all these old men to work in the winter and as soon as they could put their foot on three daisies at once to go through the country on tramp from one end to another. They liked it much better than work. They could beg on the road and were allowed one penny per mile and breakfast in the morning out of the funds,' complained James Hopkinson, a cabinet maker, recalling the 1840s.

From the 1870s, though, Thomas Kiddier, the brushmaker historian, gives a more sympathetic picture of Mogg, the old tramp:

As a personality, he was above any of us. Perhaps he was better informed than all of us . . . as a talker he was the autocrat of the shop. I myself knew nothing beyond the streets of my own city. James Mogg knew everything. He was like a book. I saw him leave. There was no more work for him. I watched him roll up his apron and stuff it in his pocket. Saw him light his pipe and go to the window and look out. Heard him say: 'Now may the winter of our discontent be made glorious summer ... That's Shakespeare. Bah! only let me put my foot upon two daisies and away I tramp right north – that's Mogg.'

The anonymous writer of the well-informed article 'Trade Tramps' in the magazine *Leisure Hours* (1868) recognised that the tramp was often better informed though less 'moral' than his stay-at-home workmate and warned the employer of the 'risk of introducing him among your apprentices' with his 'drinking habits and worse vices'.

As time went on, the 'idea of settling down grows less vivid', but the yearly round takes its toll. 'Winter is the worst season'; the tramp, 'driven into the lowest lodgings', wages a 'desperate struggle with old age, want and privation'.

Old age is relative of course, given the hardships of the road. The tramp book of William Hall, a brushmaker in his forties, shows a three-year record of wandering up and down from Halifax to Preston, Manchester to Birmingham, working a few weeks here and then on the road again (for tramps were often given the worst work), until after years on the road he is marked first sick and then the word 'dead' is written across by the Blackburn secretary. It is a most pathetic sight.

Noting that the tramps often lived on workshop collections by 'unwritten law', the writer in *Leisure Hours* asked: Why do the tradesmen tolerate it?

Manby Smith, himself a printer – a trade plagued by the casual tramp – made the same point in his memoirs (1853), declaring that what was needed was a 'little firmness and commonsense ... a point blank refusal ... an act of humanity to put an end to their miserable wanderings'.

But still the workshop collections continued even when forbidden by rule. After all, the custom had preceded the rule, and survived it, for even in the twentieth century collections were still made in hatting workshops. There were several reasons why they persisted. The relief scales, which varied from trade to trade, were 'lamentably low', said the brushmakers. Local compositors' societies recognised the problem in the 'low rate of relief, insufficient for the common needs of the road'. The expression used by the masons – 'chasing the sixpences' – speaks for itself.

Many masons knew the pressures on the tramp. 'No use to talk about principle,' said the Stafford men; 'empty bellies, empty pockets, thin clothes, bad shoes and nowhere to sleep. Tramps in this condition are obliged to take what wages are offered.'

And it must be said that the tramp was not as bad as painted, often the reverse. Several times the masons' reports published the names of alleged offenders, sometimes in insulting terms (Joseph Scurr, 'alias Scum'), only to retract later on with a plea from the corresponding secretary that more care should be taken to make only justified accusations.

As late as 1890, the masons' executive felt obliged to reply to a complaint from the Dover lodge: 'They appear to hold a light opinion of our travelling brethren, many of whom carry the society's principles with them and often open up lodges where necessary. We admit that we have been the subject of some little fraud.' But the committee believed benefit paid at home would lead to even more fraud. Henry Broadhurst, masons' leader, later claimed that the masons' tramping system was proof against fraud.

Accounts of fraud and bad behaviour, says the print union historian, were a 'very rare occurrence' and concerned only a minority. Even the threat of having to pay from their own pockets could not deter local secretaries from granting more relief than rules allowed. What, after all, could a humane branch secretary make of the ruling from the head office of the British Steel Smelters' Association in 1898: 'At least 20 miles includes 40 miles or for that matter 80 miles. A moment's consideration would make it plain that this is so. Some office bearers have paid on the assumption that it is two shillings for every 20 miles . . .'

Perhaps the most general sentiment in the minds of the rank and file was that put by a delegate to the Cordwainers' Amalgamation conference in 1844, on the subject of abuse of tramp benefit: 'It does not follow that because we have bad men that we should desert the good (hear hear).'

But 'bad men' there were, or at least men who did intolerable things. Like the compositor named in the Typographical Circular in 1849 who took tramp relief then 'entered a rat (e) hole' – i.e. worked in a shop which did not observe union conditions. What could the unions do? As early as 1812 the hatters decided to bar their turnhouses to 'foul men'. In 1839 the masons' fortnightly report published the names of twenty men who had 'worked against the society' and expelled them. But if men were expelled, they could still work against the union.

The custom among the masons and other trades was to 'treat' potential strike breakers and send them away. It was not a universally popular custom. In 1833 a writer in the *Pioneer* magazine, wrote: 'There are a sort of scamp . . . who take airs . . . threaten to go to work.' Lodges should shake off their 'silly fear' of these men, 'scout them like worms . . . let them get and suck at capital . . . initiate them not'.

But the custom continued and in April 1848 the masons' corresponding secretary was sent to Stalybridge, where a strike was in progress, after a bill for £55 had arrived from the local Moulders' Arms. 'On his arrival he found out that the scene of action for the previous fortnight had been something like a wakes or a fair instead of a strike to the utter disgrace of the officers of the lodge ... the landlord had been so simple as to allow these customers money, meat and drink in abundance under the idea of keeping these unprincipled rascals of blacks from working.' (The bill included two half barrels of ale.)

Two months later, the Sheffield lodge, finding that some men were making 'frivolous objections' to work offered them as an alternative to strike breaking, gave them tramp benefit and escorted them 'out of town in another direction'.

A more frequent cause of trouble in all trades was the tramp who tried by all devices to get more benefit than he was entitled to, by 'blotting out' dates and numbers on cards, by travelling without cards, and by falling 'sick' when his card was 'blocked' by a local branch and 'suddenly recovering' when the card was released. The accusations of 'false pretences' were many and varied and not without their humour. The 'Negro comedian' appearing at a local music hall turned out to be an engineer claiming tramp benefit under another name. Three steelworkers, 'in the habit of walking' the roads of Wales with a harpist, woke the secretary of the Cwmavon lodge to claim benefit, not only for themselves, but for the harpist, a non-union man. 'Orphan Thomas', a mason who had been in the care of the union since birth, had grown up 'a contemptible fellow not at all worthy of the society which had succoured him from infancy'.

The cordwainers decided that 'any individual suspected of making a regular livelihood by being a tramp and proved guilty of the same is to be dealt with as the section where the detection takes place may think proper to determine'. If, said the hatters, his conduct 'convinced the committee that his object was to throw himself on the funds', then he would get no benefit. Men who 'study how to "do" other people' angered the masons in 1880.

Those who 'did not care ... so long as they could live week by week and month by month upon the contributions of our good members without paying anything at all themselves' were condemned by the bricklayers in the same year.

What the Alloa printers nicknamed 'the Flying Brethren', the Birmingham brushmakers described as 'those worthies who come on pleasure' but do not linger in 'our poorly paid, much despised district'. How few, declared the Stalybridge moulders, 'look for a situation'. In between claiming benefit, charged the Cardiff masons, the habitual tramp walked round the district enough to prevent his 'muscles from getting relaxed'.

The printers discussed 'labour direction' in the 1840s, while the Journeymen Steam Engine Makers had already vested their general secretary with discretionary powers to 'remove' a member unwilling to work. The ASE passed this discretionary power down the chain of command to the branch officials backed by the branch meeting, a power also used by the General Union of Carpenters. Along with the power to remove the reluctant worker (if under 50 years of age) went the power to 'detain' if the tramp moved too quickly through the area. If the branch secretary thought work might be found with some effort, 'detention allowance' might be paid. But even 'detention allowance', the iron founders discovered, might be claimed 'tyrannically'. The engineers faced a similar problem and during the 1890s limited detention to four weeks in any area.

Before tramping among the engineers petered out in 1915, this cat-and-mouse game had reached extremes with tramps being allowed neither to stand still nor go. Any man on tramp more than six months was to be investigated. In 1899, the ASE journal reported:

Another incorrigible has been excluded in the person of James Bloxham. This man has been an old manipulator of travelling cards and has been dealt with more than once and given chances for amendment. He hailed from Bradford from which place he had made frequent excursions to ply upon the sympathy of members and to avoid work.

Four years later, James Hoy was excluded by the Farnworth branch for 'chronic laziness'. 'He was 28 years of age and unwilling to leave Farnworth district although out of work for nearly a year. So it appears pretty clear that he is no use to anybody,' said the journal, adding menacingly that 'there are still some more who ought to follow him'. James Hoy was resourceful and sued the society but lost his case.

But when a man had been excluded he could still sometimes pick up a card and travel the country at union expense, as indeed could someone who had never been a member. Branches are warned of lost cards, which might have 'fallen into the hands of any person disposed to commit a fraud on our society', of 'Fogarty a notorious vagabond . . . an imposter who has never been a mason', of 'a man representing himself a pattern maker', and even of two men pretending to be fitters when they were 'only labourers'. The cordwainers said: 'Some had been making a living of them, aye, even common cadgers who knew not how to put a bristle on a thread.'

'Engineer' John Dearden 'must be an impostor . . . about 30 years of age, short and stiff, round broad face and dark whiskers . . . has more cards than one . . . has also been going in the name of Simpson and has more cards than one.' One mason had so many cards he was known as the 'travelling lodge'. One printer provided his former brothers with 'abundant evidence of his utter want of principle', robbing workmates, swindling employers and bidding fair to find a place 'at no distant period in the Newgate Calendar'. 'He stands about 5ft 5 inches, is dark complexioned, has bushy whiskers and easy address and is very glib of tongue.'

None more glib, though, than the man 'representing himself as a Hungarian refugee', bearing a tramp certificate with a forged signature. Denouncing the forger, known as Giovanni Cassaire, the Nottingham compositors' secretary added: 'I may here say the number of "patriot" foreign printers of late has become very great.' Two had recently passed through the town, one of whom, 'by mistake filled his head with a member's hat and left his own inferior one as a matter of compensation'.

'I have had another person purporting to possess the same patriotism and liberal feeling as most have done who have come here since the struggle for liberty on the continent commenced but to whose tales I hardened my heart and turned a deaf ear.'

The parasitism of outsiders on the union tramping systems is testified to by two writers. James Greenwood, while in search for material on vagrants, met a genial individual who told him how to 'work the ticket' by attaching himself to a benefit society. If 'compelled to take a job it is easy for an unprincipled rascal to make himself objectionable' to the employers. Travelling round the societies, having made himself acquainted with the lodge nights, it was 'as easy as kissing your hand, eighteenpence a day on the road. You get your pull out of the lodge members (a collection) as much as 17s at one lodge.'

John Newton described the former lawyer who made his way by 'working the noble' near the cotton mills in Bolton. Seated on the pavement with 'out of work' chalked on one boot and 'hard up' chalked on the other, he collected 22s 9d (more than a week's wages) from passing mill workers. Taxed with his trick, he said: 'Not so many can work it as well as I can.' Such impostors, said Dunlop, had a score of tales. They had fallen from a ladder, their mill had burnt down, there was a 'trade depression, iron and steel the most convenient'.

Stories like these perhaps help to explain the apparent callous satisfaction with which the tailors' general secretary reported in 1886: 'In our obituary will be noticed the names of several men who will be familiar to many of our secretaries and who year by year received the full amount of travelling relief allowed by rule.' Noting with satisfaction that travelling benefit cost the society rather less than a halfpenny per member per week, he went on: '. . . another cause of the reduction may be due to the diminished support which the professional traveller receives in our workshops. His yearly repeated tale of hunger and no work to be got anywhere falls flat on the ears of men struggling by hard and honest toil to live honourable and respectable lives.'

A history of such cases, no matter how few, helps perhaps to explain why in 1869 the bricklayers calmly noted that John Dempsey, who had tried to obtain the sum of 1s 4d by 'falsely representing that he was a member on tramp', was sentenced to three months' imprisonment with hard labour.

Sympathy for the tramp was further reduced by the violent and degraded behaviour of an even smaller minority reported in union journals for 'misconduct' or somewhat misleadingly for 'indecency', which often enough meant drunken incontinence or emptying chamber pots out of windows. The masons either suffered more of this kind of 'shameful and insolent' abuse of landlords and landladies or they were more frank in publishing it in the hope that exposure would improve conduct or warn lodges further down the line. There was indeed some argument over whether such conduct should be made public and when in 1871 some lodges argued that references should be less specific the general secretary remarked sarcastically that 'there is no such thing as a drunken mason'. However, in that year references to indecent acts were indeed cut from the record.

The cases of bad conduct were undoubtedly few. But how many such cases could local lodges tolerate, or their hosts put up with? In 1859, the Chester lodge moved to new quarters, their host having suffered the 'fourth insult since Christmas'. In 1870 the Leeds lodge claimed that because of such behaviour they had been 'driven from street to street' until only one public house in twenty-seven would have them. The punishment during the 1840s for 'indecency' among the masons was a fine of five shillings and the stopping of benefit, raised to ten shillings in 1868. The ironfounders and engineers levied similar fines for 'nuisance' or 'misconduct' though at one point the engineers threatened 'the most severe measures'.

The punishments no doubt had their effect, but the tailors' annual report suggests another reason for the disappearance of the 'roadster':

There is evidently a distaste for travelling growing among the younger members of the trade and the men who made a business of it and lived by travelling are fast dying out.

Thanks to the rules being made more stringent and the watchfulness of a number of our branch secretaries, also a healthful public opinion arising against encouraging a class of men who have no respect for themselves and reflect no credit on us.

Paying tribute to the honest tramp, the tailors' general secretary noted:

it most unfortunately happens for these men that when work is slack in one district, it is the same for all, with a few exceptional towns which have a special trade at certain seasons. Therefore the amount of marching we demand from a member before giving him any support has anything but a beneficial effect and frequently ends in demoralising the man himself.

The fact is an out of work fund is an absolute necessity.

By the 1880s most unions had recognised this 'absolute necessity' and only in certain trades was travelling benefit the only form of out-of-work pay. But whatever form the benefit took, the cost, particularly in slump years, was colossal. It was a cost which the unions were increasingly reluctant to shoulder alone.

14 'The sooner the system is dead the better'

The year 1879, wrote the general secretary of the ASE, was the 'blackest year of all our history . . . a state of depression without parallel'. The years 1857-9 and 1868-70 had also been bad, but 1879 was far worse. 'Our speedy collapse was confidently predicted by our enemies and even our friends looked doubtful.'

Of the union's 44,000 members, 7,000 or about one in six were 'on donation' and of those just under a third chose to take the road, with over 2,000 tramp cards being issued. The union report of April 1879 required thirty-two pages to list the names of travellers and the relief they recieved.

The boilermakers declared 1879 'one of the worst years in the society's history'; the amount paid to travellers and the over-50s who were allowed to stay at home was double the 1877 figure.

But worse still was the state of the ironfounders, with 3,466 members unemployed out of 11,914 and almost as many taking out travelling cards as among the engineers. The financial burden was immense, 50 per cent more than the total subscription income. In 1878 the union's report said with wry pride: 'In no society extant has such an amount been paid for unemployed labour in the whole history of trade unionism.' In crude terms this was not strictly correct, but in expenditure per member the ironfounders led the league table in 1879 and later years, £4 13s per member against the £3 8s of the engineers, the £1 12 9d of the carpenters, the £1 17s of the boilermakers and the £2 4s of the coachmakers.

During 1879 the fourteen major craft unions paid out over £329,000 in donation, nearly three times as much as in 1869. As the engineers said, it was a state of affairs 'without parallel'. And the early 1880s brought little relief.

Reports from ninety-three union organisations, national and local, which came in to the Royal Commission on the Depression of Trade and Industry in 1886 filled out the picture. Hartlepools boilermakers: 'none have witnessed anything like the present depression'; Leeds coach makers: '1869-70, very good; 1870-75 declining; 1875-1880, never worse';

Dundee carpenters: 'I have it on good authority that nothing approaching the present depression has been experienced for the past 40 years.'

Though most unions had by now gone over to home donation, the tramping system was not discarded and the old response to bad times was dying hard. During 1879, something like 5,000 engineers, masons iron-founders and tailors took the road with tramp cards in their pockets. Few remained on the road for long, for there was little point in travelling from one workless town to another. Among the masons, where each lodge was responsible for local tramp relief, 'tramp stations' closed in scores. Among the Manchester bricklayers, relief stations closed at the rate of one a month. On average 200 ironfounders were on the move in each month of the year. The Sunderland engineers summed up the situation. In their district were 2,000 men and 1,200 boys. 'There will be about 400 men out of employment in the town and about as many more left to get work elsewhere.'

The hopeful travellers were not always welcome. As the Ashford coachmakers put it, 'When our members are out of employment we allow them travelling relief so they do not stop in one place.' The Cardiff carpenters and joiners said: 'Cardiff would be moderate if so many strangers did not enter the town.' The union reports showing Cardiff's trade as 'moderate' meant that 'our members from all parts of the country flock here and therefore it makes trade bad and very bad indeed. One of our members from the north called on me about a week ago. I could see from his travelling card that he had been from town to town for 12 weeks right off and I was obliged to send him further on in the country. That is only one case out of a hundred.'

The Journeymen Hatters Fair Trade Union reported: 'The most prominent symptoms [of depression] are seeing so many good men walking about without a penny coming in, they having run through the whole of their benefits allowed by our society.'

Benefits paid varied a great deal. The London compositors paid 12s a week; the country compositors 8s a week for six weeks in any quarter (transferring the restrictions on tramp benefit to home donation); the tailors paid 9s 4d to tramps; the brushmakers paid 'free' members 10s a week for 26 weeks, 8s for a further 26 weeks and then 7s in the second year; coachmakers payments ranged from 4s a week for a new member to 12s a week for a twelve-year member, continued for 91 days and then reducing. In most unions the benefits were less than a third of the average pay, at home or on the road, and in long depressions the most generous benefit ran out.

But from the point of view of union stability, there is no doubt which type of benefit proved more effective. During the slump, in almost every trade the membership gains made in the early 1870s were almost wiped out. The engineers, who had doubled membership each decade from 1851, counted themselves lucky to hold on to 44,000. The ironfounders, having passed the 12,000 mark, managed by great effort to get through the hard times with a loss of 600 members. But the tailors, who paid only travelling relief, saw a membership of 15,000 slide to just over 12,000, while the masons, shooting up from 12,000 to 27,000 in the mid-1870s, collapsed to 12,000 by 1880 and remained around that figure until 1890. The carpenters' 'general union', which belatedly started home benefit in the 1860s, had advanced at first but then faded away to under 2,000, while the amalgamated carpenters steadied around the 11,000, with, as the union told the Royal Commission in 1886, 'a great many . . . out of society altogether'.

The masons and the ironfounders had begun with memberships roughly equal; their average wage was in both cases around 35s a week, though the masons work was more seasonal. During the slump years of 1878–9, the masons paid out £13,000 to the travelling unemployed. During the same years the founders paid out about £90,000. Both found the burden enormous. In 1887 the founders raised their weekly subscriptions to two shillings. The masons stayed at sixpence and only later was a penny increase reluctantly agreed to put the travelling fund on a similar basis.

The different response to the crisis laid the basis for a different future for the two unions: the founders were due to go on gathering strength; the masons entered a long decline. Those unions which rode over the crisis waves did so by ruthless reorganisation and tightening up. 'All former regulations are annulled and expelled,' said the brushmakers in 1880. The boilermakers' rules revisions between 1880 and 1885 were a 'turning point in the history of the society'.

Each revision bit into the old system. The boilermakers now went over to home donation. The amalgamated hatters' union now dropped tramping from its rules. Between 1878 and 1881 the Scottish and London printers abolished travelling allowance. 'Bed and beer money are entirely done away with, in the continued trade depression we are not in a position to pay a man 3s 6d a week to travel round the country,' said the brushmakers.

The measures were adopted in a manner which, says the printers' historian, was 'narrow, parsimonious and autocratic', but from the organisational and accounting point of view, highly effective. Yet the fact that new members could count on very little from the union funds but a bed for the night if they would leave town must have hampered recruiting, much as it preserved the funds. Indeed, veterans of the building trade of the late nineteenth and early twentieth centuries have told me how they signed up men during strikes only to have them drift away when they received no benefit for the first twelve months.

But the emphasis was not on conservation. The new regulations were aimed at those, mainly tramping, members who, it was said, joined for what they could get from the funds, 'drawing out, leaving and then rejoining', as the boilermakers said, or, in the words of the tailors, '. . . many men run out of the society as soon as they had obtained full relief.' They did not mind working a while to get back in benefit, remarked one masons' lodge; 'getting a bit was all their study'.

At this distance the measures seem like a steam hammer to crack a nut, but to fund holders the drain on finances was intolerable. 'Worthy brothers, if you could only see and know of the impositions,' said the bricklayers general secretary.

The improvement in the funds, he claimed, was not 'due to improvement of trade, but the means the council has put into effect'. The means chosen by both coachmakers and boilermakers was a graduated scheme by which members got more unemployment pay the longer they were in membership – up to 12s a week for twelve years membership in the case of the coachmakers. The tailors had an elaborate grading system for members, from A to E, and in addition put a top limit of forty-five on the number of days relief which might be paid in any one year. In the aftermath of slump, masons cut relief to fourteen days in any one year, the general secretary remarking that the cuts 'tend to economise on shoe leather' as well as the funds. The free brushmaker got an elaborate passport-like travelling book in which 'pension' payments were noted; the 'non-free', a thin paper certificate which entitled him to halfpenny a mile. Boilermakers and carpenters introduced that bane of future generations of unemployed – 'waiting time', several days' delay before they might draw benefit. The card and blowing room operatives in the woollen industry allowed only three of any branch out on the road at any one time. The tailors' introduced a close season: no travelling in April, May, June, July or November, save by special order of their council, which perhaps assumed that in many of the 'open' months the weather would keep would-be travellers at home.

The debate over such revisions of the rules could be heated. The Nottingham masons sought to restore former tramp benefit so that those who had left would 'return to our ranks'. The money could be found at the expense of the fund for the disabled, which Battersea lodge declared 'monstrous in the extreme'.

The masons' new system, with a route map of club houses and a separate cheque to be handed in to the landlord in each town, a fresh one being drawn next morning, was hailed as the reason for the drastic drop in benefit payments over two years from £13,000 to just over £2,000. Not that the minority of defaulters against whom the revisions were aimed were at a loss. One lodge remarked that 'where a dozen are gathered together' ways round the restrictions could be found.

Yet another system was introduced, under which the tramp got his cheques a book at a time, 98 cheques in a book. Under the new rules, which also included slightly increased subscriptions, free members were now allowed 98 days' benefit at 1s 3d a day in any year. Fred Bower, the mason-author, has left us this verse description of the system of cheque books, a system which was to last until tramping finally faded away.

> For it was fifteen pence for a working day
> Eighteen for the day between
> And a penny for three miles over 12
> When Victoria was Queen.
> And that was six for a bed and two for a pint
> And four for a 'rough stuff' meal
> And three for an ounce of twist or shag
> To smoke when our innards did squeal.

Put that way, the tales of 'imposition' on the funds fall into perspective. If tramps 'made a living' out of the funds, then extraordinary ingenuity must have been shown. Indeed no union ever seemed able or willing to state the amount, precise or approximate, that tramps were alleged to be raking from the benefit pool.

No doubt the funds amassed with such sacrifice over the years were cherished and even a shilling lost through petty cunning or carelessness was bitterly resented. But one also gets the strong impression that the main object of the stringent economies of the 1880s was to get rid of the tramp. The welcome given by the tailors' general secretary to the appearance of tramps' names in the obituary list seems to go beyond a desire to see excessive expenditure curbed.

'Travelling from town to town in search of work has greatly decreased. The trade tramp is dying out and the sooner the system is dead the better,' the general secretary of the National Society of Amalgamated Brass-workers told a Board of Trade Inquiry in 1893. He noted that on the other hand:

'Travelling after work, where there is some evidence that it exists and where the workman receives help either from his society or his friends, is in my judgement on the increase.' Railway excursion tickets were 'cheap, frequent and speedy' and more and more unions followed the example of the metal trades which from the 1850s allowed a man his fare by 'steam, coach or ship' to the place where the job awaited him. Between the late 1860s and the early 1890s the boilermakers spent over £3,000 on it. Compositors and litho-printers paid fares or 'removal grants' and 'shifting money' was paid by the Northumberland miners' union. In some cases, as with the London compositors, the money for fares was loaned to be repaid at half a crown a week. As for tramping itself, the London printers said in 1893: 'With the growth of railway, telegraph and telephone communication the system of travelling relief was found to have served its purpose and was therefore abolished 15 years since.'

The London compositors were giving evidence to the Board of Trade Inquiry into Agencies and Methods of Dealing with the Unemployed. In 1891, 202 union societies with nearly 700,000 members had paid over £220,000 in unemployment benefit, the inquiry was told. Many of them still provided travelling benefit; some provided nothing else. As mentioned, even the Northumberland miners who were paid travel allowance were expected to 'visit three or four collieries' in search of work. The new Amalgamated Society of Railway Servants, formed in the 1870s, had adapted the old system to their new situation (they paid 1s 10d for week days, 2s 10d for the weekend).

Noting how widespread was the travelling system, the inquiry emphasised its decline under the pressure of financial stringency:

A self-governing association [should] be able to assist its members in their search for work ... and the financial interest of all its contributing members in husbanding its funds offers some stimulus to the members of the society both to endeavour to find situations for their unemployed fellow members and to watch that the society is not being defrauded by idlers who draw the out of work pay without genuinely seeking for employment.

The strong position which is occupied by trade societies with regard to their members has enabled them to experiment freely in modes of dealing with their unemployed members and the various methods at present adopted even if far from perfect are worthy of careful study, as embodying the net result of many years of experience.

And the report concluded significantly:

It may be said generally that where they have failed other agencies are not likely to succeed. For example the growing discountenance with which in many societies, travelling benefit is coming to be regarded seems a sufficient proof of the unpracticability at the present day of such a form of assistance to the unemployed on the part of an ordinary relief organisation.

Noting the job-finding role played by many of the leading unions, the Board of Trade report said of the engineers: '. . . as the trade union of this stamp is pledged by its rules to provide financial aid to its members out of work, it becomes bound as a matter of sound policy to do all it can to obtain them employment in order that the drain on its funds may be as far as possible kept down.'

In the heyday of the tramping system, of course, the tramp had been directed to the workshop where a member was foreman. But by the end of the century, as the engineers' historian has noted, 'foremen members in towns with four or five branches and 1,000 members could not know the turners, fitters and pattern makers as when there was only one branch with 200 members.' The vacant book kept behind the bar in the local club house could be as effective only as local knowledge and the recognition by the employers could make it. When the Paviors' Arms, masons' tramp station in Westminster and 'lighthouse' for the trade for half a century, ceased to receive tramps in 1889, the local lodge said they had ninety members, but only eighteen of them lived within the three miles' radius laid down by rule. The tramping system and workshop organisation of the hatters was undermined as felt-hat making was concentrated in fewer industrial centres.

The Devizes coachmakers told the Royal Commission on the Depression of Trade in 1886 that it was 'quite useless' for the unemployed to stay in 'such small towns' and 'they inevitably travel to larger places where they think they have a better chance of getting into work'. The Dundalk carpenters said: 'These last five years the country carpenters are coming into town, and labourers generally, and it is hard to procure work for them.' 'The most prominent symptoms' of depression, said the Glasgow compositors, 'are considerable numbers of men going into the large centres and swelling the overstocked labour market.' Convinced of the truth of this, the Glasgow printers had, as early as in 1879, opted for home unemployment pay, and led the way, closely followed by other Scots cities, in abolishing tramping.

The London compositors had since the 1840s discouraged the country tramp, and in 1886, when the London men were hosts to other print unions at a conference to discuss 'reciprocity', the compositors of the capital were openly hostile to the tramp.

'There is a very great desire on the part of most provincial members of the trade societies, to visit London if the opportunity offered . . .'. It was to 'be discouraged . . . the local rules were so elastic a stranger could avail himself of a holiday.' It was 'unjust and immoral to send men to London', and likewise London had 'no moral right to send to Manchester or Dublin or Leeds or Birmingham on the off chance.' Another London man added, 'Reciprocity, yes, but it is premature to apply it to London.'

When O'Reilly, the Dublin delegate, ventured on a defence of the tramps as 'by no means the worst men in the society and they probably suffered the most in the cause of union', he was met with mingled cries of 'hear, hear' and 'No'. Challenged, he declared he did not refer to the 'travelling tramp'.

With a vague promise of a committee, the conference chairman then moved the adjournment and the delegates adjourned to a celebration with seven toasts and the singing of 'I fear no foe', 'The Death of Nelson' and 'Come into the Garden, Maud'.

The tramp was a vanishing species. Even in trades where no home donation was paid men refused to take the roads. 'Good members prefer to suffer a little at home,' said the Operative Bricklayers' Society report in 1886. Robert Last, general secretary of the old carpenters' union, told his members in 1868 that there was a 'deserving class who would despise the tramp card'. The masons told the Board of Trade inquiry in 1893: 'Travelling in search of work has decreased of late years, members in the London district particularly preferring to wait for work to turn up.' Some London masons' lodges had by now set up contingent funds to provide relief at home and their leaders began to boast of it at union rallies.

Noting the London lodges' out-of-work fund, the Dover lodge had called in 1890 for travelling relief to be abolished since 'the travelling fund now acts as a back door out of society', a remark which earned the lodge a reproof from the executive for their 'light opinion of our travelling brethren'. Dover found little support, though this was on financial grounds rather than moral. 'Such schemes are not as simple as our Dover brothers imagine they are.'

A year later, when the masons' travelling fund had been stabilised by allocating a fixed $1\frac{1}{4}$d a week per member to it, Headingley lodge renewed the demand for an out-of-work fund: 'We have no wish to interfere with the freedom of travellers, but don't let us be too sentimental about them

... [they do] a great deal of good and sometimes a little harm.' Headingley proposed a subscription of one shilling a week, fourpence of which would go to an out of work fund, providing 10s a week for 14 weeks and 7s for 7 weeks. But the executive pointed out that the fund would work only if unemployment stayed below 4 per cent of membership and 'we have considerably more'.

So the travelling mason and the fund marched on into the twentieth century. The Selby lodge claimed indeed that, since trade fluctuated so much, 'until the end of time, as long as there is unity' there would be a need for it. In 1901–2 a special committee of the Provincial Typographical Association felt the system could be 'mended but not ended'.

The Board of Trade Inquiry in 1893 had noted four methods used by unions to deal with unemployment. They were unemployment benefit, travelling benefit, assistance to members in finding work, and the 'equalisation of work ... by means of short time, or by adopting some system of rotation or by other measures whereby the work may so far as possible be equally shared by all members'. The 12,000-strong Associated Shipwrights, with powerful localised organisation and ancient craft traditions, offered evidence to the inquiry not on benefits but only on work equalisation methods – fixing the number of men required to do certain classes of work, stopping a man working for two employers at once, regulating the amount of work done daily by each man, prohibiting piece or contract work, limiting overtime, or by agreeing, 'wherever practicable', to double-manning on urgent work.

Few other unions could enforce such gild-type regulation of work, though other craft unions, even where they yielded on piecework, tried to retain control of overtime working. Few could maintain the old apprentice regulations, especially the time-honoured ratio of men to boys. The London compositors endeavoured to do so – which is why they treated their city so much as a fortress against the incursions of provincial tramps. The boilermakers reaffirmed apprentice regulations in the 1890s but, under pressure from the employers, they reduced the demand from one lad to each five journeymen to two lads for seven journeymen. Among the engineers, whose industry was more widely diffused with a broad range of trades, attempts to hold on to apprentice regulations failed. The Sunderland engineers fought a dogged two-year battle in the 1880s, backed by their executive, but were defeated. Engineers' leader J. Swift, one of the old school, outlined the kind of conditions his union had to contend with in 1895. At Woolwich Arsenal, he said, 'hundreds of youths are engaged working automatic machines in connection with the production of fuses, cartridges and bullets. All that they have to do is the merest mechanical work, one operation only and this operation having to be repeated in some cases, thousands of times in one day.'

Insisting on a five-year apprenticeship, let alone the ancient seven-year term, as the means of entry to industry under such conditions was impossible. Yet the rules of the engineers and many other craft unions had insisted down the years on five years' time served as a condition of membership. This factor together with the effects of mass unemployment had helped to slow down their advance by the late 1870s.

However, during this same period the membership of unions affiliated to the Trades Union Congress, set up in 1868 on craft union initiative, had almost doubled from around 280,000 to 561,000. A great deal of the increase had come from outside the craft union areas, from those in textile and mining industries which had at last achieved stable national organisation, and from new groupings of railway and farm workers. The balance of membership of the movement was being tilted away from the older crafts although their representatives still dominated the Trades Union Congress.

It was calculated at the time that unions organised some 10 per cent of the workforce, mostly among skilled workers. Many of the remaining 90 per cent were debarred from joining by the nature of union rules, though Robert Applegarth of the Amalgamated Carpenters did assist building labourers with money and advice in forming their own organisation.

The mass unemployment, which had strained the craft union funds to breaking-point, had been a period of great suffering for the unorganised. This came to a head in the late 1880s in a series of strikes, demonstrations and a drive to organise among the poor unskilled of the East End of London – dockers, gas workers and labourers in other industries. These 'new' unions, assisted by socialist craftsmen like Tom Mann of the engineers and socialist agitators like Karl Marx's daughter Eleanor, brought an affiliation of 200,000 to the TUC in the early 1890s. They also brought a new way of looking at things.

Antipathy between 'old' and 'new' union leaders was inevitable for the new were organising men the old had considered could not and indeed ought not to be recruited. At the TUC in 1889, William Broadhurst, a mason and secretary of the TUC, and Kier Hardie, a young miners' delegate and socialist, were involved in a bitter clash in which Broadhurst denounced 'those who seek to destroy unionism by vehementaly attacking its prominent representatives'.

Frederick Engels who had shrewdly observed the English working class movement for some half a century, remarked: 'These unskilled are very different from the fossilised brothers of the old trade unions; not a trace of the old formalist spirit, of the craft exclusiveness of the engineers for instance.'

To which Swift of the engineers replied: 'If the men of the new movement, instead of shouting about the "old fossils" and reactionaries, would only apply the same amount of sincerity, self-sacrifice and faith to the trade union movement of today, we should not hear so much opposition to the theory of a living wage.'

'Fossils we may be termed', said William Hey, the ironfounders' leader, 'but we are not in the habit of striking today and going round with the hat, tomorrow.'

George Howell, former TUC secretary, took the hostility of the new unionists more personally: 'It remained for one of the most prominent and blatant of the "new trades union leaders" to revive the calumny and to speak of his colleagues at the recent TUC as aldermanic in appearance and to sneer at them for wearing tall hats.'

But the most pointed comment of new on old was the rule book of the General Railway Workers' Union, which challenged the somewhat conservative Amalgamated Society of Railway Servants in the 1890s: 'The union shall remain a fighting one and shall not be encumbered with any sick or accident fund.'

The two sides clashed head on at the TUC in 1890 and 1891 over the issue of the demand for an eight-hour day. It was not the principle, on which most were agreed. The slogan dated, indeed, from the 1830s and craft unions had fought hard first for the ten-hour then the nine-hour day. But these had been essentially 'trade' movements regulating the matter between employer and employed. Their effect on the greater number of semi-skilled and unskilled was indirect. The eight-hour day demand as it divided the TUC was for a 'legal' eight-hour day, political action to extend the benefit of shorter working hours throughout the working population, not restricting it to those strong enough to achieve it on their own.

The division was not purely 'old' versus 'new', for the miners were divided within themselves on the matter. But the demand became the focus of antagonism between two conflicting views of what the trade unions should aim for. The 'old' leaders were for strictly 'trade' matters. The TUC had indeed begun as a lobbying organisation but chiefly to secure freedom of industrial organisation, not for general political objectives.

There was another side to the matter. Engels had wickedly remarked some ten years earlier that the 'old' leaders had committed the trade unions to being the 'tail of the Great Liberal Party'. Thus the 'new' suspected the 'old' of simply trying not to embarrass their allies in the Liberal Party by independent political action. When the miners resolved their differences and, combined with the 'new' unions, carried the day over the eight-hour demand, Broadhurst resigned in protest and confirmed his opponents' argument by accepting a minor ministerial post under Gladstone.

The trade unions were slowly but surely moving towards some kind of general independent political action. In 1893, the TUC agreed in principle to set up a parliamentary fund, and the brushmakers' conference of that year was told: 'There are those who would tell us that trade unionism is a played out force and that the hope of the workers lies in politics. It may be that some of the old methods of trade unions have become obsolete and new tactics are required.' The 'new tactics' turned out to be the setting up in 1900 of the Labour Representation Committee, the forerunner of the Labour Party.

But differences on political tactics by themselves would never have made the clash between 'old' and 'new' so sharp. The new unions organised widely among the unskilled, laying down minimal conditions for membership. Since they charged new members very little they could not maintain large benefit funds; indeed, as noted, they found them an 'encumbrance'. But once the 'new' unions were moving they no longer confined themselves to dockers, or gasworkers, but ran riot through a score of industries where the semi-skilled and unskilled had been neglected by the craftsmen. Looking back on this period of mass 'poaching' which lasted from 1890 until the First World War, Sir Arthur Pugh, then a junior official in the British Steel Smelters' Amalgamated Association, wrote: 'That dockers and gasworkers in public utility undertakings should be competing with cranemen and similar occupations in iron and steel works is an indication of the lack of orderly trade unionism.'

Disorderly it was, but highly effective, as Swift of the Engineers recognised in 1895: 'Already the ASE has awakened to its deficiencies and has broadened the basis of its constitution so as to admit the new branches of the trade into its ranks.' In fact, seven years earlier the ASE had abandoned the insistence that new members should have served five years before the age of 21. It is difficult not to associate this change with

234

the sudden dramatic leap in membership. After gaining just 8,000 members in eight years, the union took in another 15,000 in the next two to reach 67,000 by 1890. Further rule changes in 1892 helped further advance. By 1899 another 17,000 had joined. Other unions responded to the same stimulus, the ironfounders rising from 11,000 in 1887 to 16,000 in 1893.

That inclusion rather than exclusion was the best answer to the breakdown of old skill-division was the lesson driven home by the 'new' unions. Brushmakers, hatters, steelworkers and others now brought in youths and women previously kept out. New textile amalgamations, who had ignored the female majority in the industry, now recruited women by the thousand.

By the end of the century the trade union movement had passed the million mark, and had changed fundamentally, with the 'new' or 'general' unions making a claim for leadership, and with the Labour Representation Committee directing energies towards political action.

By making the demand for a shorter working day political, the new unions had raised a much wider question about unemployment. G. H. Roberts, later to enter Parliament, told the 1903 delegate meeting of the Typographical Association: 'The proper solution of the surplus labour question is that the burden should be borne by the Community as well as the Association.' He thus gave expression to the kind of demand which was now put forward not only by the unions, but by the group of twenty-nine Labour MPs which appeared in Parliament along with the 1906 Liberal landslide election victory.

During the nineteenth century, the 'burden' of unemployment benefit borne by the unions had attracted the enlightened middle-class observer. In the early 1900s it attracted the attention of the man who was to be regarded as the architect of the Welfare State – William Beveridge. In his book *Unemployment* he noted that 81 of the 100 principal trade unions with a membership of around one million gave either 'stationary-local' benefit or 'travelling' benefit to members at a cost of some £650,000. Stressing the importance of these payments as a means of 'preventing distress', he outlined certain necessary requirements for industry:

To be able to follow the demand (for labour) men must possess greater powers of intelligent movement from place to place; they must possess also power to move from trade to trade or a more essential point they must have better guidance in the first choice of occupations. To be able to wait for the demand, men must have a reserve for emergencies; they must not be living from hand to mouth, they must through insurance or its equivalent be able to average wages over good and bad times and to subsist without demoralisation until they can be re-absorbed again after industrial transformations.

Speaking of the 'very important service to industry' the unions' efforts at job finding rendered, Beveridge went on to compare the tentative voluntary experiments with labour exchanges in Britain with the developing official establishments of such offices in other European countries. Beveridge was of course as much concerned to aid employers as workers, for he felt that employers had a 'natural objection' to applying to unions (via the vacant book) for labour, because of the 'not infrequent rule that men on the vacant list shall be sent to jobs in the order not of capacity but of signature'.

By maintaining at immense cost the whole system of sick and unemployment benefits the unions simply continued the duties which in pre-union days had fallen on all engaged in the trades – as Thomas Hughes noted (see Chapter 12). But Beveridge perhaps failed to see that they thus assumed a natural right to continue the craft tradition of allocating entry to the trade.

By demanding political action on unemployment the unions were trying to convert a responsibility once shared, then thrust on to their backs, once more into a charge on the whole of industry. They were looking forwards and backwards simultaneously.

Thus, when by the Act of 1909 the first labour exchanges were opened, the unions were divided in their opinions. The compositors distrusted the new exchanges which they felt suitable for the unskilled but not for the crafts whose power they diminished. Engineers feared on the one hand that the new exchanges would provide the employers with the cheapest labour. But on the other they hoped to be relieved of a problem which had burdened the unions for a long time. Painters adapted their rules to the new institution. Members wanting the 'name book' should apply to club house or labour exchange.

More universally welcome was the legislation which introduced small old age pensions (1908) after a campaign in which unions, notably the engineers, played a leading part. Payment to older members had become an increasing strain on union resources, expecially where membership stood still among the older building unions like the masons, 'Manchester' bricklayers, and 'General' carpenters. In 1905, nearly 900 of the masons' 15,000 members were 'superannuated' and the union reports lamented the failure to attract 'younger blood'.

The 'most novel and far-reaching' National Insurance Act of 1911, argued over but in the end 'uneasily' and 'circumspectly' accepted by the unions, helped some of the older organisations to survive. Under the Act workers in shipbuilding, ship repair, mechanical engineering, iron-founding, vehicle building, building, and railway and canal construction were, in return for small weekly wage deductions, insured in some degree for sickness and unemployment (7s a week for 15 weeks when out of work). Health insurance payments could be made through the unions as 'approved' friendly societies, and despite a campaign by commercial insurance companies and some Tory MPs workers in these industries were drawn into the unions as a result. Some rank-and-file members were suspicious of the schemes since they elevated 'friendly benefits' instead of the fighting capacity to improve wages and conditions, and handed over to a bureaucrat the power to judge whether a worker was 'genuinely seeking employment' before he received benefit.

But in the 'obligatory' trades the scheme went ahead, and in other trades a small Board of Trade Subsidy (a sixth of the total benefit, up to a total of 12s a week) drew in more of the older unions. The compositors used the scheme to increase the out-of-work pay they could give their members. The boot and shoe workers after centuries of tramping custom and 120 years tramping system had begun, with much hesitation, a voluntary home donation scheme based on a penny a week. At first some two per cent of the members paid in but by 1912 the union had joined the state scheme. By the outbreak of the First World War, some sort of out-of-work benefit paid at home, however meagre, had thus become general. The travelling system was clearly at an end. It was dead, but it refused to lie down.

In 1901 the compositors had reluctantly decided that they could not do more than amend the system. Mileage payments continued in fact until 1913, when they were abolished and replaced by the payment of railway fares to known work. Bursts of high employment among iron-founders between 1900 and 1910 saw nearly 7 per cent of members take out travelling cards, more on average than in some decades of the nine-teenth century. Some years an average of 130 a month were travelling. The masons saw expenditure on travelling rise from 1s 4d a member in 1898 to 6s 7½d in 1905 and then sink again to 1s 5d in 1909.

Not only did the system show remarkable signs of life in the final years, the tramp had clearly lost nothing in ingenuity. Just before Christmas 1906, the masons' Executive Committee warned lodge secretaries: 'Do not pay relief in advance. The system of travellers riding into town on their cycles where several days' relief are allowed and claiming to be paid the number of days down at once so that they can return to their home or where they started that day must not be allowed.' Among the engineers, the death of the system was more measured. In 1903 when the union had 90,000 members, there were 80 tramps on the road. In 1915, when the membership was 174,000, there were a dozen on tramp.

Unions now grew at a rate which would have amazed the old society men of a century before. Between 1900 and 1910 the total union members doubled to $2\frac{1}{2}$ million. Between 1910 and 1914 came a further increase to 4 million. Some of the increase came by courtesy of the National Insurance Act. A great deal more came from the great surge of organisation and industrial action among the unskilled and semi-skilled that preceded the 1914–18 war, with the Workers' Union increasing from 5,000 to 90,000 in three years. The miners' organisation, a federation of independent district unions, impelled by a powerful strike movement and rank and file agitation for a united 'industrial' union, now drew in nearly one million members. Rank and file activists in the craft unions – ironfounders, builders and engineers – pressed the demand for a single union in each industry. Among the spokesmen for the movement was stonemason Fred Bower, unrepentant 'roadster' who declared that the tramps had taught 'many a young man . . . the use of a union card'.

The First World War, with technological change and intensified industrial production, urged on the drive to amalgamation. In the opinion of a foundry workers' leader, it also put paid to the last tramps because the wartime control on movement made casual travelling and sleeping out extremely difficult.

During the 1914–18 war the tramp certainly disappears from union reports and statistics. The return of peace and the demobilisation of huge armed forces brought the trade union movement to an unprecedented 8 million. At the core of this now immense movement were the new 'amalgamateds', both craft and 'general': Amalgamated Engineering Union, over 300,000; Transport and General Workers' Union nearly 400,000; Amalgamated Union of Foundry Workers, 46,000; Amalgamated Union of Building Trade Workers, 75,000.

In the early 1920s the AEU had 24,000 on 'donation'; the foundry workers had over 10,000 unemployed. But neither union had any men on the road – officially. The Amalgamated Society of Woodworkers formally deleted the travelling card rule because 'the telephone and modern quick transit had made it obsolete'.

The National Union of General Workers, on the other hand, said that members on the move would get no financial assistance without a travelling card. But union funds were not to be used for the purpose.

Having lasted 120 and more years as a system, tramping was reverting again to custom. Even between the world wars, old hatters would turn up at workshop doors and be rewarded with a quick whip round among the men. Building workers, of course, continued to roam the country lanes. The irrepressible Fred Bower continued to leave his banker mark, sign of his workmanship, in the masonry of barns and churches, though after 1917 he changed his mark from anchor to hammer and sickle as one rural vicar discovered to his fury on inspecting Brother Bower's neat repair to the church porch. In the 1930s, as Duthie had done eighty years before (see Chapter 9), a union baker set off from London to tramp the roads of Germany and Austria. He was helped on his way by the German bakers with a metal ticket entitling him to free bread in each town.

Union rule books of the 1950s and 1960s show traces of the old 'tramp laws':

Members on benefit shall be free to seek employment in any district and no embargo placed against them provided they take their stand in search of employment along with members resident in the district to which they have gone. (boilermakers, 1965)

Members . . . who seek and obtain employment . . . in a district other than that in which they are residing shall . . . be entitled to the railway fare to the place . . . provided there are no suitable men signing the vacant book. (engineers, 1951)

Any craft member who has paid 12 months' contributions into the union, owes less than 15 weeks and is entitled to unemployment benefit . . . [but is disqualified for] misconduct . . . [or] if he voluntarily leaves his employment without cause or refuses suitable employment. (building workers, 1962)

[Unemployment benefit paid] twice weekly at the clubhouse. (Foundryworkers, 1964)

No member over 50 years compelled to leave the district. (boilermakers, 1965)

Faint traces of the old system remain even after the memory has died, to perplex the curious trade unionist even in the 1970s. As an Irish joiner remarked: 'I could never understand why it was when unemployment was on the increase, the old members would say "It'll soon be nothing but a tramp industry."'

15 Who? How many? How good? How bad?

'So peculiar and highly organised a system could only be erected upon a well-built foundation of custom,' wrote Professor E. J. Hobsbawm in his pioneering article on 'The Tramping Artisan' published nearly thirty years ago.

This 'well-built foundation' has been the main subject of this book, the rise of tramping from four centuries of customary dealing with 'the stranger'. The problem of the stranger was the logical outcome of the way the town craftsmen tried to secure their livelihood – by relating the number of masters, journeymen and apprentices to the available work. The ideal local balance of numbers sought in craft regulation from the fifteenth century onwards could not be achieved for none of the elements to be balanced was in itself stable – men seeking to be masters, masters seeking to employ more men and boys, both trying to restrict each other. In the course of the years, the displaced or frustrated craftsman of one town became the 'stranger' at the gates of another. Thus the 'closed shop' and the 'stranger' are linked from the start. To maintain one, the other must be 'entertained'. Thus every trade, whether migratory by nature or not, contributed to the patchwork of custom and regulation – the certificates, the guarantee of 'honest departure', the reception by a named 'brother', in larger trades by the yeomanry, the fortnight's work, the registration in the company book, the payment of quarterage or to the poor 'box', the graded status which put the new arrival behind the town freeman in the work queue, and the summoning of the stranger to the house of call. Every one of these features was present in custom or rule before the existence in any trade of the independent trade societies we see as the forerunners of the unions.

The masons moving from town to country place, working on hundreds of castles and churches, had all the problems of displacement to a much greater degree. Conscription of masons and to some extent carpenters for royal work, bringing men together from thirty counties at a time, had the special effect of overriding local loyalty and placing all 'felaus' on an equal footing. So it gave rise both to the custom of the annual 'semble' or meeting to which the mason 'must nede gon' and to regulations which were uniform throughout the country – 'The Old Charges', which existed in at least seventy or eighty versions in different towns from 1583 to 1726. The customs on which the first charges are based go back to the fifteenth century.

In the sixteenth-century 'charges' we find the first tramping system, with regulations for the reception of the 'strange felau', provision of a fortnight's work, and the 'refreshing' with money to the next lodge. Set standards of behaviour by the traveller at the hostelry where he is boarded are included.

So, as the record stands at present, the masons originated 'tramping' and not the woolcombers as has been suggested. Professor Hobsbawm supposes the system spread by 'travelling woollen workers or perhaps tramping masons from the Western quarries'. The earliest reference I have found to 'travelling' payments to woollen workers is in mid-seventeenth century at Coventry, a tantalising note in the Webb Collection. The tramping system of the woolcombers, so well known because of parliamentary scrutiny of the industry, has no record before 1700. So, while the masons' tramping system is anything but localised, masons from the West could have passed the system to the woolcombers, for whose way of life with the growth of the worsted industry in the seventeenth and eighteenth centuries it was well suited.

Did the masons' invent the system? In the earliest masons' articles, the Regius and Cooke MSS of the late fourteenth and early fifteenth century, the traveller is not mentioned, though fellows are warned to heed the counsel of others 'in logge in chamber and in every place there as masons beth'. Did they copy it from the system used by the German masons with elaborate greetings, handshakes, rules, etc? Possibly. Continental masons did work in England in the Middle Ages, and continued to leave their banker marks in English pubs until the late nineteenth century. But if borrowed, why did English craftsmen not have the continental *Wanderjahre* system – beyond, as Professor Hobsbawm remarks, a habit of young men roving before settling down. In Chapter 9 I have looked at continental tramping and it seems to me that the *wanderjahr* important as it is, is not the sole or or even the main reason for it. Journeymen were sent travelling in Germany to ease the employment situation and restrict their ability to compete with their masters. The English craftsmen was doing what the French and German did, in a different context and different traditions. Some form of 'tramping' would arise from the pressures and demands of medieval manufacture. The English could have had a similar system without borrowing. But I think the question must remain open.

Tramping in terms of piecemeal, accumulated custom and in systematic form, then, was already developing in the sixteenth and seventeenth centuries. When in the eighteenth those pressures to which journeyman mobility was a response became more insistent, the custom became more visible, more systematic. By the end of the eighteenth century it appears in the 'old' trades of woolstapler, silk and wool weaver, woolcomber, calico printer, tinplate worker, shearer, blacksmith, millwright, cabinet maker, mason, hatter, cordwainer, currier, brushmaker, tailor, compositor, and papermaker. Between 1800 and 1830 it becomes general, appearing in the trades of coachmaker, ironmoulder, framework knitter, shipwright, hemp and flax manufacture, ropemaker, bookbinder, carpenter, steam engine maker, mechanic and others, becoming increasingly systematised and uniform, perhaps with much borrowing and imitation.

Hobsbawm says: 'Its general adoption by the crafts undoubtedly reflected the need to defend local monopolies of apprenticed artisans against novel economic challenges.'

This is the kernel of the question. Though the craftsmen, at least in the older trades, did not 'adopt' tramping. The system in embryo was already part of their tradition before the 'novel' economic challenges faced them. It expanded with them into the period of change of the Industrial Revolution and played a crucial role in the transformation of local craft bodies into national class-based organisations. But in the making of the trade unions, I think, it was a catalyst. Belonging so much to the prehistory of the unions, it could not change with their changing.

As soon as the 'unions' took shape out of the tramping networks, tramping in many ways became surplus to requirements. The coachmakers, writing to the Webbs in the 1890s, dated their union from 1834, saying that before then it was 'only a federation for tramping purposes'.

However, the 'well-built' foundation could not disappear. The past had immense weight, not only in terms of the tramping system but the entire development of the unions. In this lies the historic interest of the system – what it reveals of the roots of the unions, something I examine in more detail in Chapter 16.

The mass unemployment of the 1830s and 1840s, as Hobsbawm points out, strained the system 'beyond its powers'. Indeed the effect of mass unemployment upon tramping underlies how far it was the product of earlier conditions. No one faced with the economic depressions of the 1830s and 1840s, which put anything up to a third of organised workers out of a job for long periods of time, could possibly have *invented* such a method of coping with the problem. As a system of unemployment benefit it was the worst that could be devised.

As the Stockport moulders said in 1848: 'It compels us to work again for the money for which we have already wrought.' The moulders, indeed, compared it with the workhouse treadmill, going round and round the country under intolerable conditions to get money they could have received in the much greater comfort of their homes. To the older, married men, who were the backbone of the local societies and may indeed have helped found them in their youth in the 1820s, it was even worse, for while they tramped and spent their money their families might starve.

Hobsbawm noted that a sign of the earlier roots of the system is that it was 'entirely adapted to single men'. I have found this generally though not universally the case. Some societies and unions did make allowances to families. The Glasgow printers allowed 15s to a single, 21s to a married man; the Manchester printers 10s and 15s. The London tanners allowed 1s 6d to a married tramp. The brushmakers allowed an additional one shilling for each child under 12. The cordwainers, curriers, tanners, and – now and then – the tinplate workers actually provided for the wife who tramped with her husband. The only actual photograph I have seen of a trade tramp shows the unfortunate wife trudging after him. As shown in previous chapters, the young single man was indeed the one most likely to have to go on the road if the workforce was to be reduced, on the time-hallowed principle of last in, first out.

As most major craft unions decided after mid–century, 'static' donation kept both home and family together. As the founders' historians noted, the Scots moulders' union with 'idle element' survived the 1840s better than the English with their travelling benefit. Later in the century the rival Amalgamated and General carpenters' unions (see Chapter 12) demonstrated the point again. As a stabiliser, static donation was an advance. But in another sense it was a retreat, for whatever its merits as a form of benefit it had no apparent merit as a system of finding work.

Tramping did represent an active policy of trying to find work. As such it depended much on the ability of a society in a given town to ensure that the union tramp should have work if no local man needed it. As the Old Masons' Society of Ireland agreed in 1836, English tramps should be able to find work at 'all jobs under their influence'. The 'influence' of the craft organisation over the job depended in the past on master and journeyman being in the same organisation. The Woolcombers' national rules, published in 1812, show the system at its height, making a special point that any 'fair' master 'may be ensured of having a regular supply of men who are capable of working well at the trade'. In 1826 the brush-makers cautioned members on the dangers of 'establishing masters in the trade who have no pretensions thereto' by supplying them with journey-men.

There was thus mutual benefit. The master was guaranteed skilled, time-served men. He in his turn guaranteed society men the first chance at the job. The job supply would partly be guaranteed by both parties observing the ratio of boys to men.

If all agreed, the oil of custom lubricated the wheels. If not, the men, being in the majority, could enforce it. A hat manufacturer told the Artisans and Machinery Committee in 1824 that men would not work with lads taken 'in excess' even though the lads had served seven years. Even a 'fair' boy could become 'foul'.

Q. So the fair and foul men are never mixed together in the same manufactory?
A. No, never without the fair being considered foul and placed under a fine or penalty by the fair men of the trade.

At the start of our story the Manchester and Stockport hatters laid down for the Glasgow brothers that 'foul men' should not have the benefits of the 'turn house' network.

The effectiveness of the tramping system as an answer to unemployment was thus linked with the house of call and both depended on the closed shop. Unless all elements functioned the system would not work. When in 1814 the last of the apprentice laws was repealed in the teeth of mass small-master/journeymen opposition, the trade sanctions, those of custom and organisation, had to operate alone. The incentives were still strong. The masons said in 1836: 'Experience teaches that such trades as are strict in enforcing legal apprenticeship are invariably the most powerful and best remunerated for their labour.' But a closed shop based on ap-prenticeship was a hostage to the future, as the old hand skills were fragmented by the machine and the old workshop master gave way to the factory boss. The trade societies and union strove to keep foremen inside their organisation as the bigger engineering employers complained to a parliamentary inquiry in 1856.

In 1720 and in 1800 the master tailors complained how the house of call, based as it was on the closed shop, made the men invincible. When Henry Mayhew looked the London tailoring trade over in 1850 he found the house of call as 'labour market of the trade' still worked in a limited degree, with the master 'sending to the society' and the 'workmen who stand next on the books are taken on'.

But the houses of call had diminished in number. Whereas in 1821 there had been between 5,000 and 6,000 union tailors, now there were only 3,000. And in 1867 George Druitt, London tailors' leader, told the Royal Commission on Trade Unions that the house of call system was a 'remnant of the barbarism known as statute forms'. The system now worked to the advantage of the employer, who could keep the workman 'hanging about'.

The closed shop, including master or foreman, the house of call, and tramping, then, were effective up to a point in providing jobs for members and maintaining what the Dublin men called 'influence' and the Tailors' Amalgamated referred to in some towns as 'control'. This gave the tramping system traditional prestige, and associated as it was with the effective conduct of local strikes (the men left one by one and even the Combinations Acts could not stop them) it became stamped with the mark of trade union principle. Men would rather 'walk about' than work foul. The undermining of the closed shop based on apprenticeship (the new ASE dropped the ratio rule from its book in 1852 after taking a hammering in the great lock-out of the year before) went on at different rates in different trades. But it went on remorselessly.

Deprived of the essential element (the tramp who used to shake the foreman by the hand was no longer even allowed to show his nose at the yard gate), tramping simply became a wasteful and uncomfortable way of getting unemployment benefit, and a not very efficient way of using strike funds, as the boot and shoe men found in 1859 and the tailors in 1867.

Hobsbawm says that the tailors 'did not adopt tramping until sometime before the 1860s perhaps during or after the collapse of the tight closed shops in the towns in the 1820s and 1830s'.

Yet it would have been flat against the logic of the system and its origins to enter into it when conditions were turning against it. The tailors certainly had a developed tramping custom in the eighteenth century. Francis Place says that 'it was well known [1793] that a man who brought a certificate to any leather breeches maker's shop in the country would be sure of a day's keep, a night's lodging and a shilling to start again with the next morning, and in some of the larger towns a breakfast and half a crown in money to help him along'. It sounds almost like a tramping system, and Place and his mates certainly used tramping as a strike weapon. It was so used in 1764, and as late as 1867, as the union historian says, 'in line with tradition'. But it was then futile. To the leaders of the 1867 Tailors' 'Amalgamated', indeed, tramping was an albatross, a relic of the past which they wished to get rid of.

Given that the old conditions of which tramping was part and parcel were on their way out, the mass unemployment of the 1840s served to urge on those keen to discover an alternative. This was done with 'great diffidence', said the Stockport moulders (1848), 'knowing as we do that many of our members have the greatest veneration for it and for ourselves in bygone days we have looked to it as the mainstay of the society'.

The system was to outlive the ideal conditions for many decades. It was to be kept going partly by 'veneration', partly because it had a vital spark in it, and in the building trade, for example, the rank and file saw it as a useful adjunct to local struggles to uphold conditions. And in every trade, union leaders kept it going in a perverse way by allowing non-free or less than twelve-month members no unemployment benefit, but only a bed for the night – for which they had to travel. Even among the 'free' members there were those who found 'hanging about' too frustrating, and for whom tramping was better than boredom. Thus the tailors' general secretary wrote grudgingly of his respect for those who 'sacrifice a comfortable home and drawing their card going on travel and enduring many hardships, honestly in search of employment'.

Even the stay-at-home member saw virtue in an allowance that would keep the unemployed on the move – as the 1886 inquiry into Depressions of Trade was told.

Hobsbawm sees the tramping system 'in decline' from the 1840s, and this is confirmed by everything I have read on the subject. But if we date the 'system' (as different from the custom) to the late eighteenth century, then the decline was a long one, covering almost 70 out of the 120 years life. Fifty-five years after the moulders' delegate conference of 1848 opted for home donation, more travelling cards were drawn by members of the union in 1903 (1,233) than in 1848, at the height of the crisis (1,181). The great difference is that the 1848 membership was 3,736, and the 1,181 were 'walking fairly' – to use the official phrase – through more than fifty branches, 1,038 of them even calling in Reading where there was no work, no officials and no members – only a very obliging local landlord who kept the books straight. In 1903 the 1,233 made only short journeys in search of work and on average 98 of them were on the road in any month. In 1903, too, the union membership was some four times greater than in 1848.

Estimating how many tramps were on the roads at any stage in the history of the system is difficult. Statistics are scanty in the days before national union records were kept. Even after the 1840s, few unions kept a central register of tramp cards; the engineers only succeeded in establishing one in 1865. Branch figures for tramp reliefs totalled together give only a surrealist picture of numbers of men on the road, though they convey vividly the financial burden.

We know, for example, that in 1815, 60 tramping brushmakers entered London and 76 set out. In 1816, 120 came and 113 left, perhaps reflecting post-Napoleonic War unemployment. In 1817 the figures were 48 and 34. What one does not know is what these figures represent. In 1828, when the brushmakers' tramp system was in a state of 'perfection', fifty-seven tramps were relieved at a cost of £570, more than the combined total of 800 members' subscriptions. The brushmakers could not have stood more than 6 per cent of members on tramp for many years. Tramping brushmakers were expected to walk the complete route of thirty-seven club houses strung out over 1,200 miles before getting any relief at home. Whether the fifty-seven tramps made the grand tour or not there is no way of knowing. In that year thirty-four tramps passed through Shrewsbury on their way to Chester, and eighteen passed south on their way to Wolverhampton. It may be that some had found work on the way, or perhaps they were just ignoring the rule about working the circuit. The ironmoulders complained of those not 'walking fairly' (a 1,500-mile marathon with three sea crossings). Some members, sensibly as it proved, took advantage of cheap rail fares to head straight to towns where there might be work. This threw the relief system into confusion, but within twenty years most big craft unions had adopted the 'unfair' method and were paying members fares to known jobs. The ironmoulders' records show great variations in tramp numbers. In 1841, 600 came to Manchester, 258 to St Helens, 156 to Lancaster, 145 to Bath, 69 to Dublin. The circuit was being worked harder in the industrial north where common sense indicated jobs might be had. But during the 1848 slump branch returns, whether of York, Manchester, Bristol, Stourbridge or Lancaster, were uniformly over the 1,000 mark.

During 1847–8, the moulders issued some 1,000–1,100 tramp cards. During the slump year of 1879, when home donation was the rule, nearly 2,000 tramp cards were issued. At first sight that suggests more tramps at the later date, though in 1848 a third of members took out cards and in 1879 15–16 per cent did so. In 1879, 213 on average were on the road in any month; in December 1847 1,181 were tramping, many without official relief. In December 1848, after home donation was brought in, the figure dropped to less than 100.

Similarly with the masons, there were around 1,000 on tramp in the winter of 1847–8 and roughly the same number in 1879. But at the earlier date the membership was 6,741. At the later date it was declining (rapidly) from a peak of 27,000. At the earlier date, 16 per cent were on the road; at the later less than 5 per cent.

Comparisons of this kind are difficult to make for the engineers, since statistics for the pre-amalgamation days of the 1840s exist only at branch level. One historian of the union says that at times 10 per cent of the 'Old Mechanics' went on tramp. This would mean, in the 1830s and 1840s, between 300 and 400 on the road. In 1879, which the ASE considered the 'darkest' year of its history, some 2,000 tramps took the road, though it is very difficult to say how many tramped how far. But the 2,000 figure is only 4 per cent of the membership and less than a third of the unemployed. If we look at the engineers' reports for 1865, a fairly good year, with sometimes less than 1,000 of the 29,000 members out of work, we get something of a picture of tramp movements under light pressure. During February (there are no figures for January) 65 men set out; 36 were relieved once, 17 twice, 10 three times and 2 four times. By March, 30 of them had stopped tramping, and another 97 had taken the road, making 132. In April 81 dropped off and 51 carried on, joined by another 86, bringing the total to 137. In May 99 dropped off, leaving 38, joined by another 107, making a total of 145. This continued through the summer, dwindling by autumn until in December 80 were still on the road of the 1,200 who took out cards during the year. So at any given time 10 per cent of those who had taken out cards were on the road, or less than one in 200 of the total membership.

In 1888 the ironmoulders or ironfounders, having kept fairly detailed records of tramping since the mid-1850s, were able to give a statistical breakdown of number of cards issued, number of tramps on travel on average, and the travellers related to each 1,000 members. Supplementing these 1888 figures with later records of the union, I have worked out the following general indication of the system's gradual decline. In the 1870s an average of 1623 cards a year; in the 1880s, 1257 cards; in the 1890s 911 cards; from 1900 to 1909, 680 cards; and between 1910 and 1919, 101 cards a year. During the 1860s, 126 on average were constantly travelling; during the 1870s, 100; the 1880s, 84; the 1890s, 73; from 1900 to 1909, 101 and from 1910 to 1919, 13. In these terms the decline was erratic for during the first decade of the twentieth century there was a surge of unemployment among steelworkers, ironfounders, masons and others.

Since the membership rose fairly steadily through the period the figures per 1,000 members show the relative decline more truly. During the 1860s, 11·9 per 1,000; 1870s, 10·1 per 1,000; the 1880s, 7·02 per 1,000; the 1890s, 4·78 per 1,000; 1900–1909, 5·4 per 1,000 and 1910–1919, 0·71.

Engineering union statistics analysed by union historian J. Jeffreys show a similar pattern. From 1865 to 1874, 35 per cent of the unemployed took out cards. During the 1880s this dropped to 18 per cent, in the 1890s, to 10 per cent; from 1900 to 1909, to 4 per cent and from 1910 to 1914, to 1 per cent.

Masons' statistics are less complete; indeed, at various times the general secretary complained that only between 10 and 25 per cent of lodges sent in complete returns. But from the union's fortnightly reports I calculate that in 1845 7 per cent of members were on travel; in 1848, 16 per cent; in 1851, 5 per cent; in 1860, 4·5 per cent; in 1879, approximately 8 per cent; and in 1881, 2 per cent.

Among the tailors, again from incomplete figures: 1869, 7·6 per cent; 1876, 6·8 per cent; 1884, 4·7 per cent; 1891, 2·1 per cent; 1894, 1·7 per cent; 1898, about 1 per cent.

Among the printers (outside London) where tramps were paid a penny a mile, the figure for 1863 is 180 miles a member, dwindling to nine miles a member in 1898. Out-of-work pay introduced in 1873 builds up slowly from 10d per member per year to 8s 6d in 1898. During 1879, tramping printers covered (or were paid for) 336,000 miles, 14 times round the world and three times the 1873 figure, despite the growing use of home donation.

Is the slow decline a tribute to the stubbornness of tradition or the stubbornness of the habitual tramp? Looking again at the engineers records for 1865.

Most members who took out cards did not stay long on the road. By March 1865, 35 of the February cards were still in circulation out of 65. By April 44 of the March cards were still on the move and only 7 of the February cards. By May 24 of the April cards were in use, 10 of the March cards and 5 of the February issue. In August, by which time a total of 755 cards had been issued, and 200 tramps were on the road, these included 6 from June, 1 from May, 2 from April and just 1 from February.

The man from February, who might qualify for the title of 'roadster', was 25-year-old Charles Chubb of Plymouth, who set off via Plymouth, reached Southwark by March, Deptford and Woolwich by April, Swindon and Chippenham by May, Chepstow, Gloucester and Bristol by June, Stoke on Trent, Crewe and Chester by July, and Birkenhead by August, where he vanished, perhaps finding the kind of dockyard job he may have known in Plymouth. He would seem typical of the engineering long-distance tramp whom Jeffreys thinks were 'generally the younger members'. A none too exhaustive check through the engineers records (which obligingly give the age of tramps) shows that in 1865 some three-quarters of those taking out cards were under 30 years of age. In 1879, a slump year, nearly half the tramps were over 30, in 1885 when trade was still depressed, something like 45 per cent were over 30; in 1899 and 1905 around 40 per cent were over 30. Only in 1915, before tramping vanishes from the union reports, were nine tramps out of twelve men in their fifties.

The question of the good and the bad tramp has been discussed in previous chapters. A judgement of the system, its merits and demerits is to a certain extent a matter of opinion. During the 1840s the cabinet makers said: 'If it had not been in our power to keep up our tramping transport, a universal reduction in wages would have taken place.' Of the same period, the historian of the provincial printers, whose tramping system was admittedly piecemeal, said that it 'did little to stop them (the tramps) entering unfair houses'.

While many masons' lodges were convinced that tramping kept up wages (in 1843 the Stafford lodge was categorical that 'owing to the tramp station being reduced' wages at the church were down to 22 shillings and at the jail and the asylum to 19s and 20s), moulders' lodges thought that tramps were not always proof against strike breaking.

Tramping clearly became less effective as a strike weapon the more workers were involved and the more widespread the strike. This is of course a different proposition from saying that at the latter end of the century the tramp was more likely to break a strike than his brother at the earlier time. Tramping clearly favoured the local strike, and this in turn was favoured by the local militants. National executives and central fund holders, doing all they could to control expenditure and strikes which ate into union funds, discouraged such local disputes and on the whole were more willing to consider the demerits of tramping rather than the merits.

By the end of the nineteenth century, the system, however, clearly belonged to the past of the craft unions and with the onset of the 'new' unions everything that was to do with the past and the crafts was under attack, rightly or wrongly.

With the trade union movement under pressure from its 'new' elements with eyes firmly turned towards the future, and with the new emphasis on political action rather than the time-honoured exclusive 'trade matters' approach, the whole concept of trade unions, their role, nature and even their origins was thrown into the melting-pot of debate.

When that debate (some aspects of which will be discussed in the final chapter) was over, the unions had been given a new future, and a new past as well.

As the tramp or traveller was relegated to a few lines in the regular union reports and journals and finally disappeared altogether, so the system and its significance were relegated to footnotes in the history of the trade union movement.

16   An Old Argument – the Webbs and the unions

By the early 1890s, the trade union movement had reached an important turning-point. The hard core of the movement, the 'old' craft unions, had more or less completed the period of consolidation, with stable national bodies absorbing most of the local societies in each trade. The difficult period of further amalgamation, aiming at one union in each industry, was still ahead. The 'new' unions, drawing their strength from the unskilled and semi-skilled often regardless of trade or industry, had made their decisive appearance, competing with the old unions in recruitment and obliging them to widen their conditions of membership, and challenging them for leadership of the movement. And, with the victory in the Trades Union Congress of the 'new' unions over the 'old' on the issue of the 'legal' eight-hour day, the traditional 'trade matters only' policy had been decisively changed towards one which embraced political action not only in defence of trade union rights, but over the whole range of social issues.

It was at this moment that Sidney and Beatrice Webb turned their talents for research to a study of the unions. They discovered that union activities made not a single common thread but a 'spider's web', and that what had to be written was not a 'treatise, but a history'. To know what the movement was and where it was going, one had to know what it had been and whence it had come. 'The history of trade unionism is the history of a state within our state and one so jealously democratic that to know it well is to know the English working man as no reader of middle-class histories can know him.'

So they published, in 1894, *The History of Trade Unionism*, a work on a scale to do justice to the size of the subject. They drew on the orthodox sources of economic and social history, from government reports to newspaper articles and pamphlets. But in addition they drew on the documentation of the movement itself, its reports, journals, minutes, on the histories and memoirs some of its members had written and on the personal recollections of yet others.

The mass of papers they gathered remains a major source for the historian of any aspect of trade unionism.

The *History* was, and is, an immense and valuable work, unique in two ways. Before the Webbs, there had been attempts at such a history, yet none done so systematically and on such a scale. Again, they were able to talk to veterans still alive in the 1890s who remembered the early struggles. None before them had done it so thoroughly, none afterwards would have the same opportunity to do so. Indeed, everyone coming after had to begin with the Webbs, and has been glad to do so.

Their work has remained a landmark and a monument. Not a sacred one, for G. D. H. Cole, with his critique of their writing on the 'general union' movement of the 1820s and 1830s and their concept of the 'new model' unions of mid-century, has led the way in necessary reassessment of their work. However, each reassessment leaves the *History* basically unchallenged, and no one since has felt bold enough to go over the ground they covered. So well did they do their work that many writers have been happy, with a quote from or paraphrase of the Webbs, to cover the vital formative period of the unions, giving themselves a sure launching pad for their own particular study of later history. The weight carried by the Webbs has ensured that the early days of the movement can be swiftly summed up if not disposed of, and the account proper can begin with, say, the Combination Acts or even with the Tolpuddle Martyrs of 1834. The Webbs' general view of the 'origins and early struggles of trade unions in this country' has been repeated more times than can be counted. Because of them the nature of trade union origins has been declared without hesitation and fear of contradiction.

Faced with the mountainous research of the Webbs, the reader tends to forget that their *History* was worked on and published during a period of fierce contention between opposing notions of what the trade union movement was about and what its future aims should be. The Webbs, future architects of the Labour Party Constitution, were in no doubt about which way the trade union movement should go.

In 1920, when they published a revised and amplified edition of *The History*, they made these aims clear in their statement of satisfaction with what the movement had achieved:

Its legal and constitutional status which was then [1890] indefinite and precarious, has now been explicitly defined and embodied in precise and absolutely expressed statutes. Its internal organisation has been, in many cases, officially adopted as part of the machinery of public administration. Most important of all, it has equipped itself with an entirely new political organisation, extending throughout the whole of Great Britain, inspired by large ideas embodied in a comprehensive programme of Social Reconstruction, which has already achieved the position of 'His Majesty's Opposition' and now makes a bid for that of 'His Majesty's Government'.

There can be no doubt that in publishing their original work, though they specifically aimed at 'scientific' objectivity, the Webbs were keenly aware of the struggle between 'old' and 'new' unionism. They wanted the trade union movement to face the future and turn its gaze from the past. The first chapter of the *History*, then, was a part of that controversy within the movement, and its tone was distinctly polemical. They entered the long and intermittent argument about the origins (and therefore also the nature) of the trade union movement not simply to win it, but if possible to get on to next business with no more time wasting.

They began by defining a trade union as a 'continuous association of wage earners for the purpose of maintaining and improving the conditions of their working lives'. Thus they began their story 'only with the latter part of the seventeenth century, before which date we have been unable to discover the existence in the British Isles of anything falling within our definition'.

Like any definition, their's is open to discussion. Their general statement about the 200-year history of trade unions (in the 1890s) remains basically unchallenged. But they did not leave it at that. In their search in time beyond the seventeenth century, they looked for possible 'predecessors' of the trade unions among the journeymen's fraternities, 'yeomen or bachelor companies', and the lodge organisation of the masons. They left open the verdict on the masons' lodges, but by page 11, they had disposed of the city craft organisations, of journeymen.

Then they turned to the 'outward resemblance of the trade union to the craft guild', which had 'long attracted the attention both of the friends and the enemies of trade unionism'.

Thanks to Lujo von Brentano's essay, 'The History and Development of Guilds and the Origin of Trade Unions' (1870), and a paraphrase of it which appeared in *Conflicts of Capital and Labour*, by former TUC leader and historian George Howell (1877), it was by the 1890s, said the Webbs, 'commonly accepted that the trade union had in some undefined way really originated from the craft gild'.

This view had been argued long before Howell – in the 1830s by the anonymous author of *Combinations of Trades* (1831); by the famous framework knitters' leader Gravener Henson in his history of his own trade (1831); and in the 1850s by the author friend of the engineering unions, Thomas Hughes, among others. But their opinions were lost in time. George Howell's book, and the repetition of his argument in the bad-tempered polemical work *Trade Unions New and Old* (1891), brought the matter into the area of current trade union discussion. So the Webbs were 'under the obligation of digressing to examine the relation between the medieval gild and the modern trade union'.

They digressed and returned with an emphatic answer. There was no relation:

The supposed descent in this country of the trade unions from the medieval craft gilds rests, as far as we have been able to discover, upon no evidence whatsoever. The historical proof is all the other way. In London, for instance, more than one trade union has preserved an unbroken existence from the eighteenth century. The craft gilds still exist in the city companies and at no point in their history do we find the slightest evidence of the branching off from them of independent journeymen's societies. By the eighteenth century the London journeymen had in nearly all cases lost whatever participation they may possibly once have possessed in the companies which had for the most part already ceased to have any connection with the trades of which they bore the name.

They looked not only in London, but in other cities from Sheffield to Dublin, and concluded: 'We assert indeed with some confidence that in no case did any trade union in the United Kingdom arise either directly or indirectly by descent from a craft gild.'

There were 'picturesque likenesses', between gild and union, 'regulations for admission, the box with its three locks, the common meal, the titles of the officers and so forth'. But these were shared by all kinds of friendly societies. Indeed, the 'fantastic ritual' of trade unions of 1829–34 was taken from the ceremonies of the Friendly Society of Oddfellows'. And there was common to both gild and union a purpose, the assertion of 'what was once the accepted principle of medieval society', the 'compulsory maintenance of the Standard of Life' by state intervention. 'When these regulations fell into disuse the workers combined to secure their enforcement.'

Turning from 'hypothetical origin' to 'recorded facts' – manuscript records of companies, trade pamphlets, House of Commons Journals, etc. – they discovered in the latter half of the seventeenth century 'various traces of sporadic combinations and associations some of which appear to have maintained in obscurity a continuous existence'. In the eighteenth century the House of Commons Journals were full of complaints by employers of 'combinations'. In the seventeenth century the city companies, who often spoke up to the government about trade, made no such complaints, 'which suggests to us that few, if any, such combinations existed'.

Thus, trade unions, they concluded, sprang 'not from any particular institution but from every opportunity for the meeting together of wage earners of the same occupation' – a strike, a petition to Parliament, gathering at the same public house to take a 'social pint of porter together'.

The emphasis is on spontaneous generation, passing only into 'durable' association when, due to the conditions of the Industrial Revolution, 'the great bulk of the workers had ceased to be independent producers themselves controlling the processes and owning the materials and the product of their labour and had passed into the condition of lifelong wage earners possessing neither the instruments of production nor the commodity in its finished state.'

The Webbs mention briefly the old workshop organisation of the printers' chapel, wondering briefly whether the free journeymen printers' organisation of the 1580s survived or not, the seventeenth-century 'combinations' of journeymen clothworkers and feltmakers, and then move on to the eighteenth century where they begin to trace continuous developments with the journeymen clubs which show themselves in London and other towns – tailors, coachmakers and curriers, and the handloom weavers, woolcombers and framework knitters of the country towns. They are inclined to award the latter groups the title 'pioneers of the trade union movement', distinguishing them from the 'fiercely exclusive' town artisans, 'more decisively marked off from the mass of the manual workers than from the small class of capitalist employers'.

It was these associations [woollen workers, framework knitters] that initiated what afterwards became the common purpose of nearly all 18th century combinations, the appeal to the Government and the House of Commons to save the wage earners from the new policy of buying labour like the raw material of manufacture, in the cheapest market.

(One senses here the polemical edge to the Webbs' contrast between 'exclusive' artisan clubs and the framework knitters' and woollen workers' appealing to Parliament, which has a certain parallel with 'old' and 'exclusive' unions and the 'new' unions appealing to the State for support in ensuring decent working conditions for the mass of the manual workers.)

However, no matter which trade or industrial grouping pioneered trade unionism, the argument was that unions were a more or less spontaneous response to the conditions of the Industrial Revolution by a new class of lifelong wage earners. They did not arise from any previous form of craft organisation nor have any link with such. The Webbs were quite emphatic about that.

And many succeeding writers have woven both analysis and 'assertion' into their own introductory remarks:

'In the sixteenth – seventeenth century many attempted combinations of journeymen outside the gilds for better conditions and many attempts by the gild to suppress them either directly or with the help of Parliament. These independent attempts at combination rather than the gilds themselves are to be regarded as the forerunners of trade unionism.' (G. D. H. Cole, *A Short History of the British Working Class Movement* (1948))

'. . . it would be a waste of ingenuity to connect the scattered and ephemeral combinations of a dim past with trade unions as we know them to-day. Nor is the modern trade union, as it was once fashionable to suppose, a lineal descendant of the medieval craft gild. A trade union is a permanent combination of wage earners for the protection and improvement of their conditions of employment.' (C. M. Lloyd, *Trade Unionism* (1921))

In his *History of the Tinplate Workers and Sheetmetal Workers* (1949), veteran trade unionist A. J. Kidd quotes the Webbs on the origins of trade unions. But then he extends their argument about the nature of the gilds as being primarily organisations for masters and traders to a piece of evidence sent him by a colleague – a public notice issued by 'journeymen tinplate workers' in Liverpool in 1756. He concludes that it 'savours too much of gild methods and would suggest that the warning came from an association of employers rather than a voluntary combination of journeymen . . .'. Such is the influence of the Webbs.

'The Unions of the nineteenth century were not the offspring of the past, a heritage of history, they were born from the circumstance of the time,' writes R. F. Wearmouth in *Some Working Class Movements of the 19th Century* (1948), following this with a quotation from the Webbs.

For many writers the Webbs had indeed convincingly closed the argument. But there is no harm in reopening it.

In his book *Trade Unionism New and Old* (1891) George Howell makes two statements: 'Trade unionism not only owes its origins to the old English guilds, but the earlier trade unions were in reality the legitimate successors of the craft guilds which flourished in this country down to the time of the suppression of the monasteries. . . .'

Thus he implied that the unions were at one with the gilds and the city companies which succeeded them. To link a forward-looking trade union movement in the 1890s with the by then archaic city companies, whose only functions seemed to be banquets and charitable occasions, was demanding too much. It seemed both reactionary and divisive.

But Howell also wrote this, which was not so unreasonable: 'Without the knowledge derived from a study of the gild system, the organisation rules and operations of the trade unions cannot be properly understood.'

The Webbs clearly thought such a study time-wasting and baseless. They declared next business and there matters rested. But there is no reason why today's student of trade union history should not look again at Howell's assertion. Why, indeed, did the early trade societies and the unions which followed them choose organisational forms, even ancient preambles and rules, from earlier organisations? 'Picturesque likenesses'? These might attract writers of the 1890s, in the wake of the Aesthetic movement. But why should they attract the hard-headed men of the early trade societies? When the London workers interviewed by Mayhew in 1850 used the medieval term 'craft' or 'fraternity' or when, somewhat earlier in the century, the son of Rennie the engineer, used the term 'gild' to describe organisations we would call trade unions, they made an unselfconscious and non-literary use of the terms.

Why did the Irish trade unions carry on their banners the coats of arms and charter dates of their city gilds? The Webbs investigated why a charter document of 1670 'given to the exclusively Protestant incorporation of working masters' came 'into the possession of what has always been a mainly Catholic body of wage earners'.

The Webbs came to the unflattering conclusion that it was a 'love of the picturesque', a 'trait of Irish character' that made the Dublin men claim this link with the past.

But, Mayhew noted, the London journeymen curriers carried on the title page of their union 'articles' in 1850 the craft arms with 'appropriate supporters', though the motto had been adapted to nineteenth-century trade society outlook – 'United to support not combined to injure'.

What character trait marked the English curriers, or for that matter every other English craft union which did exactly as did its Irish brothers? There was no need to go to Dublin. On the walls of the club houses of the English unions in the 1890s, between the advertisements and the gilt mirrors, hung emblems like those of the curriers. Brushmakers, bricklayers, cordwainers, coachmakers, carpenters, compositors, founders, hatters, masons, painters, plasterers, plumbers, tinplate workers, tailors, weavers, shipwrights, all had emblems containing what the brushmakers called 'the authentic sign of the craft' or the tailors 'the arms of the incorporation', complete with dates and sometimes with Latin mottoes.

So strong was the custom that later unions like the steam engine makers, boilermakers, and lithographic printers invented themselves coats of arms, sometimes borrowing from the building trade.

The Webbs, unwilling to accept the direct transmission of craft traditions, argued that early union 'ritual and regalia' was borrowed from the 'small friendly societies' around them. Committed to this argument, they then tried to prove that the Operative Builders' Union in 1834 took its clearly building trade ritual from the Leeds Woolcombers, who got it from the Rochdale Flannel Weavers, who got it from the Oddfellows' Friendly Society, who borrowed it from the Freemasons. Later historians have suggested more simply that the Leeds Woolcombers borrowed it from the builders. But if we accept that this peculiar roundabout explanation will do for the OBU ritual, will it do for the union emblems of some sixteen London-based crafts? Why should a craft organisation go outside its craft for its 'emblematic devices'? Is there no more direct line of inheritance?

Anyone who studies the activities of the craft gilds and the companies which succeeded them in London without a break cannot help but note that they had one main, overriding preoccupation. This was to regulate entry into the trade via apprenticeship, control relations within the trade by a rational balance of numbers between the masters, journeymen and apprentices working at it, and defend it from outside incursion by 'foreigners', whether masters or journeymen. The organisation's chief means of regulating the inner balance was the by-laws of the company (backed to some extent after the mid-sixteenth century by the law of the land). The chief means of regulating the balance with the outside world was through the 'right of search' guaranteed first by municipal law and later by Royal Charter.

The Webbs say that 'for the most part' the city companies had already ceased to have any connection with their trades before the eighteenth century, that is before the development of the journeymen's clubs and similar organisations. But this is not so. The first craft company to abandon formally the crucial 'right of search' was the Merchant Taylors Company (of whom more later) who did so only on the eve of the eighteenth century.

The Merchant Taylors, one of the few craft companies to climb by its wealth into the oligarchy of the 'Great Twelve' mainly trading companies, had a real direct connection with manufacture up to this point. Other merchant companies had this connection mainly through control of an 'inferior' craft company, the Haberdashers controlling the feltmakers or hatters, and the Ironmongers containing the tinplate workers within their ranks. The feltmakers and tinplate workers broke free to form independent craft companies at around the time the Merchant Taylors abandoned the right of search. But they, like the other new craft incorporations, the coachmakers and wheelwrights, secured the right of search by Royal Charter and exercised it vigorously into the eighteenth century.

So did other older companies, like the clothworkers, wheelwrights, curriers, blacksmiths, founders, silk weavers and framework knitters. As has been shown, the smaller trades retained, through a licence system, some control right into the nineteenth century. Craft companies in Bristol were assisted by magistrates to seize and burn goods well into the eighteenth century.

Writing of the gilds in 1968, Sylvia L. Thrupp divides their thousand-year history into five phases. The last 'during which gild organisation of trade and industry died out dragged on from the seventeenth into the nineteenth century'.

The right of search was not exercised willingly by those who controlled the companies, the big masters and traders, who dominated the self-perpetuating 'Courts of Assistants' which had usurped power around the middle of the sixteenth century. The companies often carried on the search under pressure – from within. After a long tussle with their journeymen, the Curriers' Company decided in 1700 to 'let the Great Seal goe about as formerly'. Indeed, in most of the bigger companies, the Court of Assistants took no active part in the search but allowed it (in the case of the tailors and the blacksmiths from the fifteenth century, and the weavers and the clothworkers from the sixteenth century) to become the main function of the 'yeomanry' within the company.

Now, anyone who studies the early union organisations and their immediate predecessors knows that their overriding function and pre-occupation, like that of their predecessors, was to regulate entry to the trade by apprenticeship and relations within the trade by preserving the ratio of apprentices and journeymen to masters, keeping out 'illegal' men or employers, and denying them employment or labour. Until 1814, when the last of the 'mercantile' laws was repealed, the early trade unions used the same laws and by-laws as the craft companies had used, supplementing the sanction when necessary with industrial pressure. When the legal sanction was removed, the industrial sanction remained, and was exercised as long as the unions could extend it – the boilermakers and compositors, for example, preserved the apprenticeship regulations and ratios down to the end of the nineteenth century.

The unions may have had the 'medieval' urge to maintain the 'Standard of Life'. But if they were only the product of the conditions of the Industrial Revolution, if they were formed spontaneously in answer to *present* need with no reference to previous 'institutions', why did they adopt and hold on to past forms of sanction, long after reason might have indicated a change? Why not immediately adopt the method of getting all workers, irrespective of how they entered the trade, into their organisation? This approach, however, was adopted reluctantly by the craft unions in one form or another only towards the end of the nineteenth century, and then chiefly under pressure of competition from the 'new' unions.

But if there were a connection between trade society and union and the craft gilds and companies which took over from them, wherein does it lie? According to the Webbs, there were journeymen's 'fraternities' which suddenly appeared in the late fourteenth and early fifteenth centuries, then disappeared. From then on there were only 'sporadic', 'isolated' and 'ephemeral' combinations of such wage earners until the late seventeenth and early eighteenth centuries, when there was a 'class of life-long wage earners' to sustain them. The journeymen could form no 'durable' organisation of their own. The 'yeoman' or 'bachelor' companies, said the Webbs, 'do not appear to have long survived the sixteenth century'.

Here one must return to the Webbs' definition of a trade union: 'a continuous association of wage earners'. At the time of stating (1894–1920), this was highly effective for it disposed of the fifteenth-century journeymen's fraternities as proto-unions. The demerit of the term 'continuous' is, however, that if applied to the nineteenth century it would exclude (at least until the 1870s) most organisations of cotton and mine workers. And since the cotton and mine workers were demonstrably industrial proletarians organising to protect a class interest, 'continuity' seems an academic matter.

The Webbs' definition, in fact, fits rather the trade club than the trade union. The essence of the actual term 'trade union', in one vital aspect, is that stated by the journeymen cordwainers in the 1790s when they were perhaps among the first to use the term a 'union of the trade' – that is the uniting of the workers at the craft not by locality, but throughout the land, as wide as possible a union to oppose the impositions of their masters. By breaking out of the degenerated *local* alliance with their masters under the old form of work organisation, and making an alliance with their fellow workmen, *wherever they were*, they were making a class alliance.

As the Bath shoemakers put it in the early 1800s, joining with their 'loving shopmaites' in other towns against their 'tyrant'.

The fraternal journeymen saddlers, cordwainers, tailors, bakers and blacksmiths, of the 1380s/1420s, could have no 'union' in the sense of the cordwainers of the 1790s. But on simple grounds of 'continuity' they can no more be dismissed than the 'ephemeral' combinations of textile workers of the 1800s. Indeed these fifteenth-century 'fraternities' were not 'ephemeral', nor were they 'sporadic'. They had their own dwelling and meeting places, the tailors in a 'house of ill repute' (said their masters), the bakers with a 'revelling' hall. The saddlers, tailors and bakers had their own 'cloathing' or livery; the cordwainers had their own 'bedel' to call them to prayer when their masters thought they ought to have been at work. They claimed (saddlers) that they had existed 'time out of mind' and even the master saddlers admitted the fraternity had existed thirteen years (see Chapter 2).

Yet if we accept them as separate organisations, where did they go? Why were the journeymen of this period, not only in London but in Coventry, Oxford and other cities, able to form stable organisations, so stable the masters had to have civic or even (in the case of Coventry) kingly help to bring them to book, while those of later centuries were not? Have we some sort of time-warp, under which the conditions for a separate organisation of wage earners, appeared at an early period and disappeared in a later one? Why were the measures against 'combination' in 1349 and 1383 less effective than the similar law of 1549? Where did the journeymen go to? Did they have any form of organisation between the false dawn of Henry IV's time and the real one of Queen Anne's? Did the English wage earner who taught the world to organise fall into some limbo for 300 years?

I don't think so. I think that the journeymen, or rather the hard core of them, had access to a form of organisation *continuously* throughout the period, and that form, however unlikely it seems, was the craft company.

I would argue that the journeymen fraternities of the 1400s were not so much separate organisations formed by journeymen as the continuance in force by the workpeople of those trades of the older craft-religious fraternities. These had once united master and man with the backing of their own solidarity and the blessing of the Church, 'to work for no one but each other' and to 'work his brother before any other'.

During the fourteenth century, the position of the masters was secured. The seven-year apprenticeship as first step to mastership was embodied

in municipal law and in London by 1376 some fifty craft gilds had secured
a share in municipal government from the ruling merchant elite. And the
purchase of the 'freedom' of the city as a further step to mastership was a
second protective wall around the masters' position. Their rights secured
by secular law, they now had less need of either craft solidarity or the
backing of the Church. The turning-point perhaps was the City proclamation of 1383 against 'conventicle and assemblies', by which these
old fraternity powers were declared illegal. After this we begin to hear of
rebellious fraternities. In their clash with authority in 1415–17 the
London journeymen tailors laid stress on fraternity rights and 'rites'
under the name of St John, patron saint of the original gild. In 1423, the
journeymen blacksmiths agreed after negotiation to accept a three-year
probation period before claiming mastership. But they secured control
over the admission of new labour to the trade. It was specifically laid down
that the journeymen should belong to the fraternity of St Loy, the blacksmiths' patron saint, 'as of old time' (see Chapter 2).

The 'journeymen fraternities' were placed 'under the governance' of
their masters and 'disappeared'. At the same time, within the craft
organisation during the fifteenth century a 'universal' development takes
place – on the one hand a 'livery' entirely masters, on the other hand a
'yeomanry', mainly journeymen. The apprentice regulations of late
fifteenth century allow the livery masters two or more apprentices, and
the ones 'outside the cloathing' only one. Thus the yeomanry begins to
develop as an organisation of journeymen and small masters, while the
livery is composed of richer masters, who secure complete control of the
running of the 'livery companies'.

With the Reformation and the Act of 1547 and the royal take-over of
religious endowments, the King's Commissioners demanded of the craft
companies 'whether or not they had any peculiar brotherhood within
their corporation. In some companies the yeomanry still constituted such
a peculiar brotherhood and in all cases where a yeomanry existed, there
was a danger that it might be so interpreted.'

The Reformation had indeed another result than the secularisation of
religious bodies. With this went the tightening of labour discipline, not
only by the 1549 Act against combinations but with the reduction of the
number of 'saints' days' and the completing of the process whereby the
'working or labouring part', the 'handytrade' organised in the yeomanry,
became a subordinate part of the livery company with no outside powers.
With each 'remodelling', not only did the journeymen lose the power of

electing the wardens of the company who embodied its powers, but the smaller masters also lost these rights which were finally vested in the livery, or a section of it.

Continuous recording of the yeomanry begins with continuous craft company records, after the Reformation, and it is evident from the records of companies like the tailors, bakers and blacksmiths that the yeomanry continued to exercise as far as they were able all the functions of the older craft fraternity.

The distinction between livery and yeomanry, say the carpenters' historians, is that between 'more prosperous and less prosperous and by and large between masters and journeymen'. The bakers' yeomanry consisted of 'free householders as well as servants'. The pewterers' yeomanry was a mixed body of 'householders and journeymen'. The clothworkers' yeomanry were the craftsmen and the livery the 'merchants who employed them'. Most companies distinguished according to charter various grades of membership, each paying a certain level of quarterage. Among the tailors, where the yeomanry or bachelors company came to include even wealthy masters, the quarterage varied from 2s 2d a year to 8d a year for the journeymen.

It is difficult to say exactly how many journeymen and how many masters were in the yeomanry of each company. The variations were considerable as, in the words of the cutlers' historian, the ranks of the yeomanry began to fill with masters queueing up for the very sparse chances of promotion to the livery – the gateway not only to prestige but to expansion of the business. There is a period towards the end of the sixteenth century when the yeomanry contains so many discontented masters that according to the company historian and economic historian, George Unwin, the journeymen became an 'appendage' to the clothworkers' company.

When the clothworkers' yeomanry was 'remodelled' after the Reformation, the merchants attempted to divide the journeymen yeomen from the small masters, but the attempt was resisted and the 'handytrade' stuck together. The two remained together with the journeymen in a 'subordinate position', says the company historian. The 'subordination' which appears to last for about a generation is a matter of opinion, for the small masters in the yeomanry complain that the journeymen 'come to work and leave off at their pleasure, yea and control their masters, if they be not served'.

By 1596 the introduction of a balloting box to 'decide all doubts and questions in variance' and in 1598 a new wage demand by the yeomanry show that the old spirit is no longer 'subordinated'. By the early seventeenth century such is the pressure of the journeymen within the yeomanry that Unwin says that the 'specific aims of the small master seem to have dropped out of sight'. The development of what Unwin, in another context, calls a 'composite class interest' of small masters and journeymen faced by dominant employers, has tentatively begun. The clothworkers' yeomanry with this class composition was to remain an active part of the company until mid-eighteenth century when the 'search' is abandoned and 'with the abolition of the Yeomanry Wardens, the end of the (company's) existence as a trade guild was very close at hand'.

The Webbs, referring to the actions of journeymen clothworkers in 1675 and 1682, treat them as ephemeral 'combinations'. 'It is not clear whether any lasting association then resulted.' But on the contrary it is fairly clear that the men involved are the yeomanry of the company.

The Webbs refer to another 'combination', that of 'Free Journeymen Printers' in 1583, and remark that it is 'uncertain' whether it managed to 'continue in existence as a trade union'. It was not a trade union, of course, but journeymen 'freemen' of the Stationers Company, negotiating within the company yeomanry over wage rates and control of apprentice intake. Journeymen compositors sought the 'freedom' of the Stationers Company until the nineteenth century. They continued their efforts to regulate industrial matters within the company until the 1790s when they decided to appeal direct to the public over the uncontrolled 'taking' of apprentices. As long as the companies were prepared to use the means at their disposal to regulate entry to the trade, and many of them went on doing this, willingly or under pressure from the yeomanry, then the journeymen together with the small masters. They found their organisation *within the company* imperfect and undemocratic, but more effective than trying to work outside it.

The situation of the yeomanry in the craft companies is summed up well by Howe and Waite in their history of the London print trade:

The Guilds contained both employers and employed. Independent action by either side was difficult. The dice were heavily loaded . . . vested interests . . . but there was the mechanism for the articulation of disputes. There was no effective higher court of appeal for the journeymen. The yeomen, the ordinary freemen were workmen or small masters. The employers comprised the livery with responsibility for control of entry, unlicensed printing offices, maintaining of wage rates and employment, relief of old age and sickness . . . the yeomanry in particular.

In the Weavers' Company, the yeomanry 'formed a bridge between the governing body and the rank and file'. The historians of the carpenters' company, referring to the late seventeenth century, say that the company, even when its powers waned, 'was still the most effective agency through which ordinary journeymen could express their demands collectively'. Or, as Unwin says of the feltworkers' journeymen, 'Though excluded from any share in its direction they had still an interest in the constitution of the company and sought to attain their objects by its means.'

The bakers' company, which continued to seek control of the trade into the nineteenth century, uniting with master bakers throughout Britain in 1779 to block a bill for 'laying open' the trade, took steps to see that journeymen paid quarterage and remained company members.

'The other side of the picture of the bakers' control over their workmen is their recognition of the men's right to employment. Journeymen free of the company had the first claim to employment.' However, in 1762 the Master and Wardens had to have help from the Mayor to control a journeymen's 'combination', and again in the 1790s.

A degree of confusion arises perhaps from the word 'combination', which is often used by the Webbs and other historians to imply an organisation, or an attempt to set one up, which proves 'ephemeral'. But in this era an organisation of their own would not necessarily be of any value for the journeymen; while the power of search, legally backed, remained in the hands of the company, indeed, they would be powerless; the companies had the power legally to drive them from the trade if they were not company members.

A 'combination' can mean more than one thing, but most often I take it to mean a movement, an action, a petition, a threat to strike, a strike. This interpretation of the word as an economic action, rather than a would-be permanent body, helps to explain why, during the period of the Combination Acts, formal bodies of journeymen openly existing might remain unmolested, only being deemed 'combinations' at the whim of their employers when an industrial dispute arose and the masters were unable to come to terms with or defeat the men.

With the newly incorporated companies of the late seventeenth century – feltmakers, tinplate workers, coachmakers, wheelwrights and others – not only did their charters lay down that journeymen should pay quarterage to the companies, but that if a journeyman wanted employment from a company master then he paid into the company as well. Payment of quarterage by the journeymen, its withholding or otherwise, became during the seventeenth and eighteenth centuries a means of internal struggle. The bakers' company, which was very tough with its yeomanry, solved the problem after a fashion in the late seventeenth century by deducting quarterage from wages. The journeymen feltmakers, whose struggles towards the end of the seventeenth century enliven the pages of many a social and economic history, are all members of the Feltmakers Company, whose incorporation they helped the masters to bring about in a protracted struggle with the Merchant Haberdashers, culminating in success in 1667.

As Unwin points out, the journeymen feltmakers withheld quarterage to put into a common fund to meet the expenses of an economic struggle with the masters, which brought its victories and defeats. During the 1690s, the masters repealed the by-laws guaranteeing one month's notice and against employing foreigners. But a few years later both by-laws were in force again, remaining in force until well into the eighteenth century. In 1698 the journeymen, beaten in the struggle, submitted and gave account of 'money contributed and the way it had been spent'. They reverted in fact to company control, to be 'obedient to the bye-laws of the company'.

The submission is temporary; by 1708, by which time the journeymen had secured links with men in other towns, they begin to pass out of the company control, and their congress in 1777, in which they make their own by-laws, coincides with the masters' securing the repeal of regulations governing the ratio of apprentices to journeymen. With the keystone to their legal associations gone, the journeymen have no choice but to rest on the power of their own independent organisation. They have entered the area of change at the other side of which lies trade unionism.

In this and in other cases we see how the exercise of company control over the trade goes hand in hand with the bigger masters' control over journeymen or working masters. Once one falls, the other cannot stand. The Webbs conclude that, since masters complain of 'combinations' to Parliament in the eighteenth but not the seventeenth century, this proves that there were no such organisations in the earlier century. There is, however, another explanation – that the masters had the means to deal with their journeymen without going to Parliament, because they held the ace in the pack, the control of the trade. As long as they exercised it in the interests of the journeymen and small masters, then they had no need to take their labour force problems to Westminster. Which brings us back to the tailors.

F. W. Galton, tailoring trade unionist, historian and partner of the Webbs, uses the same argument when discussing the emergence in London before 1710 of a tailors' journeymen's organisation. It was powerful and well organised, based on houses of call throughout the city. It could not have arisen in a moment, he considered very reasonably. But where had it come from?

The doctrine of the Webbs taught him that it could not have arisen in the seventeenth century because the masters made no complaint of it. The Webb doctrine also taught him that he should not seek the answer where it might be found, in C. M. Clode's two volumes of history and documents of the Merchant Taylors Company. Since these concerned a gild-craft company, they could not contain the answer.

As Galton put it: 'The merchant and craft gilds are therefore not referred to as they did not in any case consist exclusively of the journeymen nor does there appear to be any connection between them and the trade unions described in this volume.' Yet, as already shown, during the seventeenth century the bachelors or yeomanry of the company effectively controlled the 'labouring and working' part of it, organised in the city quarters, summoning strangers and so on. In 1601, when the yeomanry asked the company to seek a parliamentary Bill to enlarge its power over the trade, the livery replied: 'The Company has sufficient power.' In the more rampantly competitive years of the Restoration, however, when the company livery cared no more about trade regulation, the reply was: 'We are not able to domineer as in times past.' From then on the two parts of the company disputed over the right of search which a court verdict in 1691 declared 'hath bin altogether useless'. Then followed a dispute over the control of funds which the bachelors claimed the merchants had appropriated. In 1696 the yeomanry had taken the matter to the King's Court and thereafter the company records speak no more of them or for that matter of trade matters at all. As in the case of the clothworkers, the departure of the yeomanry means the end of any connection between the company and the trade.

The Webbs are content to dismiss the bachelors or yeomanry on the grounds that it was not for journeymen only and contained wealthy masters. In this they follow George Unwin when he says that in this period a yeomanry member might be a 'wealthy trader on his way to be Lord Mayor'. But he describes these types as 'birds of passage which have little to do with the yeomanry as a permanent body'. Without doubt the bachelors contained wealthy men. At the start of the eighteenth century no one was invited to apply for promotion to the Merchant Taylors' livery unless he had £1,000 a year. But the bachelors' company also contained journeymen 'free of this city and a brother of this Misterie'. The Merchant Taylors were powerful enough to be in the 'Great Twelve' and already by 1649 were trying to exclude the 'tailoring members from any place of credit'.

What we have with the bachelors of the Merchant Taylors Company is a situation not unlike that of the feltmakers who had been a subordinate part of the Haberdashers but who finally broke free by separate incorporation in 1667. It may be that the Taylors' bachelors wanted to lay hands on the money they said was theirs to pay for separate incorporation as a manufacturing company. But if so, this did not come to pass. With the close of the seventeenth century no new incorporations were being made. Nor did the 1667 incorporation of the feltmakers hold the masters and journeymen together for long. By the early 1700s the split between them was irrevocable. Perhaps a similar process (without the incorporation) carried master and journeymen tailors along united against the merchants until the end of the seventeenth century. But then, as with the feltmakers, the new divisive industrial relationship opened up in the first decades of the eighteenth century. The powerful tailors' organisation, which by 1810 had lasted 'more than a century', is not perhaps a spontaneous creation, but the former bachelors or yeomanry of the old company, without the cement of company law to hold it together, dividing into wealthy manufacturing masters on the one hand and journeymen and small masters on the other. Even in 1834 there was still a vestigial 'Operative Master Tailors' Society' supporting the journeymen. Only a decade of recorded history separates the old craft organisation from the new, though the gulf between the former and the latter state is fundamental – *even when the same men are quite likely involved*. But the time gap is narrow enough for rules, organisational forms, customs and coats of arms to cross, and it is too narrow to assert that there is 'no historical connection' between the one and the other.

In yet other London companies there is no organisational gap at all. We shall look at other trades, including some of those mentioned by the master tailors in their complaint to Parliament in 1720.

The wheelwrights' company was founded by charter in the 1660s and compelled all journeymen to be members and pay quarterage on pain of dismissal. In 1714, a journeymen's club was formed and so strong was it among the members of the company that the Court of Assistants had to rule that no member of it could be elected to the Court; this suggests that the journeymen's club contained masters as well, like the yeomanry of the older companies. Only in 1740 were members of the journeymen's club 'excused' company quarterage and the breach between parent and offspring flared into open war with prosecutions.

Among the coachmakers, likewise, the journeymen had their own club within the company, withholding quarterage when they had a tussle with their livery members. Of the 400 members of the company only 26 were on the Court, so keeping the journeymen within the company was important. As the company historian says, during the reign of the 'early Georges . . . so complete was the identity of masters and journeymen that they might fittingly be members of the same company'. Even in the second half of the century the company continued its search, and its pressure on journeymen to pay quarterage; but by 1789 the journeymen were a separate body, and wage negotiations were handled by a joint committee. However, even in 1817 when the London coachmakers had a federal link with journeymen in other towns, with a general secretary, they still had jointly with the masters a friendly society founded in the 1690s and the general secretary was reported to have urged the masters to form a joint organisation to uphold the trade.

In 1716, when there was trouble in the blacksmiths' trade in London, it was because the 'free journeymen' members of the recently reorganised 'yeomanry' would not permit the taking on of new hands.

In the 1730s, the membership of the weavers' company, masters and journeymen, reached a peak of over 6,000, perhaps as a result of the powerful company campaign to secure a government ban on cheap imported 'callimancoes', cotton goods from India – a victory for mass action and lobbying by all ranks of the company, though a short-lived one. When during the 1730s the 'search' of the trade was progressively abandoned, the membership fell by more than a thousand per decade until by 1800 it was around 900 (though all this time the 'livery' remained constant between 200 and 300).

During the 1760s, the weavers' company cut quarterage demands and even admitted new members free to try to prevent the poorer members from leaving the company to form their own organisation. In this decade, in face of desperate poverty, the journeymen weavers formed their 'cutters'' club, and were surprised by police and soldiers in the Dolphin Inn in Spitalfields taking contributions from 'terrified manufacturers', though the 1760s ended with both parties reconciled in wage negotiations.

When, later in the century, violent agitation by the weavers brought the passing of the Spitalfields Acts, one of the few government actions in favour of sustaining minimum standards for any body of workers during this period, the journeymen, when they formed their own union, did not do so in opposition to the company but to 'uphold the Act'. In the 1820s with the connivance of the larger masters the Act was repealed and the journeymen, so the company historian reports, were 'stunned' by this treachery.

Although the painters' 'yeomanry' began to vanish from the records during the seventeenth century, in 1749 a journeymen's club appears, prosecuting offenders against company apprentice regulations; and in 1800, with the passing of the Combinations Act, the company journeymen again invoked its aid to call a joint meeting with the masters, the main object of which was to regulate wages and other problems in the old way, accepting the Act as right and proper.

In 1750 master masons complained of an unlawful combination among members of the masons' company. The 'privilege of freedom of the company', they said was coming to 'destroy subordination and raise an intractable spirit in the lower class of freemen', making them, 'negligent in their calling, exorbitant in their demands and disrespectful of their superiors'.

On a smaller scale, among the tinplate workers in 1769 we see a wages petition signed by journeymen, one quarter of whom were freemen of the company. Indeed, this company was still prosecuting non-members within the trade in 1821, by which time the journeymen had linked up in a nationwide union against 'the encroachments of the masters'.

As late as 1811, two years after the launching of the union in the trade, London brass founders, journeymen freemen, were still taking matters by petition to their company court.

To borrow a phrase from the Webbs, one can assert with some confidence that almost every case of a movement, 'club', 'combination' or initiative by craftsmen of a London trade during the eighteenth century is one taken either by the freemen of the city company completely organised within it or led by a nucleus of such company freemen together with journeymen outside the company.

In certain cases referred to above it is possible to see the process of transition from freeman group within the company to journeymen group outside it, in broad outline. In the case of the curriers, whose union articles stamped with the gild coat of arms Mayhew admired in 1850, we can, thanks to the company historian, follow the process stage by stage from 1704, when the 'steward' of the Journeymen's Club appeared before the court of the company to 'substantiate' complaints against masters who have broken the rules, through one dispute after another until in the 1790s the master curriers allied themselves with employers outside the company and the journeymen 'strengthened their position by joining forces with curriers in the country' and formed a 'tramp society'. In fact, as the Webbs knew, the curriers had a tramping contact from the mid-eighteenth century. The union which grew from the tramp society eventually joined the First International in 1869.

But perhaps just as fascinating an example of the progression from one organisational form to another can be seen in the framework knitters, where the company, chartered in the seventeenth century, under pressure from journeymen and small masters enforced the regulations to such an extent that the larger masters withdrew to Nottingham and other Midland towns. The London company, again under pressure, sent deputies to Nottingham, who held searches and quarter days at public houses, spreading the organisation to the Midlands.

Gravener Henson, leader of the framework knitters, describes in his history of the trade how in 1752, at a meeting in the Crown Inn, Nottingham, the big hosiers walked out, leaving the small masters and journeymen to restructure the organisation. The journeymen freemen suggested that non-member freemen should be 'admitted' at a lower rate. That they were previously members of the company is shown by the complaint that they were paying quarterage but got no redress from the by-laws. From that time on a series of organisations were formed by the framework knitters, who only abandoned their attempt to use the company machinery in 1811, when a fully fledged union organisation with tramping system and house of call was launched.

The craftsmen of the wool trade of the seventeenth and eighteenth centuries returned time and time again to the model of the past. In Exeter the Weavers', Fullers' and Shearers' Incorporation was still in full swing at the end of the eighteenth century. West Country weavers formed bodies in the eighteenth century which a House of Commons report described as 'clubs with a common seal, tipstaffs and colours'. A later report speaks of weavers making by-laws, displaying ensigns and flags and 'assuming an arbitrary power to ascertain their wages'.

The woolcombers, some of whom had been members of larger companies embracing various parts of the wool trade, sought independence through incorporation. But the Devon woolcombers discovered in 1639 that the cost was too great for 'poor men'. A similar attempt seems to have been made in mid-century by woolcombers at Leicester, while in 1688 the woolcombers of Colchester parted from the clothiers' and fullers' company to form a 'purse' arising from their efforts to keep out intruders from the trade. One historian remarks that the woolcombers' clubs, which 'originated as benefit societies for the relief of the infirm, developed into close corporations that tried to restrict their membership to the privileged few'. In 1718, a Royal Proclamation accused the weavers' and woolcombers' organisations of having 'illegally presumed to use a Common Seal and to Act as Bodies Corporate'. In 1741 a critic said of the clubs that they were 'corporations without a charter', 'giving laws to their masters as unto themselves', and in 1794 the name 'self-constituted corporation' was thrown at the woolcombers by a Parliamentary Committee.

The woolcombers, like the handloom weavers, made little distinction between small masters and journeymen, the woolcombers being organised in gangs where one master bought the wool from the staplers on behalf of the others whom he paid. Likewise the cotton, smallware and check weavers linked together in their organisations journeymen, masters and 'undertakers' with several looms. In their relationship with the manufacturers they formed, says a historian of the cotton trade, 'an interesting link between older forms of association almost exactly the same as existing between Yeomanry and Livery companies'.

'The earlier history of trade unionism', notes Unwin, 'is mainly concerned with a composite class interest of this kind and this phase in the case of the hand-loom weavers lasted till well on into the nineteenth century.'

In 1824 the West Riding Fancy Union declared its object to be to 'prevent masters being undersold' and the Rochdale flannel weavers, at the same time, could count on one quarter of the masters in the area giving money to support strikes 'against those paying lower than the statement price'.

In 1829, the Manchester quilting weavers laid down that every master in the organisation should 'allow his journeyman or journeymen to leave at any notice' during a 'turnout', with payments for every loom 'he shall have standing ... in defence of the trade'. In the light of such organisational forms, the mottoes of early union organisations such as the Scottish ironmoulders' 'United to serve both master and man' are not to be seen with hindsight as premature class collaboration, but as a sign of attitudes and outlooks arising from centuries-old traditions – traditions based on small workshop collaborative production which in the early 1800s was still widespread.

In disputing the Webbs' 'confident' assertion that no 'historic connection' exists between unions and earlier craft organisation, one in no way disputes their main point that 'in all cases in which trade unions arose, the great bulk of the workers had ceased to be independent producers', etc.

It is a matter of how that process worked itself out and how it reflected itself in the organisational forms adopted by craft workers. Certainly the process was a prolonged one. In 1584 a journeyman printer protested to the Star Chamber that Stationers' Company regulations meant that he and his fellows were likely to be 'servants during all their life'. In the 1840s, the Glasgow master bakers, whose journeymen were fighting against almost feudal conditions of employment and a 'living-in' system, were advised that if they paid their men ordinary wages the men would no longer 'aspire to be masters'. In 1836 Sheffield filesmiths sought Francis Place's advice on how they could break the gang system in which their trade was locked and introduce a fair wage.

This period of 260 years covers the process of creation of a class of lifelong wage earners. The process accelerates to its peak between the 1780s and the 1850s, with the absolute height being reached in the early 1800s when the 'old trades' fought to hold on to their 'rights'. Thus the coming to be of the new class and the dying away of the old craft forms ran parallel for a considerable period. That the most skilled members of what was a new class derived its organisational forms from the past in no way denies the essential newness of the class, nor the revolutionary implications of its coming to be. But it recognises that among the crafts there are continuities amid the changes, and it emphatically asserts that it is unhistorical to present the history of skilled craft workers as though there was a blank period in which they were deprived of regular organisation, orphans of the economic storm, who then spontaneously awoke to the idea of trade unionism.

If we take six centuries of craft history from the thirteenth to the nineteenth, then, it falls roughly into three main overlapping periods. The first, say, of 150 years, was a period in which masters and men maintained joint interests by solidarity and Church blessing. The second lasted perhaps 250 years, in which craft companies dominated by the richer masters legally control the trade, with the 'handytrade', small masters and journeymen in varying degrees of subordination, the guarantee of livelihood being the price of their subordination.

The third stage, lasting some 150 years, the onset of the Industrial Revolution in fact, sees the decline of corporate control at varying speeds in various trades and industries, with new organisations emerging, either master–men 'corporations without a charter' or journeymen clubs first within existing craft companies and then outside them. Technological development during the eighteenth and nineteenth centuries saw trades like turner and millwright change from wood to metal, becoming the first engineers and equipping the factory centres of Industrial Revolutionary change. These tradesmen preserved traditional forms which they drew from the craft companies with which they served their time. The millwrights, said the son of John Rennie the famous engineer, 'were a particular class of skilled workmen embodied into a special gild or craft'.

In many ways, as masons, blacksmiths, carpenters and millwrights worked together building the new textile mills and fitting their power and machinery, the newer trades of boilermaker, steam engine maker and others copied the old ways, customs, rituals, even the old coats of arms and mottoes.

In general though, I would argue that the 'trade unions' of the late eighteenth and early nineteenth centuries derived a heritage from the earlier craft organisations by direct and indirect means, by links that were not only traditional and imitative, but also organisational. The unions in many trades have a prehistory as well as a history and a very long and proud one. Rather than being called 'spontaneously' into existence by the Industrial Revolution, many of them were instead utterly transformed from what they had been before. Where a craft organisation based upon, say, a score of old corporate towns spread with the spread of industry and population growth to many more new towns and fast growing villages, the old ways and traditions would become diluted and distorted. Rule books, passed from town to town, from trade to trade, were altered and amended. But the vital core, the trade and its 'rights', were preserved even long after the preservation of those 'rights' was almost a lost cause.

How were the Dublin Catholic building workers to know they were being fanciful in claiming as their own a craft organisation allegedly dominated by Protestant masters? To them the gild coat of arms was the 'sign of the trade'. To them the trade, the craft and its organisation were one, just as in the fourteenth century the 'mistery' was both the skill and the fraternity which used it.

Their formal rights in the organisation might be small; their involvement in the craft was total and its traditions were theirs as much as, if not more than, their masters'. When the earlier craft organisations passed away (though employers still pocketed the apprentice premium while expecting the journeyman to train the boy) masters affected astonishment that the members of the new unions should presume to assert old customs governing entry to the trade. In 1838, a master printer told the Select Committee on Combinations of Workmen how he had rejected the demand from his journeymen that they should have the 'binding' of the extra apprentices he wished to employ. It was not the £5 fee that moved him, he said. 'We told them we would not submit to their binding these boys, that we must have the choice of our own workmen and that if they would not allow us to do that we would give over the business.'

On such rocks the old craft unity came to grief. In 1856 an engineering employer told a Parliamentary Inquiry, with some indignation, that 'their [the union's] general endeavour seems to be to get the foremen and overlookers into these societies and by that means, as they have the right of employing those persons whom they please, they generally have the power of insisting upon the conformity of their demands'.

To convince the organised craftsmen that control of the trade was not vested in those who did the work, 'the handytrade', but in those who owned the workshop or factory, was as difficult in the nineteenth century as it had been in the eighteenth, seventeenth, sixteenth or even earlier centuries. To the Webbs, this kind of approach which the employers of the day described as 'intolerable tyranny' was 'nothing more than the rather bumptious expression of the trade unionists' feeling that they were the rightful directors of industry'.

Perhaps if the Webbs had followed the advice of George Howell that 'without a knowledge derived from a study of the Guild system the organisation, rules and operations of the trade unions cannot be properly understood', they might have taken a different view of the nature of trade union strengths and weaknesses and those stubborn peculiarities which still cropped up, and still do so, to baffle the outside observer.

Howell was right in that – the early unions do have a connection with the deep past; the organised skilled workers have both a history and a prehistory, centuries of living tradition, organisation and practical democracy.

From the academic point of view, as historian Sylvia Thrupp put it: 'The question of continuity between the old forms and the new craft unions, burial clubs, etc., intrigues historians, but the story remains incomplete.'

Incomplete it will remain since some of the links must be a matter for speculation, but this book is, in some way, an attempt towards the completion of that story.

But more important to me perhaps, the Webb school has in a sense deprived organised workers of their prehistory, and, bad or good, I believed they are entitled to every word of it.

Appendices

The Tramping Pubs

Of the seven or eight hundred 'tramping' inns and public houses I came across in researching this book perhaps only one in ten still exist, though no doubt some are disguised under other names today. I have kept to a same-name-same-street formula for greater certainty. But I included, for example, the famous Paviors' Arms, Westminster, the masons' 'lighthouse', because, although rebuilt in 1938, it is only a few yards from the original site and the tradition is, in some measure, preserved.

County/Town	House	Trade	Earliest known date
Bedfordshire			
Bedford	George and Dragon, Mill Street	Smiths	1860s
Cheshire			
Altrincham	Malt Shovel, Standford Street	Masons	1860s
Chester	Axe Tavern, Watergate Street	Masons	1860s
	Egerton Arms, Brook Street	Masons	1840s
Crewe	Angel, Victoria Street	Engineers	1860s
	Star Inn, Victoria Street	Boilermakers	1860s
Cumberland			
Carlisle	Drove Inn, Roweltown	Smiths	1860s
Derbyshire			
Buxton	Bakers' Arms, West Road	Tailors	1880s
		Masons	1850s
Derby	Masons' Arms, Edward Street	Masons	1850s
Devon			
Exeter	Papermakers' Arms, Exe Street	Moulders	1860s

County/Town	House	Trade	Earliest known date
Durham			
Chester-le Street	Joiners' Arms	Masons	1860s
Essex			
Witham	White Hart	Brushmakers	1820s
Gloucestershire			
Gloucester	New Inn, London Road	Brushmakers	1820s
Herefordshire			
Hereford	Ship Inn, Ross Road	Masons	1840s
Kent			
Bromley	Three Compasses, Widmore Road	Tailors	1880s
Dartford	Smiths' Arms, Hythe Street	Moulders	1860s
Maidstone	Union Flag, Union Street	Tailors	1880s
Sheerness	Mechanics' Arms, High Street	Bricklayers	1860s
Sydenham	Bricklayers' Arms, Dartmouth Road	Carpenters	1860s
	Golden Lion, Sydenham Road	Bricklayers	1860s
Lancashire			
Accrington	Bridge Inn, Church Street	Engineers	1860s
Ashton-under-Lyne	Crown Inn, Ashton Old Road	Carpenters, Tinplateworkers	1860s
	Highland Laddie, Ashton Old Road	Boilermakers Brushmakers	1860s
Blackburn	Grapes Hotel, Northgate	Carpenters	1860s
	Vulcan Hotel, Nab Lane	Brushmakers, Painters, Tailors	1860s
Bolton	Blue Boar, Deansgate	Masons	1850s
		Brassworkers	1860s
	Bull's Head, Bradshaw Road	Smiths	1860s
Burnley	Boot Inn, St James Street	Masons	1860s
Bury	White Boar, Radcliffe Road	Masons	1860s
Denton	Jolly Hatters, Stockport Road	Hatters	1880s

County/Town	House	Trade	Earliest known date
Denton	Jolly Hatters, Town Lane	Hatters	1880s
	Red Lion, Stockport Road	Hatters	1860s
Leigh	Lord Nelson, Bradshaw Gate	Boot and Shoe	1860s
Manchester	Crown and Cushion, Corporation Street	Engineers, Bricklayers, Tinplateworkers	1860s
	Hat and Feather, Mason Street	Brushmakers	1860s
	Pack Horse, Deansgate	Cabinetmakers	1860s
	Red Bull, Mason Street	Builders' Labourers	1840s
	Royal Oak, Didsbury	Masons	1860s
Oldham	Bath Hotel, Union Street	Engineers	1860s
Preston	Watering Trough Hotel	Boilermakers	1860s
	Wellington Inn, Glovers Court	Carpenters, Cabinetmakers	1860s
Rochdale	Woolpack Inn, Halifax Road	Smiths	1860s
Wigan	Bricklayers Arms, Hallgate	Boilermakers	1860s
Leicestershire			
Loughborough	Golden Fleece, Cattle Market	Bricklayers	1870s
Lincolnshire			
Lincoln	Crown and Anchor, Newland	Brushmakers	1860s
	Reindeer Hotel, High Street	Masons	1860s
London			
	Adams Arms, Fitzroy Square	Marble Polishers, Sawyers	1830s
	Angel Inn, Lambeth Walk	Boilermakers	1860s
	Barley Mow, Duke Street	Carpenters	1860s
	Coach and Horses, Marlborough Street, W1	Painters	1860s
	Crown, Blackfriars Road	Engineers	1860s

281

County/Town	House	Trade	Earliest known date
London	Elephant's Head, Camden High Street	Tailors	1840s
	Green Man, Poplar High Street	Carpenters	1840s
	Hole in the Wall, Mitre Court, Fleet Street	Compositors Plumbers, Smiths	1790s? 1860s
	Lamb and Flag, Covent Garden	Coachmakers	1860s
	Paviors' Arms, Page Street, Westminister	Masons	1830s
	Queen's Head, Acton Street, WC1	Carpenters	1840s
	Simon The Tanner, Bermondsey	Tanners	1840s
	Sun, Long Acre	Tailors	1790s
	White Hart, Fetter Lane	Boot and Shoe	1860s
	White Horse, White Horse Street, Stepney	Moulders	1860s
	White Swan, Greenwich High Road	Bricklayers	1860s
Nottinghamshire			
Nottingham	Arboretum Hotel	Engineers	1860s
Oxfordshire			
Banbury	Jolly Weavers, South Bar	Bookbinders	1860s
Oxford	Crown Inn, Cornmarket Street	Compositors	1860s
	Black Swan, Crown Street	Carpenters	1850s
Somerset			
Bath	Devonshire Arms, James Parade	Smiths	1860s
Staffordshire			
Stafford	Four Crosses, Sandon Road	Bricklayers	1860s
Walsall	Talbot Inn, Digbeth	Brushmakers	1860s
Surrey			
Kingston-on-Thames	Druid's Head, Market Place	Boot and Shoe	1860s

County/Town	House	Trade	Earliest known date
Kingston-on-Thames	Wheelwrights' Arms	Bricklayers	1860s
Wiltshire			
Bradford-on-Avon	Mason's Arms	Masons	1850s
Swindon	Locomotive Arms	Moulders	1860s
Yorkshire			
Bradford	Beehive, Buttershaw	Masons	1830s
Hull	Blue Bell, Market Place	Boilermakers	1860s
	Humber Tavern	Boot and Shoe	1860s
Keighley	Masons' Arms, Longcroft	Engineers	1860s
Leeds	Ship Hotel, Briggate	Brushmakers	1860s
Rotherham	Moulders' Rest	Moulders	1860s
Wakefield	Graziers' Hotel, Market Street	Masons	1860s
York	Masons' Arms, Fishergate	Masons	1850s
	Punch Bowl, Stonegate	Moulders	1860s

Bibliography

Pamphlets (p) are included together with books in each section.

SOCIAL AND ECONOMIC HISTORY

Ashley, W. J. *An introduction of English Economic History and Theory Part II* (London 1909).

Beveridge, W. H. *Unemployment, Part I* (London 1909).

Bland, A. E. (with P. A. Brown and R. H. Tawney) *English Economic History: Select Documents* (London, 1914).

Booth, Charles *Life and Labour of the People in London* (3rd edn, London, 1969).

Cipolla, C. M. (ed.) *Fontana Economic History of Europe, 16th and 17th centuries* (London, 1974).

Coulton, G. G. *Art and the Reformation* (Oxford, 1928).

Cunningham, W. *The Growth of English Industry and Commerce* (Cambridge, 1907).

Dobb, M. *Studies in the Development of Capitalism* (2nd edn, London, 1963).

Dyos H. J. and Wolff, M. (eds) *The Victorian City* (London, 1973).

Eden, Sir F. M. *Observations on Friendly Societies* (1801).
The State of the Poor (1928 edition)

Engels, F. *Condition of the Working Class in England, 1844* (Manchester, 1845).

Firth, C. H. *Cromwell's Army* (London, 1902).

Foster, John *Class Struggle and the Industrial Revolution* (London, 1974).

George, M. D. *London Life in the 18th Century* (London, 1966 edn).

Girouard, M. *Victorian Pubs* (London, 1975).

Gosden, P. H. J. H. *The Friendly Societies in England, 1815–1875* (Manchester, 1961).

Green, A. S. *Town Life in the 15th Century* (London, 1908).

Harris, M. D. *Life in an Old English Town, history of Coventry* (London, 1898).

Harrison, B. *Drink and the Victorians* (London, 1971).

Harrison, W. *Description of England* (1968 edn).

Heath, S. *Pilgrim Life in the Middle Ages* (London, 1911).

Hilton, R. *Bond Men Made Free* (London, 1973).

Hilton R. and others *The Transition from Feudalism to Capitalism* (London, 1976).

Hobsbawm, E. J. *The Age of Revolution, 1789–1848* (London, 1962).

Hoskins, W. G. *Two Thousand Years in Exeter* (Exeter, 1968).

Jervis, F. R. J. *The Evolution of Modern Industry* (London, 1961).

Judges, A. V. *The Elizabethan Underworld* (London, 1965 edn).

Jusserand, J. A. A. J. *English Wayfaring Life in the Middle Ages* (London, 1925).

Keen, M. *The Pelican History of Medieval Europe* (London, 1969).

Landes, D. S. *The Unbound Prometheus* (Cambridge, 1969).

Lipson, E. *The Economic History of England*, Vols 1, 2, 3 (London, 1931). *The Growth of English Society, a short Economic History* (London, 1949).

Lindsay, J. and Rickword, E. A. *Handbook of Freedom* (New York, 1939).

Mayhew, Henry *London Labour and the London Poor*, Vol. 3 (London, 1861).

Mitchell, R. J. with Leys, M. D. R. *A History of the English People* (London, 1950).

Oman, C. *The Great Revolt of 1381* (Oxford, 1969).

Plot, R. *History and Antiquities of Staffordshire* (1798).

Powell, E. *Rising in East Anglia* (Cambridge, 1896).

Putnam, B. H. *The Enforcement of the Statute of Labourers, 1349–1359* (Columbia, 1908).

Rabb, J. K. 'The Effects of the Thirty Years War on the German Economy' in *Journal of Modern History* Vol. XXXIV no 1, March 1962.

Razzell, P. E. and Wainwright R. W. *The Victorian Working Class* (London, 1973).

Redford, A. *Labour Migration in England, 1800–1850* (Manchester, 1964 edn).

Rogers Thorold, J. E. *Six Centuries of Work and Wages* (London, 1908).

Riley, H. T. *Memorials of London (13th–15th Century)* (London, 1868).

Rose, M. E. *The English Poor Law, 1780–1930* (Newton Abbott, 1971).

Spiller, B. *Victorian Public Houses* (Newton Abbott, 1972).

Stubbs, W. *The Constitutional History of England, Vol. II* (Oxford, 1880).

Tawney, R. H. and Power, E. *Tudor Economic Documents* (London. 1951).

Taylor, J. S. 'The Impact of Pauper Settlement 1691–1834' in *Past and Present* no. 73, November, 1976.

Thompson, E. P. *The Making of the English Working Class* (London, 1948 edn).

Thompson, E. P. and Yeo, E. *The Unknown Mayhew* (London, 1971).

Trevelyan, G. M. *English Social History* (London, 1967 edn).
 England in the Age of Wycliffe (London, 1929).

Unwin, G. *Industrial Organisation in the 16th and 17th Centuries* (Oxford, 1904).

Unwin, G. *Studies in Economic History* (London, 1958 edn).

Wilson, C. H. *England's Apprenticeship 1603–1763* (Oxford, 1965).

INDUSTRIES AND TRADES

Anon. *A General Description of All Trades* (London, 1747) (p).
 Book of Trades (London, 1811).

Burnley, James *The History of Wool and Woolcombing* (London, 1889).

Bythell, Duncan *The Handloom Weavers* (Cambridge, 1969).

Campbell, R. *The London Tradesman* (London, 1747) (p).

Cowper, Thomas *A Short Essay upon trade in general* (1741) (p).

Daniels G. W. *The Early English Cotton Industry* (Manchester, 1921).

Felkin, William *A History of Machine Wrought Hosiery and Lace Manufacture* (Cambridge 1867).

Gaskell, P. *The Manufacturing Population of England* (London, 1833).

Henson, Gravener *The Civil, Political and Mechanical History of the Framework Knitters* (Nottingham, 1831).

Howe, Ellic (ed.) *The Trade : Passages from the Literature of the Printing Craft, 1550–1935* (London, 1943).

Hurst, W. *History of the Woollen Trade for the last Sixty Years* (Leeds, 1844).

James J. *History of the Worsted Manufacture in England* (London, 1857).

Jeffreys, M. and J. B. 'Wages, Hours and Trade Customs of the Skilled Engineer in 1861' in *Economic History Review 1*, series XVII, no. 1, 1947.

Knoop, D. and Jones, G. P. *The Medieval Mason* (Manchester, 1966 edn).

Lipson, E. *The History of the Woollen and Worsted Industries* (London, 1921).

Moxon, J. *Mechanick Exercises or the Doctrine of Handywork* (1683).

Salzman, L. F. *Building in England down to 1540* (London, 1952).
 English Industries of the Middle Ages (London, 1913).

Unwin, G. *Samuel Oldknow and the Arkwrights* (Manchester, 1924).

Ure, Alexander *Dictionary of Arts, Manufacturies and Mines* (1839).

Adams, A. N. *The History of the Worshipful Company of Blacksmiths* (London, 1951).

Alford, B. W. E. and Barker T. C. *The History of the Carpenters Company* (London, 1968).

Bain, Ebenezer *A History of the Aberdeen Incorporated Trades* (Aberdeen, 1887).

Bennett, E. *The History of the Worshipful Company of Wheelwrights of the City of London, 1670–1970* (London, 1970).

Brentano, Luojo von *On the History and Development of Guilds and the Origin of Trade Unions* (London, 1870).

Bromley, J. *Armorial Bearings of the City of London* (London, 1961).

Clode, C. M. *Early History of the Merchant Taylors Company* (1888). *Memorials of the Gild of Merchant Taylors, etc.* (London, 1875).

Conder, E. *Records of the Hole Craft and Fellowship of Masons* (London, 1894).

Cruikshank, J. *Sketch of the Incorporation of Masons and the Lodge of St John* (Glasgow, 1879).

Davies, N. Z. 'A Trade Union in 16th century France' in *Economic History Review 2* vol. XIX 1/1966.

Ebblewhite, E. A. *A Chronological History of the Worshipful Company of Tinplate Workers alias Wire Workers* (London, 1896).

Elkington, G. *The Coopers, Company and Craft* (London, 1933).

Girtin, T. *The Golden Ram: A Narrative History of the Clothworkers Company, 1582–1958* (London, 1958).

The Mark of the Sword: A Narrative History of the Cutlers Company, 1189–1975 (London, 1975).

Gould, R. F. *History of Freemasonry* (ed. H. Poole) (London, 1951).

Gross, C. *The Gild Merchant* (Oxford, 1927 edn).

Halliwell, J. O. *The Early History of Freemasonry* (London, 1840).

Hibbert, A. B. 'The Economic Policies of Towns' in *Cambridge Economic History of Europe*, vol. 3 (Cambridge, 1963).

Hibbert W. N. *The History of the Worshipful Company of Founders* (London, 1925).

Illife, Lord (commissioned by) *A History of the Worshipful Company of Coachmakers and Coach Harnessmakers of London* (London, 1937).

Jupp, E. B. *An Historical Account of the Worshipful Company of Carpenters* (London, 1848).

Kellett, J. R. 'Breakdown of Gild and Company Control in London' *Economic History Review* in EH/R 1958, vol. 2 X, p. 381.

Knoop, D. and Jones, G. P. *The Evolution of Masonic Organisation* (London, 1932).

The London Mason in the 17th Century (London, 1935).

Kramer, Stella *The English Craft Gilds and the Government* (Columbia, 1905).

Lambert, J. M. (Malet) *Two Thousand Years of Gild Life* (London, 1891).

Longe, Francis D. 'The Law of Trade Combinations in France' in *Fortnightly Review* N.S., vol. 2 (1867).

Ludlow, J. M. 'Old gilds and New Friendly Societies' in *Fortnightly Review*, N.S. vol. 6 (1869).

Marsh, B. (ed.) *Records of the Carpenters Company 1654–1694*

Masons, *Court Minute Books of Worshipful Company of Masons 1677–1720* (Guildhall Library).

Mayer, E. *The Curriers and the City of London* (London, 1968).

Plummer, A. *The London Weavers' Company, 1600–1970* (London, 1972).

Pooley, Sir E. *The Guilds of the City of London* (London, 1945).

Saint Leon E. M. *Le Compagnonnage* (Paris, 1901).

Schanz, G. *Zur Geschichte der Deutschen Gesellen Verbanden* (Leipzig, 1877).

Smith, Toulmin *English Guilds* (London, 1870).

Trade Guilds of Europe: Reports from the Consuls of the United States (Washington, 1885).

Thrupp S. L. *A short History of the Worshipful Company of Bakers of London* (London, 1933).

'Medieval Gilds Reconsidered' in *Journal of Economic History*, II, (1942).

'The Gilds' in *Cambridge Economic History of Europe*, vol. 3, chapter 5 (Cambridge, 1963).

'Gilds' in *International Encyclopedia of Social Science*, vol. 6.

Unwin, G. *The Guilds and Companies of London* (London, 1938 edn).

Warner, O. *A History of the Tinplate Workers Alias Wireworkers Company of the City of London* (London, 1964).

Williams, W. M. *Annals of the Founders Company* (London, 1867).

TRADE UNIONS AND TRADE SOCIETIES

General Studies

Aspinall, A. *The Early English Trade Unions* (London, 1948).

Baernraether, J. M. *English Associations of Working Men* (London, 1889).

Bray, J. F. *Labour's Wrongs and Labour's Remedy* (1839).

Busteed, T. *Trades' Unions, Combinations and Strikes* (London, 1860).

Challoner, W. H. *The Skilled Artisans During the Industrial Revolution 1750–1850* (London, 1969) (p).

Cole, G. D. H. *Attempts at General Union, 1818–1834* (London, 1953).

A short history of the British Working Class movement 1789–1947 (London, 1948).

Dunning, T. J. *Trades Unions and Strikes, Their Philosophy and Intention* (London, 1860) (p).

Galton, F. W. *Workers on their Industries* (London, 1895).

Hammond, J. L. and B. *The Skilled Labourer 1760–1832* (London, 1965 edn).

Hobsbawm, E. J. *Labouring Men* (London, 1964).

Howell, G. *Conflicts of Capital and Labour* (London, 1878).

Trade Unionism, old and new (London, 1891).

Hughes, T. *Tracts on Christian Socialism (IV)* (London, 1850).

Hutt, G. A. H. *British Trade Unionism: A Short History* (London, 1941).

Jevons, S. *A lecture on trade societies* (London, 1868).

Johnstone, T. *The history of the working classes in Scotland* (Glasgow, 1921).

The Records of an Ancient Friendly Society – the Bo'ness United General Sea Box (1890).

Leeson, R. A. *Strike: A Live History, 1887–1971* (London, 1973).

United We Stand: An illustrated history of trade union emblems (Bath, 1971).

Lloyd, C. M. *Trade Unionism* (London, 1921).

Ludlow, J. M. and Jones, L. *Progress of the Working Class* (London, 1867).

Morton, A. L. and Tate, G. *The British Labour Movement, 1770–1920* (London, 1956).

Musson, A. E. *Trade Unions and Social Studies* (London, 1974).

Pelling, H. M. *A History of British Trade Unionism* (London, 1963).

Paris, Comte de *The Trade Unions of England* (London, 1869).

Potter, E. *Some Opinions on Trades' Unions and the Bill of 1869* (p).

Samuelson, James *Trades Unions and Public Houses* (London, 1871) (p).

Trant, W. *Trade Unions, Their origins and objects, influence and efficiency* (London, 1884).

Trades: *On Combinations of Trades* (London, 1831) (p).

Tufnell, H. *The Character, Object and Effects of Trade Unions* (London, 1834) (p).

Wearmouth, R. F. *Some Working-class movements of the nineteenth century* (London, 1948).

289

Webb, S. and B. *The History of Trade Unionism* (London, 1894).

    Industrial Democracy (London, 1920 edn.).

Williams, F. *Magnificent Journey : The Rise of the Trade Unions* (London, 1954).

Labour Disputes in the early days of the Industrial Revolution 1758–1780 (New York, 1972) (p).

Rebirth of the Trade Union Movement, 1838–1847 (New York 1972) (p).

First Annual Trade Union Directory (London, 1861).

Trade Clubs, Unions, strikes, Conferences, etc., 1836–45 (Place Collection, Set 53).

TRADE UNIONS AND TRADE SOCIETIES (INDIVIDUAL)

Boot and Shoe Operatives *Fifty Years History of National Union 1874–1924.* (in Webb Coll.)

Collins, H. and Fyrth, J. *The Foundry Workers: A Trade Union History* (AUFW, 1959).

Cummings, D. C. *A History of the Boilermakers' Society, 1834–1904* (Newcastle, 1905).

Dickson, J. J. *Manchester Typographical Society: A Centenary Souvenir* (Manchester, 1897).

Galton, F. W. *Select Documents illustrating the history of trade unionism* (i) *The Tailoring Trade* (London, 1896).

Gillespie, S. C. *A hundred years of progress, the record of the Scottish Typographical Association* 1853–1952 (Glasgow, 1953).

Higenbotham, S. *Our Society's History* (Amalgamated Society of Woodworkers, Manchester, 1939).

Hilton, W. S. *Foes to Tyranny: A History of the Amalgamated Union of Building Trade Workers* (AUBTW, 1963).

Howe, Ellic and Waite, H. E. *The London Society of Compositors* (London, 1848).

Jeffreys, J. B. *The Story of the Engineers* (London, 1946).

Kidd, A. T. *History of the Tinplate Workers and Sheet Metal Workers and Braziers Societies* (NUSMW, 1949).

Kiddier, W. *The Old Trade Unions: from unprinted records of the Brushmakers* (London, 1931).

McLaine, W. *The Engineers' Union, Book 1 : The Millwrights and "Old Mechanics"* (Unpublished Thesis, University of London, 1939).

Mortimer, J. E. *History of the Boilermakers' Society, vol. I 1834–1906* (London, 1973).

Mosses, W. *History of the Pattern makers 1872–1922* (London, 1922).

Musson, A. E. *The Typographical Association, origins and history up to 1949* (Oxford, 1954).

Postgate, R. W. *The Builders' History* (London, 1923).

Pugh, Sir A. *Men of Steel, by One of Them* (Iron and Steel Trades Confederation, 1951).

Slatter, H. and Hackett, R. *The Typographical Association: A Fifty Years' Record 1849–1899* (Manchester Typographical Association, 1899).

Smith, J. H. *The Hatters* (pamphlet history of the Felt Hatters' and Trimmers' Unions).

Stewart, M. and Hunter, L. *The Needle is Threaded, The History of an Industry* (London, 1964).

Tailors, *The Case of the Journeymen Tailors* (London, 1720) (p).

Tuckett, A. *The Blacksmiths' History* (London, 1974).

TRADE UNION AND TRADE SOCIETY DOCUMENTS

Bakers:	Notes on union and trade in Webb Collection AXLV
Basketmakers:	as above
Boilermakers:	Monthly Reports, 1918–1919 (Nuffield Library)
	rule books, 1912, 1919, 1965 (Nuffield Library)
Brassworkers:	rule book, 1918 (Nuffield Library)
Bricklayers:	Operative Bricklayers Society:
	Annual Reports, 1862–1870 (Modern Records Centre)
Bricklayers:	Manchester United Order of Bricklayers:
	Monthly Reports, 1868–1892 (Modern Records Centre)
Brushmakers:	assorted records, correspondence, travelling cards, etc., covering period from 1806, though with considerable gaps (National Union of Brushmakers' Headquarters)
Building Workers:	Amalgamated Union of Building Trade Workers: 1921 rule book of new amalgamation (Modern Records Centre).
Carpenters:	Amalgamated Society of Carpenters and Joiners:
	Annual Reports, 1860–1870 (Modern Records Centre)
	Travelling Cards, 1870s, 1884–86, 1901, 1916 (Modern Records Centre)
	ASCJ rule book, 1917 (Nuffield Library)
Carpenters	General Union of Friendly Operative Carpenters and Joiners:
	Annual Reports, 1866–1872 (Modern Records Centre), rule book, 1916 (Modern Records Centre)

Coachmakers:	Notes on UK Society of Coachmakers, 1840–1897 (Webb Collection AXLV 5 318–409)
	rule book (undated) of UK society (Nuffield Library)
Engineers:	Amalgamated Society of Engineers:
	Delegate Meeting Reports, 1852, 1853, 1885, 1892
	Abstract Reports, 1862–63 and 1888–90
	(Webb Collection ED 74)
	ASE:
	Monthly Reports, 1851–1901
	Monthly Report and Journal, 1906–1920
	(Amalgamated Union of Engineering Workers HQ)
	ASE rule books, 1897, 1907, 1912, 1915 (Nuffield Library)
	Amalgamated Engineering Union rule books, 1923, 1951 Nuffield Library)
	Journeymen Steam Engine and Machine Makers Friendly Society:
	Delegate Meeting Reports, 1842, 1843, 1847 (Webb ED 74)
Founders:	Friendly Society of Ironfounders:
	Half-yearly Reports, 1848–1866
	Yearly Reports, 1864–1914 (Modern Records Centre)
	FSIF rule book, 1917 (Nuffield Library)
	National Union of Foundry Workers:
	Journal and Report, 1922–1925 (Nuffield Library)
Framework knitters:	Articles and Regulations of a Society for Obtaining Parliamentary Relief and the Encouragement of Mechanics in the Improvement of Mechanism, Nottingham, 1813 (Webb Collection, Sec. A.1)
General Workers:	National Union of General Workers:
	rule book, 1922 (Nuffield Library)
Hatters:	Amalgamated Society of Journeymen Felt Hatters:
	Records, assorted, 1870s and 1880s (Felt Hatters' and Trimmers' Union HQ)
	Journeymen Hatters of Great Britain and Ireland:
	rule book, 1862
	Journeymen Hatters Fair Trade Union:
	rule book, 1898
	(Felt Hatters' and Trimmers' Union HQ)

Masons: Operative Society of Masons:

Fortnightly Returns, 1834–1912 (Modern Records Centre)

rule books, 1849, 52, 55, 59, 62, 68, 71, 78, 81, 89, 91 (Modern Records Centre)

rule book, 1919 (Nuffield Library)

Mechanics: Friendly Society of Mechanics of the City of Bath (1824) (Working Class Movement Library)

Rules of the Mechanics Friendly Institution of Leeds, 1824 (Working Class Movement Library)

Painters: National Amalgamated Society of Operative Ship and House Painters:

rule book, 1919 (Nuffield Library)

Shipwrights: Shipconstructors and Shipwrights Association Rule book, 1912 (Nuffield Library)

Spinners: Proceedings of a Delegate Meeting of the Operative Spinners of England, Ireland and Scotland, December 1829 (Manchester Free Library)

Steel: British Steel Smelters Association:

Annual Reports, 1886–1907 (Iron & Steel Trades Confed. HQ)

British Steel Smelters, Mill, Iron Tinplate and Kindred Trades:

rule book, 1917 (Nuffield Library)

Smiths: Rules to be observed by the members of the United Order of Smiths, Derby 1839 (Working Class Movement Library)

Rules and Orders to be observed by the Friendly Smiths Society, Derby 1823 (Working Class Movement Library)

Associated Blacksmiths' Society Travelling card, 19th century (Working Class Movement Library)

Tailors: Yearly Reports of the Amalgamated Society of Tailors, 1884–1898 (Webb Collection)

Amalgamated Society of Tailors and Tailoresses (Women's Section):

rule book, 1912, 1918 (Nuffield Library)

Typographical: Provincial Typographical Association:

Half-yearly Reports, 1848–1855 (Modern Records Centre)

Conference of Typographical Associations and Societies, London 1886 (Webb Collection)

Weavers: Rules of the Friendly Associated Society of Quilting
          Weavers of Manchester and its Neighbourhood, 1829
          (Manchester Free Library)

Note on above sources: I have indicated where I found the documents listed, but this by
no means indicates the immense range of other relevant documents to be found in the
Modern Records Centre (Warwick University) which is very strong on union reports;
the Webb Collection in the London School of Economics, which has many early rule
books and reports; and the Nuffield Library, Oxford, which is strong on later rule books,
journals etc. The collection of trade union records, rule books, etc. in the Working Class
Movement Library – the life work of Ruth and Edmund Frow of Manchester – while
not restricted to this, is strong on the metal trades. The Amalgamated Union of
Engineering Workers (Peckham) and the British Iron and Steel Trades Confederation
(London, Grays Inn Road) have remarkably complete sets of their own records. The
National Society of Brushmakers (Watford) and the Felt Hatters and Trimmers Union
(Denton) have less complete but no less fascinating collections of papers.

PARLIAMENTARY AND OTHER PUBLIC PAPERS

Parliament (House of Commons): First (Sixth) Report from the Select
Committee on Artisans and Machinery, 1824.

Report from the Select Committee on the Combination Laws, 1825.

Report to the Home Office by Nassau Senior on Repeal of 5 Geo. IV c 95,
1830.

First Report of the Select Committee on Combinations of Workmen
(1838).

Report of the Royal Commission on the Poor Law, 1834 (PP vol. XXVII).

Masters and Workmen: Select Committee of the House of Commons on
Causes of Strikes and the Desirability of Establishing Equitable Councils
of Conciliation, 1856.

Trade Societies and Strikes: Report of the Committee on Trade Societies
to the National Association for the Promotion of Social Science, Fourth
Annual General Meeting, Glasgow, 1860.

First Report of the Commissioners appointed to enquire into the Organisation and rules of trade unions and other associations, London,
1867.

First Report of the Royal Commission on the Depression of Trade and
Industry, 1886.

Parliamentary Accounts and Papers, Session 1893–94: Report on Agencies
and Methods of Dealing with the Unemployed (Board of Trade), Part
II, Section 1: The Action of Trade Societies in Relation to their
Unemployed Members (PP vol. Lxxxll, 377).

NEWSPAPERS, JOURNALS, ETC.

(excluding union journals which appear in the Trade Union documents section)

Cobbett's Political Register
Crisis
Economic History Review
Fortnightly Review
Freemason
Gentlemen's Magazine
Gorgon
Journal of Economic History
Leisure Hours
North British Review
Notes and Queries
Past and Present
Pioneer
Plebs
Poor Man's Guardian
Shipwrights' Journal
Trades Advocate and Herald of Progress
The Trades Weekly Messenger

BIOGRAPHIES, MEMOIRS, ETC

Acorn, George *One of the Multitude* (London, 1911).

Bower, Fred *Rolling Stonemason* (London, 1936).

Bray, J. F. *A Voyage from Utopia* (ed. M. F. Lloyd) (London, 1957).

Broadhurst, H. *The Story of His Life* (London, 1907).

Brown, John *Autobiography of J. B. The Cordwainer* (London, 1867).

Burton, Anthony *Josiah Wedgwood* (London, 1976).

Dunning, T. *Reminiscences of Thomas Dunning (1813–94) and the Nantwich Shoemakers strike of 1834* (ed. W. H. Challoner) (Lancs and Ches. Antiquarians' Society Transactions, vol. LIX, 1947).

Duthie, Wm. *A Tramp's Wallet, stored by an English Goldsmith during his Wanderings in Germany and France* (London, 1858).

Frost, Thomas *Forty Years' Recollections* (London, 1880).

Gent, Thomas *The Life of Thomas Gent Printer of York* (London, 1832).

Hopkinson, James *Memoirs of a Victorian Cabinet Maker* (ed. J. B. Goodman) (London, 1968).

Moritz C. P. *Travels Through Several Parts of England*, (vol. II of J. Pinkerton's *Collection of Best Voyages and Travels* London, 1808).

Pollitt, Harry *Serving My Time* (London, 1940).

Smith, Charles Manby *The Working Man's Way in the World* (London, 1853).

Place, Francis *Autobiography, 1771–1854* (ed. Mary Thale) (Cambridge, 1972).

Thomson, Christopher *Autobiography of an Artisan* (London, 1847).

A Working Man *Reminiscences of a Stonemason* (London, 1908).

Wallas, G. *The Life of Francis Place* (London, 1908).

Wright, Thomas *The Great Unwashed* (London, 1868).

MISCELLANEOUS

Greenwood, James *On Tramp* (London, 1883).

Dunlop, John *Philosophy of Artificial and Compulsory Drinking Usage in Great Britain and Ireland* (London, 1839).

Newton, William *Secrets of Tramp Life Revealed: A guide to the public* (London, 1886).

Timbs, John *Clubs and Club Life in London* (London, 1872).

Hone, W. *The Everyday Book* (May 1826).

Phillips, Sir R. *A Morning's Walk from London to Kew* (London, 1817).

Smith, Sir Thomas *A Discourse of the Commonweal of this Realm* (1581).

Notes

INTRODUCTION

page

13   *Manchester Hatters' letter :* Home Office papers, 42/124, quoted in A. Aspinall, *The Early Trade Unions*, p. 121.

15   *tramping :* The Glasgow potters thought it 'suited only for trades requiring comparatively little skill'. *See Report on Trade Societies' Rules* (National Association for Promotion of Social Science, September 1860).

15–16   *tramping procedure :* The description is based on records, rules, etc., of the Felt Hatters' and Trimmers Unions of Great Britain and on a union pamphlet, *The Hatters*, by J. H. Smith.

16   *emblems :* See R. A. Leeson, *United We Stand*. The most complete emblem collection is in the library at TUC headquarters.

18   '*. . . a peasant at heart*' : G. D. H. Cole, *A Short History of the British Working Class Movement, 1789–1847*, p. 4.

CHAPTER I

page   *gild rules :*

23   *Lincoln fullers :* Toulmin Smith, *English Guilds*, p. 180.

    Norwich Cordwainers : See S. Campion, *The Gentle Craft*, etc.

    Lincoln tilers' entertainment : Toulmin Smith, op. cit., p. 184.

    coppersmiths' 'misdeeds' : H. T. Riley, *Memorials of London*, pp. 158–9.

    hatters and debts : ibid., p. 240.

    tests of skill :

24   *pewterers :* E. Lipson, *Economic History of England*, vol. 1, p. 324.

page

24   *founders*: W. M. Williams, *Annals of the Founders' Company*,
        p. 7.

        carpenters: E. B. Jupp and W. W. Pocock, *An Historical
        Account of the Worshipful Company of Carpenters*.

        York Minster: D. Knoop and G. P. Jones, *The Medieval
        Mason*, p. 224.

        blacksmiths: A. J. Ashley, *An Introduction to English
        Economic History and Theory*, Part II, p. 117.

        Bristol fullers: L. F. Salzman, *English Industries in the
        Middle Ages*, p. 229.

        Exeter Cordwainers: Toulmin Smith, op. cit., pp. 331–3.

        '*covenant hynd*': Salzman, op. cit., p. 227.

        covenant pay rates: S. Thrupp, *A Short History of the Wor-
        shipful Company of Bakers*, p. 112.

        Beverley Minstrels: Malet Lambert, *Two Thousand Years of
        Guild Life*, pp. 132–7.

        masons: Knoop and Jones, op. cit., p. 196.

        Portland Quarrymen: P. E. Razzell and R. W. Wainwright
        (ed.), *The Victorian Working Class*, pp. 36–8.

        London weavers v. burrellers: A. S. Green, *Town Life in the 15th
        Century*, pp. 161–2.

        masons' work-to-rule: G. M. Trevelyan, *English Social History*
        1967 edn., p. 54n.

        London builders' pickets: L. F. Salzman, *Building in England
        down to 1540*, pp. 73–4.

24–5   *Royal proclamation*: R. W. Postgate, *The Builders' History*, p. 4.

25   '*work his brother*': B. W. E. Alford and T. C. Barker, *The
        History of the Carpenters*, p. 17.

        modern authority: S. L. Thrupp in *Cambridge Economic
        History of Europe*, vol. 3, pp. 232–3.

        Norfolk gilds: R. Hilton, *Bond Men Made Free*, p. 217.

        '*social*' *gilds*: J. M. Ludlow, *Fortnightly Review*, vol. 6, 1869.

        '*parish*' *gilds*: S. L. Thrupp, *International Encyclopedia of
        Social Science*, vol. 6, p. 186.

        '*poor or middling sort*': Toulmin Smith, op. cit., p. 178.

        gild rules: Toulmin Smith, ibid., pp. xxxvi, 143, 192, 231, 291,
        etc.

25–6   *masons' grave*: Postgate, op cit., p. 156n.

        '*overt aggression*': Thrupp, op. cit., p. 186.

25–6   *London blacksmiths and church:* A. N. Adams, *The History of the Worshipful Company of Blacksmiths.*

          'gild' definition: See Thrupp, op. cit., p. 184, and A. B. Hibbert, *Cambridge Econ. History of Europe,* vol. 3, p. 210.

27   *women and gilds:*

          masons: J. P. Halliwell, *Early History of Freemasonry.*

          Lincoln fullers: Toulmin Smith, op. cit., p. 180.

          carpenters: Alford and Barker, op. cit., p. 16.

          blacksmiths: A. N. Adams, op. cit.

          coopers: A. N. Elkington, *The Coopers, Company and Craft,* pp. 23–7.

          women in town crafts: R. J. Mitchell and M. D. R. Leys, *A History of the English People,* pp. 177, 180, 196.

27–8   *crafts and church:* Adams, op. cit., and G. Unwin, *Studies in Economic History,* p. 160.

          Chesterfield blacksmiths: Toulmin Smith, op. cit., p. 170.

          Coventry crafts: Salzman, *English Industries,* p. 236.

28   *gilds in Italy:* S. L. Thrupp, *Cambridge Economic History of Europe,* vol. 3, pp. 236–40.

28   *'false goods':* Riley, op. cit., pp. 91, 136, 212.

          girdlers' specifications: Riley, op. cit., p. 216.

          spurriers' 'deception': Riley, op. cit., pp. 226–7.

28–9   *cutlers' 'deception':* T. Girtin, *The Mark of the Sword,* p. 218.

29   *'strict' shops:* Operative Society of Masons' *Fortnightly Returns,* July 22, 1836.

          apprenticeship spread: G. Unwin, op. cit., p. 96.

          return to masters: OSM, *Fortnightly Returns,* August 28, 1862.

29–30   *apprentice death rate:* S. L. Thrupp, op. cit., p. 264.

30   *apprentices' fathers:* A. Plummer, *The London Weavers' Company 1600–1970,* p. 85.

          Royal masons': Salzman, *Building in England,* op. cit., p. 70.

          masons' pay: Knoop and Jones, op. cit., p. 184.

          master/employer: *Book of Trades, 1811,* and W. Kiddier, *The Old Trade Unions,* p. 56.

          'journey' payment: T. Girtin, *The Golden Ram, a Narrative History of the Clockworkers' Company,* p. 296.

          journeymen, non-apprenticed: O. Lipson, vol. 1, p. 324.

30–1   *saddlers:* Riley, op. cit., pp. 156–9.

31   *weavers/burrellers:* Green, op. cit., p. 162.

31 *haberdashers/hatters:* E. Pooley, *The Guilds of the City of London*, p. 17, and G. Unwin, *Industrial Organisation in the 16th and 17th Centuries*, p. 106.

31–2 *merchant gilds:* C. Cross, *The Guild Merchant*, p. 6, and A. S. Green, op. cit., p. 53.

32 *merchants and Henry III:* J. E. Thorold Rogers, *Six Centuries of Work and Wages*, p. 108.

  London Merchants and war loans: Riley, op. cit., pp. 147 and 208–11.

  merchant gild ambivalence: See A. B. Hibbert, op. cit., pp. 188–92, 198–205, 219, etc.

  merchant gilds excluding craftsmen: Unwin, *Studies in Econ. History*, op. cit., p. 88, Gross, op. cit., and G. M. Trevelyan, op. cit., p. 99.

  crafts in merchant gilds: Hibbert, op. cit., p. 192; Malet Lambert, op. cit., p. 60; Toulmin Smith, op. cit.; Harris, op. cit., pp. 96–7.

  crafts meet outside towns: Riley, op. cit., pp. 180–1.

33 *pilgrimages:*

  Canterbury: S. Heath, *Pilgrim Life in the Middle Ages*, p. 29.

  . . and politics: J. A. A. Jusserand, *English Wayfaring Life in the Middle Ages*, pp. 339–42.

  secular control: Trevelyan, op. cit., pp. 56–7, and M. Keen, *Pelican History of Medieval Europe*, pp. 280–1.

  pilgrims abroad: Heath, op. cit., p. 29.

  'wanton songs': Heath, ibid., pp. 43–4.

34 *minstrels and 'artificers':* Jusserand, op. cit., pp. 208–11.

  pilgrims 'under colour': Jusserand, ibid., pp. 266–79.

  carpenters to cities: Tawney and Power, *Tudor Economic Documents*, vol. 1, p. 94, and Alford and Barker, op. cit., pp. 31–3.

  gilds and pilgrimages: Toulmin Smith, op. cit., pp. 143, 180, 231.

  inter-town agreements: Green, op. cit., p. 53.

35 *town contact in 1381 Revolt:* Trevelyan, *England in the Age of Wycliffe*.

  German 'city leagues': Hibbert, op. cit., p. 187, and Keen, op. cit., pp. 228–9.

page

35   '*Regiment of Rogues*': A. V. Judges, *The Elizabethan Under-world*, p. 411.

        Flemish crafts: Keen, op. cit , pp 247–8.

35–36   *complaints of 'Flemynges'*: Riley, op. cit., pp. 149 and 352, and R. Hilton, op. cit., p. 195.

36   *alien cobblers*: Riley, op. cit., pp. 538–9 and 570.

        castles: Mitchell and Leys, op. cit., p. 61; Knoop and Jones, op. cit., p. 244.

        masons:

          in London: Riley, op. cit., p. 280.

          outside London: Knoop and Jones, op. cit., pp. 244–7.

36–7   *assembly*: Knoop and Jones, ibid., p. 197.

37   *assembly ban*: Salzman, *Building in England*, op. cit., pp. 47, 73.

        marks: Salzman, ibid., p. 127. See also F. Bower, *Rolling Stonemason*.

        minstrels: Malet Lambert, op. cit., pp. 132–7.

38   *London wages*: Riley, op. cit., 253–7.

        Statute of Labourers: B. H. Putnam, *Enforcement of the Statute of Labourers*, and Thorold Rogers, op. cit., p. 251.

        rovers, charity: Jusserand, op. cit., p. 270.

        Langland and craftsmen: quoted in Jusserand, p. 270n.

39   *masons/serfs*: Knoop and Jones, op. cit., p. 246.

        Gravesend in 1381 Revolt: J. Lindsay, E. Rickword, *Handbook of Freedom*, pp. 31–2.

        craftsmen and 1381 Revolt: Hilton, op. cit., pp. 177–9 and 221.

        King and serfs: Lindsay, Rickword, op. cit., p. 42.

40   *1388 law on movement*: Jusserand, op. cit., pp. 274–6.

        1388 gild registration: Toulmin Smith, op. cit., pp. xxiv–v.

CHAPTER 2

41   *blacksmiths*: Ashley, op. cit., Part II, p. 117.

        London proclamation: Riley, op. cit., pp. 480–1.

        population estimates: Thorold Rogers, op. cit., pp. 116–17.

41–2   *Norwich gilds*: Salzman, *English Industries*, op. cit., p. 239.

42   *bowyers' rules*: Riley, op. cit., p. 352.

        Chester weavers: Lipson, op. cit., vol. 1, p. 407.

        shearmen, etc. disputes: Riley, op. cit., pp. 247 and 307.

        Bristol cobblers: Lipson, op. cit., vol. 1, pp. 393–4.

48   *takeovers :* Pooley, op. cit., p. 17.

         tailors' livery : Clode, *Early History, etc.,* op. cit., Part I, p. 37.

48–9   *'upset' fees :* Lipson, op. cit., vol. 1, pp. 414–16.

49   *printers' 'servitude' :* E. Howe and H. E. Waite, *London Society of Compositors,* pp. 6–7.

         carpenters' livery : Alford and Barker, op. cit., p. 25.

         bakers : S. L. Thrupp, *Bakers Company,* op. cit., pp. 95–9.

         tailors : Clode, *Memorials,* op. cit., p. 9.

         cutlers : T. Girtin, *Mark of the Sword,* p. 117.

50   *Reformation charities :* Clode, op. cit., p. 22; Unwin, op. cit., p. 230.

         holidays : Salzman, *Building in England,* op. cit., pp. 65–6.

         women and employment : Girtin, *Clothworkers,* op. cit., p. 22; Thrupp, *Bakers,* op. cit., p. 113.

51   *'confederacies' :* Thorold Rogers, op. cit., p. 397.

         internal disputes : Williams, op. cit., p. 14, and Thrupp, op. cit., pp. 94–5.

         bakers' apprentices : Thrupp, op. cit., p. 107.

51–2   *rich members :* Thrupp, *Cambridge Econ. History of Europe,* vol. 3, p. 269.

52   *clothworkers' employment :* Girtin, op. cit., p. 15.

         petition on aliens : Mander, op. cit., p. 64.

         May Day : Green, op. cit., p. 126n; A Tuckett, *The Blacksmiths' History,* p. 25; Sir Thomas Smith, *A Discourse of the Common weal of this Realm* (1581).

         'Evil May Day' : E. B. Jupp, *A Historical Account of the Worshipful Company of Carpenters,* and Girtin, *Mark of the Sword,* p. 9.

52–3   *Edinburgh crafts :* T. Johnston, *The History of the Working Classes in Scotland,* p. 131.

53   *'masterless men' :* Judges, op. cit., p. xv.

         'extortioners' : Quoted in Lindsay-Rickword, op. cit., p. 64.

         vagrants : Sir F. Eden, *The State of the Poor,* pp. 3–14.

54   *'rogues' and craftsmen :* Judges, op. cit., pp. 15 and 386 et. seq.

         vagrant dyers : Quoted in Bland, Brown and Tawney, *English Economic History, Select Documents,* p. 143.

55   *Thomas More, Crowley :* Quoted in Lindsay Rickword, op. cit., pp. 27, 59–68 and 83.

page
64 woollen wages: Lipson, Woollen Industry, op. cit., pp. 106–10.
    emigration: Trevelyan, op. cit., p. 224.
    Poor Law: Eden, op. cit., pp. 16–23.
65 amalgamation: Unwin, Industrial Organisation, op. cit., pp. 38–40.
    'hammermen': Tucket, op. cit., pp. 17–31.
    'search' regulation: Unwin, Guilds of London, op. cit., p. 341.
    'search' and yeomanry: A. Plummer, op. cit., p. 43; Clode, Memorials, op. cit., p. 561.
    yeomanry meeting room: Plummer, pp. 210–11: Clode, p. 564.
65–6 tailors' search: Clode, op. cit., pp. 561–3.
66 Hull tailors: Malet Lambert, pp. 236–49.
    weavers/strangers: Plummer, op. cit., pp. 56, 61–4.
    weavers, 'national' search: Unwin, Industrial Organisation, op. cit., p. 204.
67 weavers' internal dispute: Plummer, op. cit., pp. 44–5.
    'engine' loom: ibid., pp. 164–6.
    framework knitters: W. Felkin, A History of Machine Wrought Hosiery, p. 75, and Lipson, Economic History, op. cit., vol. II, p. 282.
68 disputes over funds: Girtin, Clothworkers, op. cit., pp. 89–90; Clode, op. cit., 566.
    'handytrade': Ashley, op. cit., Part II, p. 115.
    clothworkers' livery: Girtin, op. cit., pp. 114–15.
    masons' funds: Records of Worshipful Company of Masons, 27 April 1677.
    'wage earners': Alford and Barker, op. cit., p. 90.
    'vital difference': Lipson, op. cit., vol. 1, p. 375.
69 glovers/feltmakers: Unwin, op. cit., pp. 197–8 and 211.
    clothworkers stay in company: Girtin, op. cit., p. 85.
69–70 company disputes: Clode, op. cit., pp. 24–5; Girtin, Cutlers, op. cit., p. 283; Thrupp, Bakers, op. cit., p. 95; Unwin, op. cit., p. 207; Williams, op. cit., pp. 109–10.
70–1 weavers': Unwin, op. cit., pp. 207–8; Plummer, op. cit., pp. 48–9.
71 vagrancy after Civil War: Eden, op. cit., pp. 26–7.
    ex-servicemen: J. H. Firth, Cromwell's Army, p. 274.
    'King's Freemen': Johnstone, op. cit., p. 134.
    jobless weavers: Lipson, Economic History, vol. II, p. 286.

71   *Rye ban on soldiers:* Lipson, op. cit., vol. II, p. 286.

71–2   *post-war vagrants:* Firth, op. cit., pp. 274, 277.

72   *Act of Settlement:* Eden, op. cit., pp. 26–31.

        craftsmen and settlement: B. & S. Webb, *English Poor Law History*, vol. I, p. 335.

        Hull and married journeymen: Lambert, op. cit., p. 219.

73   *Settlement Act:* For a critique of the 'liberal' condemnation of the Settlement Act, see J. S. Taylor, *Past and Present*, No. 73, November 1976, pp. 49–67.

        parish dole: Trevelyan, op. cit., p. 292.

        trade disputes:

            printers: Howe and Waite, op. cit., p. 7.

            feltmakers: Unwin, *Industrial Organisation*, pp. 216–20.

            tailors: Clode, *Memorials*, pp. 24–8.

            weavers: Plummer, op. cit., pp. 56 and 293.

73–4   *travelling weavers' payment:* Webb Collection, Sec. A, Item 1.

74   *masons' signs:* quoted in E. Conder, *Records of the Hole Craft and Fellowship of Masons*.

        London masons: Company Ordnances, 1677.

        breakdown of relations: Alford and Barker, op. cit., p. 90.

        masons' search: London company records, 1677–1700.

        Worcester carpenters: Toulmin Smith, op. cit., p. 209.

75   *Norwich worsted trade:* Lipson, *Woollen Industry*, op. cit., vol. III, p. 287.

        printers' journeymen: Howe and Waite, op. cit., p. 6.

        clothiers break rules: Lipson, op. cit., vol. III, p. 288.

        bakers' livery: Thrupp, *Bakers*, p. 108.

        'idle' poor: Trade of England Revived (1681).

75–6   *clothiers, etc.:* Lipson, op. cit., vol. III, p. 293, and Lipson, *Woollen Industry*, pp. 104–5.

76   *tailors' disputes:* Clode, *Memorials*, pp. 28–9, 247–8.

        painters' yeomanry: Postgate, op. cit., p. 6.

        bakers' yeomanry: Thrupp, op. cit., pp. 95–6.

        mason's yeomanry: London company records, 25 September 1694.

77   *wheelwrights:* E. Bennett, *History of the Worshipful Company of Wheelwrights*, pp. 52–5.

        feltmakers: Unwin, *Industrial Organisation*, pp. 217–23.

77   *wool trade :* Lipson, *Economic History*, vol. III, pp. 390, 1, 7, and Unwin, op. cit., p. 226.

78   *London sawyers :* Unwin, op. cit., pp. 212–13.

        woolcombers' purse : Lipson, op. cit., vol. III, p. 387.

CHAPTER 4

        (In Chapters 4 and 5 the source of reference to Home Office papers is A. Aspinall's *The Early English Trade Unions*.)

79   *'free trade' :* Lipson, *Woollen Industry*, pp. 115–17.

        framework knitters : Felkin, op. cit., p. 80.

        Mansfield judgement : G. W. Daniels, *The Early English Cotton Industry*, pp. 51–2.

80   *'tide of luxury' :* T. Smollett, *Humphrey Clinker*, p. 35.

        South Sea Bubble : E. Mayer, *Curriers of the City of London*, p. 124.

        blacksmiths' inventions, trade control in London : J. R. Kellet, *Breakdown of Gild and Corporation Control. EHR*, 1958, vol. 2, p. 381.

80–1   *blacksmiths' amalgamations :* Tuckett, op. cit., pp. 17–32.

81   *wood to metal :* R. Campbell, *The London Tradesman*, and Daniels, op. cit., pp. 40–1.

82   *weavers' company membership :* Plummer, op. cit., pp. 32–3.

        'numerous' tailors : Campbell, op. cit.

        tailors 'forced out' : The Case of the Journeymen Tailors (1721).

        cordwainers' 'wandering' : HO 42/79; Aspinall, op. cit., p. 82.

        'useless' widows : H. Collins and J. Fyrth, *The Foundry Workers*, p. 14.

82–3   *Wedgwood on wages :* A. Burton, *Josiah Wedgwood*, pp. 94 and 115.

83   *James Watt :* quoted in W. McLaine, *The Engineering Union*, unpublished thesis, London, p. 80.

84   *calico printers and apprentices :* Bland, Brown and Tawney, op. cit., pp. 574–5, and A. Redford, *Labour Migration in England, 1800–1850*, p. 31.

        Cartwright's machine : James Burnley, *History of Wool and Woolcombing*.

84–5   *coachmakers' regulations :* Illife, *History of the Worshipful Company of Coachmakers*, p. 73.

page
85   *curriers' apprentices:* Mayer, op. cit., pp. 124, 135.

clothworkers: Girtin, op. cit., p. 120; Unwin, *Guilds of London*, p. 349.

tinplateworkers: O. Warner, *History of the Tinplate Workers' Company*, pp. 39–40.

wheelwrights' dispute: Bennett, op. cit., p. 530.

'illegal shop': Lipson, *Woollen Industry*, p. 115.

Manchester checkweavers: Daniels, op. cit., p. 48n.

86   *workhouse supervisors:* HO, 42/168; Aspinall, op. cit., p. 235.

woollen wages' apprenticeship: Lipson, op. cit., pp. 116–17.

hatters' apprenticeship: B. and S. Webb, *History of Trade Unionism*, p. 30.

'40 Acts . . .': Aspinall, op. cit., p. ix.

87   *silkweavers' campaign:* Plummer, op. cit., pp. 293 et. seq.

master tailors: B. and S. Webb, op. cit., pp. 31–2.

framework knitters: G. Henson, *Civil, Political and Mechanical History*, pp. 94–6.

woollen workers' actions: Lipson, op. cit., pp. 114–15 and 124, and HO, 42/26; Aspinall, op. cit., p. 19.

'cutters' movement: Plummer, op. cit., pp. 325–7.

88   *checkweavers:* T. Percival, *A Letter to a Friend* (1759).

cordwainers: HO, 42/79; Aspinal, op. cit., p. 83.

cabinet makers: S. Higenbotham, *Our Society's History*, p. 2.

Birmingham tailors: F. W. Galton, *Select Documents Illustrating the History of Trade Unionism I, The Tailoring Trade*, p. 74.

woolcombers: House of Commons Journals, xlix, p. 324.

compositors: Howe and Waite, op. cit., p. 48.

weavers' wage list: Plummer, op. cit., p. 327.

88–9 *cordwainers on 'scabbs':* HO, 42/79; Aspinall, op. cit., p. 89.

89   *bookbinders' strike:* W. Galton, *Workers on Their Industries*, pp. 143–4.

journeymen hatters: Unwin, *Industrial Organisation*, p. 215.

'jurisdiction': HO, 42/20; Aspinal, op. cit., pp. 4–5.

bakers' control: Thrupp, op. cit., p. 113.

wheelwrights: Bennett, op. cit., pp. 52–5.

90   *searches:*

        coachmakers: Illife, op. cit., pp. 25–6.

        blacksmiths: Adams, *Blacksmiths' Company*.

96   *tinplateworkers:* Kidd, op. cit., p. 99.

    '*abandon work*': Webb, *Collection*, Section A, Item 1.

    Fairbairn's 'indentures': McLaine, op. cit., pp. 59–60.

96–7 '*run away*': Master Millwrights' petition to Parliament, House of Commons Journal, 5 April 1799, quoted in J. B. Jeffrey, *They Story of the Engineers*, pp. 11–12.

97   *17 trades:* Listed in Chapter 15.

    Spitalfields: Plummer, op. cit., p. 330.

    '*insubordination*': HO, 102/6; Aspinall, op. cit., p. 18.

97–9 *Sheffield mechanics:* HO, 42/20; Aspinall, op. cit., pp. 4–5.

98   *tailors conscripted:* Johnstone, op. cit., p. 379.

    friendly societies: Sir F. Eden, *Observations Upon Friendly Societies*, and P. H. Gosden, *The Friendly Societies in England*, pp. 2–6.

98–9 *corresponding societies:* A. L. Morton and G. Tate, *The British Labour Movement, 1770–1920*, p. 31.

99   '*odious*' *law:* Aspinal, op. cit., p. xii.

CHAPTER 5

100 *Combination Acts:* These are well summarised in Aspinall, *Early Unions*, op. cit., pp. x–xvii.

    Nottingham mayor: HO, 43/23/9–11; Aspinall, op. cit., p. 171.

101 *Wilberforce:* quoted in Aspinall, p. xii.

    '*contagion*': Eden, *Observations . . .*, p. 24.

    '*fresh race*': HO, 42/95; Aspinal, p. 151.

    Scots weavers: Aspinall, p. 18.

    corresponding societies: Aspinall, p. 90.

    '*democratical fury*': Aspinall, p. 22.

    '*Pitt's health*': John Foster, *Class Struggle and the Industrial Revolution*, p. 38.

    Cobbett '*Levellers*': Political Register, 2 November 1816; Gorgon, 5 September 1818.

102 '*mob oligarchy*': HO, 42/180; Aspinal, 286.

102–3 *Industrial Revolution:* F. Engels, *Condition of the Working Classes in England*, pp. 7, 9, 15.

103 '*Aristocracy of Labour*': *Typographical Gazette*, 3 June 1846.

104 *Combination Acts* '*evaded*': HO, 42/133; Aspinall, pp. 161–2.

    '*dead letter*': Aspinall, p. xix.

104–5 *inadequacy of Acts: Artisans and Machinery*, 17 February

104–5   1824, and *Select Committee on Combination Laws*, Proceedings, 27 April 1825.

105   '*supply and demand*': G. Wallas, *The Life of Francis Place*, pp. 213–14.

'*immense number in jail*': *Gorgon*, 14 November 1818.

105   *should Government prosecute?*: HO, 42/79, 48/13; Aspinall, pp. 91–2, and 94–5.

close public houses?: HO, 48/17, 42/165, 42/23/9–11; Aspinall, pp. 171, 217–17, 233.

106   *no prosecutions*: HO, 42/140; Aspinall, pp. 179–80.

Shields arrests: HO, 42/146; Aspinall, p. 206.

Merthyr Tyddfil: HO, 42/159; Aspinall, p. 229.

informers: HO, 43/24/377–8; Aspinall, pp. 219, 232.

Wolverhampton: Kidd, *Tinplateworkers*, op. cit., p. 74.

derisory sentences: HO, 40/17/13, 36, 67, and 42/146; Aspinall, pp. 190 and 358.

'*reluctance*': Aspinall, pp. 59 and 275–6; Foster, op. cit., pp. 49–50.

107   *Oldham industry*: Foster, ibid., pp. x and 225.

'*tyrant*' *of Accrington*: Operative Society of Masons, *Fortnightly Returns*, 3 March 1837.

'*deserted*': HO, 42/79; Aspinall, p. 92.

'*Prince Regent*': HO, 42/118, Aspinall, p. 118.

Manchester hatters: HO, 42/198, Aspinall, p. 339.

'*defaulting*' *blacksmiths*: Tuckett, op. cit., p. 38.

107–8   *masters and lodges*: OSM Returns, 24 April 1847 and 24 June 1834.

108   *Henson as King Ludd?*: Wallas, op. cit., p. 207; Felkin, op. cit., p. 231.

109   '*in power of masters*': *Artisans and Machinery*, 2nd Report, 23 February 1824.

'*Foul shop*': *Artisans, etc.*, 2nd Report, 1 March 1824.

calico printers unemployment: Petition to Parliament quoted in Bland, Brown and Tawney, op. cit., pp. 574–5.

'*cheapest rate*': Select Committee on Combinations, 2 July 1838.

children as strike-breakers: Select Committee, etc., 2 July 1838.

109–10   *child migration*: Redford, op. cit., pp. 24–5, 115.

110   '*abuse*' *of Settlement Act*: Taylor, *Past and Present*, op. cit.

110   *workhouses:* H. Mayhew, *London Labour and the London Poor*, vol. III, pp. 368–70.

weavers' petition: Plummer, op. cit., p. 335.

engineering apprentice rules: J. B. Jeffreys, *Story of the Engineers*, p. 102.

masons' rules: OSM *Returns*, 19 July 1849.

111   *foundry 'boys':* Collins and Fyrth, op. cit., p. 20.

coachmakers: Webb, *Collection*, AXLV 5, 318.

'strictness': OSM *Returns*, 22 July 1836.

Whigs-Tories: Gorgon, 23 May 1818.

'independence': Gorgon, 28 November 1818.

111–12   *'federal' networks:* McLaine, op. cit., p. 108; Collins and Fyrth, op. cit., p. 21.

boot and shoe workers: Artisans and Machinery, 3rd Report, 8 March 1824.

brushmakers' 'divisions': Union Circular, 20 January 1859.

papermakers: Select Committee on Combinations, 22 May 1825.

woolcombers' congress: Aspinall, op. cit., pp. 127–36.

framework knitters: J. L. and B. Hammond, *The Skilled Labourer*, pp. 230–2.

coachmakers: Webb, *Collection*, AXLV 5.

tinplateworkers: Kidd, op. cit., pp. 135–47.

steam enginemakers: McLaine, op. cit., pp. 108–9.

mechanics/smiths: Rule books, 1823 and 1824.

papermakers: Select Committee on Combinations, 22 May 1825.

shipwrights: Select Committee on Combinations, 22 May 1825.

cotton printers: Aspinall, op. cit., p. 61.

Oddfellows: Gosden, op. cit., p. 26.

112   *'Commonly called tramps':* E. J. Hobsbawm, *Tramping Artisan* in *Labouring Men*, p. 39.

shearmen: HO, 42/65; Aspinall, op. cit., p. 42.

flax workers: HO, 42/78; Aspinall, p. 70.

'similar combinations': HO, 42/79; Aspinall, p. 91.

hospitality: Articles of the London Brushmakers, 1806.

cabinet makers: Higenbotham, op. cit., p. 5.

printers: H. Slatter and R. Hackett, *The Typographical Association, 50 Years' Record*.

joiners: Postgate, op. cit., p. 25.

coachmakers: Webb, *Collection*, AXLV 5.

moulders: Friendly Society of Ironmoulders, *Half-Yearly Reports*, May–November 1848.

tinplateworkers: Kidd, op. cit., p. 141.

113

Combination Acts 'avoided': quoted in B. and S. Webb, *Trade Unionism*, p. 77.

'leave man by man': *Artisans and Machinery, 2nd Report,* 1 March 1824.

friendly societies: Gosden, op. cit., p. 5.

Earl Fitzwilliam: HO, 42/133; Aspinall, op. cit., p. 161.

Bath shoe makers: HO, 42/79; Aspinall, p. 75.

1795 protest: Tuckett, op. cit., p. 35.

1800 protest: G. Howell, *Trade Unions New and Old*, p. 41.

Combination Acts protests: Aspinall, op. cit., pp. xiii, xiv; HO, 43/11/224–5; Aspinall, p. 26.

1809 delegate meeting: Nassau Senior's *Report to the Home Office, 1830.*

1814 trades committee: HO, 42/133; Aspinall, pp. 161–3.

London tailors: HO, 42/165; Aspinall, p. 232.

'Philanphropic': G. D. H. Cole, *Attempts at General Union*, pp. 9–13.

'Men in need': J. F. Bray, *Voyage from Utopia* (preface).

mechanics: HO, 79/3/300–1; Aspinall, p. 281.

printers/brushmakers: Kiddier, op. cit., pp. 24–6.

'itinerant orators': HO, 42/178; Aspinall, p. 251.

shoemakers: HO, 42/79; Aspinall, p. 79.

woolcombers: Aspinall, p. 130.

framework knitters: Hammonds, op. cit., pp. 230–2.

'tramping': Bath Mechanics, rules, 1823.

116

Gladstone: *Weekly Star*, 6 February 1892.

Place and Combin. Acts Repeal: Wallas, op. cit., pp. 219–20, and Place to *Artisans and Machinery, 1st Report*, 20 February 1824.

Nassau Senior: Webb, *Collection*, Sec. A., Item 1.

networks: Brushmakers *Circular*, 18 April 1826.

mechanics: McLaine, op. cit., p. 109.

carpenters: Higenbotham, op. cit., p. 25.

bricklayers: Postgate, op. cit., p. 54.

117   *spinners:* Proceedings of a Delegate Meeting of the Operative
           Spinners of England, etc. (1829).
         Operative Builders Union: Postgate, op. cit., Chapter 3, and
           W. S. Hilton, *Foes To Tyranny*, Chapter 4.
         OBU membership: Hilton, op. cit., p. 36.
118   *'general attack':* Postgate, op. cit., p. 72.
119   *Strike 'production':*
           tailors: Thale (Place biog.), op. cit., p. 113.
           masons: Postgate, op. cit., p. 10.
           carpenters: Postgate, p. 23.
           blacksmiths: Tuckett, op. cit., p. 402.
         'visionary scheme': OSM *Returns*, 13 and 29 August 1840.
         'swallowed Owenism': Cole, *Short History*, op. cit., p. 82.
119–20   *collapse of GNCTU:* Cole, *General Union*, op. cit., pp.
           115–36.

CHAPTER 6

         (In this and succeeding chapters, the source for references to
           Henry Mayhew's *Morning Chronicle* articles is Thompson
           and Yeo, *The Unknown Mayhew*.)
122   *universal function: Committee on Trade Societies Report
           to Society for Promotion of Social Science*, Glasgow,
           1860.
         spinners reject: Proceedings of Spinners' Delegate Meeting,
           Isle of Man, 1829.
         Northumberland miners: Board of Trade Report (1893) on
           *Agencies and Methods of Dealing with the Unemployed,
           Part II, Sec. 1.*
123   *'traveller':* Tuckett, op. cit., *Appendix B.*
         'treating strangers': Artisans and Machinery, 3rd Report,
           2 March 1824.
         moulders: Collins and Fyrth, op. cit., p. 22.
         'commonly called tramps': Hobsbawm, op. cit., p. 38.
         tinplateworkers: Kidd, op. cit., p. 146.
         brushmakers: Union Circular (Witham), 1829.
         'a tramp': Engels, op. cit., p. 215.
123–4   *masons' system:* Knoop and Jones, op. cit., pp. 248–53.
124   *papermakers:* Select Committee on Combination Laws, 22
           May 1825.

131   *sawyer on tramp*: *Manchester Times*, 26 December 1840.

CHAPTER 7

132   '*drinking system*': John Dunlop, *Philosophy of Artificial and Compulsory Drinking Usage in Great Britain* (1839).

    vacant book: Operative House Painters, *Rules*, 1919.

    '*cadgers*': *Leisure Hours*, 1 June 1868 ('Trade Tramp').

    Cork journeymen: Rules in *Trade Guilds of Europe* (1885), Appendix on trade unions.

132–3 *Cock Inn*: Cited in Mayer, *Curriers . . .*, p. 118.

133   *Pubs*:

    carpenters: Alford and Baker, op. cit., p. 46.

    weavers: Plummer, op. cit., p. 150.

    wheelwrights: Bennett, op. cit.

    blacksmiths: Adams, op. cit.

    masons: *London Company Records*, 11 December 1701.

    tailors: Clode, *Memorials*, pp. 561–2.

    framework knitters: Henson, op. cit., pp. 94–6.

    '*cutters*': Plummer, op. cit., p. 324.

    master tailors: Galton, *The Tailoring Trade*, p. 3.

    '*Flints and Dungs*': *Gorgon*, 10 March 1818.

134   *boot and shoe*: HO, 42/79; Aspinall, op. cit., p. 73.

    framework knitters: Hammonds, op. cit., pp. 230–1.

    bakers' 'diatribe': Ure, *Dictionary of Manufactures*, p. 182.

    House of Commons: Hilton, op. cit., p. 75.

    '*King Pippin*': Kidd, op. cit., p. 150.

135   *pubs and tramping routes*: Harrison, *Drink and the Victorians*, p. 51.

    (Public houses quoted on these pages are from union rule books, route cards and *First Annual Trade Union Directory*, 1861.)

136   '*lighthouse*': OSM *Returns*, 7 March 1889.

    tramp welcomed: In Thos. Wright, *The Great Unwashed*.

137   *clean beds*: OSM *Returns*, 29 August 1850.

    moulders' beds: FSIM *Half Yearly Reports*, January–June 1848.

    moving pubs: McLaine, op. cit., p. 44; Manchester Unity of Operative Bricklayers' *Reports*, 21 December 1882; Kiddier, op. cit., p. 106.

    Sydney pub: OSM *Returns*, 24 March 1841.

141   *curriers:* Mayer, op. cit., p. 144.

141–2   *Publicans and Combination Acts:* Aspinall, op. cit., xxiv; HO,
        43/23/9–11 and 42/179; Aspinall, pp. 171 and 280.

142   *Chartists:* B. Harrison, in *The Victorian City*, p. 175.

        Republicans: OSM *Returns*, August 1848.

        '*wet rent*': Eden, *Observations*, op. cit., pp 23–4

        '*obligatory*': Place, *Autobiography*, pp. 110–11; Higenbotham,
        op. cit., p. 3.

        drink allowance: Derby Smiths' *Rules*, 1839; Manchester
        Typographical Society *Souvenir History*; Cummings, op.
        cit., p. 30.

        '*entomologists*': J. M. Ludlow, *Progress of the Working Classes*,
        p. 19.

        pot ticket: London Brushmakers' *Rules*, 1806.

        '*drinking out of turn*': McLaine, op. cit., and Tuckett, op.
        cit.

        Huddersfield engineers: Article in *Plebs*, June 1922.

        Franklin: Howe and Waite, op. cit , pp. 39–40.

        shipwright: Trades Advocate, 13 July 1850.

        '*touching regard*': Salzman, *English Industries*, op. cit.

145   *clothworkers:* Girtin, op. cit., p. 15.

        sedition: Eden, *Observations*, op. cit., p. 23.

        machines 'never drunk': Jeffreys, op. cit., p. 16.

        boilermakers: H. Pollitt, *Serving My Time*, pp. 59–60.

        '*three days*': HO, 42/20; Aspinall, op. cit., p. 4.

146   *fines and footings:*

        coopers: Elkington, op. cit., p. 160.

        cordwainers: HO, 42/79; Aspinall, op. cit., p. 85.

        coachmakers: Webb, *Collection*, AXLV, 5.

        brushmakers: Union Circular, 1826.

        NUWC: Harrison, *Victorian City*, op. cit., p. 175.

        Sheffield filesmiths: Place Collection, *Set. 53.*

146–7   *Oddfellows hall:* C. Thomson, *Autobiography of an Artisan.*

147   *spinners abstain:* Select Committee on Combinations, 14 June
        1838.

        moulders' allowance:Half Yearly Reports, January–May 1848.

        printers: Manchester Typographical *Souvenir History*, 1843.

        steam engine makers: Delegate Meeting, 1842.

        moulders 'aloof': FSIM, *Half Yearly Reports*, July 1851.

147 *Dublin carpenters:* Select Committee on Combinations, 27 July 1838.

  'wet rent': Manchester, *typo,* op. cit., July 1843.

  tinplateworkers: Kidd, op. cit., p. 109.

  bookbinders: Dunning, in *Workers on their Industries,* ed. Galton, op. cit.

  compositors: Howe and Waite, op. cit., pp. 103, 109–10.

CHAPTER 8

  shoemakers: Reminiscences of Thomas Dunning, ed. Challoner, pp. 97–8.

148–9 *'The Difference':* quoted in Tuckett, op. cit., p. 45.

149 *masons:* OSM *Returns,* 13 October 1837.

  moulders debate: FSIM, *Half Yearly Reports,* January–July 1848.

  brushmakers: Union *Circular,* 1829.

  'valuable': OSM, *Returns,* 13 October 1838.

  'shop steward': OSM, *Returns,* 6 July 1838.

  'no disgrace': Musson, op. cit., p. 51.

  'respect' tramp: Amalgamated Society of Tailors, *Reports,* January–December 1884.

  'preservative': Brushmakers' *Circular,* 1829.

  'walk fairly': FSIM, *Half Yearly Reports,* May–December 1847.

  'Old Mechanics': Plebs, September 1922.

  'wondrous kind': T. Wright, in *The Great Unwashed.*

150 *trade tramp: Leisure Hours,* 1 June 1868.

  Will Crooks: quoted in Beveridge, *Unemployment,* p. 249.

  'denial of work': Reminiscences of a Stonemason (1908).

  Moritz on trade tramps: Travels Through Several Parts of England (1808).

  tramps' ideas: Preface to J. F. Bray, *Voyage From Utopia.*

151 *printer-tramp:* C. Manby Smith, *The Working Man's Way In The World,* pp. 9–12.

  'no garroter': Thos. Wright, *The Great Unwashed.*

  trade tramp/professional: H. Mayhew, *London Labour* ..., vol. III, pp 112–13

  tramp organisers: McLaine, op cit, pp 67–8; Collins and Fyrth, op cit., p. 20.

151–2   *travelling bakers: Pioneer*, 1 March 1834.

152   *masons:* Hoskins, op. cit., p. 99. Also OSM *Returns*, 6 February
        and 1 May 1835; 24 June 1836; 31 March and 27 October
        1847.

        boilermakers: Cummings, op. cit., pp. 82 and 105.

        masons: Broadhurst, op. cit., pp. 21–3; F. Bower, *Rolling
        Stonemason.*

        'independence': Place in Wallas, op. cit.

        leatherseller: quoted in B. and S. Webb. *Industrial Democracy*,
        pp. 161–2.

        compositors: Manby Smith, op. cit., pp. 19–20.

152–3   *trade tramp: Leisure Hours*, 1 June 1868.

153   *'roadsters':* Bower, *Rolling Stonemason.*

        woolcombers: Thos. Cowper, *A Short Essay on Trade in General.*

        tailors: Place/Thale *Autobiography*, p. 113.

        boot and shoe: Mayhew, Letter XXXII, *Morning Chronicle*,
        4 February 1850.

        calico printers: HO, 42/138; Aspinall, op. cit., p. 168. Also
        Webbs, *Industrial Democracy*, pp. 161–2.

        masons: OSM *Returns*, 12 June 1835 and 8 January 1836.

153–4   *shipowner and strikebreakers:* Select Committee on Combina-
        tion Laws, 6 August 1825.

        building strikebreakers: Pioneer, 16 January 1833.

        masons' strikes: OSM *Returns*, 25 April 1839, 9 May 1839,
        15 January 1842.

        'blacks': OSM *Returns*, 18 July 1861.

        tinplateworkers: Kidd, op. cit., pp. 141 and 146.

        compositors: Musson, op. cit., p. 30.

        'compensation': Hilton, op. cit., p. 59.

154–5   *'treadmill':* OSM, 23 May 1859.

155   *master millwrights:* House of Commons *Journal*, liv, 405–6,
        5 April 1799.

        'leave man by man': Artisans and Machinery, 2nd Report,
        1 March 1824.

        'no warrant': Select Committee on Combinations, 1838.

        pickets: Nassau Senior report to Home Office, 1830; also *On
        Combinations of Trades* (1831).

155–6   *sawyers: Manchester Times*, 19 and 26 December 1840.

156   *witness removed:* Henson, op. cit., pp. 410–13.

156   *shearmen:* HO, 42/66; Aspinall, op. cit., pp. 52 and 65.

     shoemakers: Dunning, *Reminiscences*, op. cit., pp. 99–109.

CHAPTER 9

157   *crowd of tramps:* W. Duthie, *A Tramp's Wallet*, p. 49.

     jeweller: Duthie, op. cit., p. x.

158   *Berlin artisan:* ibid.

     viaticum: Duthie, pp. 34 and 40.

     two shillings: Duthie, p. vii

     'a right': Duthie, p. 41.

     Saxony: Duthie, p. xii.

     'vile den': Duthie, p. 53.

159   *tinsmith:* Duthie, p. 40.

     passport: Duthie, pp. ix, x.

     'broken hearted': Duthie, p. xi.

160   *Moritz: Travels Through England.*

     artisan and state: Duthie, p. 52.

     French workmen: Duthie, p. 141.

160–1   *English workman:* Duthie, p. 52; Unwin, *Industrial Organisation*, p. 227; also Lujo von Brentano, *On The History and
Development of Guilds*, p. clxvi (n).

161   *laissez-faire:* Unwin, op. cit., p. 226.

161–2   *fraternities:* G. Schanz, *Geschichte der Gesellen Verbande.*

162   *apprenticeship:* Brentano, op. cit., p. cl.

     sons exempt: ibid., p. cli.

     city leagues: See A. B. Hibbert, in *Cambridge Economic
History of Europe*, vol. 3, pp. 187–8.

163   *compagnons:* E. M. St Leon, *Le Compagnnage.*

     hatter: Mayhew, Letter LXXXVII, *Morning Chronicle*,
7 November 1850.

     gilds and labour mobility: S. L. Thrupp, *Cambridge Econ.
History*, vol. 3, p. 280.

     herberge: Brentano, op. cit., pp. cliv–vi.

     greeting: G. G. Coulton, *Art and The Reformation*, p. 168.

164   *fortnight's work:* Duthie, op. cit., p. xvi.

     French journeymen's gild: N. Z. Davies, in *EHR* 2, vol. XIX,
no. 1, 1966.

     printers' 'chapel' customs: Howe and Waite, op. cit., p. 41;
Thos. Gent, op. cit., p. 16.

164 *French trades:* F. D. Longe, in *Fortnightly Review*, vol. II, 1867.

 German law: Redford, op. cit., pp. 87–8.

165 *German framework:* Felkin, op. cit., p. 541.

 'aristocratic': *Trade Guilds of Europe*, op. cit., on German gilds.

 1791 decree: Longe, op. cit.

166 *German trades: Trade Guilds of Europe.*

 George Sand: Les Compagnons de Tour de France.

166–7 *legislation:* J. M. Baerrneither, *English Associations of Working Men*, p. 7.

CHAPTER 10

171 *cabinet makers:* Higenbotham, op. cit., p. 18.

 print jobless: Musson, op. cit., pp. 49–65.

 moulders' jobless: FSIM *Half Yearly Reports*, June–December 1841, June–December 1842, June–December 1847.

 masons' jobless: OSM *Returns*, 23 April 1840.

 moulders: FSIM *Half Yearly Reports*, June–December 1848.

 cabinet makers: Mayhew, *Morning Chronicle*, 1 August 1850.

171–2 *London trades: Trades Weekly Messenger*, 16 March 1848.

172 *workhouse numbers:* Mayhew, *London Labour*, vol. III, p. 376.

 Huddersfield poor: Plebs, June 1922.

 Chartists: John Brown, *Autobiography.*

 moulders: FSIM *Reports*, December 1847–June 1848.

 Chartist movement: A. L. Morton, *People's History of England*, pp. 436–7.

173 *engineers:* Jeffreys, op. cit., p. 22.

 'beyond example': Musson, op. cit., p. 53; FSIM *Reports*, June–December 1847.

 'wandering': McLaine, op. cit., p. 182.

 'walk fairly': FSIM *Reports*, June–December 1847.

 printers: Musson, op. cit., p. 50.

 Reading: FSIM *Reports*, June–December 1841, June–December 1848.

173–4 *'Hurtful':* Cummings, op. cit., p. 54.

174 *masons:* OSM *Returns*, 4 May 1843.

 'humiliation': Provincial Typographical Association, *Half Yearly Reports*, June–December 1852.

page

184   *moulders:* FSIM *Reports*, June–December 1864, and *Annual Reports*, 1868, 1869, 1878

184–5   *Liverpool:* PTA *Half Yearly Reports*, July 1851, December 1851, July 1852

185   *hatters:* Fair Trade Union *Rules*, 1898, No. 8.

    printers: Musson, op. cit., pp. 282–4.

    carpenters: Higenbotham, op. cit., pp. 49–52; *emblem*, Leeson, op. cit., opp. p. 27.

186   *printers:* Musson, op. cit., p. 284.

    'forswear realm': Mitchell and Leys, op. cit., pp. 149–52; Judges, op. cit., p. xxxvi.

    60,000 emigrants: Trevelyan, op. cit., pp. 224–6.

    framework knitters: Felkin, op. cit., p. 441.

186–7   *'transportation':* Redford, op. cit., pp. 24–5 and 113.

187   *'capitalist remedy':* Bray, *Labour's Wrong and Labour's Remedy*, and Hurst, *History of the Woollen Trade*; see also, Poor Law Commissioners Report, pp. 484–92, and Redford, op. cit., p. 110.

187–8   *emigration appeal:* quoted in Burton, *Josiah Wedgwood*, p. 188.

188   *English abroad:* D. S. Landes, *Unbound Prometheus*, pp. 148–9.

    'resort to colonies': W. Cunningham, *Growth of English Industry and Commerce*, vol. II, Part 2, p. 756.

    'swarms': *Gorgon*, 7 November 1818.

    warning: FSIM *Reports*, December 1847–June 1848.

188–9   *masons:* OSM *Returns*, 8 May 1849.

189   *statistics:* quoted in *Trade Guilds of Europe*.

    masons in United States: R. Samuel, in Dyos and Wolff, *The Victorian City*, p. 124.

189–90   *Sydney masons:* OSM *Returns*, 24 March 1842.

190   *engineers abroad:* Jeffreys, op. cit., pp. 61–2; ASE Delegate meeting report, 1885, and Jeffreys, pp. 128–9.

    carpenters: Amalgamated Society of Joiners and Carpenters, *Rules*, 1886.

    hatters' cards: In *Union Archives*, Denton, Manchester.

    travel system: Board of Trade Inquiry, 1893, op. cit., Part II, Section 1.

    hatters 'foul': J. F. Smith, *The Hatters*, p. 13.

190–1   *bookbinders:* Webb *Collection*, BL CXIX.

191   *masons abroad:* OSM, 2 March 1842, 23 March 1843.

        Melbourne: OSM *Returns*, January 1861.

        engineers' warnings: ASE *Monthly Reports* during 1863 and 1873.

        founders' warnings: Friendly Society of Ironfounders, *Annual Report*, 1876.

        hatters: Smith, op. cit., p. 13.

192   *last tramp:* ASE *Journal*, March 1915.

CHAPTER 12

194   *Shortt, mason:* Hilton, op. cit., p. 65.

        'technical sense': Thomas Hughes, *Tracts on Christian Socialism*, IV.

        strike-breaking: FSIM *Report*, December 1847–June 1848.

        'desperadoes': ASE Delegate *Conference Report*, 1885.

195   *membership:* ASE *Monthly Reports*, 1865–8.

        cordwainers: Northern Star, 20 October, 2 November 1844.

        tailors: Northern Star, 16 April 1844.

        boot and shoe strike, 1859: Report by J. Ball in *Trade Societies and Strikes*, Social Science Congress, 1860.

196   *tailors' strike:* Stewart and Hunter, op. cit., p. 107.

        membership: Amalgamated Tailors' *Reports*, 1885.

        boot and shoe union: Fifty Years, History of the National Union of Boot and Shoe Operatives, 1824.

        basket makers: Webb *Collection*, AXLV.

196–7   *National Typographical Association:* Gillespie, op. cit., pp. 32–3; Musson, op. cit., Provincial Typographical Association *Half Yearly Reports*, June 1850, December 1850, December 1851.

197   *Relief Assoc.:* Slatter and Hackett, *The Typographical Association, 50 Years History*; Gillespie, op. cit., p. 81.

198   *hatters:* J. Smith, op. cit., pp. 3 and 8.

        bricklayers: Operative Bricklayers' Society *Annual Report*, 1864, Manchester Unity Operative Bricklayers *Monthly Report*, November 1872; Hilton, op. cit., pp. 149–52.

198–9   *carpenters:* Higenbotham, op. cit., p. 24; Royal Commission on Trade Unions, *First Report*, 9 April 1867.

199   *equalisation:* Higenbotham, op. cit., p. 33.

        union rally: ASCJ, *Annual Report*, 1866.

page

199–200   '*General Union*': Higenbotham, op. cit., p. 33; General Union of Carpenters, *Annual Report*, 1866–7.

200   *cabinet makers*: Higenbotham, op. cit., p. 15.
     Irish masons: OSM *Returns*, 4 June 1840.
     Harnott: Hilton, op. cit., p. 139.
     carpenters and strikes: Higenbotham, op. cit., p. 73
     printers and The Times: Musson, op. cit., pp. 58–9.
     '*Would to God . . .*': Ludlow and Jones, op. cit., p. 219.

200–1   *closed shop*: Hilton, op. cit., p. 139; OSM *Returns*, April 1850

201   *masons' emblem*: Leeson, op. cit., p. 28.
     boilermakers: Cummings, op. cit., pp. 42, 67, 83.

201–2   '*travelling*': Royal Commission on *Trade Unions*, 26 May 1867.

202   *founders dispute*: FSIF, *Annual Report*, 1862.
     masons' rules: OSM *Returns*, 20 July 1838.

203   *bricklayers' rules*: OBS, *Annual Report*, 1868.
     founders' expenditure: FSIF *Half Yearly Report*, January–December 1867.
     engineers' expenditure: ASE *Monthly Reports*, 1861–70.
     carpenters' expenditure: General Union of Carpenters, *Annual Report*, 1868–9.
     '*useless*': OSM *Returns*, 26 October 1871.

204   *thrift*: Engels, op. cit., p. 125.
     insurance: Baernreither, op. cit., p. 196.
     Lord Elcho: Quoted in Ludlow and Jones, op. cit., p. 212n.
     '*indebted*' *to workers*: Mayhew, in Letter LXV, *Morning Chronicle*, 15 August 1850.
     '*Bastille*': OSM *Returns*, 23 April 1840.

205   *Tid Pratt*: In Poor Law Commissioners' *Report*, pp. 340–1.
     '*experience*': Charles Booth, *Life and Labour . . .*, p 314.
     levies:
       engineers: Jeffreys, op. cit., p. 60.
       brushmakers: Kiddier, op. cit., p. 19.
     hatters' '*discipline*': F. Knowles, *Hatters' Work*, 1889.
     '*all the bad*': FSIF *Annual Report*, 1868.

206   *1867 Elections*: General Union of Carpenters, *Annual Report*, 1867–8.
     temperance: Girouard, *Victorian Pubs*, pp. 171–2.

206–7   '*no more sotting*': Aspinall, op. cit., p. 84.

207   '*done away with*': quoted in Harrison, op. cit., p. 309.

207   *better habits:* Ludlow and Jones, op. cit., p. 22; Higenbotham, op. cit., p. 50.

'*70 per cent':* British Steel Smelters Assoc. *Journal,* April 1906.

'*Temperance Party':* Arthur Pugh in *Men of Steel,* pp. 22–3; BSSA *Journal,* December 1907.

cricket match: ASCJ *Report,* 1866.

208   *house of call:* George Druitt, London Tailors, to Royal Commission on Trade Unions, *Tenth Report,* 1867.

bakers: Letter in Webb *Collection,* AXLV.

accommodation: ASE Amended *Rules,* 1892 Delegate Meeting. *Belfast:* ASE *Report,* May 1861.

bricklayers: MUOBS *Report,* February 1869.

Doncaster races: ASE *Report,* September 1863.

Gladstone lobbied: Higenbotham, op. cit., p. 78.

209   '*respected':* ibid., p. 30.

'*refuse of the tap':* FSIM *Half-Yearly Report,* 1847–8.

'*vulgarly called':* G. Howell, *Trade Unionism New and Old,* p. 112.

'*politer terms':* S. Campion, *The Gentle Craft.*

209–10   *emblem changes:* Leeson, op. cit., pp. 27, 32, 34, 40, 42, 46.

210   '*don't call':* Tailors *Rules,* 1885; Masons *Rules,* 1865; ASE *Journal,* September 1860; FSIM *Half-Yearly Report,* December 1844–June 1845.

CHAPTER 13

211   *rule changes:* Masons' *Rules,* 1887; Tailors, 1912; Ironfounders, 1917.

engineers: See Chapter 15 for statistics.

212   *punishments:* Pugh, *Men of Steel,* p. 112.

'*lazy':* ASE *Journal,* September 1899.

213   *workhouse walls:* Rose, *The English Poor Law.*

'*easy touches':* *Trade Tramp,* in *Leisure Hours,* June 1868.

'*Harry Welford':* Steel Smelters' *Reports* during 1907.

workhouse boys: Mayhew, *London Labour . . .,* vol. III, pp. 368–70.

grass crop . . . : R. Samuels, in Dyos/Wolff, op. cit., pp. 123–4.

'*foot on daisies':* Kiddier, op. cit., p. 215.

'*mendicity':* Howell, *Conflicts of Capital and Labour.*

214   '*licensed pauper':* *Pioneer,* 16 January 1833.

moulders: FSIM *Half-Yearly Report,* 1847–8.

214   *workhouse keepers:* Mayhew, op. cit., vol. III, p. 371.
       sickness: OSM *Returns*, 22 January 1846.
       '*demoralised*': Amalgamated Tailors *Yearly Report*, 1894.
       '*lounging*': Manby Smith, op. cit., pp. 19–20.
       '*three in a bed*': FSIM, *Half Yearly Report*, 1847–8.
       Scots printers: Gillespie, op. cit., p. 79.

214–15 '*they wander*': Tailors *Rules*, 1867, 1912.

215   '*good tailor*': Tailors *Report*, 1894.
       young men: FSIF *Auditors' Report*, 1862; *Half-Yearly Reports*
           (FSIM), 1847–8.
       '*foot on daisies*': J. Hopkinson, *Memoirs of a Victorian Cabinet
           maker*, p. 24.

215–16 *Mogg the Tramp:* Kiddier, op. cit., p. 215.

216   '*lamentable*': Letter from Sheffield Brushmakers to Leeds
           brothers, 15 March 1847.
       low relief: Provincial Typographical Association, *Half-Yearly
           Report*, December 1852.
       sixpences: OSM *Returns*, 21 July 1859.
       '*empty bellies*': OSM *Returns*, 4 May 1843.

217   '*alias Scum*': ibid., 25 October 1838.
       '*light opinion*': ibid., 27 November 1890.
       fraud-proof: H. Broadhurst, *His Life*, p. 23.
       rare: Musson, op. cit., pp. 274–5.
       '*at least 20 miles*': Steel Smelters Assoc. *Reports*, 31 July 1898.
       cordwainers: Northern Star, 20 October 1844.
       '*rat hole*': PTA *Report*, December 1849–June 1850.
       '*scamp*': Pioneer, 16 January 1833.

218   '*a wakes*': OSM *Returns*, 13 April 1848, 22 June 1848.
       '*Negro comedian*': Jeffreys, op. cit., pp. 60, 61.
       harpist: Pugh, op. cit., p. 138.
       '*Orphan Thomas*': OSM *Returns*, 19 June 1862.
       cordwainers: Northern Star, 12 April 1845.
       rules:
           hatters: Union *Rules*, 1859.
           masons: OSM *Returns*, 22 December 1880.
           bricklayers: MUOBS *Report*, 1880.
       '*flying brethren*': Gillespie, p. 78; Brushmakers *Circular*, 1862.

219   *labour direction:*
           printers: Musson, p. 53.

219   *steam engine makers:* 1842 Delegate Conference *Report.*
        engineers: ASE Delegate Conference *Report,* 1885.
        '*tyrannical*': FSIM *Half Yearly Reports,* December 1847.
        '*incorrigible*': ASE *Journal,* September 1899, February
            1903.
        imposters: ASE *Report,* June 1857.

220   '*travelling lodge*': OSM *Returns,* 22 February 1843.
        '*Newgate . . .*': PTA *Half-Yearly Report,* July 1852.
        '*Hungarian . . .*': ibid , December 1852.
        outsiders: cited in James Greenwood *On Tramp* and John
            Newton, *Secrets of Tramp Life Revealed.*
        jailed: MUOBS *Report,* 4 March 1869.
        '*drunken*': OSM *Returns,* 26 October 1871.

221   *lodges moving:* OSM *Returns,* 4 March 1859, 31 March 1870.
221–2   *fines:* OSM *Rules,* 1849 and 1868.
        severe: ASE *Journal,* December 1879.
222   *dying out:* Tailors *Annual Report,* 1885.

CHAPTER 14

223   '*blackest year*': ASE *Annual Report,* 1880.
        '*worst years*': Cummings, op. cit., p. 105.
        expenditure: FSIF *Annual Reports,* 1878 and 1879.
        comparison: Tables published in Howell, *Trade Unionism New
            and Old,* p. 114.
223–4   *depression:* Reports to *Royal Commission on Depression of Trade
            and Industry,* 1886, *First Report,* Appendix D.
224   *5000 tramps:* calculations based on *Monthly, Fortnightly,
            Annual Reports* of masons, engineers, tailors, founders.
        Sunderland: R. C. on Depression of Trade, op. cit.
        benefits: from union *Rule Books* and *Reports.*
225   *membership:* from union *Reports.*
        masons/founders: FSIF *Annual Reports,* 1879, 1887; OSM
            Biennial Report, November 1879; *Auditors' Report,* 1891.
        rules revision: Brushmakers' *Circular,* February 1880; Cum-
            mings, op. cit., p. 116; Felt Hatters' *Rules,* 1886.
        printers: Musson, op. cit., pp. 229 and 277.
226   '*drawing out*': Cummings, op. cit., p. 116; Tailors *Report,*
            1892.
        bricklayers: MUOBS *Annual Report,* 1880.

243   *Manchester :* Dickson, *Manchester Typographical Centenary Souvenir.*

tanners : Mayhew, *Morning Chronicle,* 15 November 1850.

tramping wives : See Chapter 6; picture from J. H. Crawford, *Autobiography of a Tramp.*

Irish masons : OSM *Returns,* 22 July 1836.

244   *woolcombers :* Aspinall, op. cit., pp. 127–37.

'*establish masters*' : Kiddier, op. cit., pp. 51–66.

'*fair/foul*' : *Artisans and Machinery, 2nd Report,* 1 March 1824.

'*strictest*' : OSM *Returns,* 22 July 1836.

foremen : Select Committee on Causes of Strikes, 1856.

master tailors : in Galton, *Select Documents,* p. 3; also HO, 42/54; Aspinall, pp. 33–5.

244–5 *house of call :* Mayhew, Letter LXIII, 1 August 1850; XVI, 11 December 1849, *Morning Chronicle.*

245   *engineers '*ratio*' :* Jeffreys, op. cit., p. 102.

tailors' closed shop : Hobsbawm, op. cit., pp. 36–7.

245–6 *tailors tramping :* Place/Thale, op. cit., p. 113; J. Lindsay, 1764, p. 246; Stewart and Hunter, op. cit., p. 107.

246   '*respect tramp*' : Tailors *Annual Report,* 1885.

246–7 *number on road :* FSIM *Half-Yearly* and FSIF *Annual Reports;*

247   Brushmakers' *London Society Reports,* 1815–17; Brushmakers' *National Circular,* 1828.

'*moulders' marathon*' : calculated from money figures given in *1848 conference report,* see Chapter 10.

tramp numbers :

    moulders : Half Yearly Reports, FSIM.

    masons : OSM *Annual Reports.*

248   '*Old Mechanics*' : 10 per cent suggested by article in *Plebs,* June/September 1922.

engineers : ASE *Monthly Reports.*

249   *percentages :* Jeffreys, op. cit., pp. 61, 128; also OSM and Amalgamated Tailors *Annual Reports.*

printers : Slatter and Hackett, op. cit.

250   *cabinet-makers :* Higenbotham, op. cit., p. 18.

printers : Musson, op. cit., p. 51.

Stafford masons : OSM *Returns,* 4 May 1843.

moulders' views : FSIM *1848 Delegate Conference Report.*

252   (Webb quotations in this chapter are from the 1920 edition of
         B. and S. Webb, *History of Trade Unionism.*)
         '*state within*': Webbs, op. cit., 1894, preface, pp. vii–ix.

253   *G. D. H. Cole critique*: in Cole, *Attempts at General Union*,
         pp. 2, 3, 38–9, 42–3; *Some Notes on British Trade Unionism
         in the Third Quarter of the 19th Century*, in Carus-Wilson,
         ed., *Essays in Economic History*, vol. III, 1962.

253–4   *movement's aims*: Webbs, op. cit., *Introduction*, p. v.

254   *definition of trade union*: ibid., p. 1.
         '*resemblance*': ibid., pp. 12–13.

254–5   *Thomas Hughes*: in *Tracts on Christian Socialism*, IV.

255   '*supposed descent*': Webbs, op. cit., pp. 13–14.
         '*ritual*': ibid., p. 19.
         '*Standard of Life*': p. 21.

255–6   *companies*: ibid., pp. 21–2.

256   '*social pint*': ibid., p. 23.
         '*ceased to be*': ibid., p. 26.
         printers: ibid., p. 27.
         '*pioneers*': ibid., p. 46.
         appeal to Government: ibid., pp. 46–7.

257–8   *George Howell: Trade Unions New and Old*, pp. 1–2.

258   *Irish '*character*'*: Webbs, op. cit., pp. 721, 2, 3.
         curriers: Mayhew, Letter LXXVIII, *Morning Chronicle*,
         15 November 1850.
         emblems: Many reproduced in Leeson, op. cit.

259   '*ritual*': Webbs, op. cit., pp. 19 and 125–7; for comment on
         this see B. Springett, *The Freemason*, 25 March 1925.
         '*ritual*': See also, Cole, *General Union*, p. 72; Higenbotham,
         op. cit., pp. 10–13; Hilton, op. cit., pp. 28–30.
         companies – '*no connection*': Webbs, op. cit., pp. 13–14.

260   *trade control*: See G. Unwin, *Guilds of London*, p. 344; J. R.
         Kellett, in *EHR*, 1958, vol. 2, X, 381; see also S. L. Thrupp,
         on *Gilds* in *International Encyclopedia of Social Science*,
         vol. 6, p. 184, and J. Latimer, *Annals of Bristol in the 18th C.*,
         p. 155.
         '*great seal*': Mayer, op. cit., p. 116.

261   *yeoman companies*: Webbs, pp. 2–3.
         '*not survived*': ibid., p. 6.

Index

Benefit Societies, *see* Friendly Societies

Benefits, other than travelling and unemployment 13, 14, 98, 112, 122, 128, 129, 130, 137, 142, 149, 173, 203, 204, 205, 209, 226, 233, 234, 236, 237, 239

Berlin 157, 158

Bermondsey 135

Beveridge, Sir W. 205, 235, 236

Beverley 24, 32, 34, 47

Bewick, Thomas 93, 94, 166

Bilbao 190

Birmingham 41, 88, 118, 123, 140, 194, 197, 204, 218

Blackburn 128, 216

Black Death 38, 62

Black Friars 38, 43

'Blacks' 130, 154

Blacksmiths: craft or trade 24, 41, 46, 80, 92, 103, 270, 275; fraternity/gild 26, 27, 28, 32, 262, 263, 264; craft company 48, 67, 80, 81, 92, 133, 260; livery 46, 89, 134; yeomanry 41, 45, 46, 89, 262, 263, 264, 270; trade society 96, 103, 107, 108, 275; union 112, 120, 125, 126, 128, 137, 143, 148, 149, 193; travelling custom/ system 14, 122, 123, 124, 125, 126, 128, 129, 135, 148, 242

Blanks 13, 15, 95, 98, 112, 115, 125, 126, 129, 191; *see also* certificate and travelling card

Boilermakers: craft or trade 88, 96, 103, 111, 124, 125, 126, 148, 231, 260, 275; trade societies 88, 96, 103, 128, 137; union, Order of Friendly B . . . 120, 122, 124, 141, 143, 148, 209, 210, 259; United Society of B . . . 111, 115, 152, 192, 209, 210, 223, 226, 231, 260; travelling custom/system 14, 115, 122, 124, 125, 126, 148, 173, 176, 201, 202, 208, 209, 210, 223, 226, 228, 242

Bolton 136, 141, 192, 220

Bombay 190

Bookbinders 14, 89, 147, 157, 190, 191, 242

Booth, Charles 205

Boston (US) 191

Boulton 83

Bower, Fred (stonemason) 153, 189, 227, 238, 239

Bowyers, 42

Bradford 174, 219

Brassworkers, National Union of 227, 228

Bray, J. F. 115, 150, 151, 187, 191

Brazil 184

Brentano, Lujo von 161, 162, 163, 166, 254

Bricklayers 14, 64, 117, 135, 137, 189, 198, 203, 208, 221, 224, 230, 236, 258

Brighton 147, 197

Bristol 24, 35, 41, 42, 44, 45, 54, 56, 66, 89, 153, 154, 172, 179, 189, 247

Broadhurst, Henry (stonemason) 127, 128, 152, 232

Brushmakers: craft or trade 30, 56, 117, 126, 127, 242, 244; craft organisation 56, 127; trade societies 115, 127, 138, 139, 243; union 111, 117, 120, 123, 125, 126, 128, 137, 143, 146, 180, 183, 184, 205, 225, 226, 234, 235; travelling custom/ system 14, 95, 112, 123, 125, 126, 127, 128, 129, 138, 139, 149, 178, 194, 216, 217, 226, 242, 247

Buffalo (US) 190, 191

Builders' Parliament 117

Building workers 36, 49, 74, 117, 118, 119, 123, 128, 132, 137, 138, 152, 182, 192, 194, 239, 259; Operative Builders' Union 117, 118, 119, 120, 259

Building Trade Workers, Amalgamated Union of 239

Buntingford 39

Burnley 135

Burrellers 31, 41, 54; *see also* clothiers

Bury, Lancashire 114, 178

Bury St Edmunds 47, 56

Butley, C. 175

Cabinet makers 14, 88, 92, 95, 112, 120, 142, 143, 171, 200, 215, 242, 250

Cade, Jack 42, 54

Caldecott (govt informer) 114

Calico printers 14, 84, 96, 108, 109, 110, 153, 154, 242

Callimancoes 73, 82, 270

Canada 184, 188, 189, 190, 191

Canterbury 33, 38, 65, 73

Capper, W. (shoemaker) 156

Cardiff 135, 219, 224

Carlisle 114, 122

Carpenters: craft or trade 14, 24, 36, 37, 39, 41, 49, 56, 78, 83, 190, 240, 275; fraternity/gild 24, 25, 27; craft company 45, 47, 69, 74, 78, 133; livery 47, 49; yeomanry 49, 56, 78; trade societies 118, 147, 200, 224; union: General

POLITICS

CLASS INEQUALITY AND POLITICAL ORDER
Frank Parkin   £1.50
How can we account for the persistence of class and status
differences in the modern industrial world? Frank Parkin confronts
these problems with a careful appraisal of the influence of working-
class movements, political ideologies and the agencies of moral
control.

DAILY SKETCHES: A CARTOON HISTORY OF BRITISH
TWENTIETH-CENTURY POLITICS   Martin Walker   £1.95
A wide-ranging survey of a much-overlooked art-form. 'A
stimulating guide.' Norman Shrapnel, *The Guardian*. Illustrated.

THE INTERNATIONAL URBAN CRISIS   Thomas L Blair 60p
A lucid and disturbing analysis of the facts behind planning
blight, suburban sprawl, traffic congestion, and human alienation.

MARX'S GRUNDRISSE   David McLellan   £1.25
A substantial set of extracts from the classic work in which Marx
develops an account of the process of alienation, analyses the
nature of work and develops a vision of the fully automated
society in which social wealth could be devoted to the all-round
development of the faculties of each individual. Edited by one of
Britain's leading Marxist scholars.

THE SLOW-BURNING FUSE   John Quail   £1.95
The activities, triumphs, disasters, influence and personalities of
the British anarchist movements; a history long neglected.

THE LORE AND LANGUAGE OF SCHOOLCHILDREN
Iona and Peter Opie   £2.50
The classic study of the mysterious world and underworld of
schoolchildren – the games, the chants, the rites and the rituals
performed generation after generation by children all over Britain.

MAGIC AND MILLENNIUM   Bryan Wilson   £2.50
'Civilised' man's impact on the Third World has thrown up many
strange millenarian religions. This classic of the sociology and
anthropology of religion casts light on the very bases of man's
hopes and fears for the future and for redemption.

MYTHOLOGIES   Roland Barthes   £1.25
An entertaining and elating introduction to the science of semiology
– the study of the signs and signals through which society expresses
itself, from the leading intellectual star.

THE NEW TOWN STORY   Frank Schaffer   75p
A comprehensive review of the whole of Britain's post-war
New Town movement from its early origins to likely developments
in the year 2000 and beyond.

THE SOCIAL PHILOSOPHERS Robert Nisbet £2.50

This provocative absorbing essay in social and intellectual history shows that Western social philosophy has been preoccupied with man's perennial quest for community: military, religious, revolutionary, ecological and plural.

STEPS TO AN ECOLOGY OF MIND Gregory Bateson £2.50

This book develops a new way of thinking about the nature of order and organisation in living systems, a unified body of theory so encompassing and interdisciplinary that it illuminates all areas of study of behaviour and biology.

SUBURBIA David Thorns 60p

Is the suburb the successful fusion of town and country or a mirror of the most depressing feature of urban existence? A critical analysis of the origin and components of suburbia.

VILLAGES OF VISION Gillian Darley £2.50

A lively study of the many villages in Britain that have evolved and developed naturally but were 'planted' artificially. An entertaining and unusual piece of social history. Illustrated.

All these books are available at your local bookshop or newsagent, or can be ordered direct from the publisher. Just tick the titles you want and fill in the form below.

Name ....

Address ....

....

Write to Granada Cash Sales, PO Box 11, Falmouth, Cornwall TR10 9EN.

Please enclose remittance to the value of the cover price plus:

UK: 30p for the first book, 15p for the second book plus 12p per copy for each additional book ordered to a maximum charge of £1.29.

BFPO and EIRE: 30p for the first book, 15p for the second book plus 12p per copy for the next 7 books, thereafter 6p per book.

OVERSEAS: 50p for the first book and 15p for each additional book.

Granada Publishing reserve the right to show new retail prices on covers, which may differ from those previously advertised in the text or elsewhere.